CBT: Science Into Practice

Series Editor

Nikolaos Kazantzis, Cognitive Behavior Therapy Research Unit, Melbourne, VIC, Australia

This series addresses topics that reflect current thinking in the field of cognitive behavior therapy, the most widely accepted form of therapy across mental health disciplines. Despite the consensus that CBT is an effective treatment modality, much of the existing clinical literature focuses on single facets, such as specific disorders or populations. Mostly it does not take into account the latest evidence for transdiagnostic change mechanisms and processes. This series provides guidance on how the latest evidence can be translated into practice. Volumes focus on enhancing flexibility in both the selection and delivery of techniques tailored to individual clients. Each provides clinical insights enhanced by case studies and vignettes to ensure relevance for the practicing professional.

Nicholas A. Livingston • Brian A. Feinstein
M. Paz Galupo
Editors

Addressing Minority Stress and Enhancing Resilience with Diverse LGBTQ+ Clients

Springer

Editors
Nicholas A. Livingston
National Center for PTSD, Behavioral Science Division, VA Boston Healthcare System
Boston, MA, USA

Department of Psychiatry
Boston University Chobanian & Avedisian School of Medicine
Boston, MA, USA

Brian A. Feinstein
Department of Psychology
Rosalind Franklin University of Medicine and Science
North Chicago, IL, USA

M. Paz Galupo
Brown School of Social Work
Washington University in St. Louis
St. Louis, MO, USA

ISSN 2946-5419 ISSN 2946-5427 (electronic)
CBT: Science Into Practice
ISBN 978-3-031-92835-2 ISBN 978-3-031-92836-9 (eBook)
https://doi.org/10.1007/978-3-031-92836-9

This Springer imprint is published by the registered company Springer Nature Switzerland AG
The registered company address is: Gewerbestrasse 11, 6330 Cham, Switzerland

Contents

Part I
Orientation and Setting the Stage

Chapter 1
Setting the Stage for LGBTQ+ Affirmative Therapy

Nicholas A. Livingston, Brian A. Feinstein, and M. Paz Galupo

Our Positionality

We are a group of researchers, educators, and clinicians in psychology and social work at various stages in our careers. We represent a range of gender and sexual identities (agender, cisgender man, bi/pansexual, queer, heterosexual) and racial/ethnic identities (Biracial, Filipinx, White) and collectively, we share a professional and personal commitment to supporting the health and wellbeing of LGBTQ+[1] people through research, clinical practice, and advocacy. Two of the authors are clinically trained, one of whom currently works with clients in a VA Medical Center and one of whom supervises trainees in a University clinic that serves uninsured

[1] We generally use LGBTQ+ rather than sexual and gender minority (SGM) throughout this book because it is more commonly used within the community (i.e., outside of academia). However, some authors use variations (e.g., LGBTQIA2S) to reflect the language used within specific communities of interest. In addition, authors vary in their Main Textidentity-first language (e.g., bisexual man) for intentional reasons (e.g., based on the setting in which they provide care and the language used by a specific client/patient). For more on LGBTQ+ language conventions see Veldhuis et al. (2024).

N. A. Livingston (✉)
National Center for PTSD, Behavioral Science Division, VA Boston Healthcare System, Boston, MA, USA

Department of Psychiatry, Boston University Chobanian & Avedisian School of Medicine, Boston, MA, USA
e-mail: Nicholas.Livingston@va.gov

B. A. Feinstein
Department of Psychology, Rosalind Franklin University of Medicine and Science, North Chicago, IL, USA

M. P. Galupo
Brown School of Social Work, Washington University in St. Louis, St. Louis, MO, USA

N. A. Livingston et al. (eds.), *Addressing Minority Stress and Enhancing Resilience with Diverse LGBTQ+ Clients*, CBT: Science Into Practice,
https://doi.org/10.1007/978-3-031-92836-9_1

community members. Both are trained in a range of cognitive-behavioral approaches, including third-wave interventions (e.g., Acceptance and Commitment Therapy), specialize in the treatment of mood and anxiety disorders, obsessive-compulsive and related disorders, posttraumatic stress disorder (PTSD), and substance use disorders, and have expertise in working with LGBTQ+ clients. Our intention in doing this work was to produce a resource that can help mental health professionals across discipline, therapeutic orientation, treatment setting, and career stage to expand their knowledge of, and support for, the diverse needs of LGBTQ+ clients.

Setting the Stage: Minority Stress, Resilience, and LGBTQ+ Mental Health

Mental health disparities among lesbian, gay, bisexual, transgender or gender diverse, and queer (LGBTQ+) people have been documented for over four decades (e.g., Meyer, 2003; Pachankis et al., 2020a, b; Wilson et al., 2024; Wittgens et al., 2022). These disparities are evident as early as childhood (e.g., Blashill et al., 2021; Feinstein et al., 2024) and persist throughout the lifespan (e.g., Feinstein et al., 2023; Fredriksen-Goldsen et al., 2013, 2014a). In addition, a massive body of literature now links higher prevalence of negative mental health outcomes to minority stressors (e.g., discrimination, victimization) and related social determinants of health (e.g., financial insecurity, housing instability; Dürrbaum & Sattler, 2020; Manalastas et al., 2024; Pachankis et al., 2020a, b; Wilson et al., 2024). These stressors are multilevel, spanning systems at the interpersonal micro-level (e.g., peers, family), exo-level (e.g., schools, clinics, neighborhoods), and macro-level (e.g., federal and state policies; Hatzenbuehler, 2009, 2016; Shipherd et al., 2019). The frequency of these experiences is chronic for some, and can also vary in intensity from subtle daily slights (e.g., microaggressions) to severe forms of violence and trauma, all of which have been shown to have significant negative impacts on LGBTQ+ individuals' mental health. Importantly, exposure to minority stressors varies by geography, specific gender and sexual identity, other aspects of identity (e.g., race, ethnicity, disability), and time (e.g., generation). These life experiences are not only impactful when they occur, but can also serve as predisposing factors to later distress and impairment, particularly in the form of negative automatic thoughts and core beliefs.

Foundational works document the various types of minority stressors experienced by LGBTQ+ people, the range of psychiatric outcomes that stem from them, and the transdiagnostic ways in which they impact LGBTQ+ people's felt sense of safety, trust, and self-worth (Brooks, 1981; Fredriksen-Goldsen et al., 2014b; Hendricks & Testa, 2012; Meyer, 2003; Shipherd et al., 2019). Although each prevailing model of LGBTQ+ health highlights unique features of LGBTQ+ people's lived experience, each model is aligned in the position that the etiology of mental health concerns exists outside the person. Prejudicial attitudes—including heterosexism, monosexism, and cissexism—that give rise to, or fail to prevent, discriminatory laws, policies, or violence against LGBTQ+ people are indeed pathological. Without these looming and enacted threats, LGBTQ+ people appear no more likely to develop mental health concerns than non-LGBTQ+ people (Livingston, 2023).

Discussion of the links between minority stressors and mental health among LGBTQ+ people is incomplete, and less clinically useful, without acknowledgement of the ways in which these stressors lead to adverse outcomes. Hatzenbuehler (2009) was the first to articulate, and provide summarized empirical evidence for, "how stigma gets under the skin". In this framework, minority stressors (e.g., discrimination, victimization) lead to internalizing (e.g., depression, anxiety) and externalizing disorders (e.g., substance use disorders) by way of the "general" psychological processes that pertain to all people, as well as the "group-specific" processes that are unique to LGBTQ+ people. Specifically, general psychological processes include the depletion of coping resources and the use of maladaptive emotion regulation strategies (e.g., rumination, using substances to cope), social isolation and social norms (e.g., permissive attitudes that normalize substance use), and cognitive processes such as learned helplessness, negative views of the self, and beliefs that distress can be ameliorated via hazardous coping strategies (e.g., self-injury, substance use). Group-specific processes that can be activated by minority stressors include internalization of negative societal attitudes toward LGBTQ+ people, expectations of future rejection, and efforts to conceal one's minoritized identity as a means of self-protection. Hatzenbuehler's articulation of these causal processes provided an initial framework to help clinicians to conceptualize the distress experienced by LGBTQ+ clients, and to target interventions using the insights and skills outlined in front-line cognitive-behavioral therapies (CBT).

At the same time, reactions to minority stressors often reflect proportional adaptations that confer safety and survival advantage. Although the prejudices that warrant these adaptations are unjust, understanding the sources of these adaptations, their functions, and validating that they may be (or once were) warranted is an important step toward developing a mutual and balanced understanding of the client, and to prevent overpathologizing necessary adaptations to extreme stress (Livingston et al., 2020a, b). For some, uniform or situational (with certain people or in specific places) identity concealment may be a means of preventing discrimination and violence. On the other hand, concealment is associated with higher levels of social isolation and estrangement, vigilance, shame, and internalizing disorders such as depression (Pachankis, 2007; Pachankis et al., 2020a, b).

The focus on minority stress as a prevailing framework is understandable given the pervasive health disparities experienced by LGBTQ+ persons. Although LGBTQ+ specific resilience (e.g., identity affirmation, community connectedness and engagement) has been shown to mitigate the effects of minority stress on mental health (Katz et al., 2023; Meyer, 2015; Parmenter & Galliher, 2023), minority stress theory has been critiqued for promoting a deficit model of LGBTQ+ experience and for not fully integrating an understanding of resilience and joy (Lee et al., 2024;

McLean et al., 2024). Clinicians should be careful to avoid defining LGBTQ+ clients primarily based on their experiences of oppression and instead focus on ways to highlight positive experiences and build strength based on resilience, resistance, healing, joy, and liberation (Matsuno & Israel, 2018; Parmenter et al., 2024; Puckett et al., 2025; Singh & Chun, 2015).

Overarching Considerations for Providing LGBTQ+ Affirmative Care

The eventual negative mental health outcomes of singular, sporadic, or chronic minority stressors can vary widely and may include symptoms of mood and anxiety disorders, PTSD, substance use disorders, and eating disorders, to name a few (Feinstein & Dyar, 2017; Hatzenbuehler, 2009; Hendricks & Testa, 2012; Manalastas et al., 2024; Meyer, 2003; Livingston et al., 2017, 2019, 2020a, b, 2022; Pachankis et al., 2020a, b; Salomaa et al., 2022; Shipherd et al., 2019, 2021; Wilson et al., 2024; Wittgens et al., 2022). Variability in the constellation of symptoms presents challenges to clinicians, particularly in cases of comorbidity or when the needs of clients require deviations from, or modifications to, protocol-driven evidence-based practices (Livingston et al., 2020a, b; Salomaa et al., 2024). In conceptualizing risk and mental health concerns among LGBTQ+ people, and what to do about it, it is important to balance knowledge of the commonalities that may pertain to LGBTQ+ people as a whole with, quite critically, the variability across subgroups, regions, and over time. For these reasons, it is beneficial to have individualized conversations with LGBTQ+ clients who present to your offices or clinics to gain an accurate appraisal of their stressors, their impacts, individuals' strengths, and desired intervention approaches rather than relying solely on the belief that minority stress is the leading, or even a relevant, cause of their distress. For some, it may be primary, while for others, it may be secondary, tertiary, or not at all relevant to their presenting concerns. We advocate for due consideration of these nuances, and in this book, authors provide a wide range of considerations and illustrations about how to provide LGBTQ+ affirming care.

For many LGBTQ+ people, effectively responding to minority stress, or processing traumas and their enduring effects, includes skill development and practice that goes beyond boilerplate content of manualized protocols. Relevant strategies to consider incorporating in these protocols include, but are not limited to, (1) building social and community supports with safe and LGBTQ+ affirming people, (2) developing interpersonally effective boundary setting skills (e.g., to prevent exposure to harmful treatment from others or to defend one's self from such treatment in the moment when prevention is not possible); (3) fostering self-empowerment, including through empowerment-based self-defense training (Berke et al., 2024; Salomaa et al., 2024), as a means of building both confidence and self-efficacy when assertive or defensive action is needed; and (4) practicing existing or developing new emotional regulation skills to help restore a sense of safety and calm following exposure to minority stressors. These recommendations are not meant to suggest that the onus is on LGBTQ+ people to adapt to abject circumstances while others who perpetuate harms are given a free pass. It is not the fault of LGBTQ+ people that they experience minority stressors, but it is their right to fortify themselves against such threats to self, safety, or belonging. Clinicians can support this by helping to equip clients with the skills that may help prevent undue consequences associated with these experiences (e.g., substance use, self-harm; see Livingston et al., 2020a, b; Shipherd et al., 2019).

Persistent Service Gaps and the "Invisibility" of LGBTQ+ People in Clinical Research

Unfortunately, despite an impressive amount of research linking mental health disparities to minority stress and other adverse social determinants of health among LGBTQ+ individuals, there is insufficient research on therapeutic strategies to effectively offset their negative impacts. There are numerous evidence-based cognitive-behavioral interventions for mental health concerns such as depression (e.g., *Behavioral Activation*; Martell et al., 2022; *Interpersonal Psychotherapy*; Weissman et al., 2018), anxiety (e.g., *the Unified Protocol*; Barlow et al., 2020); PTSD (e.g., *Cognitive Processing Therapy*; Resick, et al., 2017; *Prolonged Exposure*; Foa et al., 2019; *Written Exposure Therapy*; Sloan & Marx, 2019; *Eye Movement Desensitization and Reprocessing*; Shapiro, 2018), and substance use disorder (Daley & Marlatt, 2006; Daley & Douaihy, 2023; DeMarce et al., 2014; Epstein & McCrady, 2007; Kadden & Litt, 2011). However, LGBTQ+ identity information is rarely reported in randomized clinical trials (Harper et al., 2022; Heck et al., 2017; Flentje et al., 2015), which undermines confidence in the degree to which evidence-based interventions generalize to LGBTQ+ people.

Some of the most efficacious treatments focus on challenging and reprogramming negative automatic thoughts and core beliefs, trauma processing, and habituation to trauma and related triggers as mechanisms of recovery. Although LGBTQ+ people can and often do benefit from targeting these processes in treatment, accumulating evidence suggests that they may not benefit as much or as quickly as their cisgender and heterosexual peers (Beard et al., 2017; Hollinsaid et al., 2020; Rimes et al., 2019). There is also some evidence that LGBTQ+ individuals report worse perceptions of and less satisfaction with care (Beard et al., 2017; Benjamin et al., 2023; Hollinsaid et al., 2020), as well as negative healthcare experiences (e.g., microaggressions from providers; Livingston et al., 2019; Morris et al., 2020). Together, these findings raise questions about the extent to which existing evidence-based interventions are meeting the needs of LGBTQ+ individuals, which is likely related to the limitations of existing protocols—namely, they rarely include appropriate and LGBTQ+ affirmative language, considerations or strategies for addressing minority stressors, guidance for working with people who are oppressed and living in active or looming threat situations, or how to tailor treatment when stressors or symptoms require clinicians to deviate from existing protocols (Livingston et al., 2020a, b; Shipherd et al., 2019).

Emerging Trends in Evidence-Based and Patient-Centered Care for LGBTQ+ People

More research is needed to determine if and when existing evidence-based treatment protocols need to be adapted, or whether new treatments need to be developed under certain circumstances. In the meantime, it is clear that existing CBT protocols do not provide adequate guidance for clinicians to be responsive to the needs of LGBTQ+ individuals, including how to (1) validate or challenge automatic thoughts and negative core beliefs that stem from minority stress; (2) prevent overpathologizing normal reactions and adaptations to stress; (3) attend to concerns relating to concurrent trauma (bias related or not) and minority stress; and (4) balance cognitive restructuring with skill building, particularly when the skills that seem warranted are those that help the client navigate unjust circumstances effectively (e.g., coping with discrimination when discrimination is itself the issue); all while (5) affirming authentic identity development and expression, and promoting resilience, resistance, and liberation.

There are a number of efforts published that help to establish an evidence-base for tailored interventions that target minority stress processes as drivers of mental health among LGBTQ+ people (e.g., *ESTEEM;* Pachankis et al., 2015, 2022; *EQuIP;* Pachankis et al., 2020a, b). The specific strategies utilized across these interventions differ, but they share a focus on minority stress experiences and reactions, including educating clients about the range of ways in which minority stress can affect psychosocial functioning and wellbeing, and teaching clients adaptive ways of coping with minority stressors and their unfair consequences. These interventions also leverage LGBTQ+ people's unique strengths to promote self-worth, pride, and healthy relationships. Accumulating evidence supports the efficacy of these tailored interventions, and they provide a foundation for clinicians to work from when providing care to LGBTQ+ individuals. Still, this literature is in its infancy, and there remains a need for clinical guidance on how to support LGBTQ+ clients using a range of affirming strategies.

Our Motivation and Aims in Developing This Book

CBT, and some behavioral therapies in particular, have a tarnished legacy in the LGBTQ+ community (Comer et al., 2024). Sexual orientation and gender identity change efforts ("reparation" or "conversion" therapies), such as systematic desensitization (Barlow, 1973) and covert sensitization (Hayes et al., 1983), have been opposed and denounced by every major practice organization (Comer et al., 2024). These practices are ineffective, harmful, and can have lasting adverse effects on LGBTQ+ people (see Comer et al., 2024). Estimates vary but as many as 11–34% of LGBTQ+ people have been subjected to these practices (Comer et al., 2024), suggesting widespread use and the potential for mistrust of helping professionals among members of the LGBTQ+ community.

As a corrective step forward, one motivation for this book was to elevate voices from the community to share their collective wisdom and insights into how to provide LGBTQ+ affirming care. We prioritized clinical wisdom from clinicians and scholars from diverse gender and sexual identities, racial and ethnic groups, and fields of study, and carefully selected contributors with demonstrated expertise in LGBTQ+ affirmative care practices who actively resist efforts to use therapy as a medium to suppress, convert, persecute, or subjugate LGBTQ+ people. We also selected contributors with experience providing care across diverse treatment settings (e.g., academic and non-academic settings, federal and private hospitals, college counseling centers, private practice), and across various career stages (e.g., senior, mid-career, and early-career professionals and trainees). In this book we aimed to be inclusive of a variety of interventions under the broad umbrella of CBT, and to illustrate ways that readers can seamlessly integrate LGBTQ+ affirming care practices regardless of their preferred theoretical orientation.

What You Can Expect From This Book

Treatment development and research are slow in relation to the exigent need for patient-centered care practices. Additional research and intervention development and evaluation are needed, but LGBTQ+ people and providers who care for them need not wait. Fortunately, providers in the field have been adapting evidence-based practices 'on the fly' and providing outstanding clinical care for LGBTQ+ people for years. This book provides a collection of works from leaders in LGBTQ+ health and CBT who are at the forefront of treatment development, adaptation, and real-world implementation and application.

This book is specifically designed for clinicians, clinical researchers, and students, with varying degrees of expertise, who are hoping to learn cutting-edge approaches to assess, treat, and mitigate the negative effects of minority stress on the mental health of LGBTQ+ individuals. The primary objective of this book is to translate the state of the science and practice into clear and practical guidance and recommendations that readers can implement today. We accomplish this through applied and diverse case examples, clinical dialogue, and lessons learned from expert clinicians in every chapter. We also prioritize increasing the visibility of under-represented topics (e.g., person-centered assessment, co-occurring trauma and minority stress, relationships and consensual non-monogamy) and populations within the LGBTQ+ community (e.g., Black, Indigenous, and People of Color [BIPOC], veterans, older adults, and people with disabilities). At the same time, we emphasize the need to consider systems of power, privilege, and oppression more so than demographic characteristics of the people featured in this book.

Throughout this book we highlight cultural and intersectional considerations for practice, and share practical guidance for tailoring clinical care in a manner that is responsive to individual and within-community differences. Importantly, every chapter focuses on applied skills and recommendations for clinical practice, tailored to its respective topic. In the first part of the book, we begin with an orientation to the essential building blocks of evidence-based and person-centered care with LGBTQ+ clients, including screening, assessment, and case formulation (Chap. 2) and affirming approaches to clinically addressing experiences of minority stress (Chap. 3). Given high prevalence of both minority stress and other traumas among LGBTQ+ people, and the challenges with addressing these co-occurring stressors and their impacts, our foundational part also includes a chapter devoted to treating minority stress among people receiving trauma-focused therapy for PTSD (Chap. 4). We conclude Part I with a chapter on helping LGBTQ+ people to heal from sexual orientation and gender identity change efforts (Chap. 5).

In Part II, we showcase works that address developmental and lifespan considerations. We present considerations and applied skills for facilitating LGBTQ+ identity development (Chap. 6) and helping LGBTQ+ youth and their families with affirmative therapeutic practices (Chap. 7). The remaining works in this part concern strategies for addressing ageism and its intersections with heterosexism and cissexism among LGBTQ+ older adults (Chap. 8), as well as ableism and health promotion among LGBTQ+ people with developmental and acquired disabilities (Chap. 9).

In our final part, we cover timely topics and emerging best-practices for addressing the different types of prejudice and discrimination affecting historically underrepresented groups within the LGBTQ+ community. The first chapter in this part provides strategies for how clinicians can prioritize radical healing and liberation for LGBTQ+ BIPOC (Chap. 10). Following this, our contributors address considerations and provide recommendations for interrupting cissexism and binary conceptualizations of gender/sex when working with transgender, nonbinary, and gender diverse people (Chap. 11), as well as how to counter anti-bisexual prejudice and monosexism (Chap. 12). The next chapters help readers to challenge compulsory sexuality and romanticism to support asexual- and aromantic-spectrum individuals (Chap. 13), and to address relationship stigma while supporting LGBTQ+ individuals in diverse types of relationships (e.g., consensual non-monogamy; Chap. 14). In our last chapter, we address the invisible concerns of LGBTQ+ military veterans (Chap. 15), including strategies for working with patients who have been subject to harsh treatment within deeply entrenched hierarchical systems, which is relevant to all readers regardless of whether they work clinically with veterans.

Reflections and Conclusions

We are mindful of the fact that much has changed in our social and political climate since we began assembling this book nearly 3 years ago. What began as a passion project for us has now become a matter of urgent concern. In 2024, there were over 570 anti-LGBTQ+ bills across the U.S. (ACLU, 2024), and the number of bills targeting transgender and gender diverse individuals specifically increased five-fold (Trans Legislation Tracker, 2024). These bills seek to limit all aspects of life including health care, public accommodations, access to accurate identification documents, civil rights and nondiscrimination protections, free speech and expression, and even what content can be discussed in schools. Some of the more extreme bills attempt to criminalize health care professionals for providing care to trans youth, and threaten child abuse charges for parents who support their child's transition (Hughes et al., 2021; Kraschel et al., 2022).

Providing affirming and culturally attuned care for LGBTQ+ clients requires professionals to navigate the constantly shifting socio-political landscape. Macro-level laws, policies, and even political discourse can have immediate and dramatic effects on the health, wellbeing, and safety of LGBTQ+ people directly (Haas & Lannutti, 2024; Kuroki, 2021; Price et al., 2021), and indirectly through greater polarization, fractured social and family relationships (e.g., Price et al., 2021), and increased rates of discrimination and victimization that can lead to or exacerbate worsened mental health outcomes. The contents of this book were relevant and timely prior to these socio-political shifts and have now become critical.

What we hope that readers will take away from this book is a greater appreciation for the types of stressors that disproportionately affect LGBTQ+ people, the unique strengths that they possess, and how they relate to case conceptualization and treatment. We hope that readers finish each chapter better equipped and more confident in their ability to provide LGBTQ+ affirming care. Last, we hope that this book will be a resource to you, the reader, and to institutions of higher education charged with training future generations of helping professionals.

Disclaimer Statement The views expressed in this chapter are those of the authors and do not reflect the official policy or position of the U.S. Department of Veterans Affairs nor the U.S. Government.

References

ACLU. (2024). *Mapping attacks on LGBTQ rights in U.S. State Legislatures*. Available from: https://www.aclu.org/legislative-attacks-on-lgbtq-rights-2024 (Accessed 15 Dec 2024).

Barlow, D. H. (1973). Increasing heterosexual responsiveness in the treatment of sexual deviation: A review of the clinical and experimental evidence. *Behavior Therapy, 4*(5), 655–671. https://doi.org/10.1016/S0005-7894(73)80158-3

Barlow, D. H., Farchione, T. J., Sauer-Zavala, S., et al. (2020). *Unified protocol for transdiagnostic treatment of emotional disorders: Workbook* (2nd ed.). Oxford University Press.

Beard, C., Kirakosian, N., Silverman, A. L., Winer, J. P., Wadsworth, L. P., & Björgvinsson, T. (2017). Comparing treatment response between LGBQ and heterosexual individuals attending a CBT- and DBT-skills-based partial hospital. *Journal of Consulting and Clinical Psychology, 85*(12), 1171–1181. https://doi.org/10.1037/ccp000025

Benjamin, I., Rodriguez-Seijas, C., & Zimmerman, M. (2023). Differences in patient satisfaction across sexual orientation and gender identity in an acute care setting. *Psychology of Sexual Orientation and Gender Diversity, 10*(1), 117–127. https://doi.org/10.1037/sgd0000505

Berke, D. S., Miller, M., & Palatnik, J. (2024). Empowerment self-defense for sexual and gender minority populations. In L. Orchowski & J. Hollander (Eds.), *Empowerment self-defense: Theory, research and practice*. Academic Press.

Blashill, A. J., Fox, K., Feinstein, B. A., Albright, C. A., & Calzo, J. P. (2021). Nonsuicidal self-injury, suicide ideation, and suicide attempts among sexual minority children. *Journal of Consulting and Clinical Psychology, 89*, 73–80.

Brooks, V. R. (1981). *Minority stress and lesbian women*. Lexington Books.

Comer, J. S., Georgiadis, C., Schmarder, K., Chen, D., Coyne, C. A., Gudiño, O. G., Kazantzis, N., Langer, D. A., LeBeau, R. T., Liu, R. T., McLean, C., Sloan, D. M., Williams, M. T., & Pachankis, J. E. (2024). Reckoning with our past and righting our future: Report from the behavior therapy task force on sexual orientation and gender identity/expression change efforts (SOGIECEs). *Behavior Therapy, 55*(4), 649–679. https://doi.org/10.1016/j.beth.2024.05.006

Daley, D. C., & Douaihy, A. B. (2023). *Managing substance use disorder: Practitioner guide* (3rd ed.). Oxford University Press.

Daley, D. C., & Marlatt, G. A. (2006). *Overcoming your alcohol or drug problem: Effective recovery strategies: Therapist guide* (2nd ed.). Oxford University Press.

DeMarce, J. M., Gnys, M., Raffa, S. D., & Karlin, B. E. (2014). *Cognitive behavioral therapy for substance use disorders among veterans: Therapist manual*. U.S. Department of Veterans Affairs.

Dürrbaum, T., & Sattler, F. A. (2020). Minority stress and mental health in lesbian, gay male, and bisexual youths: A meta-analysis. *Journal of LGBT Youth, 17*(3), 298–314. https://doi.org/10.1080/19361653.2019.1586615

Epstein, E. E., & McCrady, B. S. (2007). *Overcoming alcohol use problems: A cognitive-behavioral treatment program* (1st ed.). Oxford University Press.

Feinstein, B. A., & Dyar, C. (2017). Bisexuality, minority stress, and health. *Current Sexual Health Reports, 9*, 42–49.

Feinstein, B. A., Katz, B. W., Benjamin, I., Macaulay, T., Dyar, C., & Morgan, E. (2023). Disparities in depression and anxiety related to sexual orientation and gender identity among older adults: The role of age discrimination. *Stigma and Health*. Advance online publication. https://doi.org/10.1037/sah0000462

Feinstein, B. A., van der Star, A., Dorrell, K., & Blashill, A. J. (2024). Sexual orientation and mental health in a US cohort of children: A longitudinal mediation study. *Journal of Child Psychology and Psychiatry, 65*(2), 188–198. https://doi.org/10.1111/jcpp.13873

Flentje, A., Bacca, C. L., & Cochran, B. N. (2015). Missing data in substance abuse research? Researchers' reporting practices of sexual orientation and gender identity. *Drug and alcohol dependence, 147*, 280–284. https://doi.org/10.1016/j.drugalcdep.2014.11.012

Foa, E. B., Hembree, E. A., Rothbaum, B. O., & Rauch, S. A. M. (2019). *Prolonged exposure therapy for PTSD: Emotional processing of traumatic experiences: Therapist guide* (2nd ed.). Oxford University Press.

Fredriksen-Goldsen, K. I., Kim, H. J., Barkan, S. E., et al. (2013). Health disparities among lesbian, gay, and bisexual older adults: Results from a population-based study. *American Journal of Public Health, 103*(10), 1802–1809.

Fredriksen-Goldsen, K. I., Cook-Daniels, L., Kim, H.-J., Erosheva, E. A., Emlet, C. A., HoyEllis, C. P., Goldsen, J., & Muraco, A. (2014a). Physical and mental health of transgender older adults: An at-risk and underserved population. *The Gerontologist, 54*(3), 488–500. https://doi.org/10.1093/geront/gnt021

Fredriksen-Goldsen, K. I., Simoni, J. M., Kim, H.-J., Lehavot, K., Walters, K. L., Yang, J., & Hoy-Ellis, C. P. (2014b). The Health Equity Promotion Model: Reconceptualization of lesbian, gay, bisexual, and transgender (LGBT) health disparities. *The American Journal of Orthopsychiatry, 84*(6), 653–663. https://doi.org/10.1037/ort0000030

Haas, S. M., & Lannutti, P. J. (2024). "They are giving folks permission to discriminate and hate": A 4-year longitudinal analysis of perceived impact of the Trump administration on LGBTQ+ individuals and relationships, 2017–2020. *Sex Research and Social Policy, 21*(1), 62–75. https://doi.org/10.1007/s13178-023-00843-x

Harper, K., Hinds, Z., Benevides, E., & Livingston, N.A. (2022). Increasing visibility of transgender and gender diverse individuals in trauma and PTSD research. International Society for Traumatic Stress Studies: Stress Points Newsletter. https://istss.org/public-resources/trauma-blog/2022-march/increasing-visibility-of-transgender-andgender-di

Hatzenbuehler, M. L. (2009). How does sexual minority stigma "get under the skin"? A psychological mediation framework. *Psychological Bulletin, 135*(5), 707–730. https://doi.org/10.1037/a0016441

Hatzenbuehler, M. L. (2016). Structural stigma: Research evidence and implications for psychological science. *American Psychologist, 71*(8), 742–751. https://doi.org/10.1037/amp0000068

Hayes, S. C., Brownell, K. D., & Barlow, D. H. (1983). Heterosocial-skills training and covert sensitization. Effects on social skills and sexual arousal in sexual deviants. *Behaviour Research and Therapy, 21*(4), 383–392. https://doi.org/10.1016/0005-7967(83)90007-4

Heck, N.C., Mirabito, L.A., LeMaire, K., Livingston, N.A., & Flentje, A. (2017). Omitted data in randomized controlled trials for anxiety and depression: A systematic review of the inclusion of sexual orientation and gender identity. *Journal of Consulting and Clinical Psychology, 85*(1), 72–76. http://dx.doi.org/10.1037/ccp0000123

Hendricks, M. L., & Testa, R. J. (2012). A conceptual framework for clinical work with transgender and gender nonconforming clients: An adaptation of the Minority Stress Model. *Professional Psychology: Research and Practice, 43*(5), 460–467. https://doi.org/10.1037/a0029597

Hollinsaid, N. L., Weisz, J. R., Chorpita, B. F., Skov, H. E., The Research Network On Youth Mental Health, & Price, M. A. (2020). The effectiveness and acceptability of empirically supported treatments in gender minority youth across four randomized controlled trials. *Journal of Consulting and Clinical Psychology, 88*(12), 1053–1064. https://doi.org/10.1037/ccp0000597

Hughes, L. D., Kidd, K. M., Gamarel, K. E., Operario, D., & Dowshen, N. (2021). "These laws will be devastating": Provider perspectives on legislation banning gender-affirming care for transgender adolescents. *Journal of Adolescent Health, 69*(6), 976–982. https://doi.org/10.1016/j.jadohealth.2021.08.020

Kadden, R. M., & Litt, M. D. (2011). *Overcoming alcohol use problems: Therapist guide: A cognitive-behavioral treatment program*. Oxford University Press.

Katz, B. W., Chang, C. J., Dorrell, K. D., Selby, E. A., & Feinstein, B. A. (2023). Aspects of positive identity buffer the longitudinal associations between discrimination and suicidal ideation among bi+ young adults. *Journal of Consulting and Clinical Psychology, 91*(5), 313–322. https://doi.org/10.1037/ccp0000788

Kraschel, K. L., Chen, A., Turban, J. L., & Cohen, I. G. (2022). Legislation restricting gender-affirming care for transgender youth: Politics eclipse healthcare. *Cell Reports Medicine, 3*(8), 100719. https://doi.org/10.1016/j.xcrm.2022.100719

Kuroki, M. (2021). The rise in extreme mental distress among LGBT people during Trump's rise and presidency. *Economics and Human Biology, 43*, 101034. https://doi.org/10.1016/j.ehb.2021.101034

Lee, S. Y., Vergara-Lopez, C., Jennings, E., Nugent, N. R., Parade, S. H., Tyrka, A. R., & Stroud, L. R. (2024). How can we build structural resilience? Integration of social-ecological and minority stress models. *American Psychologist, 79*(8), 1012–1024. https://doi.org/10.1037/amp0001252

Livingston, N. A. (2023). Trauma, minority stress, and disproportionate health burden among LGBTQ+ people. *National Center for PTSD Research Quarterly, 34*(4).

Livingston, N. A., Flentje, A., Heck, N. C., Szalda-Petree, A., & Cochran, B. (2017). Ecological momentary assessment of daily discrimination experiences and nicotine, alcohol, and drug use among sexual and gender minority individuals. *Journal of Consulting and Clinical Psychology, 85*(12), 1131–1143. https://doi.org/10.1037/ccp0000252

Livingston, N. A., Berke, D. S., Ruben, M. A., Matza, A. R., & Shipherd, J. C. (2019). Experiences of trauma, discrimination, microaggressions, and minority stress among trauma-exposed LGBT veterans: Unexpected findings and unresolved service gaps. *Psychological Trauma: Theory, Research, Practice, and Policy, 11*(7), 695–703. https://doi.org/10.1037/tra0000464

Livingston, N. A., Berke, D., Scholl, J., Ruben, M., & Shipherd, J. (2020a). Addressing diversity in PTSD treatment: Clinical considerations and guidance for the treatment of PTSD in LGBTQ populations. *Current Treatment Options in Psychiatry, 7*(2), 53–69. https://doi.org/10.1007/s40501-020-00204-0

Livingston, N. A., Flentje, A., Brennan, J., Mereish, E., Reed, O., & Cochran, B. (2020b). Real-time associations between discrimination and anxious and depressed mood among sexual and gender minorities: The moderating effects of lifetime victimization and identity concealment. *Psychology of Sexual Orientation and Gender Diversity, 7*(2), 132–141. https://doi.org/10.1037/sgd0000371

Livingston, N. A., Lynch, K. E., Hinds, Z., Gatsby, E., DuVall, S. L., & Shipherd, J. (2022). Identifying posttraumatic stress disorder and disparity among transgender veterans using nationwide Veterans Health Administration electronic health record data. *LGBT Health, 9*(2), 94–102. https://doi.org/10.1089/lgbt.2021.0246

Matsuno, E., & Israel, T. (2018). Psychological interventions promoting resilience among transgender individuals: Transgender resilience intervention model (TRIM). *The Counseling Psychologist, 46*(5), 632–655. https://doi.org/10.1177/0011000018787261

Manalastas, E. J., Sain, K. S., Blumenau, H. S., Katz, B. W., & Feinstein, B. A. (2024). Associations between antibisexual discrimination from heterosexual versus lesbian/gay sources and bisexual people's depression, anxiety, and psychological distress: A systematic review and meta-analysis. Psychology of Sexual Orientation and Gender Diversity. Advance online publication. https://doi.org/10.1037/sgd0000795.

Martell, C. R., Dimidjian, S., & Herman-Dunn, R. (2022). *Behavioral activation for depression: A clinician's guide* (2nd ed.). Guilford Press.

McLean, K. C., Fish, J., Rogers, L. O., & Syed, M. (2024). Integrating systems of power and privilege in the study of resilience. *American Psychologist, 79*(8), 999–1011. https://doi.org/10.1037/amp0001260

Meyer, I. H. (2015). Resilience in the study of minority stress and health of sexual and gender minorities. *Psychology of Sexual Orientation and Gender Diversity, 2*(3), 209–213. https://doi.org/10.1037/sgd0000132

Meyer, I. H. (2003). Prejudice, social stress, and mental health in lesbian, gay, and bisexual populations: Conceptual issues and research evidence. *Psychological Bulletin, 129*(5), 674–697. https://doi.org/10.1037/0033-2909.129.5.674

Morris, E. R., Lindley, L., & Galupo, M. P. (2020). "Better issues to focus on": Transgender microaggressions as ethical violations in therapy. *The Counseling Psychologist, 48*(6), 883–915. https://doi.org/10.1177/0011000020924391

Pachankis, J. E. (2007). The psychological implications of concealing a stigma: A cognitive-affective-behavioral model. *Psychological Bulletin, 133*(2), 328–345. https://doi.org/10.1037/0033-2909.133.2.328

Pachankis, J. E., Hatzenbuehler, M. L., Rendina, H. J., Safren, S. A., & Parsons, J. T. (2015). LGB-affirmative cognitive-behavioral therapy for young adult gay and bisexual men: A randomized controlled trial of a transdiagnostic minority stress approach. *Journal of Consulting and Clinical Psychology, 83*(5), 875–889. https://doi.org/10.1037/ccp0000037

Pachankis, J. E., Mahon, C. P., Jackson, S. D., Fetzner, B. K., & Bränström, R. (2020a). Sexual orientation concealment and mental health: A conceptual and meta-analytic review. *Psychological Bulletin, 146*(10), 831–871. https://doi.org/10.1037/bul0000271

Pachankis, J. E., McConocha, E. M., Clark, K. A., Wang, K., Behari, K., Fetzner, B. K., Brisbin, C. D., Scheer, J. R., & Lehavot, K. (2020b). A transdiagnostic minority stress intervention for gender diverse sexual minority women's depression, anxiety, and unhealthy alcohol use: A randomized controlled trial. *Journal of Consulting and Clinical Psychology, 88*(7), 613–630. https://doi.org/10.1037/ccp0000508

Pachankis, J. E., Harkness, A., Maciejewski, K. R., Behari, K., Clark, K. A., McConocha, E., Winston, R., Adeyinka, O., Reynolds, J., Bränström, R., Esserman, D. A., Hatzenbuehler, M. L., & Safren, S. A. (2022). LGBQ-affirmative cognitive-behavioral therapy for young gay and bisexual men's mental and sexual health: A three-arm randomized controlled trial. *Journal of Consulting and Clinical Psychology, 90*(6), 459–477. https://doi.org/10.1037/ccp0000724

Parmenter, J. G., & Galliher, R. V. (2023). Experiences of community resilience and inequity among LGBTQ+ people: A person-centered analysis. *The Counseling Psychologist, 51*(1), 84–112. https://doi.org/10.1177/00110000221124274

Parmenter, J. G., Gao, S., Khan, N. S., Lê, D., Staton, D., & Galupo, M. P. (2024). "My healing journey gives back to my communities": Experiences of intersectional resilience and liberation among queer and trans black, indigenous, and people of color. *Psychology of Sexual Orientation and Gender Diversity*. Advance online publication. https://doi.org/10.1037/sgd0000750

Price, S. F., Puckett, J., & Mocarski, R. (2021). The impact of the 2016 US presidential elections on transgender and gender diverse people. *Sex Research and Social Policy, 18*(4), 1094–1103. https://doi.org/10.1007/s13178-020-00513-2

Puckett, J. A., Glozier, K., Kimball, D., Matsuno, E., MacBeth, M., Olko, A., Clements, Z., & Galupo, M. P. (2025). "I was resilient before I knew that resilience was a thing": Transgender and nonbinary people's perspectives on resilience. *Journal of Prevention and Health Promotion, 6*(2), 275–300. https://doi.org/10.1177/26320770241308397

Resick, P. A., Monson, C. M., & Chard, K. M. (2017). *Cognitive processing therapy for PTSD: A comprehensive therapist manual* (2nd ed.). Guilford Press.

Rimes, K. A., Ion, D., Wingrove, J., & Carter, B. (2019). Sexual orientation differences in psychological treatment outcomes for depression and anxiety: National cohort study. *Journal of Consulting and Clinical Psychology, 87*(7), 577–589. https://doi.org/10.1037/ccp0000416

Salomaa, A., Livingston, N. A., Bryant, W., Herbitter, C., Harper, K., Sloan, C., Hinds, Z., Gyuro, L., Valentine, S., & Shipherd, J. (2022). A bottom-up approach to developing a unified trauma-minority stress model for transgender and gender diverse people. *Psychological Trauma: Theory, Research, Practice, and Policy*. Advance online publication. https://doi.org/10.1037/tra0001373

Salomaa, A. C., Berke, D., Harper, K., Valentine, S. E., Sloan, C. A., Hinds, Z., Gyuro, L., Herbitter, C., Bryant, W. T., Shipherd, J. C., & Livingston, N. A. (2024). A patient-centered model of mental health care for trauma and minority stress in transgender and gender diverse people: A bottom-up network analysis. *Psychology of Sexual Orientation and Gender Diversity*. Advance online publication. https://doi.org/10.1037/sgd0000705

Shapiro, F. (2018). *Eye movement desensitization and reprocessing (EMDR) therapy: Basic principles, protocols, and procedures* (3rd ed.). Guilford Press.

Shipherd, J., Berke, D., & Livingston, N. A. (2019). Trauma recovery in the transgender and gender diverse (TGD) community: Extensions of the minority stress model for treatment planning. *Cognitive & Behavioral Practice, 26*(4), 629–646. https://doi.org/10.1016/j.cbpra.2019.06.001

Shipherd, J. C., Lynch, K., Gatsby, E., Hinds, Z., DuVall, S. L., & Livingston, N. A. (2021). Estimating prevalence of PTSD among veterans with minoritized sexual orientations using electronic health record data. *Journal of consulting and clinical psychology, 89*(10), 856–868. https://doi.org/10.1037/ccp0000691

Singh, A. A., & Chun, K. Y. S. (2015). Multiracial/multiethnic queer and transgender clients: Intersections of identity and resilience. In *Casebook for counseling: Lesbian, gay, bisexual, and transgender persons and their families* (pp. 197–209). Wiley.

Sloan, D. M., & Marx, B. P. (2019). *Written exposure therapy for PTSD: A brief treatment approach for mental health professionals*. American Psychological Association.

Trans Legislation Tracker. (2024). *2023 anti-trans legislation*. https://translegislation.com/bills/2023

Veldhuis, C. B., Cascalheira, C., Delucio, K., Budge, S., Matsuno, E., Huynh, K., Puckett, J. A., Balsam, K., Velez, B., & Galupo, M. P. (2024). Guidelines for writing up and publishing LGBTQIA+ research. *Psychology of Sexual Orientation and Gender Diversity, 1*(3), 365–396. https://doi.org/10.1037/sgd0000722

Weissman, M. M., Markowitz, J. C., & Klerman, G. L. (2018). The guide to interpersonal psychotherapy (Updated and expanded ed.). Oxford University Press.

Wilson, L. C., Newins, A. R., Kassing, F., & Casanova, T. (2024). Gender minority stress and resilience measure: A meta-analysis of the associations with mental health in transgender and gender diverse individuals. *Trauma, Violence & Abuse, 25*(3), 2552–2564. https://doi.org/10.1177/15248380231218288

Wittgens, C., Fischer, M. M., Buspavanich, P., Theobald, S., Schweizer, K., & Trautmann, S. (2022). Mental health in people with minority sexual orientations: A meta-analysis of population-based studies. *Acta Psychiatrica Scandinavica, 145*(4), 357–372. https://doi.org/10.1111/acps.13405

Nicholas A. Livingston, PhD, [he/him] is a Principal Investigator and Staff Psychologist in the National Center for PTSD, Behavioral Science Division, VA Boston Healthcare System; and an Assistant Professor of Psychiatry at Boston University Chobanian & Avedisian School of Medicine. For over 15 years he has studied the effects of trauma, discrimination, and minority stress on health among LGBTQ+ individuals. Other primary research interests include PTSD and substance use and disorder (SUD) comorbidity, treatment access and outcomes, and adverse events (e.g., relapse, overdose, suicide). Primary clinical expertise includes evidence-based SUD and PTSD treatment and patient centered adaptations to evidence-based care for LGBTQ+ people. Dr. Livingston is an Associate Editor of *Behavioral Medicine*, Contributing Editor of *StressPoints* for the International Society for Traumatic Stress Studies, and serves on the editorial boards of *Psychology of Sexual Orientation and Gender Diversity* and *Cognitive and Behavioral Practice*.

Brian A. Feinstein, PhD, [he/him] is a Professor in the Department of Psychology at Rosalind Franklin University of Medicine and Science and a Licensed Psychologist in Illinois. His program of research focuses on understanding and reducing the health disparities affecting sexual and gender minority (SGM) populations, especially bisexual, pansexual, and queer (bi+) individuals. In particular, his work focuses on understanding how different types of stress (e.g., discrimination, internalized stigma, rejection sensitivity) influence mental health, substance use, sexual behavior, and relationship functioning among SGM individuals and couples, and developing and testing interventions to improve health and relationships in these populations. He is an Associate Editor for *Psychology of Sexual Orientation and Gender Diversity* and *Behavior Therapy* and serves on the editorial board of the *Journal of Consulting and Clinical Psychology*.

M. Paz Galupo, PhD, [they/them] is the Audre Lorde Distinguished Professor of Sexual Health and Education at Washington University in St. Louis and Director of QT-CREW (Queer/Trans Collective for Research on Equity & Wellness). Dr. Galupo's research centers the intersection of sexual orientation and gender identity, with a particular focus on understanding non-binary expressions of bisexual/plurisexual and transgender experience, as well as on queer and trans BIPOC. Dr. Galupo is currently Editor for *Journal of Bisexuality*, and the Editor for the official Division 44 APA journal, *Psychology of Sexual Orientation and Gender Diversity*.

Chapter 2
Person-Centered Screening, Assessment, and Case Formulation for Diverse LGBTQ+ Individuals

Kelly L. Harper, Joelle T. Taknint, Anna C. Salomaa, Alison Duncan, and Sarah E. Valentine

Highlights

- LGBTQ+ people are frequently overpathologized and stigmatized in mental healthcare settings, including being provided highly stigmatizing and inaccurate diagnoses.
- Person-centered (i.e., centering the voice, experiences and preferences of the client), collaborative, and affirming assessment and case conceptualization with LGBTQ+ clients can help reduce inaccurate diagnosis and stigma.
- Collaborative/Therapeutic Assessment (Collaborative/Therapuetic Assessment) is an assessment approach that focuses on addressing the questions the client has

K. L. Harper (✉)
National Center for PTSD, Behavioral Science Division, Boston, MA, USA

Chobanian & Avedisian School of Medicine, Psychiatry Department, Boston University, Boston, MA, USA
e-mail: kelly.harper@va.gov

J. T. Taknint · S. E. Valentine
Chobanian & Avedisian School of Medicine, Psychiatry Department, Boston University, Boston, MA, USA

Boston Medical Center, Boston, MA, USA

A. C. Salomaa
Chobanian & Avedisian School of Medicine, Psychiatry Department, Boston University, Boston, MA, USA

VA Boston Healthcare System, Boston, MA, USA

A. Duncan
Chobanian & Avedisian School of Medicine, Psychiatry Department, Boston University, Boston, MA, USA

N. A. Livingston et al. (eds.), *Addressing Minority Stress and Enhancing Resilience with Diverse LGBTQ+ Clients*, CBT: Science Into Practice, https://doi.org/10.1007/978-3-031-92836-9_2

about themself and working collaboratively to select assessment materials to address these questions.
- In this chapter we review Collaborative/Therapuetic Assessment strategies and apply them to a case example to demonstrate person-centered, collaborative assessment, and case conceptualization with an LGBTQ+ client.
- We also provide recommendations for future research and practice on screening, assessment, and case conceptualization among LGBTQ+ people.

Positionality

Kelly Harper, PhD (she/they) identifies as atheist, white, pansexual, and non-binary. They are United States-born, from an upper-middle class SES background, are of European descent, and are without developmental or acquired disability. They are a licensed clinical psychologist, trained from a cognitive-behavioral theoretical orientation. Their research and clinical expertise is in trauma, posttraumatic stress disorder (PTSD), LGBTQ+ minority stress, and adapting evidence-based interventions to address the intersection of trauma and minority stress.

Joelle Taos Taknint, PhD, MSc (she/her) is an agnostic, straight, multiethnic, cisgender women of Amazigh (indigenous North African), European, and Middle Eastern descent. She is a US born second-generation immigrant of a middle SES background without developmental or acquired disability. She is a licensed clinical psychologist with research expertise in immigrant and refugee mental health, identity development, and discrimination. Her clinical expertise is in immigrant mental health care and psychological assessment.

Anna Salomaa, PhD (she/her) identifies as atheist, white, bisexual, and a cisgender woman. She is United States-born, from a middle class SES background, of European descent, and is without developmental or acquired disability. She is a licensed clinical psychologist, trained from cognitive-behavioral and psychodynamic theoretical orientations. Her research and clinical expertise are in LGBTQ+ minority stress and primary care mental health integration.

Alison Duncan, MD (she/her) is a generation x, pagan/unitarian universalist, lesbian, white, cisgender femme with butch adornments. She is second-generation Irish-American. She is without developmental or acquired disability. She is a board-certified child, adolescent and adult psychiatrist and her clinical work is primarily with children, adolescents and transitional-age adults. Her research focuses on psychiatric emergency care, suicide prevention, quality improvement, and parent-adolescent communication in the context of ADHD.

Sarah Valentine, PhD (she/her) is an atheist, straight, White, ciswoman of European descent. She is US-born of low-middle income SES background to two military veteran parents from the United States and the United Kingdom. She is without developmental or acquired disability. She is a licensed clinical psychologist with research expertise in community-engaged adaptation and implementation of evidence-based treatments for PTSD, with a focus on reducing racial and socioeconomic inequities in access and quality of treatment in usual care settings in the US. Her clinical expertise is in the application of cognitive and behavioral interventions for PTSD.

Introduction

Although there is a growing body of research that aims to quantify components of the minority stress framework (Brooks, 1981; Hendricks & Testa, 2012; Meyer, 2003), integrated models for assessment, case conceptualization, and treatment planning are limited. As such, LGBTQ+ individuals continue to be misdiagnosed and have their normative responses to interpersonal and sociocultural systems of oppression pathologized. Expected responses to chronic invalidation and interpersonal harm, or experiences of gender dysphoria, are often misdiagnosed as personality disorders due to both clinician and measurement biases (Rodriguez-Seijas et al., 2021). Additionally, limitations in measures and screening tools complicate accurate screening and assessment. For example, screening and assessment tools may perform differently in LGBTQ+ and non-LGBTQ+ samples (Bauerband et al., 2019; Borgogna et al., 2021), often use gendered and heterosexist language, and lack norming data with LGBTQ+ populations.

To address these limitations, screening, assessment, and case formulation for LGBTQ+ clients should be informed by the clients' past and current sociopolitical and psychosocial contexts (including the client's historical and current experiences of discrimination), identification of what is adaptive responding to unsafe circumstances, and awareness of limitations to assessment measures. In this chapter, we provide strategies for conducting affirming, person-centered (i.e., centering the voice, experiences, and goals of the client) assessment and case conceptualization for LGBTQ+ clients. We review strategies of Collaborative/Therapeutic Assessment, a psychological assessment framework that is collaborative and flexible, and describe a clinical case using Collaborative/Therapeutic Assessment approaches with a fictitious LGBTQ+ client. Lastly, we provide additional assessment recommendations for researchers and clinicians.

Assessment and Conceptualization Framework

Collaborative/Therapeutic Assessment is a modality of psychological assessment that may be particularly useful with LGTBQ+ clients because of its foundational values of collaboration, respect, humility, compassion, openness, and curiosity (Smith, 2016). Collaborative/Therapeutic Assessment is focused on addressing the questions the client has about themself and collaboratively working together to select assessment materials to address these questions. Within the Collaborative/Therapeutic Assessment framework, test data are shared and interpreted with clients collaboratively, and conclusions are drawn in partnership with the client throughout the assessment process (see Fig. 2.1 for an adaptation of the steps to Collaborative/Therapeutic Assessment from Therapeutic Assessment Institute, n.d.).

The process of ongoing collaboration, sharing of information, and interpretation of the meaning of information in partnership with the client likely reduces power

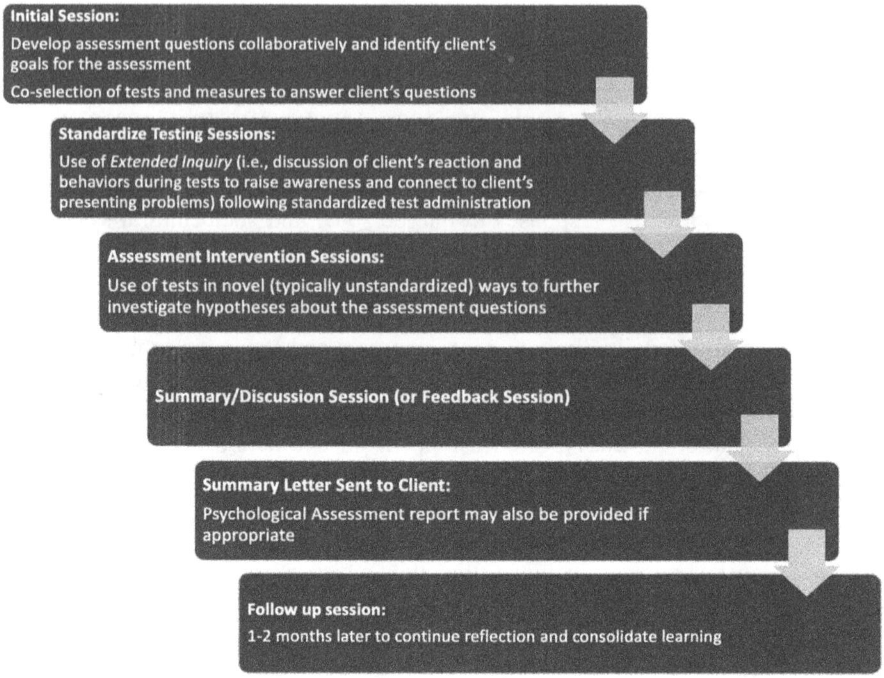

Fig. 2.1 Overview of Collaborative/Therapeutic Assessment Steps, as outlined by the Therapeutic Assessment Institute (n.d.)

differentials that are inherent in mental health assessment settings. Collaborative/Therapeutic Assessment may be especially useful among LGBTQ+ communities, as these communities have experienced historical stigmatization and discrimination from the medical community, including from mental health care professionals, resulting in understandable distrust of medical and mental health providers (e.g., Brenick et al., 2017; Cahill, 2017). Collaborative/Therapeutic Assessment helps to center individuals' experiences and enables individuals to be active agents in their healthcare assessment, interpretation and understanding of their experiences, and treatment planning. Although Collaborative/Therapeutic Assessment can act as a stand-alone psychological intervention,[1] components or aspects of Collaborative/Therapeutic Assessment can be used in screening, assessment, and case conceptualization to increase person-centeredness, collaboration, and affirmation without the full model needing to be implemented.

To illustrate the use of Collaborative/Therapeutic Assessment strategies as a collaborative and affirming assessment practice with LGBTQ+ communities, we

[1] Collaborative/Therapuetic Assessment has demonstrated enhanced client (e.g., improved self-efficacy, self-esteem, increased readiness for and engagement in treatment, decreased psychological symptomatology) and treatment process (e.g., improved treatment alliance, hopefulness) outcomes (Aschieri et al., 2016; Durosini & Aschieri, 2021).

provide a fictionalized case example, which is an amalgamation of several clients. Throughout the case example we discuss ways Collaborative/Therapeutic Assessment strategies were applied. We have changed all identifying information for this case example.

Case Example

Sol (pronouns: they/them), a 22-year-old nonbinary, pansexual, Mexican American person, was referred for psychological assessment by a licensed independent clinical social worker (LICSW) within a chronic pain clinic for diagnostic clarity and treatment recommendations. A licensed clinical psychologist trained in Collaborative/Therapeutic Assessment conducted the assessment. Sol self-identified as neurodivergent and requested formal evaluation for attention deficit-hyperactivity disorder (ADHD). In addition, they sought psychological assessment for diagnostic clarification regarding the effects of trauma, symptoms of anxiety and depression, and psychological effects of coping with chronic pain on their current well-being and functioning. Of note, Sol also presented with acculturative stress related to their Mexican American identity and frequent moves between Mexico and the United States as a child and young adult. They noted that their extended family was not accepting of their gender identity and worried they would never be accepted by their family given their family's cultural and religious beliefs. Sol reported distress related to feeling like they do not "belong anywhere" and concern that if they do not have ADHD, they will lose access to the neurodivergent queer community they were part of. Sol was seen in a short-term assessment clinic[2] where assessments tend to be completed in 3–5 sessions that range from 1–2 h per session and include a feedback session.[3]

First Session (90-Minute Initial Appointment)

The primary goal of the initial appointment was to figure out Sol's own questions for the assessment and what they wanted to get out of the assessment, consistent with a Collaborative/Therapeutic Assessment approach. The clinician and client worked together to discuss the current problems they were having (e.g., inattention,

---

[2]Therapeutic assessments typically range from 3–10 sessions (Durosini & Aschieri, 2021). Brief models of therapeutic assessment (e.g., collection of assessment questions, delivery of MMPI-2, feedback appointment) have also been found to improve symptomology and self-esteem (Finn & Tonsager, 1997). Therefore, aspects of Collaborative/Therapeutic Assessment can be used in assessment settings with only 1–2 visits.

[3]Assessment sessions were divided into relatively shorter assessment sessions than typical due to the client's fatigue, pain, and difficulty concentrating. Additionally, the provider read some self-report test items aloud to the client to reduce fatigue and pain.

Table 2.1 Case example Sol's assessment questions

"Why do I have so much trouble paying attention?"
"Is this just depression? Why do I feel so overwhelmed and so fatigued all the time?"
"How has trauma affected me?"
"Can I get better? What would help?"

extreme fatigue, hopelessness, constant worry) and to reframe these problems as questions that could be co-investigated over the course of the assessment. Table 2.1 presents Sol's questions, generated during the initial session.

In the first session, to begin to elicit Sol's conceptualization of their presenting concerns, the assessor administered sections one and two of the Diagnostic and Statistical Manual for Mental Disorders, 5th edition (*DSM*-5) Cultural Formulation Interview. These sections are focused on assessing the cultural definition of the problem and cultural perception of cause, context, and support for the problem (APA, 2013; Aschieri et al., 2016).[4] Examples of questions or prompts the assessor used from the Cultural Formulation Interview are presented in Table 2.2. In addition to these Cultural Formulation Interview questions and prompts, the assessor also included questions to facilitate hypothesis generation with Sol about potential answers to the assessment questions, as client hypothesis generation and eliciting client curiosity are core components of Collaborative/Therapeutic Assessment. This process is also helpful for collaboratively discussing the client's conceptualization and understanding of the problem while also beginning to shift the client's focus from a place of distress to one of curiosity as they explore their own initial hypotheses about the answers to their questions.

Through this conversation, Sol hypothesized that if they have ADHD, it was likely overlooked by teachers and other health care providers because they presented as a girl in childhood and teachers and providers often attributed attentional difficulties to the client being "a sad, quiet child". They also hypothesized that they had been targeted for sexual assault in adolescence due to their gender identity, sexual orientation, and ethnicity.

Following the first session, collateral information was collected from the referring provider and past mental health providers. Sol had an extensive mental health history in the context of integrated behavioral medicine due to experiencing chronic headaches; however, they had not undergone a formal diagnostic evaluation before. Thus, their previous diagnoses were generally nonspecific and included: anxiety disorder, unspecified; depressive disorder, unspecified; and a rule out of personality disorder, unspecified.

[4] Strand and Bäärnhielm (2022) provide recommendations for ways to enhance the delivery of the Cultural Formulation Interview to increase the therapeutic effect.

Table 2.2 Examples of questions and prompts used from the Cultural Formulation Interview

Interview domain	Example questions or prompts
Perceptions of cause, context, and support	"Tell me more about when the problem began…"
	"Why do you think this is happening to you? What do you think are the causes of the problem?"
Stressors and supports	"What are factors or contexts that increase or decrease the problem?"
	"Are there any kinds of stresses or contexts that make the problem worse?"
Self-coping	"Tell me more about the ways in which you have attempted to cope with the problem include…"
	"How effective have these strategies been?"
Collaborative/Therapeutic assessment hypothesis generation	"Any initial ideas you have about potential answers to the assessment questions?"

Assessment Sessions

The following assessment sessions included: (1) collection of the client's developmental history, (2) collaborative selection of initial test measures, (3) administration of measures, (4) extended inquiry[5] into test responses and client's behaviors and experiences during test administration, and (5) ongoing review of test results and exploration of Sol's evolving hypotheses about their assessment question. Initial sessions were focused more on administration of tests and later sessions were focused more on exploring client's reactions to tests and exploring different hypotheses during test administration.

Developmental Background and Selection of Measures Following the initial appointment, the assessor collected Sol's developmental history as it pertains to the assessment questions, including prior experiences with mental health and healthcare. The assessor asked open-ended questions about Sol's past experiences with mental health care and their perceptions of those experiences.[6] Sol reported dissatisfaction with previous mental health providers and noted feeling they had to re-explain their history and problems without any clarity on their diagnoses or clear treatment recommendations. Sol reported feeling uncertain about the appropriateness of their diagnoses and feeling confused about "what was really going on with

[5] Extended inquiry involves joint discussion between assessor and client on the client's reactions, behaviors, and experiences during tests to help raise awareness and understanding of the experience and connect it with the client's assessment questions and presenting problems.

[6] See *DSM-5 Cultural Formulation Interview* for examples of questions to assess past perceptions of and experiences with mental health care. Many LGBTQ+ individuals have had past negative experiences with mental health care, which can impact their openness and willingness to seek care in the future. Assessing these experiences and providing an affirming, supportive space to discuss these experiences can: (1) inform ways that mental health care can be more affirming and supportive for the client, and (2) validate the experiences the client has had in the past.

them", which informed the questions they generated for this assessment (e.g., diagnostic clarity).

Regarding symptoms, Sol reported a long history of difficulty focusing, forgetfulness, and disorganization since early childhood that negatively impacted their schoolwork. They also reported struggling with schoolwork and in social contexts due to frequently moving between Mexico and the United States, which made it difficult to have continuity in schoolwork and friendships. Sol indicated that they often felt "othered" and like an outsider.

Regarding other symptoms, they reported experiencing symptoms of depressed mood, low self-esteem, low motivation, and sleep difficulties, including nightmares, that began in mid-childhood and progressed throughout adolescence and early adulthood. Sol indicated that these symptoms worsened during late childhood/early adolescence during which time they began outwardly exploring their gender identity and gender expression (e.g., dressing less feminine, cutting their hair short). Sol endorsed experiencing significant rejection from friends, family, and community, including harassment at school from peers and teachers and from their family members (e.g., calling them slurs, bullying, exclusion, and attempts to control their gender expression from family and teachers). Additionally, they were sexually assaulted by a peer in adolescence, which they attributed to be due to their ethnicity, sexual orientation, and gender identity. They reported feeling like they weren't safe anywhere and endorsed significant anxiety/worry and physiological symptoms consistent with panic attacks (e.g., heart racing, sweating, difficulty breathing, stomach upset, dizziness). Lastly, Sol reported a history of somatic and physical health difficulties, including chronic and severe headaches, fatigue, and gastrointestinal problems beginning in adolescence and worsening throughout early adulthood.

Following the collection of developmental history, the assessor selected initial test measures that were responsive to Sol's specific assessment questions (e.g., selecting the Minnesota Multiphasic Personality Inventory-3 [MMPI-3; Ben-Porath & Tellegen, 2020] to broadly assess presence of psychological symptoms for diagnostic clarity regarding depression and impacts of trauma). See Table 2.3 for the full list of assessment measures delivered throughout the assessment. Consistent with Collaborative/Therapeutic Assessment, psychological tests selected for the assessment were used as "empathy magnifiers," meaning that they are tools to increase the assessor's understanding and empathy for the client and their experiences (e.g., a way to step into the client's perspective while also maintaining a separate view of the experience) (Finn & Tonsager, 1997). In order to cultivate trust in the utility of the assessment process and develop a collaborative assessment partnership, it is helpful to include face valid measures that speak to the client's specific concerns in the early stages of the assessment (Finn, 2020).[7] For example, the assessor included the Barkley Adult ADHD Rating Scale-IV (BAARS-IV; Barkley, 2011) childhood and adult report (self and informant report) and the Behavior Rating Inventory of Executive Function for Adults (self and informant report; Gioia et al., 2000) in the

[7] Face valid measures for our case are noted with ** in Table 2.3.

initial assessment session as these are face-valid measures for ADHD and attentional difficulties which were Sol's primary concerns.

In addition to selecting measures relevant to Sol's concerns, the assessor collaborated with Sol regarding test selection (and which tests to not include) and explained how each test was relevant to the client's concerns. For example, Sol had an existing and nuanced understanding of how minority stress and their own intersecting identities were marginalized through structural oppression (e.g., housing discrimination, health care discrimination, school-based discrimination) and how these factors impact their mental health. This was largely elucidated during the Cultural Formulation Interview. For this reason, the assessor and client did not think there would be strong incremental validity in adding discrete measures of minority stress to the assessment battery. Rather, the assessor used the client's conceptualization garnered through the Cultural Formulation Interview throughout the assessment process and situated assessment results within this context. However, other

Table 2.3 Selection of measures and conceptualization process

Client's assessment questions	Measure selection	What was learned (diagnostically)	Narrative shifts (co-created through the assessment)
"Why do I have so much trouble paying attention?"	BAARS-IV childhood report and adult report (self and informant reports)** BRIEF-A (self and informant reports)** SCID-5 ADHD module** Conners continuous performance test (CPT-3)	Criteria for *attention deficit/hyperactivity disorder, predominantly inattentive presentation, mild* had been met since childhood. *This predated the onset of PTSD and persistent depressive disorder (PDD) (see column below).* Criteria for PTSD was also met beginning in childhood in the context of parental physical abuse. *Hypervigilance in childhood contributed to attentional difficulties, but did not fully explain ADHD symptomatology.* In adulthood, PDD and generalized anxiety disorder (GAD) were further exacerbating problems with attention in the form of distracting ruminative thinking (GAD), feeling cognitively slowed down and having low motivation (PDD).	I am neurodivergent (I have ADHD) and that's *part* of my story. I have *also* had to be so aware all the time throughout my life to keep myself safe as an abused kid, and as a queer, nonbinary teen and adult. Feeling unsafe is really distracting. My depression has made it hard for me to get things done. It's like wearing an invisible weighted vest. My anxiety has made me doubt myself and yanks me to the past rather than letting me stay in the now. I guess, who wouldn't be distracted?

(continued)

Table 2.3 (continued)

Client's assessment questions	Measure selection	What was learned (diagnostically)	Narrative shifts (co-created through the assessment)
"Is this just depression? Why do I feel so overwhelmed and so fatigued all the time?"	MMPI-3 (Spanish) SCID-5 anxiety and depressive disorders modules Yale Brown obsessive compulsive scale-clinician administered (YBOCS) Cognitive distortions scale (CDS)** Metacognitions questionnaire—30 item (MCQ-30)** Pain self-efficacy Questionnaire-2	Client presented with both depression (persistent depressive disorder, with early onset, with intermittent major depressive episodes, with current episode; PDD) and anxiety (generalized anxiety disorder; GAD) that was not better explained by PTSD alone.	This is depression, but not "just depression." depression is serious and PDD is a serious form of depression. I've had it for more of my life than not. Depression, anxiety, trauma, ADHD, and my chronic health conditions. These are all weights put on my vest that have overwhelmed me, slowed me down, and made me feel so tired. People can't see the weights so they may not understand, but it's real. When I have a panic attack, that's like knocking me down in a hole and then asking me to climb back out with my weights on. It's hard but I want to be more compassionate towards myself for getting through every day with all of these weights I am carrying.
"How has trauma affected me?"	MMPI- 3 (Spanish) LEC-5 CAPS-5 PCL-5 (Spanish)**	Identification of discrete traumatic life events linked to the PTSD diagnosis and the physical, psychological, and relational effects of discrimination (interactions of cissexism, racism, ableism), and chronic day-to-day traumas (family conflict, housing insecurity, food insecurity).	Trauma has affected me in all ways in my life. I developed a lot of strategies when I was younger to try to keep my parents happy and keep myself safe. They don't work so well anymore, but they are hard to let go of. I am scared to let go, but I can see how those things may be distracting me and keeping me anxious. Maybe that is something I will think about with my therapist.

(continued)

Table 2.3 (continued)

Client's assessment questions	Measure selection	What was learned (diagnostically)	Narrative shifts (co-created through the assessment)
"Can I get better? What would help?"	All measures selected were to also clarify this question, in addition to inquiries and real-time elicitation of difficulties and potential solutions during the assessment.	See recommendations section	I think and hope I can get better. There are some treatments I haven't tried. This is the first time I have diagnoses that describe all the things happening for me. Connecting with other people with the same problems might make me feel less alone too.

Note: BAARS-IV = Barkley Adult ADHD Rating Scale-IV; BRIEF-A = Behavior Rating Inventory of Executive Functioning for Adults; SCID-5 = Structured Clinical Interview for DSM-5; MMPI-3 = Minnesota Multiphasic Personality Inventory-3; LEC-5 = Life Events Checklist for DSM-5; CAPS-5 = Clinician Administered PTSD Scale for DSM-5; PCL-5 = PTSD Checklist for DSM-5
**Face valid measures

assessment cases may benefit from more formal assessment of minority stress, both the experience of stressors and reactions to those stressors. See Table 2.4 below for a non-exhaustive list which we adapted from Livingston et al.'s (2020) list of minority stress measures. Regarding test specifications, the assessor worked with the client on selecting the language of tests and discussed gender norms. For example, when Spanish versions of measures were available, Sol preferred these for answering questions about their emotional states, as they found it easier to think about and access emotions in Spanish.[8] Many assessment measures have binary gender norms, which have generally excluded transgender and gender expansive (TGE) individuals from norms. Therefore, it is recommended clinicians use tests without gender norms or use the combined gender norms (i.e., norms that are combined for men and women) when possible (e.g., Beck Depression Inventory; Beck et al., 2011). If not possible, then it is recommended to analyze the test with norms for both men and women and compare the results, discussing similarities and differences with the client (American Psychological Association, 2020). For the current assessment, the assessor and client chose to select measures that did not use gender norms or used combined gender norms (e.g., MMPI-3; Ben-Porath & Tellegen, 2020).

[8] Resources on selecting measures in English and Spanish can be found elsewhere (Puente et al., 2013). However, in general, it is recommended that test language selection should be done collaboratively with the client, standardized tests that have been normed with the population that is representative of the client's cultural and linguistic background should be selected, and a variety of tests should be used and synthesized instead of the overreliance on a single test given how bias may play a part in results. Lastly, it is important to consider how bilingualism may impact test results (e.g., cognitive or learning tests).

Table 2.4 Review of minority stress measures adapted from Livingston et al.'s (2020) list of measures

Measure	Description	Reference
Everyday Discrimination Scale (9 items)	Measure of day-to-day experiences of discrimination based on different aspects of identity.	Williams, D. R., Yu, Y., Jackson, J. S., & Anderson, N. B. (1997). Racial differences in physical and mental health: Socio-economic status, stress and discrimination. Journal of health psychology, 2(3), 335–351.
Heterosexist Harassment, Rejection, and Discrimination Scale (14 items)	Measure of recent experiences of sexual orientation-related harassment, rejection, and discrimination.	Szymanski, D. M. (2006). Does internalized heterosexism moderate the link between heterosexist events and lesbians' psychological distress?. Sex Roles, 54, 227–234.
LGBT People of Color Microaggressions Scale (18 items) or the brief version, LGBTQ+ POC Microaggressions Scale-Brief (12 items)	Measure of microaggressions experienced by LGBTQ+ people of color.	Balsam, K. F., Molina, Y., Beadnell, B., Simoni, J., & Walters, K. (2011). Measuring multiple minority stress: the LGBT People of Color Microaggressions Scale. Cultural Diversity and Ethnic Minority Psychology, 17(2), 163.
		Huynh, K. D., Bricker, N. L., Lee, D. L., & Balsam, K. F. (2022). Development and validation of the LGBTQ+ POC Microaggressions Scale—Brief (LGBTQ+ PCMS-B). Stigma and Health.
Daily Heterosexist Experiences Questionnaire (50 items)	Measure of various forms of minority stressors (e.g., vigilance, harassment/ discrimination, victimization).	Balsam, K. F., Beadnell, B., & Molina, Y. (2013). The Daily Heterosexist Experiences Questionnaire: Measuring minority stress among lesbian, gay, bisexual, and transgender adults. Measurement and Evaluation in Counseling and Development, 46(1), 3–25.
Lesbian, Gay, and Bisexual Identity Scale (27 items)	Measure of different facets of minority stress, including identity concealment.	Mohr, J. J., & Kendra, M. S. (2011). Revision and extension of a multidimensional measure of sexual minority identity: the Lesbian, Gay, and Bisexual Identity Scale. Journal of Counseling Psychology, 58(2), 234.
Bisexual Identity Inventory (24 items)	Measure of minority stress for bisexual people (e.g., internalized and anticipated binegativity) and identity affirmation.	Paul, R., Smith, N. G., Mohr, J. J., & Ross, L. E. (2014). Measuring dimensions of bisexual identity: Initial development of the Bisexual Identity Inventory. Psychology of Sexual Orientation and Gender Diversity, 1(4), 452.

(continued)

Table 2.4 (continued)

Measure	Description	Reference
Brief Anti-Bisexual Experiences Scale (8 items)	Measure of discrimination against bisexual people from both heterosexual and lesbian/gay people.	Dyar, C., Feinstein, B. A., & Davila, J. (2019). Development and validation of a brief version of the Anti-Bisexual Experiences Scale. Archives of Sexual Behavior, 48(1), 175–189.
Gender Minority Stress and Resilience Measure (58 items)	Measure of different facets of minority stress and resilience factors for transgender and gender expansive people.	Testa, R. J., Habarth, J., Peta, J., Balsam, K., & Bockting, W. (2015). Development of the gender minority stress and resilience measure. Psychology of sexual orientation and gender diversity, 2(1), 65.
Transgender Identity Survey (52 items)	Measure of internalized transphobia and cissexism.	Bockting, W. O., Miner, M. H., Swinburne Romine, R. E., Dolezal, C., Robinson, B. B. E., Rosser, B. S., & Coleman, E. (2020). The Transgender Identity Survey: A measure of internalized transphobia. LGBT Health, 7(1), 15–27.
Internalized Homophobia Scale (5 items)	Measure of internalized heterosexism.	Herek, G. M., Gillis, J. R., & Cogan, J. C. (2009). Internalized stigma among sexual minority adults: Insights from a psychological perspective. Journal of Counseling Psychology, 56(1), 32–43. https://doi.org/10.1037/a0014672
Trauma Symptoms of Discrimination Scale (21 items)	Measure of distress related to discrimination.	Williams, M. T., Printz, D. M. B., & DeLapp, R. C. T. (2018). Assessing racial trauma with the Trauma Symptoms of Discrimination Scale. Psychology of Violence, 8(6), 735–747. https://doi.org/10.1037/vio0000212

Test Administration, Review of Results, and Differential Diagnostic Considerations

In the following assessment sessions, the assessor administered tests, reviewed results with the client, considered differential diagnoses, and selected additional measures, as needed. Ongoing review of test results and selection of additional measures is meant to continue a collaborative understanding of the tests and results while also linking responses to the client's assessment questions and experiences of the problems in day-to-day life. For example, following completion of the MMPI-3, the assessor shared the results with Sol (e.g., elevations on most Somatic/Cognitive Dysfunction and Internalizing Scales) and potential interpretations from the test while facilitating a discussion with them about how these results mapped onto their perception of their difficulties and their assessment questions. Sol identified with the interpretations, including struggling with (1) emotional dysfunction (e.g., feeling overwhelmed, worrying, difficulty concentrating, significant depression, low energy, beliefs that they cannot overcome their problems or reach goals, and feelings of worthlessness, incompetence, and shame), (2) cognitive/somatic complaints (e.g., diffuse somatic problems, including headaches, gastrointestinal distress, fatigue, and sleep difficulties) and (3) interpersonal dysfunction (e.g., feeling uncomfortable around others, anxious and nervous in social situations, and thinking they are viewed as socially awkward). Although they related to these interpretations, Sol noted that this did not provide clarity on the presence (or absence) of depression, whether their experience is "just depression" (i.e., one of their assessment questions), or the specific impacts of trauma. Collaboratively, Sol and the assessor selected diagnostic interviews and self-report measures that would help provide diagnostic clarity regarding depression and to rule-out other possible diagnoses. These included the anxiety and depressive disorder modules and ADHD module of the Structured Clinical Interview for DSM-5 (First et al., 2016), the Yale Brown Obsessive Compulsive Scale-clinician administered (YBOCS; Goodman et al., 1989),[9] and the Clinician Administered PTSD Scale for DSM-5 (CAPS-5; Weathers et al., 2013c).

To clarify potential impacts of trauma, the assessor administered the CAPS-5. During the administration, the assessor engaged in collaborative inquiry with the client regarding which traumatic event to focus on for the interview. Sol initially chose to focus on the sexual assault in adolescence; however, they denied re-experiencing symptoms (e.g., intrusive memories, nightmares) during the CAPS-5 administration, which was inconsistent with their self-report during the developmental history collection. The assessor and Sol reflected on this difference together. They re-visited the Life Events Checklist (LEC; Weathers et al., 2013a, b) to determine whether there was another experience they should be focusing on for the assessment. Sol identified having unwanted memories and nightmares about multiple physical abuse and neglect experiences from childhood, and stated that when they are reminded of those experiences, then they tend to think of other experiences of victimization, including the sexual assault. Therefore, collaboratively, they decided to index the CAPS-5 to experiences of physical abuse in childhood, as these experiences occurred first developmentally and served as internal reminders and triggered ruminative thinking about other traumatic experiences. Results of the CAPS-5 indicated that Sol met criteria for PTSD since childhood with marked re-experiencing symptoms (e.g., intrusive memories, nightmares, trauma-related panic attacks), avoidance (e.g., constantly listening to music/watching TV/being on social media, avoiding social activities and crowds), negative beliefs about the self, others, and the world (e.g., "I am not safe anywhere"), anhedonia, shame, hypervigilance (e.g., checking locks of their home repeatedly), and sleep difficulties.

[9] Elevations on the Emotional Dysfunctional scales indicated significant worry, anxiety, and repetitive thinking; therefore, the client and assessor chose to evaluate the potential presence or absence of obsessive-compulsive and related disorders.

Throughout the assessment process, Sol and the assessor discussed the timeline and course of symptoms to situate the findings within Sol's experience and conceptualization of their symptoms. For example, during the administration of the ADHD module of the SCID-5, the assessor and Sol established that the symptoms of inattention began in early childhood and predated the onset of other types of symptomatology that may explain inattention (e.g., PTSD [which also began in childhood], depression, anxiety, chronic pain). Sol and the assessor also discussed how these symptoms of inattention significantly worsened overtime likely related to distal stressor experiences (e.g., trauma, minority stress) and the psychological sequelae of these experiences. This timeline and onset of inattention was also corroborated with Sol's and their informant's reports on ADHD measures (e.g., BAARS-IV).

Sol and the assessor also collaboratively ruled out other diagnoses by exploring what may be better explained by other experiences (e.g., PTSD). Sol reported experiencing significant anxiety (e.g., heart racing, sweating, tension), worry, intrusive thoughts about "bad things that may happen", and avoiding social situations since adolescence, which was also present on the MMPI-3. While some of these symptoms (e.g., avoiding trauma reminders, hypervigilance) were attributable to PTSD, Sol's report of anxiety appeared more diffuse and generalized than only being trauma-related. During the administration of the anxiety disorders module of the SCID-5 and the YBOCS, the following diagnoses were ruled out: panic disorder (i.e., panic attacks were only triggered by trauma-reminders), agoraphobia (i.e., Sol's avoidance was attributable to realistic threats related to their ethnicity, sexual orientation, and gender identity and avoidance of trauma-reminders), and social anxiety disorder (i.e., Sol's concerns regarding judgment and rejection from others were better explained by anticipatory rejection concerns related to their identities), and obsessive compulsive and related disorders because the client's reported intrusions were intrusive memories of traumatic experiences and the compulsions appeared to be better explained by PTSD (e.g., repeatedly checking to see if their house is locked while they are inside due to concern that someone will break in).

Sol met criteria for generalized anxiety disorder (GAD) characterized by excessive worrying about day-to-day activities (e.g., being late, missing medical appointments), their health, and catastrophic thinking about the future (e.g., they will never be able to function independently and will never be able to work). Their experience of worry, particularly ruminative worry, also occurred during testing, which allowed the assessor and Sol to discuss how worry is clinically impacting them. Collaborative/Therapeutic Assessment allows for the opportunity to use reactions to tests in real time as information related to the areas of concern and provides opportunities to use assessment as intervention. For example, on the Continuous Performance Test (CPT-3) (Homack & Riccio, 2006), which was administered to assess Sol's inattention difficulties, Sol found themself distracted and having difficulty concentrating on subsequent tests. Sol and the assessor discussed the difficulty that arose during the CPT-3 administration and collaboratively selected additional measures to better understand this ruminative tendency (i.e., the Meta-Cognitions Questionnaire-30 [MCQ-30]; Wells & Cartwright-Hatton, 2004). Sol and the assessor used single test items (e.g., "I need to worry in order to remain organized", "If I did not control a worry, and then it happened, it would be my fault", and "Worrying helps me cope") on the MCQ-30 as launching discussion points to further explore the utility of worry, how it is tied into perceived executive functioning deficits, and the role of past trauma, which resulted in a high need for control and a tendency to blame themself for any perceived errors or mistakes. This also allowed Sol to see ways in which their worry was negatively impacting them in the moment (e.g., contributing to distraction and difficulty focusing), which increased their openness to reduce worry despite its perceived usefulness for coping.

As one of Sol's assessment questions was whether their experience was "just depression", the assessor and client focused on assessing the presence of depression and potential differential diagnoses, while discussing the cumulative health burden of having multiple psychiatric and medical conditions. As a result of the SCID-5 depressive disorders module, the client met criteria for current major depressive episode and persistent depressive disorder (PDD) beginning in adolescence, including symptoms that were not attributable to other diagnoses (e.g., PTSD). Due to the significant overlap between PTSD, PDD, and GAD symptoms, the assessor and client discussed unique symptoms of depression that were not better explained by PTSD and GAD. For example, Sol identified experiencing significant psychomotor retardation, low energy, periods of both decreased and increased appetite, hopelessness/helplessness, and chronic passive suicidal ideation, along with shared symptoms with PTSD and GAD (i.e., depressed mood, low self-esteem/self-worth, other negative beliefs about themself, anhedonia, agitation/irritability, sleep disturbances). Additionally, per Sol's report and MMPI-3 results, they had a history of chronic pain, which appeared to be interrelated with psychiatric diagnoses and was negatively impacting their functioning. To provide clarity for Sol's question, "Is this just depression? Why do I feel so overwhelmed and so fatigued all of the time?", the impact of chronic pain on their presenting concerns was assessed. Based on administration of the Pain Self-Efficacy Questionnaire-2 (Nicholas et al., 2015), they endorsed having extremely low self-efficacy in their ability to cope with pain and their ability to live their desired life despite pain. The pain and low self-efficacy to cope with pain contributed to feelings of low self-worth, helplessness/hopelessness, and also worry about their future and their ability to work.

Shifting the Client's Self-Narrative Consistent with Collaborative/Therapeutic Assessment, Sol and the assessor worked together throughout the assessment to shift their narrative surrounding their difficulties toward better understanding, reducing experiences of shame and self-judgment, and opening up the possibility of other ways of being. For example, Sol and the assessor worked to better understand how the adaptiveness of certain behaviors evolved over time (e.g., vigilance vs. hypervigilance, realistic threat appraisal vs. catastrophic thinking in relation to past or current stressors) and begin to shift the narrative the client has regarding these symptoms. Sol and the assessor identified how these thoughts and behaviors functioned semi-successfully in anticipating and attempting to avoid triggers for parental abuse and family conflict during development. In considering how these were maintained and reinforced over time and reorienting to Sol's present context, they were able to also elucidate the ways in which the same behaviors had lost their adaptiveness and had begun to cause impairment in adulthood. Using scores and single responses on measures such as the MCQ-30 and Cognitive Distortions Scale (CDS; Covin et al., 2011), the assessor and Sol discussed how their tendency to engage in all-or-nothing thinking, catastrophizing, and overgeneralization was learned over time in an attempt to protect themself from future realistic harms and also perceived disappointments and failures, but is currently keeping them from engaging in activities that are important to them (e.g., making and maintaining affirming friendships). This process helped to create a new narrative which both honored the utility of these past behaviors and opened a door for experimenting with new ways of being.

Another example of a narrative shift was generated by Sol's and the assessor's discussion about the ways that their symptoms overlap with each other (e.g., low motivation and fatigue can be a symptom of PTSD, depression, and generalized anxiety disorder and related to chronic pain) and the interconnectedness of symptoms (e.g., worry makes it difficult to concentrate and difficulty concentrating makes them worry more; depressed mood leads to low motivation, but low motivation and not engaging in activities makes them more depressed; they worry about their health and chronic pain, but worry and anxiety exacerbate their pain). The assessor also provided psychoeducation on the interactive effects of having multiple psychiatric diagnoses, the effects of chronic pain, and about their cumulative health burden. This discussion and psychoeducation helped Sol shift their thinking from conceptualizing their experience as "just depression" to better understand the interrelated symptom burden they experience. This helped shift their narrative from a place of self-judgment to a place that allows space for self-compassion. See Table 2.3 for additional examples of Sol's narrative shifts that occurred throughout the assessment process related to the assessment questions and the measures administered.

Results of the Assessment

Through the process of administering measures, discussing results, extended inquiry, and beginning to shift narratives in partnership with the client, the assessment was concluded with the diagnoses presented below:

- Persistent depressive disorder, with early onset, with intermittent major depressive episodes, with current episode
- Generalized anxiety disorder
- ADHD, predominantly inattentive presentation, mild
- Posttraumatic stress disorder, with dissociative symptoms and panic attacks

Recommendations and Referrals

- Evidence-based psychotherapy for PTSD was recommended as a first line of treatment due to the conceptualization that if PTSD were effectively treated the remaining mental health burden would be reduced and subsequent interventions would be more effective. Treating the PTSD with a cognitive behavioral therapy approach may be particularly useful given the co-occurring diagnoses of PDD, GAD, ADHD, and chronic pain. Developing cognitive behavioral skills through PTSD treatment may enable Sol to apply these skills related to other diagnoses and pain and thus may be the most efficient course of treatment.
- The client was also referred to group psychotherapy for GAD due to a waitlist for individual treatment for PTSD as a way to increase efficient access to care.
- The client was provided information on peer support groups for adults with ADHD given the centrality of these symptoms to the client's identity as a neurodivergent person. The client was provided an ADHD workbook and mental health apps to increase self-support while awaiting connection to individual psychotherapy for PTSD.
- To reduce the need for additional psychotherapy referrals, the assessor provided Sol with psychoeducation on the biopsychosocial model of chronic pain and recommendations on coping with chronic pain (e.g., pacing activities), and on sleep hygiene and sleep stimulus control.
- The client was provided resources for queer Latine community organizations given the client's difficulty with acceptance of gender identity within their family and perceived incompatibility with cultural values.
- The assessor offered to meet with the client in 4–6 weeks to consolidate assessment gains, consistent with a Collaborative/Therapeutic Assessment approach.

Feedback (Summary/Discussion) Session

It is recommended that family members, partners, and support people are invited to the feedback session as needed and preferred by the client within Collaborative/Therapeutic Assessment; however, in this case, Sol chose to present to the appointment alone. A goal of a Collaborative/Therapeutic Assessment feedback session is to facilitate the client's understanding of themself and their experiences while also developing a new narrative with realistic, collaboratively generated alternative ways of dealing with difficulties. Additionally, the goal of the feedback session is to review treatment recommendations as potential "next steps". As there were many recommendations for Sol, these were phrased as "possible next steps" instead of implying these are steps they "must" or "should" take. Additionally, another goal of feedback sessions is for the client to feel validated and affirmed and offer an opportunity for discussion about whether the findings from the assessment fit with the client's conceptualization of their difficulties and discuss the ways these findings will be presented, and to whom.

At the feedback session, Sol commented on feeling like they had increased understanding of their problems, answers to their assessment questions, and a clearer path for seeking help. They also noted feeling like they had a better understanding about the interrelatedness of their difficulties (e.g., worry, self-blame) and how their strategies to cope with these difficulties may contribute to attention-related difficulties. Additionally, Sol felt understood and validated by the assessment experience, especially the focus on attention-related difficulties, as membership with the neurodivergent community is important to them. They also appreciated the space to explore how different stressors (e.g., acculturation, familial non-support, trauma and victimization) had contributed to their distress, which was perceived as validating and consistent with their conceptualization of their problems.

Future Directions for Testing, Assessment, and Case Conceptualization

In this chapter, we reviewed strategies for conducting person-centered, affirming assessments using components of the Collaborative/Therapeutic Assessment framework, and applying these components in a case example of an LGBTQ+ client. Although these recommendations are useful steps forward in conducting assessments and case conceptualizations, additional work in both research and clinical avenues is needed to continue improving assessment and case conceptualization in LGBTQ+ communities.

While the assessment context is one where power differentials can lead to LGBTQ+ clients' perspectives being overlooked, it also holds potential to provide corrective experiences, validation, and insight. This requires that assessors directly leverage the perspectives of LGBTQ+ people throughout the assessment process. Additionally, it requires assessors to engage in their own self-reflection of power and privilege, and identity (see Table 2.5 resources). In assessing and conceptualizing the impacts of minority stress on LGBTQ+ individuals, clinicians are capable of effective work even without shared lived experiences, given openness to learning more and reflective engagement. It is also true that those who do have overlapping identities should be mindful of avoiding overidentification with their clients, so as to not assume understanding more than is accurate.

Future assessment research should use methodologies that center voices of LGBTQ+ people, such as community-based participatory research and qualitative studies, especially with underrepresented or excluded communities. TGE people, as compared with cisgender sexual minority people, have been historically underrepresented in research on assessment and case formulation, as well as the clinical literature. Although research on the conceptualization and assessment of mental health and minority stress among TGE people has grown (Salomaa et al., 2022; Valentine et al., 2023), most research has collapsed across binary and nonbinary gender identities despite the unique experiences for people within and between these

Table 2.5 Resources for clinicians to increase awareness of positionality, identity, power and privilege

Resource	Description	Reference
Sexual Orientation Counselor Competency Scale (SOCCS)	The SOCCS is a measure that assesses clinicians' competency and comfort providing care to lesbian, gay, and bisexual individuals, and can inform areas of growth for clinicians to seek further education and training.	Bidell, M. P. (2000). The development and validation of the Sexual Orientation Counselor Competency Scale (SOCCS). University of California, Santa Barbara.
The Gender Book	The Gender Book is "a visual primer on the world of gender" and it includes a useful and informative survey that encourages readers to reflect on their own experience of gender and identity.	Reiff Hill, M., & Mays, J. (2013). The gender book: Inspired by the gender explorations of Boston Davis Bostian. Marshall House Press.
Reflective local practice	Reflective local practice encourages clinicians to reflect on and expand their self-awareness of their own cultural influence and their knowledge and experience of their local culture through practice.	Sandeen, E., Moore, K. M., & Swanda, R. M. (2018). Reflective local practice: A pragmatic framework for improving culturally competent practice in psychology. Professional Psychology: Research and Practice, 49(2), 142–150. https://doi.org/10.1037/pro0000183
Readings on Intersectionality	1) The statement developed through years of Black Lesbian Feminist consciousness-raising and activism. Often acknowledged as a fore-runner to Kimberlé Crenshaw's theory of intersectionality.	1) Taylor, K. Y. (Ed.). (2017). How we get free: Black feminism and the Combahee River Collective. Haymarket Books
	2) A collection of key essays defining the concept of intersectionality.	2) Crenshaw, K. W. (2017). On intersectionality: Essential writings. The New Press.
	3) Theoretical framework applying intersectionality to psychological work with gender and sexually diverse clients.	3) Dunlop, B. J., & Lea, J. (2023). It's not just in my head: An intersectional, social and systems-based framework in gender and sexuality diversity. Psychology and Psychotherapy: Theory, Research and Practice, 96(1), 1–15.

communities. However, relying on studies focused on TGE people to build this evidence base is insufficient; rather, it is recommended that *all* measure and assessment validation studies include participants with diverse sexual orientations and gender identities, and that they collect diverse sexual orientation and gender identity demographic information.

Particular focus is needed on expanding the breadth of measures that assess the intersectionality in discriminatory and stigma-based experiences; in particular, we recommend the expansion of measures that capture experiences of oppression that are applicable across a range of intersecting identities, and that are sensitive to the emotional, cognitive, and behavioral sequelae of these experiences. For example, measures that focus on specific intersectional identities that due to the social and political context experience notable oppression, such as Black transgender women, or target experiences that are common across holding a minoritized identity, such as social exclusion or 'othering' (Singh et al., 2021) may be particularly useful.

Finally, as new measures are being developed, it is important to consider the utility of gender norms in assessment, given how use of gender norms upholds binary conceptualizations of gender and limits applicability to those who live outside of this binary. As we leverage the voices of LGBTQ+ people to develop measures that are more inclusive, we overall aim to become more person-centered, collaborative, and culturally responsive in our assessments and case conceptualizations with LGBTQ+ people.

Disclaimer The views expressed in this chapter are those of the authors and do not necessarily reflect the official policy or position of the U.S. Department of Veterans Affairs nor the U.S. Government.

Funding Kelly Harper was supported by the U.S. Department of Veterans Affairs (Clinical Sciences Research and Development Service) under Career Development Award # **1IK2CX002629**.

References

American Psychiatric Association. (2013). Diagnostic and statistical manual of mental disorders (5th ed.).

American Psychological Association. (2020). *Psychological and neuropsychological assessment with transgender and gender nonbinary adults*. https://www.apa.org/pi/lgbt/resources/transgender-gender-nonbinary

Aschieri, F., Fantini, F., & Smith, J. D. (2016). *Collaborative/therapeutic assessment: Procedures to enhance client outcomes.*

Barkley, R. A. (2011). *Barkley adult ADHD rating scale-IV (BAARS-IV)*. Guilford Press.

Bauerband, L. A., Teti, M., & Velicer, W. F. (2019). Measuring minority stress: Invariance of a discrimination and vigilance scale across transgender and cisgender LGBQ individuals. *Psychology & Sexuality, 10*(1), 17–30.

Beck, A. T., Steer, R. A., & Brown, G. (2011). *Beck depression inventory–II* [Data set]. https://doi.org/10.1037/t00742-000

Ben-Porath, Y., & Tellegen, A. (2020). Minnesota Multiphasic Personality Inventory-3 (MMPI-3): Manual for administration, scoring, and interpretation. University of Minnesota Press.

Borgogna, N. C., Brenner, R. E., & McDermott, R. C. (2021). Sexuality and gender invariance of the PHQ-9 and GAD-7: Implications for 16 identity groups. *Journal of Affective Disorders, 278*, 122–130.

Brenick, A., Romano, K., Kegler, C., & Eaton, L. A. (2017). Understanding the influence of stigma and medical mistrust on engagement in routine healthcare among black women who have sex with women. *LGBT Health, 4*(1), 4–10.

Brooks, V. R. (1981). *Minority stress and lesbian women*. Free Press.

Cahill, S. (2017). *LGBT experiences with health care.*

Covin, R., Dozois, D. J., Ogniewicz, A., & Seeds, P. M. (2011). Measuring cognitive errors: Initial development of the Cognitive Distortions Scale (CDS). *International Journal of Cognitive Therapy, 4*(3), 297–322.

Durosini, I., & Aschieri, F. (2021). Therapeutic assessment efficacy: A meta-analysis. *Psychological Assessment, 33*(10), 962.

Finn, S. E. (2020). *In our clients' shoes: Theory and techniques of therapeutic assessment* (1st ed.). https://doi.org/10.4324/9781003064459

Finn, S. E., & Tonsager, M. E. (1997). Information-gathering and therapeutic models of assessment: Complementary paradigms. *Psychological Assessment, 9*(4), 374.

First, M. B., Williams, J. B. W., Karg, R. S., & Spitzer, R. L. (2016). *User's guide for the SCID-5-CV structured clinical interview for DSM-5® disorders: Clinical version*. American Psychiatric Publishing, Inc..

Gioia, G. A., Isquith, P. K., Guy, S. C., & Kenworthy, L. (2000). *Behavior rating inventory of executive function: BRIEF*. Psychological Assessment Resources.

Goodman, W. K., Price, L. H., Rasmussen, S. A., Mazure, C., Delgado, P., Heninger, G. R., & Charney, D. S. (1989). The yale-brown obsessive compulsive scale: II. Validity. *Archives of General Psychiatry, 46*(11), 1012–1016.

Hendricks, M. L., & Testa, R. J. (2012). A conceptual framework for clinical work with transgender and gender nonconforming clients: An adaptation of the Minority Stress Model. *Professional Psychology: Research and Practice, 43*(5), 460–467. https://doi.org/10.1037/a0029597

Homack, S., & Riccio, C. A. (2006). Conners' continuous performance test (CCPT-II). *Journal of Attention Disorders, 9*(3), 556–558.

Livingston, N. A., Berke, D., Scholl, J., Ruben, M., & Shipherd, J. C. (2020). Addressing diversity in PTSD treatment: Clinical considerations and guidance for the treatment of PTSD in LGBTQ populations. *Current Treatment Options in Psychiatry, 7*, 53–69.

Meyer, I. H. (2003). Prejudice, social stress, and mental health in lesbian, gay, and bisexual populations: Conceptual issues and research evidence. *Psychological Bulletin, 129*(5), 674–697. https://doi.org/10.1037/0033-2909.129.5.674

Nicholas, M. K., McGuire, B. E., & Asghari, A. (2015). A 2-item short form of the pain self-efficacy questionnaire: Development and psychometric evaluation of PSEQ-2. *The Journal of Pain, 16*(2), 153–163. https://doi.org/10.1016/j.jpain.2014.11.002

Puente, A. E., Zink, D., Hernandez, M., Jackman-Venanzi, T., & Ardila, A. (2013). Bilingualism and its impact on psychological assessment. *Guide to Psychological Assessment with Hispanics*, 15–31.

Rodriguez-Seijas, C., Morgan, T. A., & Zimmerman, M. (2021). Is there a bias in the diagnosis of borderline personality disorder among lesbian, gay, and bisexual patients? *Assessment, 28*(3), 724–738.

Salomaa, A. C., Livingston, N. A., Bryant, W. T., Herbitter, C., Harper, K., Sloan, C. A., Hinds, Z., Gyuro, L., Valentine, S. E., & Shipherd, J. C. (2022). A bottom-up approach to developing a unified trauma-minority stress model for transgender and gender diverse people. *Psychological Trauma: Theory, Research, Practice, and Policy*. https://doi.org/10.1037/tra0001373

Singh, R. S., Bhambhani, Y., Skinta, M. D., & Torres-Harding, S. R. (2021). Measurement of intersectional microaggressions: Conceptual barriers and recommendations. *Perspectives on Psychological Science, 16*(5), 956–971. https://doi.org/10.1177/1745691621991855

Smith, J. D. (2016). Introduction to the special section on cultural considerations in collaborative and therapeutic assessment. *Journal of Personality Assessment, 98*(6), 563–566.

Strand, M., & Bäärnhielm, S. (2022). Could the DSM-5 Cultural Formulation Interview Hold Therapeutic Potential? Suggestions for Further Exploration and Adaptation Within a Framework of Therapeutic Assessment. *Culture, Medicine and Psychiatry, 46*(4), 846–863. https://doi.org/10.1007/s11013-021-09761-2

Therapeutic Assessment Institute. (n.d.). *Overview of therapeutic assessment*. https://www.therapeuticassessment.com/question3.php

Valentine, S. E., Smith, A. M., Miller, K., Hadden, L., & Shipherd, J. C. (2023). Considerations and complexities of accurate PTSD assessment among transgender and gender diverse adults. *Psychological Assessment, 35*, 383–395.

Weathers, F.W., Blake, D.D., Schnurr, P.P., Kaloupek, D.G., Marx, B.P., & Keane, T.M. (2013a). *The Clinician-Administered PTSD Scale for DSM-5 (CAPS-5)* [Assessment]. Available from www.ptsd.va.gov

Weathers, F.W., Blake, D.D., Schnurr, P.P., Kaloupek, D.G., Marx, B.P., & Keane, T.M. (2013b). *The Life Events Checklist for DSM-5 (LEC-5)*. Instrument available from the National Center for PTSD at www.ptsd.va.gov

Weathers, F.W., Litz, B.T., Keane, T.M., Palmieri, P.A., Marx, B.P., & Schnurr, P.P. (2013c). *The PTSD checklist for DSM-5 (PCL-5)*. Scale available from the National Center for PTSD.

Wells, A., & Cartwright-Hatton, S. (2004). A short form of the metacognitions questionnaire: Properties of the MCQ-30. *Behaviour Research and Therapy, 42*(4), 385–396.

Chapter 3
Affirming Therapy in Response to Minority Stress Among LGBTQ+ Clients

Matthew D. Skinta, Sérgio A. Carvalho, and Ashley Bryan

Highlights

- This chapter illustrates particular ways that minority stressors are described in relation to presenting problems.
- Particular attention is paid to the unique challenges that may be experienced by gender diverse people and are not shared with sexual orientation diverse people.
- The important role of intersectionality is also highlighted, as all of a client's meaningful identities shape their experiences with and exposure to bias.
- Specific contextual behavioral strategies are described that clinicians might incorporate into their work.
- The processes described emphasize a process-based approach. As no two individuals might be subject to the same forms of bias or experience the same difficulties in responding, emphasis is placed on targeting the specific behaviors that are no longer working for a client that they wish to change.
- The strategies in this chapter include questions and prompts that may aid in clarifying how minority stress affects an individual client in their unique context.

Positionality

We are three researchers, educators, and clinicians in psychology at various stages of our careers: internship, early, and middle career. Our sexual identities are all queer/gay, with two of us based in the United States (a White, cisgender man and Black, Caribbean woman), and an Iberian-Portuguese cisgender man. All of the authors have been clinically trained and spend at least some of their time conducting

M. D. Skinta (✉) · A. Bryan
Roosevelt University, Chicago, IL, USA
e-mail: mskinta@roosevelt.edu

S. A. Carvalho
University of Coimbra, Coimbra, Portugal

N. A. Livingston et al. (eds.), *Addressing Minority Stress and Enhancing Resilience with Diverse LGBTQ+ Clients*, CBT: Science Into Practice,
https://doi.org/10.1007/978-3-031-92836-9_3

psychotherapy based upon contextual, or third-wave, cognitive behavioral approaches (e.g., Acceptance and Commitment Therapy, Compassion-Focused Therapy). All three of us have worked clinically and trained in both community mental health and medical settings, and have specific expertise in working with LGBTQ+ clients. Collectively, all of the authors share a professional and personal commitment to supporting the health and wellbeing of LGBTQ+ people through practice, advocacy, and research.

Introduction

Over 40 years ago, Virginia Brooks (1981) proposed a model of minority stress to describe how societal animus might trickle through the internal, interpersonal, and social worlds of lesbians that was subsequently expanded to gay, bisexual, transgender, queer, and other sexual orientation and gender minoritized (LGBTQ+) people (e.g., Hendricks & Testa, 2012; Meyer, 2003). As research has more broadly clarified these mechanisms and their associations with mental health, it is important to consider how minority stress might guide affirmative treatment for work with LGBTQ+ clients. In this chapter, we will explore how a well-informed clinician might use minority stress theory to craft an affirming experience in psychotherapy.

Minority Stress Theory

Empirical evidence on the mental health of LGBTQ+ individuals suggests that there are measurable mental health disparities between LGBTQ+ individuals and their cisgender and heterosexual counterparts in youth (e.g., Russell & Fish, 2016; Wilson & Cariola, 2020), adults (e.g., Wittgens et al., 2022), and older adults (e.g., King & Richardson, 2017; Yarns et al., 2016). These disparities are especially salient for transgender and gender diverse (TGD) people (e.g., Su et al., 2016), who present higher levels of anxiety and depression (e.g., Borgogna et al., 2019), and have an elevated risk for suicidality (e.g., Bränström et al., 2022). These disparities are often attributed to structural inequities and interpersonal stigma arising from cis-heteronormative society that affect LGBTQ+ individuals' mental health.

Minority stress theory (Brooks, 1981; Meyer, 2003) is the most researched paradigm to describe and understand the risk and protective factors related to mental health amongst LGBTQ+ individuals (Frost & Meyer, 2023). It posits that LGBTQ+ individuals experience unique sexual- or gender-related social stressors at different levels such as institutional (e.g., anti-LGBTQ+ legislation; e.g., Ogolsky et al., 2019), interpersonal (e.g., discrimination, microaggressions; e.g., Calabrese et al., 2015), and individual levels (e.g., the internalization of anti-LGBTQ+ sentiment; e.g., Puckett et al., 2017), which contribute to an individual's vulnerability to mental health challenges. Stressors that are *distal*, such as victimization, harassment, abuse, and social and family rejection, are known contributors to these mental health disparities (e.g., Argyriou et al., 2021), evidenced in samples of adolescents and young adults (de Lange et al., 2022). Additionally, *proximal* stressors are internal stress processes resulting from learned societal cisheteronormative biases, such as internalized stigma, shame, and rejection sensitivity.

Internalized stigma, such as internalized homophobia, is observed to vary across populations, racial and ethnic groups, and age (e.g., Newcomb & Mustanski, 2010), though as the world has become more interconnected, harmful myths about LGBTQ+ communities may not impact younger generations in the same manner as older individuals (e.g., Wickham et al., 2021). Alternately, rejection sensitivity has been described as a cognitive-affective process through which a sexual or gender minority individual becomes vigilant to the possibility of rejection when faced with ambiguous treatment or unclear acceptance by others, closely tied with histories of familial rejection (e.g., Feinstein, 2020). Rejection sensitivity is positively associated with social anxiety, generalized anxiety, and posttraumatic stress in gay and bisexual men (Cohen et al., 2016), and helps explain the connection between discrimination and depression and social anxiety in sexual minority (SM) people (Feinstein et al., 2012). All of these factors can be intertwined with distal factors (e.g., Douglass & Conlin, 2020) and can negatively impact LGBTQ+ mental health (e.g., Helsen et al., 2022; Walch et al., 2016).

Diamond and Alley (2022) have argued that the harmful impact of stigma and overall minority stressors is not exclusively tied to what happens to an individual, but also reflects one's current perception of potential future threats. Social safety (i.e., social connection, belongingness, inclusion, recognition, and protection), or lack thereof, is proposed as the key element underlying the impact of stigma in LGBTQ+ people. From harassment to instances of microaggressions, LGBTQ+ individuals encounter social interaction situations where social safety cues are absent (e.g., empathetic facial expressions, validating nods and gestures). As a result, social environments can become coded as stress-eliciting threats. Social unsafety resulting from actual instances of threat-related stress might result in avoidance strategies, such as concealment of sexual orientation or gender identity, or hypervigilance or the overperception that heterosexual, cisgender people might secretly harbor threatening beliefs in daily social interactions that contribute to interpersonal guardedness. The role of social safeness in the mental health of LGBTQ+ individuals has not been extensively explored. However, this might be an intrapersonal cognitive-emotional source of resilience for LGBTQ+ individuals. One study found that social safeness was negatively correlated with self-criticism and internalized sexual stigma, and positively correlated with well-being, in a sample of SM participants (Petrocchi et al., 2020).

Even though one may expect that an increase in societal acceptance of LGBTQ+ identities and progress in pro-LGBTQ+ legislation would lessen these disparities (e.g., Du Bois et al., 2018; Hatzenbuehler et al., 2012), empirical data fails to corroborate this (e.g., Liu et al., 2019; Wittgens et al., 2022). Historic societal anti-LGBTQ+ sentiment has long-lasting effects (i.e., its psychological effects outlive structural anti-LGBTQ+ discrimination), and reports have suggested a push-back to

LGBTQ+ progress and a current threat to overturn societal legal protections thought of as guaranteed (e.g., the threat to the overturn of Obergefell v. Hodges in the USA; the loss of same-sex parenting rights in Italy). This tentatively suggests the need for micro-level interventions (e.g., psychological interventions), both for support during ongoing stressors as well as for individual healing following painful lived experiences of mistreatment or interpersonal rejection.

Minority stress can constitute interpersonal trauma (*see* Cardona et al., 2022), sharing several of the same brain and body signaling pathways as posttraumatic stress, such as an easily triggered fight-or-flight response, heightened startle response, or the distraction of constantly monitoring the environment for safety (Nicholson et al., 2022). In addition to negative impacts on mental health, minority stress can also have an adverse effect on one's physical health (e.g., immune response, including at the level of gene expression, HIV-related outcomes, blood pressure and heart rate, and hormone outcomes, especially cortisol levels; Flentje et al., 2020). Important resilience factors shown to protect against mental health challenges do exist, however, such as family acceptance and perceived social support (e.g., Szymanski & Gonzalez, 2020). Strength-based and empowering strategies, such as self-affirmation and engaging in LGBTQ+ activism, have been reported as sources of resilience against the detrimental impacts of discrimination (Dunn & Szymanski, 2018).

A Closer Look at Minority Stress in Transgender and Gender Diverse (TGD) People

TGD individuals are becoming increasingly more visible in the public sphere (e.g., GLAAD, 2020), so while responses to minority stress are quite varied among sexual minoritized people, we believe it is particularly important to consider the unique experiences of TGD people. This change in visibility and public awareness has been deemed as both positive and negative based on safety concerns that have been raised and increased vulnerability to stigma (Bockting et al., 2020). Gender minority stressors are drivers of depression and suicidality experienced by TGD individuals. More specifically, proximal factors, such as expectations of rejection and internalized transphobia (Pellicane & Ciesla, 2022), are theorized to account for the negative impact of distal factors on mental and physical health (e.g., Testa et al., 2014). Misgendering can be especially stressful to TGD individuals, as these are not only instances of identity invalidation, but also a reminder of how others perceive their transgender identity or misread their gender (McLemore, 2018). TGD people may choose to conceal their identity in response to experiences or expectations of discrimination, but identity concealment can also have negative consequences. One study found that shame was positively associated with the desire to be perceived as cisgender (Bockting et al., 2020), and another study found that non-disclosure of gender identity was associated with lower life satisfaction and more internalized transphobia (Flynn & Bhambhani, 2021).

The interconnection of distal and proximal gender-related stressors may also lead to health challenges, which is also influenced by a lack of access to healthcare (e.g., Safer et al., 2016). TGD individuals might internalize transphobic stigma, which can further lead to avoidance of healthcare (e.g., Drabish & Theeke, 2022). Avoiding healthcare, however, leads to risks of worsening health problems or the later assessment of progressive health conditions, resulting in a higher burden of care for more complex medical concerns accompanied by greater levels of personal distress. Compared to cisgender people, TGD individuals are less likely to have a strong support network, which may lead to fewer feelings of safety (Jackman et al., 2018), and might manifest as social avoidance and isolation (e.g., Wilson & Liss, 2022). Such social avoidance may result in a reluctance to pursue mental health care as needed, as well as a greater likelihood of relational ruptures early in treatment that then may reduce continuation in therapy. Although these avoidant coping mechanisms may be warranted as a way of protecting TGD individuals against distal stressors, these coping strategies may have a negative impact on their mental health (Lindley & Bauerband, 2022).

Nonbinary/genderqueer individuals experience more stressors and poorer mental health compared to trans men and trans women (Lefevor et al., 2019), which may be attributed to their non-conformity with the expected gender binary and resulting increases in misgendering or other forms of mistreatment. In fact, evidence suggests that nonbinary/genderqueer people may go through unique social challenges. Some of these challenges are particularly likely to lead to misunderstandings or mistreatment by well-meaning providers only familiar with binary trans narratives, such as a greater diversity in desired affirming medical interventions, non-alignment with the narrative of "transition", stress resulting from others using wrong pronouns, as well as experiences of invisibility and illegitimacy. For example, it may be more challenging for an individual to seek affirming medical procedures that are not intended to result in being recognized as a binary gender, such as low doses of hormones with the intent of an appearance that is not strictly feminine or masculine. Therapists may possess unchallenged beliefs that the client's gender after intervention must be perceived as binary by others, or even hold implicit assumptions about sexual attractiveness that serve as barriers in supporting a client's goals (Ashley, 2023). Alternately, the development of a personal sense of gender identity and cultivating self-worth and a hopeful stance towards the future are reported resilience factors (Singh et al., 2011). Also, community connection seems to be a key factor to resilience and a buffer against proximal minority stressors (Jones et al., 2022).

Sexual and Gender Minority Stress and the Mental Health of LGBTQ+ Black, Indigenous and People of Color (BIPOC)

More researchers have begun to explore the importance of conducting fine-tuned and nuanced research on the impact of minority stress for individuals who are part of multiple marginalized groups (Singh et al., 2021). There is a lack of research on the intersection of ethnic/racial and sexual and gender identities, specifically how multiple minority stress compounds and affects the health of Black, Indigenous, and People of Color (BIPOC) LGBTQ+ individuals, as well as sources of strengthened resilience (Follins et al., 2014; Williams et al., 2012). Research has been inconclusive whether or not BIPOC LGBTQ+ individuals present with more mental health challenges because of multiple minority stress, either due to small sample sizes (e.g., Krieger et al., 2008) or studies with samples that may not generalize broadly (e.g., Mereish & Bradford, 2014). Intersectional stressors, such as disapproval of queerness in some ethnic/racial or religious backgrounds, are socially taxing for BIPOC LGBTQ+ people.

Intra-minority stressors, specifically for gay and bisexual men, can promote rigid in-group norms related to race, masculinity, attractiveness, body type, age, and HIV status (Burton et al., 2020), which can impact the health of LGBTQ+ individuals above and beyond minority stress (Pachankis et al., 2020a, b, c). BIPOC LGBTQ+ individuals report racism in LGBTQ+ environments as well as cisheterossexism in ethnic/racial communities (e.g., Levitt & Ippolito, 2014). For example, one study found that Black LGBTQ+ individuals report higher ethnic/racial stigma in queer spaces, however, that connection to the queer community is a buffer against the impact of stigma on stress only for White LGBTQ+ individuals (McConnell et al., 2018). This suggests that clinicians should take a more nuanced approach when conducting therapy and promoting community-related resilience with BIPOC LGBTQ+ communities.

The Science of Minority Stress-Informed Interventions

There are multiple lenses that might be applied in the development of empirically supported interventions to mitigate the effects of minority stress. One of the early challenges to the field was how a broad range of discriminatory influences, expressed either via broad societal messages or interpersonal acts of discrimination or violence, might result in diverse forms of psychological distress or substance use. One model that has received the greatest attention suggests that minority stress 'gets under the skin' of LGBTQ+ people through adversely affecting emotion regulation skills, social/interpersonal functioning, and cognitive processes (such as hopelessness and negative self-schemas; Hatzenbuehler, 2009). Other models have suggested a parallel pathway through experiential avoidance (e.g., an unwillingness to experience certain thoughts, feelings, or emotions; Mann et al., 2022).

Such models have had a powerful impact in guiding intervention work, as the therapeutic tools for improving emotion regulation skills or reducing experiential avoidance already exist, and might orient therapists wishing to target these processes. Targeting coping, interpersonal behaviors, unhelpful thoughts and emotion dysregulation have led to the first randomized controlled trials of treatments specifically targeting minority stress experiences and reactions (Pachankis et al., 2015, 2020a, b, c), as well as a number of pilot studies adapting other cognitive behavioral therapy (CBT) interventions such as dialectical behavior therapy (Linehan, 1993) to target minority stress (e.g. Cohen et al., 2021). Similarly, a number of small pilot studies have explored the utility of targeting experiential avoidance, specifically using acceptance and commitment therapy (ACT) given the close theoretical association between ACT and the construct of experiential avoidance (Fowler et al., 2022).

While preliminary work on what makes these treatments work has shown promise, it is important to remember that each facet of minority stress can impact an LGBTQ+ person, and the form and severity of these exposures and their impacts can vary across environments. Not all LGBTQ+ people are subjected to the same amount of overt or covert discrimination, and some individuals come out to welcoming and loving families and friends. Internalized stigma varies broadly across demographic characteristics and may not influence all individuals (e.g., Newcomb & Mustanski, 2010), many who now grow up in a world full of openly LGBTQ+ television characters and celebrities. A history of parental rejection, however, is strongly associated with subsequent rejection sensitivity, even when later adult relationships might have been more accepting (e.g., Pachankis et al., 2008).

For these reasons, it is important to consider that therapies may selectively target specific components described within minority stress theory. For example, given the relative importance of social safeness, rejection sensitivity appears to be an important target in that behavioral repertoires of interpersonal guardedness serve to continually undermine connection. Both theoretical and treatment models have been described that highlight the treatment of rejection sensitivity (respectively, Feinstein, 2020; Rincón et al., 2023). For example, functional analytic psychotherapy generally encourages interpersonal risk taking. Speaking openly about one's feelings, or expressing a need, creates an opportunity for an LGBTQ+ person to challenge their fears or uncertainties in a relationship based on the response of the person they are with. Such work requires both the acknowledgment of real risks, as well as a recognition of how past experiences might have interfered with exploring greater openness in relationships when there might not be a risk of harm. Discriminating between relationships where an LGBTQ+ individual might wish to invite someone more fully into their life is key, as being responded to in a loving and accepting manner can allay overactive fears of rejection and provide corrective learning experiences (Skinta et al., 2018). While this particular approach is rooted in behavior therapy, similar practices have been proposed in recent interpersonal psychodynamic models (Medley, 2021), as well as attachment-based approaches intended to repair severed relationships between LGBTQ+ individuals and rejecting parents (Diamond et al., 2022). Before expanding upon these models, it is worth highlighting that minority stress arises from discriminatory social processes, not intrapersonal origins. Therapists should be cautioned from allowing individual efforts at healing by clients to suggest that their distress is their fault; no LGBTQ+ individual is to blame for the biased experiences they have encountered in the world (Meyer, 2020).

A Process-Driven Model for Intervention

As described above, sexual and gender minority stress might affect individual clients differently according to the relative impact of different aspects of discrimination or discriminatory environments to which they have been exposed. A person raised in an environment where discrimination or violence is widespread and frequently witnessed might express greater hypervigilance than a person raised in a religious environment where shame dominates their inner world. For these reasons, the vignette below illustrates a model grounded in process-based approaches to contextual behavior therapy, and specifically a conceptualization grounded in the knowledge that no behavior or action makes sense outside of the cultural context that it occurs in (e.g., Hayes & Toarmino, 1995). At its heart, process-based psychotherapy considers how empirically-supported techniques might be fit against the client's presenting problems, regardless of their diagnosis and without reliance on a treatment manual (Hofmann & Hayes, 2019).

Examples of process-based, contextual behavioral approaches to respond to minority stress include acceptance and commitment therapy (ACT; Hayes et al., 1999), functional analytic psychotherapy (FAP; Kohlenberg & Tsai, 1991), and compassion-focused therapy (CFT; Gilbert, 2010). Each of these approaches share an emphasis on orienting toward the present moment, leaning toward or remaining present with unwanted thoughts or emotions, and noticing the response of others when attempting a new behavior, rather than overfocusing on one's own emotional responses or efforts to control them. An excellent general guide to the integration of these three approaches as a general behavioral stance is available to guide this work (Tirch et al., 2014), as well as a guide on the integration of these approaches through a minority stress lens for work with sexual orientation and gender diverse clients (Skinta, 2020). Specifically, ACT emphasizes a framework grounded in the present moment that dances between acceptance processes, such as willingness to feel unwanted emotions and noticing how differently painful thoughts or beliefs (e.g., "my family will never love me") affect behavior when they are experienced as more or less believable on any given day, and action processes that include both awareness of what is most meaningful in life and efforts to behave in alignment with those values. FAP is closely related, and emphasizes interpersonal values such as authenticity and genuineness, and acceptance of the fearful emotional consequences of expressing one's needs or setting boundaries. Finally, CFT introduces the importance of choosing compassion, specifically self-compassion, as a value that might be acted upon, and the greater awareness of the present moment that comes from viewing one's self from a perspective of care and non-judgment. These processes complement one another in mitigating the effects of minority stress, which reduces agency in life and particularly in relationships, wherein some people experience expectations of bias, rejection, or a reflection of one's unlovability. The integration of these processes and how they impact LGBTQ+ people is described in Fig. 3.1, and the unfolding of these processes in clinical work can be seen in the illustrative case example that follows.

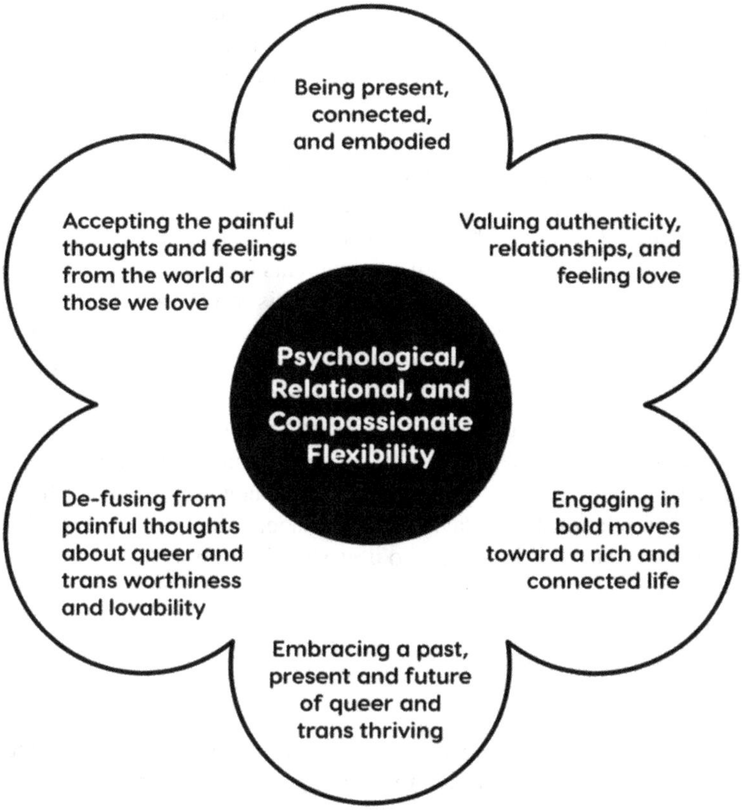

Fig. 3.1 A model of contextual behavior therapy processes important in work with LGBTQ+ individuals

Case Example

Client Demographics

The following case example is inspired by a variety of clinical experiences, specifically working with the LGBTQ+ community in a variety of clinical settings (e.g., academic medical centers, private practice, safety net hospitals, integrated behavioral health) by the third author, though with the therapist also representing some attributes of her clinical mentors. The goal of this clinical example is to highlight the impact of minority stress and explore affirmative therapeutic approaches when working with sexual minority individuals, particularly those with a history of trauma. John is a 27-year-old Black, cisgender, queer individual who uses he/him pronouns. His mother has a history of depression and he has an estranged relationship with his biological father, who left the family unit when he was a child. John's mother remarried a White man, who moved into his family home with his 17-year old son when John was in the sixth grade. John reported that his stepfather fulfilled the role of a father figure in his life. However, the patient has mixed feelings about this relationship due to the complex and inappropriate behavior of his stepbrother toward him when he was young, and his stepfather's dismissal of this behavior. Specifically, his stepbrother would frequently find opportunities when alone with John to play sexually explicit videos in front of him, and would tease John that he was aroused or overly interested when men's bodies or genitals were visible on screen. When John tried to tell his stepfather, he was told that his stepbrother would never engage in "gay stuff" and that those incidents must have another explanation. Moreover, his stepfather appeared to be proud of his son for watching pornographic material, almost as if it were a rite of passage into "manhood." As a result, John felt that his sexual development was "tainted" by these experiences, which led to immense feelings of guilt and shame around his sexuality. John mentioned that being raised in a predominantly White neighborhood, his experiences with his stepbrother, and being invalidated by his father figure made him subconsciously feel more inclined to date other White men. This has influenced the sexual challenges he is having in his relationship today. John's provider, Arya Baker, is a 27-year-old, Latina, cisgender, queer individual who uses she/her pronouns.

Presenting Concern(s)

John sought therapy services in order to better understand how his childhood trauma may have influenced his sexual identity development. John's intersecting identities (i.e., queer, Black) and invalidating experiences regarding his sexuality growing up increased his risk of being impacted by minority stress. For example, John highlighted how fear of rejection, victimization, and being forced to adhere to heteronormative cultural norms led to experiences of low mood, anxiety, and internalized homophobia. John has endorsed currently experiencing symptoms of depression and anxiety. John's symptoms of depression include depressed mood, loss of interest/pleasure, decreased concentration, inappropriate guilt, and fatigue. John reported that his symptoms of anxiety involve restlessness, irritability, and excessive worry. John shared that his symptoms of depression and anxiety coincide with one another and he has trouble regulating these symptoms.

Therapist and Client Exchange

John: I feel horrible about myself. I feel like this is often true in my blended family as well as in my career. I have deep-seated insecurities, which I think started when I realized I did not fit in with the other kids at school because I was one of two Black students in a predominately White school until I went to college. I guess the nature of my relationship with my stepbrother also made me feel strange in my skin… I think these things feed into how I feel today and my ongoing imposter syndrome.

Therapist: It seems like being one of two Black students during your formative educational experiences was challenging and isolating in a way. And as a result, I see someone who is resilient but has not felt very empowered. You also mentioned that your relationship with your stepbrother has also negatively influenced the way you view yourself, which we haven't talked too much about yet. Can you tell me more about that?

John: Hmm…I've always felt pretty insecure, especially growing up in a blended household. I don't know, I guess I felt like my parents took my stepbrother more seriously than me. Even when I was the one who got straight A's, it was never enough. And then to not be believed when something was happening… I don't know. Then to top it off, I'm constantly working underneath White folks at my job. It feels like there is no running away from White supremacy. There is also code-switching, which I inherently have to do—sometimes it all feels hopeless, it's either I am too Black for some spaces or I'm too White for spaces—and I'm not even White, my mom decided to remarry to a White man!

Therapist: It sounds like you have constantly been in spaces where you have not had space to live authentically. You mentioned feeling like a Black sheep in a blended family growing up, which has been replicated in many of your workspaces. What would it feel like to have compassion for your child self who struggled with feeling seen and connected to those around you?

John: I guess I feel sad for him and … I guess it also makes me feel sad for myself now because I do not know how to have compassion for myself in general. I have always been hard on myself because I would rather blame myself than the people around me. It just somehow always feels like it is my fault.

Therapist: You made a great point John about why compassion may be challenging for you– there's a part of you that notices you have existed in a world where you have not felt protected by your parents and there's another part of you noticing that you exist in a world that often is unsafe for Black queer people. If you have constantly been exposed to situations that have caused you harm and in return blame yourself for the harm done to you, where does that leave space for compassion or those moments where you created safety for yourself in challenging circumstances?

John: Hmmm, I guess I never really stopped to think about it that way.

Therapist: It can be challenging to find space for that when our minds are constantly prioritizing the newest challenge, but that is why taking a moment to focus on our breathing can help to slow us down amidst all the chaos. I appreciate your vulnerability in this conversation, and I can acknowledge that this conversation may feel like a lot. How are you feeling right now, in this space, with me?

John: Tense in my hands and chest, a bit overwhelmed I guess. Ugh, I wish that I did not feel this way. I'm glad it's with you, though, it feels safe. I feel seen.

Therapist: I'm glad it feels safe to be overwhelmed with me, too. I really hope what we work on brings this safety out into the rest of the world. Previously we discussed using mindfulness to help you pause and take a few moments to ground yourself. Do you think we could do that right now in session? The goal is to reduce the power of these feelings of being overwhelmed by decreasing the influence that these painful feelings have over you. How does that sound?

John: Sure, let's give it a try.

Therapist: Great! We are going to practice a mindfulness exercise that involves your five senses. First, I want you to bring your attention to five things that you see. Pick something that you don't normally notice in this room… it could be a shadow or a small crack in the wall.

John: Uh okay, well first I see a book about mindfulness on your bookshelf (chuckles).

Therapist: (chuckles) Good! Let's name four more things you see in the room.

John: I see a dent in the wall behind you, pens on your desk, a lamp in the corner of the room, and a bird outside of the window.

Therapist: Excellent, now try to bring your awareness to four things that you can feel. Remember we are talking about senses, not things you are feeling inside. Rather things that you are feeling externally.

John: Okay, well I feel a light breeze from the vents on my skin, the velvet from the arm of the chair, the tightness of the shoes on my feet, and the texture of my pants on my legs.

Therapist: Great, you're doing very well at this. Next, I want you to take a moment to listen and share three things that you hear in the background.

John: I hear the children playing at the school next door, a car alarm going off, and birds chirping outside.

Therapist: Wonderful, now bring your awareness to what you smell and name two things that you smell right now.

John: First, I smell the flowers in the room, which are very nice by the way. And I also smell myself because I'm a little smelly right now (chuckles).

Therapist: (chuckles) Very good. Now focus on one thing that you can taste at this moment.

John: I taste the coffee that I was just drinking before I started the session.

Therapist: That's great! How are you feeling right now after taking a moment to check in with your senses?

John: Well, I feel like I barely remember what we were talking about before. I guess I also feel more relaxed and my mind isn't racing in a million directions for once.

Therapist: That is great John. This is a quick and easy exercise that I would encourage you to use to help you ground and bring yourself back to the present moment. Often when we are beginning to feel overwhelmed, our mind ventures into a million directions like you just shared. This is something that you can add to your toolbox whenever you are feeling overwhelmed. How does that feel?

John: It felt silly at first, but I do like how I feel after trying that out. So, I will give it a go.

Assessment Approach and Considerations

The model described above offers us a guide in where to approach John's struggle. In order to gain a better understanding of John, the clinician should begin by exploring the function of his behavior (e.g., a functional analysis) to better understand the areas of life that he feels "stuck" in, including beliefs or fears related to his sexual orientation. In order to do so, the clinician should consider the client's psychological, relational, and compassionate flexibility, such as his ability to stay present and embodied, or to accept the difficult or painful thoughts and feelings within his experience. In other words, the clinician should be considering where *inflexibility* is arising, such as fusion (e.g., treating his thoughts as if they were completely believable or true) when painful ideas about his own worth and lovability arise. The clinician wants to explore if he is living in the past, considering his losses and rejections, or stuck in a feared future, so the mindfulness activity above emphasizes a connection to the present in an embodied way. Future sessions might continue to explore what John finds most meaningful, and how he translates that into action in ways that are self-compassionate and create room for mistakes.

In working with John, the therapist began by probing for a sense of the role of cognitive fusion (*see* Table 3.1). Cognitive fusion refers to the process of being stuck or "fused" to our thoughts, best assessed by asking a series of questions that allows for an understanding of where John gets "caught up" or "entangled" in his own thoughts (Hayes et al., 2012). The clinician should then assess how the client engages in avoidance, characterized by the attempts to suppress, avoid or get rid of unwanted feelings, thoughts, and memories. For John, the experience of both fusion and avoidance of unwanted thoughts and feelings are related, and John's low willingness to experience his emotions and memories may lead him to fuse with negative thoughts about himself (i.e., "I am worthless," "No one can love me").

Fusion can also occur in relation to how one experiences the self, particularly as it relates to stories about one's past or future. In asking John about the memories and images of himself he is most stuck in, we will better understand how he sees himself. Some LGBTQ+ people also struggle with memories of shame and rejection from their childhood, and those histories of shame might be easily reawakened by current relationships (e.g., Matos et al., 2017). Process-based therapies suggest flowing through therapeutic tasks based upon what is in front of the clinician in any given moment. For these reasons, in moments John is expressing a willingness to

Table 3.1 Questions to explore the function of behaviors with LGBTQ+ clients

Are there any painful memories, particularly when you reflect on your sexual orientation or gender identity, that you frequently find yourself stuck in?
How do you act when those memories are present?
How much time do you spend in the past/future?
Are there specific thoughts, feelings, or judgments from others you find yourself avoiding?
Is it easier or harder to work with me since we share (or do not share) certain identities?
Adapted from Harris, 2009

feel difficult emotions and does not appear fused with the believability of painful thoughts, the therapist's task is to move toward identifying those things that make life and relationships meaningful, and practicing behaviors that move him toward them. It can be challenging for John, like any queer or transgender person, to feel like he can live a meaningful life if he has not previously had opportunities and reinforcement from others for identifying the things in his life that bring him joy, purpose, and solace (e.g., creativity, community, self-compassion, openness). Many LGBTQ+ clients have been raised in family homes or discriminatory environments where one's self-worth might feel dependent on the judgment of others, sometimes labeled contingent self-worth, so John may have learned that living up to the values of others is more important than identifying his own (e.g., Pachankis & Hatzenbuehler, 2013).

Intervention Approach and Considerations

John's initially stated goal for therapy was to better understand how his childhood trauma may have influenced his sexual identity development. From a contextual behavioral perspective, the clinician would aim to promote psychological, relational, and compassionate flexibility as illustrated in Fig. 3.1, which involves helping the client connect with the present moment while remaining open to their experiences and engaging in behaviors guided by their values as a whole, authentic person. The six processes listed, derived from ACT, FAP, and CFT, have been described through the lens of minority stress theory for work with LGBTQ+ clients as being grounded in the present moment, authentically and vulnerably connected in our relationships, and accepting our embodied experiences of our feelings, gender, and sexual desires. Taking bold moves that align with what feels most meaningful in life, while embracing one's full worthiness and lovability, are at the heart of this approach (Skinta & D'Alton, 2016).

John appears to struggle with acceptance of painful inner experiences, which may involve opening up about his trauma history and making room for the painful feelings, sensations, and emotions related to his past. As a result, John is working on opening up and accepting the feelings in order to create a space where he can make room for these uncomfortable emotions, which is the first step to reengaging with a meaningful life. While willingness to feel these powerful emotions is important, so is a sense of safety in the room and compassion within himself. One helpful exercise might be a compassionate figure meditation, which will allow him to try on the sensations of receiving warmth from another person in a manner that is less overwhelming than moments of connection in daily life that are hard to stay present within (e.g., Petrocchi et al., 2016). The therapist should consider the value of self-disclosure, particularly if the therapist is a member of an LGBTQ+ community, and to remember that the therapeutic space might allow for the gradual practice of both vulnerability and receiving compassion from the therapist in difficult moments. Building upon the mindfulness practice described in the vignette, the therapist might gently orient the client toward an awareness that he is not alone in the room in this present moment. Rather, he is being seen by another, experiencing the presence of another, and this is an integral and potentially evocative piece of the present moment. He is not just being encouraged to sit with whatever shame or pain arises, he is being asked to do so while another person can see him, and to connect with the vulnerability that this context allows to arise.

John is practicing how to use himself as the context, which involves understanding that his emotions, thoughts, and experiences are frequently changing and experiences are not fixed. Using the self as context also helps to remind the client that thoughts, feelings, and experiences may change but the core part of yourself that views and notices those changes throughout life never changes. The therapist helps John see that his experiences from childhood, such as being excluded and not fitting in with his family, have translated to other areas of his adult life. The therapist might share "There's a part of John that notices he has existed in a world where he did not feel protected by his parents and there's another part of John noticing that he exists in a world that often is unsafe for Black queer people." Through such statements, the therapist is planting seeds for John to begin viewing himself as more than his experiences in order to promote a flexible view of himself. It is important to note that such language, such as noting how unsafe the world is for Black queer people, may hold different meaning for John when said by a Black queer therapist versus a White straight therapist. To do this work, it is important that the therapist be willing to note how clients respond to their own stated and perceived identities, to accept it, and to model a willingness to explore and discuss it.

Within this vignette, the therapist did not directly engage John in values work. However, throughout the course of treatment, the therapist will help John identify what gives his life meaning or purpose. This could be done by asking John "What would it look like, as a Black queer man, to be your fullest and most authentic self in the world? To live a life that brings you joy to look back on?" The therapist can use whatever answers arise to encourage John to engage in behaviors rooted in his values, and many clients resonate with the metaphor of values working like a compass that gives us direction on our ongoing journey. Lastly, the therapist might encourage the creation of specific and measurable goals, guided by values, and then doing the work to achieve those goals, even while it brings forth pain and discomfort. At the end of treatment, John is likely to feel as though he has made moves towards living a meaningful life, regardless of the unwanted and difficult experiences that life throws his way.

Conclusion

The process described in this chapter of conducting process-based, contextual behavior therapy may serve as one model that can affirm and support LGBTQ+ clients affected by minority stress. It merits repetition in the close of this chapter that minority stress is the result of societal bias—harm done upon LGBTQ+ people by the collective and individual actions of politicians, media misrepresentations, societal movements, or rejection from loved ones and family, which ultimately shape and stamp themselves upon the inner and outer behaviors of LGBTQ+ individuals and maintain or perpetuate instances of harm. These therapies alone will not free LGBTQ+ people from oppression or create a safer world. They may, however, reduce suffering due to carrying painful histories, promote resilience and thriving, and encourage more vulnerable and meaningful relationships. Process-based, affirming, contextual behavior therapies provide one path forward in responding to the harms of minority stress.

References

Argyriou, A., Goldsmith, K. A., & Rimes, K. A. (2021). Mediators of the disparities in depression between sexual minority and heterosexual individuals: A systematic review. *Archives of Sexual Behavior, 50*, 925–959.

Ashley, F. (2023). Interrogating gender-exploratory therapy. *Perspectives on Psychological Science, 18*(2), 472–481.

Bockting, W., Barucco, R., LeBlanc, A., Singh, A., Mellman, W., Dolezal, C., & Ehrhardt, A. (2020). Sociopolitical change and transgender people's perceptions of vulnerability and resilience. *Sexuality Research and Social Policy, 17*, 162–174.

Borgogna, N. C., McDermott, R. C., Aita, S. L., & Kridel, M. M. (2019). Anxiety and depression across gender and sexual minorities: Implications for transgender, gender nonconforming, pansexual, demisexual, asexual, queer, and questioning individuals. *Psychology of Sexual Orientation and Gender Diversity, 6*(1), 54.

Bränström, R., Stormbom, I., Bergendal, M., & Pachankis, J. E. (2022). Transgender-based disparities in suicidality: A population-based study of key predictions from four theoretical models. *Suicide and Life-threatening Behavior, 52*(3), 401–412.

Brooks, V. R. (1981). *Minority stress and lesbian women*. Lexington Books.

Burton, C. L., Clark, K. A., & Pachankis, J. E. (2020). Risk from within: Intraminority gay community stress and sexual risk-taking among sexual minority men. *Annals of Behavioral Medicine, 54*(9), 703–712.

Calabrese, S. K., Meyer, I. H., Overstreet, N. M., Haile, R., & Hansen, N. B. (2015). Exploring discrimination and mental health disparities faced by Black sexual minority women using a minority stress framework. *Psychology of Women Quarterly, 39*(3), 287–304.

Cardona, N. D., Madigan, R. J., & Sauer-Zavala, S. (2022). How minority stress becomes traumatic invalidation: An emotion-focused conceptualization of minority stress in sexual and gender minority people. *Clinical Psychology: Science and Practice, 29*(2), 185–195.

Cohen, J. M., Feinstein, B. A., Rodriguez-Seijas, C., Taylor, C. B., & Newman, M. G. (2016). Rejection sensitivity as a transdiagnostic risk factor for internalizing psychopathology among gay and bisexual men. *Psychology of Sexual Orientation and Gender Diversity, 3*(3), 259–264.

Cohen, J. M., Norona, J. C., Yadavia, J. E., & Borsari, B. (2021). Affirmative dialectical behavior therapy skills training with sexual minority veterans. *Cognitive and Behavioral Practice, 28*(1), 77–91.

de Lange, J., Baams, L., van Bergen, D. D., Bos, H. M., & Bosker, R. J. (2022). Minority stress and suicidal ideation and suicide attempts among LGBT adolescents and young adults: A meta-analysis. *LGBT Health, 9*(4), 222–237.

Diamond, L. M., & Alley, J. (2022). Rethinking minority stress: A social safety perspective on the health effects of stigma in sexually-diverse and gender-diverse populations. *Neuroscience & Biobehavioral Reviews, 138*, 104720.

Diamond, G. M., Boruchovitz-Zamir, R., Nir-Gotlieb, O., Gat, I., Bar-Kalifa, E., Fitoussi, P. Y., & Katz, S. (2022). Attachment-based family therapy for sexual and gender minority young adults and their nonaccepting parents. *Family Process, 61*(2), 530–548.

Douglass, R. P., & Conlin, S. E. (2020). Minority stress among LGB people: Investigating relations among distal and proximal stressors. *Current Psychology*, 1–11.

Drabish, K., & Theeke, L. A. (2022). Health impact of stigma, discrimination, prejudice, and bias experienced by transgender people: a systematic review of quantitative studies. *Issues in Mental Health Nursing, 43*(2), 111–118.

Du Bois, S. N., Yoder, W., Guy, A. A., Manser, K., & Ramos, S. (2018). Examining associations between state-level transgender policies and transgender health. *Transgender Health, 3*(1), 220–224.

Dunn, T. L., & Szymanski, D. M. (2018). Heterosexist discrimination and LGBQ activism: Examining a moderated mediation model. *Psychology of Sexual Orientation and Gender Diversity, 5*(1), 13–24.

Feinstein, B. A. (2020). The rejection sensitivity model as a framework for understanding sexual minority mental health. *Archives of Sexual Behavior, 49*(7), 2247–2258.

Feinstein, B. A., Goldfried, M. R., & Davila, J. (2012). The relationship between experiences of discrimination and mental health among lesbians and gay men: An examination of internalized homonegativity and rejection sensitivity as potential mechanisms. *Journal of Consulting and Clinical Psychology, 80*(5), 917–927.

Flentje, A., Heck, N. C., Brennan, J. M., & Meyer, I. H. (2020). The relationship between minority stress and biological outcomes: A systematic review. *Journal of Behavioral Medicine, 43*, 673–694.

Flynn, M. K., & Bhambhani, Y. (2021). Internalized transphobia, nondisclosure of gender identity, and life satisfaction among transgender and non-binary adults: The moderating roles of psychological flexibility and inflexibility. *Journal of Contextual Behavioral Science, 20*, 194–201.

Follins, L. D., Garrett-Walker, J. J., & Lewis, M. K. (2014). Resilience in Black lesbian, gay, bisexual, and transgender individuals: A critical review of the literature. *Journal of Gay & Lesbian Mental Health, 18*(2), 190–212.

Fowler, J. A., Viskovich, S., Buckley, L., & Dean, J. A. (2022). A call for ACTion: A systematic review of empirical evidence for the use of Acceptance and Commitment Therapy (ACT) with LGBTQI+ individuals. *Journal of Contextual Behavioral Science, 25*, 78–89.

Frost, D. M., & Meyer, I. H. (2023). Minority stress theory: Application, critique, and continued relevance. *Current Opinion in Psychology*, 101579.

Gilbert, P. (2010). *Compassion focused therapy: Distinctive features*. Routledge.

GLAAD. (2020). *Where we are on TV 2019-2020*. https://www.glaad.org/sites/default/files/GLAAD%20WHERE%20WE%20ARE%20ON%20TV%202019%202020.pdf

Harris, R. (2009). *ACT made simple: An easy-to-read primer on acceptance and commitment therapy*. New Harbinger Publications.

Hatzenbuehler, M. L. (2009). How does sexual minority stigma "get under the skin"? A psychological mediation framework. *Psychological Bulletin, 135*(5), 707–730.

Hatzenbuehler, M. L., O'Cleirigh, C., Grasso, C., Mayer, K., Safren, S., & Bradford, J. (2012). Effect of same-sex marriage laws on health care use and expenditures in sexual minority men: A quasi-natural experiment. *American Journal of Public Health, 102*(2), 285–291.

Hayes, S. C., Pistorello, J., & Levin, M. E. (2012). Acceptance and commitment therapy as a unified model of behavior change. *The Counseling Psychologist, 40*(7), 976–1002.

Hayes, S. C., Strosahl, K. D., & Wilson, K. G. (1999). *Acceptance and commitment therapy: An experiential approach to behavior change*. Guilford Press.

Hayes, S. C., & Toarmino, D. (1995). If behavioral principles are generally applicable, why is it necessary to understand cultural diversity? *The Behavior Therapist, 18*, 21–23.

Helsen, V., Enzlin, P., & Gijs, L. (2022). Mental health in transgender adults: The role of proximal minority stress, community connectedness, and gender nonconformity. *Psychology of Sexual Orientation and Gender Diversity, 9*(4), 466–477.

Hendricks, M. L., & Testa, R. J. (2012). A conceptual framework for clinical work with transgender and gender nonconforming clients: An adaptation of the Minority Stress Model. *Professional Psychology: Research and Practice, 43*(5), 460.

Hofmann, S. G., & Hayes, S. C. (2019). The future of intervention science: Process-based therapy. *Clinical Psychological Science, 7*(1), 37–50.

Jackman, K., Edgar, B., Ling, A., Honig, J., & Bockting, W. (2018). Experiences of transmasculine spectrum people who report nonsuicidal self-injury: A qualitative investigation. *Journal of Counseling Psychology, 65*(5), 586–597.

Jones, A. K., Wehner, C. L., Andrade, I. M., Jones, E. M., Wooten, L. H., & Wilson, L. C. (2022). Minority stress and posttraumatic growth in the transgender and nonbinary community. *Psychology of Sexual Orientation and Gender Diversity*. Advance online publication. https://doi.org/10.1037/sgd0000610

King, S. D., & Richardson, V. E. (2017). Mental Health for Older LGBT Adults. *Annual Review of Gerontology & Geriatrics*, 37(1).

Kohlenberg, R. J., & Tsai, M. (1991). *Functional analytic psychotherapy: Creating intense and curative therapeutic relationships*. Springer.

Krieger, N., Chen, J. T., Waterman, P. D., Hartman, C., Stoddard, A. M., Quinn, M., et al. (2008). The inverse hazard law: Blood pressure, sexual harassment, racial discrimination, workplace abuse and occupational exposures in US low-income Black, White and Latino workers. *Social Science & Medicine, 67*, 1970–1981.

Lefevor, G. T., Boyd-Rogers, C. C., Sprague, B. M., & Janis, R. A. (2019). Health disparities between genderqueer, transgender, and cisgender individuals: An extension of minority stress theory. *Journal of Counseling Psychology, 66*(4), 385–395.

Levitt, H. M., & Ippolito, M. R. (2014). Being transgender: Navigating minority stressors and developing authentic self-presentation. *Psychology of Women Quarterly, 38*(1), 46–64.

Lindley, L., & Bauerband, L. (2022). The mediating role of avoidant and facilitative coping on the relation between discrimination and alcohol use among transgender and gender-diverse individuals. *Transgender Health*. Online ahead of print: https://doi.org/10.1089/trgh.2021.0173

Linehan, M. M. (1993). *Cognitive-behavioral treatment of borderline personality disorder*.

Liu, R. T., Sheehan, A. E., Walsh, R. F., Sanzari, C. M., Cheek, S. M., & Hernandez, E. M. (2019). Prevalence and correlates of non-suicidal self-injury among lesbian, gay, bisexual, and transgender individuals: A systematic review and meta-analysis. *Clinical Psychology Review, 74*, 101783.

Mann, A. M., Naugle, A. E., & Lieberman, E. (2022). Experiential avoidance and emotion dysregulation as mediators in the LGBTQ minority stress model. *Archives of Sexual Behavior, 51*(7), 3443–3456.

Matos, M., Carvalho, S. A., Cunha, M., Galhardo, A., & Sepodes, C. (2017). Psychological flexibility and self-compassion in gay and heterosexual men: How they relate to childhood memories, shame, and depressive symptoms. *Journal of LGBT Issues in Counseling, 11*(2), 88–105.

McConnell, E. A., Janulis, P., Phillips, G., II, Truong, R., & Birkett, M. (2018). Multiple minority stress and LGBT community resilience among sexual minority men. *Psychology of Sexual Orientation and Gender Diversity, 5*(1), 1–12.

McLemore, K. A. (2018). A minority stress perspective on transgender individuals' experiences with misgendering. *Stigma and Health, 3*(1), 53–64.

Medley, B. (2021). Recovering the true self: Affirmative therapy, attachment, and AEDP in psychotherapy with gay men. *Journal of Psychotherapy Integration, 31*(4), 383–402.

Mereish, E. H., & Bradford, J. B. (2014). Intersecting identities and substance use problems: Sexual orientation, gender, race, and lifetime substance use problems. *Journal of Studies on Alcohol and Drugs, 75*(1), 179–188.

Meyer, I. H. (2003). Prejudice, social stress, and mental health in lesbian, gay, and bisexual populations: Conceptual issues and research evidence. *Psychological Bulletin, 129*(5), 674–697.

Meyer, I. H. (2020). Rejection sensitivity and minority stress: A challenge for clinicians and interventionists. *Archives of Sexual Behavior, 49*(7), 2287–2289.

Newcomb, M. E., & Mustanski, B. (2010). Internalized homophobia and internalizing mental health problems: A meta-analytic review. *Clinical Psychology Review, 30*(8), 1019–1029.

Nicholson, A. A., Siegel, M., Wolf, J., Narikuzhy, S., Roth, S. L., Hatchard, T., et al. (2022). A systematic review of the neural correlates of sexual minority stress: Towards an intersectional minority mosaic framework with implications for a future research agenda. *European Journal of Psychotraumatology, 13*(1), 2002572.

Ogolsky, B. G., Monk, J. K., Rice, T. M., & Oswald, R. F. (2019). As the states turned: Implications of the changing legal context of same-sex marriage on well-being. *Journal of Social and Personal Relationships, 36*(10), 3219–3238.

Pachankis, J. E., Clark, K. A., Burton, C. L., Hughto, J. M. W., Bränström, R., & Keene, D. E. (2020a). Sex, status, competition, and exclusion: Intraminority stress from within the gay community and gay and bisexual men's mental health. *Journal of Personality and Social Psychology, 119*(3), 713–740.

Pachankis, J. E., Goldfried, M. R., & Ramrattan, M. E. (2008). Extension of the rejection sensitivity construct to the interpersonal functioning of gay men. *Journal of Consulting and Clinical Psychology, 76*(2), 306–317.

Pachankis, J. E., & Hatzenbuehler, M. L. (2013). The social development of contingent self-worth in sexual minority young men: An empirical investigation of the "Best Little Boy in the World" hypothesis. *Basic and Applied Social Psychology, 35*(2), 176–190.

Pachankis, J. E., Hatzenbuehler, M. L., Rendina, H. J., Safren, S. A., & Parsons, J. T. (2015). LGB-affirmative cognitive-behavioral therapy for young adult gay and bisexual men: A randomized controlled trial of a transdiagnostic minority stress approach. *Journal of Consulting and Clinical Psychology, 83*(5), 875–889.

Pachankis, J. E., Mahon, C. P., Jackson, S. D., Fetzner, B. K., & Bränström, R. (2020b). Sexual orientation concealment and mental health: A conceptual and meta-analytic review. *Psychological Bulletin, 146*(10), 831–871.

Pachankis, J. E., McConocha, E. M., Clark, K. A., Wang, K., Behari, K., Fetzner, B. K., Brisbin, C. D., Scheer, J. R., & Lehavot, K. (2020c). A transdiagnostic minority stress intervention for gender diverse sexual minority women's depression, anxiety, and unhealthy alcohol use: A randomized controlled trial. *Journal of Consulting and Clinical Psychology, 88*(7), 613–630.

Pellicane, M. J., & Ciesla, J. A. (2022). Associations between minority stress, depression, and suicidal ideation and attempts in transgender and gender diverse (TGD) individuals: Systematic review and meta-analysis. *Clinical Psychology Review, 91*, 102113.

Petrocchi, N., Matos, M., Carvalho, S., & Baiocco, R. (2016). Compassion-focused therapy in the treatment of shame-based difficulties in gender and sexual minorities. In M. D. Skinta & A. Curtin (Eds.), *Mindfulness and acceptance for gender and sexual minorities* (pp. 69–86). New Harbinger.

Petrocchi, N., Pistella, J., Salvati, M., Carone, N., Laghi, F., & Baiocco, R. (2020). I embrace my LGB identity: Self-reassurance, social safeness, and the distinctive relevance of authenticity to well-being in Italian lesbians, gay men, and bisexual people. *Sexuality Research and Social Policy, 17*(1), 75–86.

Puckett, J. A., Horne, S. G., Herbitter, C., Maroney, M. R., & Levitt, H. M. (2017). Differences across contexts: Minority stress and interpersonal relationships for lesbian, gay, and bisexual women. *Psychology of Women Quarterly, 41*(1), 8–19.

Rincón, C. L., Muñoz-Martínez, A. M., Hoeflein, B., & Skinta, M. D. (2023). Enhancing interpersonal intimacy in Colombian gay men using functional analytic psychotherapy: An experimental nonconcurrent multiple baseline design. *Cognitive and Behavioral Practice, 30*(1), 82–95.

Russell, S. T., & Fish, J. N. (2016). Mental health in lesbian, gay, bisexual, and transgender (LGBT) youth. *Annual Review of Clinical Psychology, 12*, 465–487.

Safer, J. D., Coleman, E., Feldman, J., Garofalo, R., Hembree, W., Radix, A., & Sevelius, J. (2016). Barriers to health care for transgender individuals. *Current Opinion in Endocrinology, Diabetes, and Obesity, 23*(2), 168–171.

Singh, A. A., Hays, D. G., & Watson, L. S. (2011). Strength in the face of adversity: Resilience strategies of transgender individuals. *Journal of Counseling & Development, 89*(1), 20–27.

Singh, R. S., Bhambhani, Y., Skinta, M. D., & Torres-Harding, S. R. (2021). Measurement of intersectional microaggressions: Conceptual barriers and recommendations. *Perspectives on Psychological Science, 16*(5), 956–971.

Skinta, M. D. (2020). *Contextual behavior therapy for sexual and gender minority clients: A practical guide to treatment*. Routledge.

Skinta, M. D., & D'Alton, P. (2016). Leaving shame behind: Mindfulness and acceptance for malignant shame. In M. D. Skinta & A. Curtin (Eds.), *Mindfulness and acceptance for gender and sexual minorities: A clinician's guide to fostering compassion, connection, and equality using contextual strategies*. New Harbinger Publications.

Skinta, M. D., Hoeflein, B., Muñoz-Martínez, A. M., & Rincón, C. L. (2018). Responding to gender and sexual minority stress with functional analytic psychotherapy. *Psychotherapy, 55*(1), 63.

Su, D., Irwin, J. A., Fisher, C., Ramos, A., Kelley, M., Mendoza, D. A. R., & Coleman, J. D. (2016). Mental health disparities within the LGBT population: A comparison between transgender and nontransgender individuals. *Transgender Health, 1*(1), 12–20.

Szymanski, D. M., & Gonzalez, K. A. (2020). The role of resilience in sexual and gender minority mental health. In *The Oxford handbook of sexual and gender minority mental health* (pp. 429–442). Oxford University Press.

Testa, R. J., Jimenez, C. L., & Rankin, S. (2014). Risk and resilience during transgender identity development: The effects of awareness and engagement with other transgender people on affect. *Journal of Gay & Lesbian Mental Health, 18*(1), 31–46.

Tirch, D., Schoendorff, B., & Silberstein, L. R. (2014). *The ACT practitioner's guide to the science of compassion: Tools for fostering psychological flexibility*. New Harbinger Publications.

Walch, S. E., Ngamake, S. T., Bovornusvakool, W., & Walker, S. V. (2016). Discrimination, internalized homophobia, and concealment in sexual minority physical and mental health. *Psychology of Sexual Orientation and Gender Diversity, 3*(1), 37–48.

Wickham, R. E., Gutierrez, R., Giordano, B. L., Rostosky, S. S., & Riggle, E. D. (2021). Gender and generational differences in the internalized homophobia questionnaire: An alignment IRT analysis. *Assessment, 28*(4), 1159–1172.

Williams, D. R., Kontos, E. Z., Viswanath, K., Haas, J. S., Lathan, C. S., MacConaill, L. E., et al. (2012). Integrating multiple social statuses in health disparities research: The case of lung cancer. *Health Services Research, 47*, 1255–1277.

Wilson, C., & Cariola, L. A. (2020). LGBTQI+ youth and mental health: A systematic review of qualitative research. *Adolescent Research Review, 5*, 187–211.

Wilson, L. C., & Liss, M. (2022). Belonging and loneliness as mechanisms in the psychological impact of discrimination among transgender college students. *Journal of LGBT Youth*, 1–19.

Wittgens, C., Fischer, M. M., Buspavanich, P., Theobald, S., Schweizer, K., & Trautmann, S. (2022). Mental health in people with minority sexual orientations: A meta-analysis of population-based studies. *Acta Psychiatrica Scandinavica, 145*(4), 357–372.

Yarns, B. C., Abrams, J. M., Meeks, T. W., & Sewell, D. D. (2016). The mental health of older LGBT adults. *Current Psychiatry Reports, 18*, 1–11.

Chapter 4
Patient-Centered Treatment for Co-Occurring Trauma and Minority Stress

Colleen A. Sloan, Christine R. Serpe, and Claire M. Burgess

Highlights

- Trauma and minority stress often co-occur for LGBTQ+ people, jointly contributing to distress and impairment for many LGBTQ+ people.
- Minority stress theories provide useful frameworks for understanding how systemic injustices and identity-based stigma contribute to health problems, but they are limited regarding treatment implications.
- Evidence-based trauma focused therapies are inadequate if they do not integrate minority stress, and therefore may be limited in their utility for LGBTQ+ communities.
- This chapter aims to address this gap by describing both general guidelines and some concrete, specific modifications that can be implemented when treating co-occurring minority stress and trauma related problems in LGBTQ+ people.

Positionality

We begin by providing a positionality statement to both acknowledge aspects of our own identities and lived experiences and to transparently name those that align with and differ from the diverse identities and lived experiences represented via vignettes within this chapter. All authors are white cisgender women and hold class privilege related to educational attainment. Two of the three coauthors identify as lesbian, and one identifies as bisexual. All authors are nonveteran civilians, presently employed with the Veterans Health Administration (VHA); all come from families with veterans and servicemembers. We acknowledge that the diverse identities represented

C. A. Sloan (✉) · C. R. Serpe · C. M. Burgess
VA Boston Healthcare System, Boston, MA, USA

Chobanian & Avedisian School of Medicine, Psychiatry Department, Boston University, Boston, MA, USA
e-mail: Colleen.Sloan2@va.gov

N. A. Livingston et al. (eds.), *Addressing Minority Stress and Enhancing Resilience with Diverse LGBTQ+ Clients*, CBT: Science Into Practice,
https://doi.org/10.1007/978-3-031-92836-9_4

within this chapter, in almost all ways, do not reflect our own, and we therefore are limited in our understanding. We honor the inherent wisdom that exists within lived experiences, particularly for those who are most marginalized; we include literature from an intersectional lens where possible and acknowledge limitations in research that does not identify or acknowledge minoritized experiences. We similarly believe it is important to leverage the power that arises from unearned privilege in a way that draws attention to and contextualizes the experiences of those who are rendered less power within our society and that aims to promote equity, access, and justice.

Background: Inequities and Health Disparities for LGBTQ+ People

Discriminatory experiences, identity concealment efforts, and internalization of sociocultural hostilities and indignities directed toward LGBTQ+ people result in adverse mental and physical health outcomes (Meyer, 2003). And, larger disparities exist for certain communities within the broader LGBTQ+ "umbrella." For example, in a recent meta-analysis conducted by Marchi et al. (2023) examining post-traumatic stress disorder (PTSD) in LGBTQ people, results showed that transgender people were at highest risk for PTSD followed by bisexual people. Indeed, bisexual-specific disparities have been well documented. Studies combining systematic review and meta-analysis have revealed bisexual persons to be at highest risk for anxiety and depression symptomatology and diagnoses (Ross et al., 2018), as well as greater endorsement of suicidal ideation and history of suicide attempt, as compared with lesbian/gay and straight counterparts (Salway et al., 2019).

Minority stress theories (Brooks, 1981; Hendricks & Testa, 2012; Meyer, 2003) provide frameworks for understanding the presence of health disparities in minoritized people. Minority stress can contribute to negative health outcomes both directly via *distal stress* factors, which are experiences within the larger environment such as identity-based discrimination, interpersonal violence, traumatization, and inadequate access to healthcare, and indirectly via *proximal stress* factors, which manifest as internalization of distal stressors (e.g., internalized anti-trans prejudice). Minority stressors within the larger environment can include but are not limited to identity-based traumatic stressors such as being physically or sexually assaulted because of one's identity. And, at the same time, minority stressors may not necessarily be traumatic stressors. For example, being fired from one's job because of one's sexual orientation and/or gender identity or expression is a minority stressor but is not a traumatic stressor. Likewise, being in a life threatening automobile accident is a traumatic stressor but is not a minority stressor. Non-traumatic minority stressors may exacerbate and/or drive trauma-related symptoms. For example, being called an identity-related slur is not considered a Criterion A traumatic stressor per DSM-5, but may nevertheless serve as a trauma-related cue and/or contribute to/exacerbate trauma-related symptoms including those consistent with PTSD (e.g., hyperarousal). Likewise, minority stressors may present on a daily basis (and even several times throughout 1 day), so perhaps unsurprisingly, may negatively impact mental and physical health.

Increased attention has been paid to addressing minority stress therapeutically by targeting the underlying and modifiable cognitive and affective processes that drive minority stress (Hatzenbuehler, 2009). Generally speaking, efforts to reduce minority stress (and its effects) and increase resilience (e.g., community connectedness, affirming social support, and positive or prideful feelings) are targets of these interventions. Despite these important efforts and work, specific treatments for trauma-related mental health diagnoses complicated by minority stress essentially do not exist. Thankfully, there has been burgeoning literature regarding client-centered, evidence-informed guidance and clinical considerations and recommendations (e.g., Hope et al., 2022; Levenson, et al., 2023; Livingston et al., 2020; Puckett, 2019; Shipherd et al., 2019; Salomaa et al., 2023, 2024). The present chapter aims to supplement existing literature by more concretely demonstrating the implementation, application, and integration of evidence-based treatments for PTSD with culturally-responsive clinical recommendations and guidelines (e.g., Livingston et al., 2020) when treating with LGBTQ+ people with trauma-related mental health diagnoses complicated by minority stress.

Application of Adapted Evidence-Based Trauma Focused Therapy

In this section, we provide two case vignettes to demonstrate the implementation of culturally-responsive, affirming, and tailored evidenced-based treatments for PTSD when treating LGBTQ+ clients who present with trauma-related mental health diagnoses and co-occurring minority stress. Generally, evidence-based treatments for PTSD conceptualize PTSD as a disorder of non-recovery, maintained via emotional, cognitive, and behavioral avoidance. As such, treatments directly address avoidance and aim to reduce symptoms in an effort to promote recovery. The first vignette depicts utilization and tailoring of Cognitive Processing Therapy (CPT; Resick et al., 2016) with a veteran client who is a white, bisexual, cisgender man. The second vignette depicts utilization and tailoring of Prolonged Exposure (PE; Foa et al., 2019) with a Black, pansexual, nonbinary person. For each vignette and related treatment approach, a brief overview of the treatment, relevant mechanisms of change, and rationale for use is discussed.

Vignette 1—Cognitive Processing Therapy (CPT)

The Client—Charlie (He/Him Pronouns)

Charlie is a 41-year-old, married, white, bisexual, cisgender man, and veteran of the Army (dates of service: 2000–2010). Charlie met and married his wife, Alison (she/her pronouns), after his military career. They lived together with their 9-year old daughter in a rented apartment in a large metropolitan city. While their family was financially stable at the start of treatment, a period of financial and housing instability early in their marriage was a source of ongoing distress. Additionally, Charlie had never shared with Alison that he began drinking shortly after he experienced a military sexual trauma. Charlie was 5 years sober, which he attributed to medication for alcohol use disorder and an early sobriety group in which he participated through his local VA Medical Center.

Charlie had one older brother and was raised in a working class suburb. His parents were loving but often absent from the home due to the demands of their work schedules. To offset the childcare expenses, Charlie was frequently cared for by grandparents, aunts, and uncles. One of his uncles began to sexually abuse Charlie when he was 6 years old, which persisted until age 13. Charlie believed his sexuality was strongly influenced by the sexual abuse he experienced (despite a lack of empirical evidence for such a connection), and that if the abuse never had occurred, he would be straight or, in his words, "normal." Charlie felt significant shame associated with his bisexual identity and guilt secondary to believing that he had been responsible for the abuse repeatedly occurring. A lack of access to other bisexual people or queer community, mental health professionals, or education likely contributed to this inaccurate belief about the genesis of his sexual identity, contributing to feelings of isolation that allowed for trauma related stuck points (i.e., alterations to thoughts or beliefs following trauma that impact recovery from trauma) to fester.

Charlie enlisted in the Army after high school and after learning about college and other financial incentives otherwise unavailable to him. Colloquially known as Don't Ask, Don't Tell, Charlie's enlistment occurred while Public Law 103-160 (10 U.S.C. § 654) was still under effect, which allowed lesbian, gay, and bisexual people to serve in the military but not openly, or risk retribution, discharge from the military, and legal action (Bumiller, 2011; Herek, 1993; Burks, 2011). For Charlie, the effects of serving under Don't Ask, Don't Tell were central to his suffering. Already navigating sexual identity concerns and persistent negative beliefs that his sexual identity was the result of childhood trauma, Don't Ask, Don't Tell caused him to work even harder to conceal and dismiss his identity. Three years into his service, he was sexually assaulted by another cisgender man in his unit. Charlie understood the already toxic climate around military sexual violence and reporting and knew the consequences of reporting under Don't Ask, Don't Tell could include immediate discharge. Charlie remained silent, and while he appeared to be outwardly functioning well, the trauma-related consequences had started to take their toll on his mental health. Efforts to manage fears that he would be attacked again or that others in his unit would find out about the sexual assault led to marked hypervigilance. This, coupled with consistent efforts to conceal his sexual identity culminated in exhaustion. As a result, Charlie began to use alcohol to cope with the trauma-related distress and internalized biphobia. Charlie's suffering could be contextualized within a framework of oppression and erasure at the interpersonal and systemic levels.

The Therapist—Emilia (She/Her Pronouns)

Emilia is a 35-year-old, Biracial, bisexual, cisgender woman, and nonveteran civilian. She was a psychologist within a PTSD Clinical Team at Charlie's local VA Medical Center. While Emilia's core practice includes the provision of evidence-based psychotherapies (EBPs) for PTSD, she considers the unique and culturally-formed needs of all her clients and thus practices through the lens of cultural humility to make treatment more collaborative and client-centered. Cultural humility guides therapists to take responsibility to educate themselves on their client's cultural background, while also remaining genuinely curious and responding to clients' corrections non-defensively (Hook et al., 2013; Mosher et al., 2017). Emilia attends to cultural factors in the counseling space, and uses her clients' experiences to shape the therapy process. By balancing the directive nature of evidence-based psychotherapies with open and responsive cultural humility, clients may in turn feel more invested and empowered by the counseling process.

Clinical Intervention

Intake and Assessment

When Charlie arrived for his appointment, he completed standardized screening tools to evaluate lifetime trauma exposure (Life Events Checklist, LEC; Gray et al., 2004), PTSD symptoms (PTSD Checklist for DSM-5, PCL-5; Blevins et al., 2015), and suicide risk (Columbia Suicide Severity Rating Scale, CCRS; Posner et al., 2011). Charlie completed most symptom based questionnaires with ease, but felt anxious when filling out the demographic form. He struggled to validate his identity by initially checking "bisexual." He then reflected on past experiences with healthcare providers who questioned if he was "actually gay" when discussing his marital status and identity. Charlie observed his own internal struggle, questioning himself, wondering "Am I really bisexual?" Charlie then checked "straight" in effort to avoid another invalidating discussion and subsequent shame.

Conceptualized as insidious trauma, Root (1992) explained that while not always blatant, overt, or meeting the definition of Criterion A trauma, daily and repeated degradations on the basis of identity have the power to culminate into distress or disorder. These daily and repeated indignities, also known as microaggressions (Sue, 2010), have the power to inflict great suffering (Nadal et al., 2016). Further, emerging research on antibisexual discrimination and internalized biphobia indicates that in addition to Criterion A trauma, bisexual oppression and internalization is uniquely related to trauma symptoms, further exacerbating health disparities between bisexual and monosexual populations (Arnett III et al., 2019). Thus, in addition to assessing for Criterion A trauma using the LEC, Emilia explored sexual minority stress using the brief version of the Antibisexual Experiences Scale (ABES; Dyar et al., 2019), based on the original work by Brewster and Moradi (2010). Responses to these items revealed childhood sexual abuse, military sexual trauma, and multiple sources of anti-bisexual stress and discrimination.

While Charlie's PCL-5 score of 68 was above the clinical cutoff (31–33 points) and suggestive of probable PTSD, Emilia planned to use a well-validated clinical interview for confirmation (Bovin & Marx, 2023), the Clinician Administered PTSD Scale for DSM-5 (CAPS-5; Weathers et al., 2018) to assess for PTSD presence and severity. During assessment, Emilia was careful to observe and take note of responses that were not identity related and typically consistent with PTSD, and others that were more consistent with minority stress. This process allows for understanding affective and cognitive processes that may be either identity-salient or more general, so that treatment can be more effectively matched to the client. Consistent with Criterion B of PTSD, impacts of sexual abuse and antibisexual discrimination revealed frequent and distressing intrusions about these events and subsequent avoidance of trauma-related cues (e.g., avoiding memories of the event, efforts to escape feelings of shame, avoiding sex) captured by Criterion C. Charlie also reported feeling so shamed and punished by antibisexual discriminatory experiences that he made efforts to avoid thinking about his identity, even with his wife who had expressed open support and affirmation. A pattern of identity-related avoidance (e.g., avoiding LGBTQ+ events) was used to "maintain straightness" and avoid further discrimination and identity-related distress. Criterion D revealed inaccurate beliefs about his role in causing his own experiences of sexual abuse, and in turn that the abuse somehow "caused" his bisexual identity. In other words, changes in thinking resulted in self-blame and diminished self-worth, stemming from the sexual abuse and what he had come to believe about bisexuality (e.g., "I'm unlovable because of my sexual identity"). Based on the disempowerment he experienced in early childhood and repeated sexual identity rejection, he feared that if he reported his experience of military sexual trauma, he would be disbelieved or discharged under Don't Ask, Don't Tell for participating in "homosexual behavior." He experienced chronic shame and fear about the abuse and his identity, and he appeared to have internalized biphobia (e.g., "bisexuality is dirty"). Criterion E symptoms revealed a chronic pattern of sleep dysregulation, difficulties with concentration, hyperarousal, and irritability.

Emilia provided Charlie with diagnostic feedback, conceptualization, and treatment options. Charlie learned that he met the DSM-5 criteria for PTSD (American Psychiatric Association, 2013), and that his early childhood experiences shaped his sense of self, including his perception and understanding of his sexuality. Tailoring

Minority Stress Theory (Meyer, 2003) and insidious trauma (Root, 1992) to bisexual experiences (Arnett III et al., 2019; Feinstein & Dyar, 2017) provided a collaborative and exploratory framework to label the contributions of distal stressors that include trauma and distal minority stressors (e.g., Criterion A traumas, bisexual rejection, assumptions about indiscriminate sexual behavior), and reactions to these stressors including psychiatric symptoms and proximal minority stress (e.g., PTSD symptoms, internalized biphobia, belief that sexual identity was a result of trauma). Conceptualization also included discussion of sexual identity formation influenced by antibisexual negativity and erasure (e.g., "bisexuality isn't real"), and how sexual trauma and discrimination were both contributing to chronic feelings of shame. Anticipatory rejection served to contextualize Charlie's efforts to conceal and avoid his identity and trauma history. Further, Emilia and Charlie explored his military service and collaboratively conceptualized that the military sexual trauma occurring under Don't Ask, Don't Tell had exacerbated childhood trauma-related symptoms and identity-related distress. Emilia provided education about the documented adverse effects of minority stress on health, and outlined that trauma recovery includes confronting the sources of suffering, which frightened Charlie. Emilia normalized his distress and validated short term effectiveness of avoidance, while highlighting the longer-term impacts identified directly by Charlie. Next, they explored the various EBPs for PTSD and collaboratively determined that Cognitive Processing Therapy (CPT; Resick et al., 2016) would be most effective for Charlie's symptoms and presentation, particularly given his ongoing proximal stress, self-blame, and other negative beliefs.

Treatment

Cognitive Processing Therapy is an evidence-based treatment for PTSD that is based on a social cognitive theory of PTSD and conceptualizes PTSD as a disorder of non-recovery (Resick et al., 2016). CPT conceptualizes PTSD as manifesting via faulty beliefs about *why* a traumatic event occurred. Treatment is aimed at changing cognitions to access and facilitate "natural" emotions and in turn promote recovery. CPT includes psychoeducation about PTSD and trauma recovery, and providers work with clients to identify and challenge faulty and unhelpful thoughts. Through Socratic dialogue, "stuck points" (i.e., faulty beliefs) are examined and challenged, thereby fostering a more balanced and accurate understanding of the cause of the traumatic event. Cognitive restructuring facilitates emotional processing by allowing clients to directly experience the natural emotions associated with the trauma(s), thereby allowing emotions to run their course instead of being protracted (i.e., avoided) by stuck points.

Cognitive Processing Therapy may be well suited to address internalized stigma and minority stress by targeting unhelpful beliefs shaped by discrimination and social attitudes (Binion & Gray, 2020). Emilia planned to use CPT flexibly by retaining the core underpinnings of the treatment model while also incorporating psychoeducation about bisexual health disparities tailored to Charlie's needs and helping Charlie explore and examine the connection between childhood sexual abuse and beliefs about bisexual identity. Emilia tailored the initial sessions to include information about minority stress theory and the connection between distal and proximal stress. Next, Charlie was assigned the impact statement, a standard component of CPT that asks clients to explore their beliefs about the cause of a single traumatic event (even if there are multiple events from which to choose) as well as the effects on five core themes: safety, trust, power/control, intimacy, and esteem. Charlie shared, "I really don't know where to start, they all just feel equally bad but for different reasons." Emilia validated this and encouraged Charlie to begin with the first instance of sexual abuse, with encouragement to write about what he had been telling himself about why the abuse continued thereafter. The impact statement is a first step in a client's processing of their experiences and is also used to derive what CPT describes as "assimilated" (e.g., "It was my fault I was abused") and "over-accommodated" stuck points (e.g., "I can't trust anyone"; "I am bisexual because of the abuse") for future challenging.

Charlie's impact statement revealed numerous assimilated stuck points (e.g., "I should have fought harder," "Because this happened more than once, I must have wanted it"), other-blame (e.g., "my parents should have known"), and gendered beliefs about the severity of the abuse (e.g., "it's not as bad for boys"). Assimilated stuck points also revealed inaccurate beliefs about sexual identity development (e.g., "I am bisexual because of the abuse") and a connection between credibility about the abuse (e.g., "no one will believe me") and sexual identity (e.g., "because I am married to a woman, no one will believe I am bisexual"). Over-accommodated stuck points were revealed in all five themes, with prominent distress appearing in esteem (e.g., "If I come out, I will be rejected," "if I work harder, I can be straight," and "I am damaged because of the abuse"). They collaboratively filled out his stuck point log, and Emilia took notice of the prominence of self-blame beliefs about the childhood sexual abuse and his identity.

Socratic dialogue is a central technique in CPT and is used at the very start of treatment to begin to engage clients in a collaborative and guided exploration of their thoughts and beliefs about the trauma, leading to observation of inconsistencies and inaccuracies. Thus, whereas a therapist may understand that a client is not to blame for their abuse, and in Charlie's case, know that it was also not the cause of his sexual identity, Socratic dialogue helps clients answer these questions for themselves, strengthening self-efficacy and natural learning. Balancing the tenets of the therapy while taking care to provide education and promote trust between her and Charlie, Emilia shared, "we're going to work together to address stuck points, and I want to help you get there on your own, so that you can see things in a balanced way for yourself. However, based on your impact statement, I am also wondering if it might be helpful to talk on the front end about how we think sexual identity develops?" Charlie expressed appreciation for the information, and noted feeling less like something was fundamentally wrong with him.

Charlie's reports of repeated identity invalidation, such as rejection on the basis of identity, being told that "bisexuality isn't real," that he was "just going through a phase," or that "bisexual persons are greedy and promiscuous," contributed to an overall negative self-view and image. By helping clients experience and label their underlying emotions as valid and challenge societal norms and assumptions, they may in turn create new mechanisms for change. To account for the proximal identity-related distress that may be maintaining PTSD symptoms, Emilia targeted over-accommodated or identity-related stuck points earlier in treatment than would be recommended through a fidelity course of care (Farmer et al., 2017; Resick et al., 2016).

Socratic dialogue supports therapist-client dialogue by using open-ended questions and genuine therapist curiosity. It is also critical to balance questioning with validation at times when beliefs may reflect an accurate experience for marginalized people. In Charlie's case, Emilia was careful to balance validation with gentle Socratic questioning around statements that may reflect the cultural climate around bisexuality. For example, in response to the belief "bisexuality is immoral," Emilia validated this belief as a reasonable response to punishment that Charlie and many bisexual people have experienced, while helping him to contextualize these statements within the narrative of social preference for monosexual or straight identities. Socratic dialogue, balanced with cultural humility, also proved an effective tool to challenge distressing beliefs about abuse as the cause of his identity:

Charlie: "I know we've talked about how the abuse wasn't my fault, and I can see that now. I know that my uncle is the one who is at fault here. But I can't shake this feeling like it was the abuse that made me this way."

Emilia: "Can you tell me more about the effect that this has been having on you?"

Charlie: "I just feel so much shame. Shame that sexual abuse messed me up, and shame about being bisexual."

Emilia: "Tell me more about how you came to know this – that your sexual identity was caused by the sexual abuse?"

Charlie: "Well, I don't know when I started thinking it exactly. I just always felt like this, even when I was little, that I liked boys and girls. And because my uncle made me do sexual stuff with him, I must have learned to like it."

Emilia: "It wasn't too long ago that you shared you were afraid and disgusted by your uncle."

Charlie: "I was really afraid of him. I hated it, and felt too terrified to say anything. I really didn't like what he was doing to me and I wished it would have stopped."

Emilia: "That makes sense, he was an adult abusing his power. You did nothing wrong."

Charlie: "I know it wasn't my fault."

Emilia: "You mentioned that you 'must have learned to like it.' Can you help me understand that?"

Charlie: "Well, it happened enough, I must have wanted it… but I know that's not true either. I know I was really confused when I was little, and grew to really hate him and hate what was happening when I got older and understood more."

Emilia: "So, how would it make sense that repeated sexual abuse that made you feel afraid caused you to experience attraction to people of the same gender?"

Charlie: "… okay, it doesn't actually make sense when I think about it more. Why am I so convinced of this?"

Emilia: "How does it relate to your other experiences with bisexual identity? What are the ways people have talked about it?"

Charlie: "People say really awful things all the time, I've heard stuff like 'bisexuality isn't real,' or that it's 'dirty.'"

Emilia: "How does this sound like what you're saying to yourself now? That the abuse is what caused you to be bisexual?"

Charlie: "I think I've lived my whole life thinking that I was dirty because of the sexual abuse, and that because bisexuality can't be real, that something must have happened to me to make me this way, that it can't just be a part of who I am. I don't think I want to keep believing this stuff."

Emilia: "You've taken on a lot of the negative narrative about bisexuality, and it's hard to escape when it's so prevalent. Let's help you think about new ways of relating to yourself and tending to your identity and needs."

Socratic dialogue is critical to helping clients come to their own conclusions, which instills more powerful learning than when simply provided with corrective feedback. Emilia would continue to help Charlie evaluate his beliefs, while empowering him to come to new conclusions.

Later sessions of CPT include more focused exploration of the five themes (safety, trust, power/control, esteem, and intimacy). For example, one activity asks clients to engage in one pleasurable activity per day "just because" and without strings attached to facilitate a sense of inherent self-worth, fostering growth and personal resilience. The prominence of Charlie's self-esteem related stuck points were connected to internalized beliefs that he was an "imposter" and that bisexuality was "dirty." Through collaborative discussion, Charlie shared that he was able to more fluidly label and challenge internalized biphobia, and that he wanted to develop more affirming behaviors in his day to day. Emilia introduced the *#StillBisexual* campaign, a now grass-roots organization, devoted to bisexual individuals affirming their identity no matter their relationship structure, and is a direct push-back against bisexual erasure and invalidation (Gonzalez et al., 2017). Charlie agreed to look at some materials for homework. The following session, Charlie reported that he had asked his wife to look at the materials with him, and that he felt relief after her validation and encouragement. Whereas Charlie's wife had been a source of support for him, he had dismissed any discussion about his identity for years. Charlie shared that this was a positive step for him.

In his final session, they reviewed his new impact statement. Charlie was tearful, and shared that he was stunned by the unhelpful and harmful beliefs he had previously internalized. Now, he was able to appropriately assign blame for the abuse, and no longer misattributed his sexual identity to the abuse. In addition to a subthreshold PCL-5 score of 15, Charlie reported that he felt more able to deflect anti-bisexual discrimination and felt much more affirmed in his identity and experiences.

Vignette 2—Prolonged Exposure (PE) Therapy

The Client—Justice (They/Them Pronouns)

Justice is a 29 year-old, Black, pansexual nonbinary person. They have worked as a freelance web designer for the past 3 years, and they live alone in a rented apartment. At the time of treatment, they were single, having recently separated from a long term partner. They were feeling more depressed since the end of this relationship and increasingly isolated. Isolation impacted relationships with supportive others and work productivity, which in turn negatively impacted their finances resulting in concerns about their ability to pay rent and other bills.

Justice was born and raised in Georgia, a southern state in the U.S. Justice recalled always feeling "a little different" from their peers and felt most comfortable wearing clothing that was less stereotypically gendered. Their parents insisted that they "look and act like a boy." They often would change clothes at school, which led to negative reactions from teachers and peers. They reported a history of bullying during childhood and adolescence, based on gender and race. Regarding gender, they reported having been called "it" by school-aged peers, and they reported that teachers never intervened. At one point, they reported that a teacher told them that they could avoid harassment if they "would just dress normally." In high school, they were part of a school integration program, which bussed students from areas that were predominantly Black and African American to schools in areas that were predominantly white. Throughout high school, they were told that they should "go back to where they came from" on a regular basis. On one occasion, white students staged a "walk out" in protest of the integration program, and Justice was deliberately tripped while walking into school. When they began to confront the white student who tripped them, a police officer forced them to the ground, shouting both racist and transphobic remarks to them. After this incident, they began avoiding school. Their grades dropped, and they ultimately did not graduate with a diploma. They later earned their GED.

At 19, they began working as a bartender. They entered into a romantic relationship with a patron who frequented the establishment where they worked. This relationship became serious rather quickly, and Justice moved into their partner's apartment within 3 months. Over time, the relationship became hostile, and Justice experienced significant intimate partner violence (IPV), marked by verbal, emotional, and physical abuse. Frequently during arguments, their partner would threaten to call the police, knowing that this was triggering to Justice given their history. Justice grew intensely afraid of their partner. Due to ongoing depression, they became completely isolated from others, and over time, Justice became increasingly helpless and hopeless. They attempted to die by suicide via overdose, and they were involuntarily hospitalized. The hospital facility where they were admitted utilized a medical record system that relied on sex assigned at birth and legal name for identification, forcing Justice to be misgendered and identified by their deadname on their wristband. Likewise, the psychiatric inpatient facility had no designated spaces for gender-diverse people, only designated spaces for "male" and "female" inpatients, and Justice was housed on the male ward.

During their hospitalization, they were constantly misgendered and deadnamed, despite their repeated requests to be addressed by their affirmed name and pronouns. Justice also expressed discomfort about being housed with men and asked about other options; a nurse then accused Justice of trying to be housed with women, which then led to additional conflict and invalidation. Justice then clarified and explained that they were uncomfortable with men and asked if it would be possible for them to have access to private space. They were told that this request would be considered "special treatment" and that "all patients were treated equally." Justice felt further invalidated and was especially eager to leave the inpatient facility; they effectively engaged with their inpatient treatment providers in order to leave as soon as possible. They were offered resources for employment and housing, which enabled them to successfully remain separated from their former partner. They were also connected with outpatient mental health treatment for trauma-related and depressive symptoms.

The Therapist—Julian (He/Him Pronouns)

Julian is a white, gay, cisgender man. He has been practicing as part of a group private practice for the past 5 years. He specializes in evidence-based treatments for PTSD, having been formally trained in both CPT and Prolonged Exposure (PE). Julian has deliberately sought training experiences relevant to LGBTQ+ health, although he has not had very much experience working with TGD clients. As such, he appropriately reached out to colleagues who have more relevant experience and expertise for consultation, and he sought out additional training resources relevant to TGD health. For example, he participated in multiple webinars regarding TGD health offered by the National LGBTQIA+ Health Education Center through the Fenway Institute. Prior to Justice's intake evaluation, Julian ensured that the office administrative staff knew to address Justice by their affirmed name in lieu of their legal, given name, and that they used they/them pronouns. Julian also ensured that staff knew where all restrooms were located within the facility including a single stall, all gender restroom, in case this was most comfortable to Justice.

While Julian was making efforts to increase his own competency and environmental affirmation, he was also mindful that he had a different lived experience as compared to Justice, leading him to embrace a culturally-humble and responsive approach to working with Justice. With this in mind, he was careful to avoid relying on Justice to educate him about pansexual experiences, nonbinary experiences, Black experiences, and experiences of Black, nonbinary, pansexual people. Likewise, he also worked to acknowledge that Justice's experiences do not represent those of all Black, nonbinary pansexual people. He spent time on social media and other sites, following nonbinary, Black, and pansexual influencers and learning more about relevant lived experiences and content. Additionally, Julian ensured that he was knowledgeable and up-to-date on relevant legislation, understanding the impact that policies have on the health and well-being of marginalized people including Black, nonbinary people.

Clinical Intervention

Intake and Assessment

When Justice arrived for their first appointment, the administrative staff person appropriately addressed them by their affirmed name and asked that they complete the clinic standard intake packet. Justice was also asked to complete standardized screening measures to evaluate lifetime trauma exposure (LEC; Gray et al., 2004), PTSD symptomatology (PCL-5; Blevins et al., 2015), as well as the Gender Minority Stress and Resilience measure (GMSR; Testa et al., 2015) and the Racial Trauma Scale—Clinical Version (RTS; Williams et al., 2022). Justice felt relief when completing the demographic questionnaire, as each item allowed for free text response, enabling Justice to openly describe their identity characteristics and avoid difficulties selecting categorical responses that may not represent their identities. Justice also noted that this form asked about their pronouns. Justice experienced some distress but also validation when completing the GMSR, noting having never been asked about these very real stressors in any past mental health treatment. While responding to these items, they reflected on how impactful these experiences have been, and they thought "finally, some paperwork that actually has questions about *my* personal experiences." Justice was curious, somewhat suspicious, but also grateful in response to being asked about past experiences in healthcare, especially because so many of their past experiences had been so negative. They were wondering, "maybe this time, therapy will be different?"

When Julian introduced himself to Justice, he shared his pronouns, which put Justice at ease and normalized sharing. Justice also noticed nonbinary and pansexual symbols within Julian's office space, which offered some relief to Justice's anxiety, given their past negative experiences in healthcare. Julian worked to practice a culturally responsive and humble approach when first meeting with Justice:

Julian: "So, Justice, I just want to take some time here at the beginning of our work together to acknowledge our identities and lived experiences and to take note of some of the differences that may exist between the two of us. I'll start by noting that I'm a white, cisgender, gay man, and I'm aware of my own privilege in this space. I'll hopefully get to know you more over the course of our work together, and from what I know about you so far, I'm aware that some aspects of your identity and lived experiences differ from mine. I do just want to be clear that I know I have some work to do in order to better understand your experiences as a Black, pansexual, nonbinary person. I also want to be clear that I know it is not your responsibility to educate me about your experiences. Having said this, there may be times when I make mistakes; I'll do my best to be mindful of these mistakes and work to correct them. At the same time, I would like to ask, if you're okay with it, to make me aware of my mistakes and allow me the opportunity to correct them. I'm really hoping that our work together will allow you to feel comfortable and empowered to do this and to let me know when any problems come up. What do you think about all of this?"

Justice: "Uh…wow…ok? I've never really had anyone, definitely not a doctor, ever say anything to me like this before. If I'm being honest, it feels a little weird. [nervously laughs] But, I do appreciate it."

Julian: "Ha, I'm not that surprised to hear that you've not had this particular discussion with other health professionals in the past. And, I also can totally appreciate that it feels weird, and that you're not sure how it will go if something does come up."

Justice: "I mean, I've sometimes been really good at speaking up for myself, but not always. But, I can definitely say that I've never been asked to do this, so that's pretty cool."

Julian: "I'm happy to hear that. I consider myself as someone who has expertise in trauma-related symptoms and treatment, and with this in mind, I do think I can help you. And, at the same time, you are the expert in your own experiences, so I am hoping that we can work together to help you feel better."

Justice: "Ok, that makes sense. Thank you."

Julian: "Of course. Now, why don't we spend some time going over your responses to the questionnaires you completed. Does that sound okay?"

Justice: "Yes."

Justice and Julian collaboratively reviewed Justice's responses to questionnaires. Justice endorsed a history of multiple Criterion A traumatic stressors including physical assault, IPV, including sexual assault, and witnessing someone be killed. A score of 63 on the PCL-5 indicated clinically significant past month symptoms of PTSD, anchored to the incident in which Justice was assaulted by a police officer in high school. Justice also endorsed racial trauma, as indicated by a score of 91 on the Racial Trauma Scale (recommended cutoff is 48; Williams et al., 2022), with elevated scores in all three subscales (Lack of Safety; Negative Cognitions; Difficulty Coping). Likewise, Justice endorsed an overall elevated score on the Gender Minority Stress and Resilience Measure (Testa et al., 2015); subscales scores indicated elevations of gender minority stress consistent with gender-related discrimination, rejection, and victimization, non-affirmation of identity, internalized transphobia, and negative expectations about the future, as well as low sense of pride and community connectedness. Given recent suicidal behavior, Julian also conducted a thorough risk assessment and engaged in safety planning with Justice. Finally, Julian conducted the DSM-5 Cultural Formulation Interview (American Psychiatric Association, 2013), as recommended by Williams, Malcoun, Sawyer, et al., (2014) to provide Justice with an opportunity to describe their presenting problems in their own words. Assessment concluded across two sessions.

Julian shared his conceptualization with Justice, indicating that Justice likely met criteria for PTSD per DSM-5 (American Psychiatric Association, 2013). As part of this feedback, Julian clearly acknowledged Justice's history of traumatic stress, minority stress, and invalidation based on multiple components of their identities. Julian was thoughtful in communicating to Justice that traumatic stressors are not considered "worse" or even more impactful than minority stressors, and that minority stressors can also drive and/or exacerbate PTSD symptoms. Julian again named Justice's intersecting identities and how Justice has been living within oppressive systems that have increased their risk of negative experiences and mental health symptoms. Importantly, Julian was careful to clearly communicate that Justice's experiences of identity-related distress *do not* indicate that Justice's identities are pathological.

Julian: "So, I just want to make sure that this is all making sense, Justice. Do you have any questions about this feedback?"

Justice: "Um, I don't think so. So, I do have PTSD? And, that's why I'm afraid all the time?"

Julian: "Well, I think it's likely that you do have PTSD, *and* I am not sure that is the only reason you feel afraid a lot. I do want to be clear we didn't do a full diagnostic interview for PTSD. However, you did complete a self-report measure, and your score was much higher than the recommended cut-off. So, let's talk a little more about PTSD. PTSD is a mental health diagnosis that can result after person experiences what we call a 'traumatic stressor' such as a life threatening event or something similar - we don't need to go into the full list here, but we both know you've had your fair share of those kinds of stressors—and then, the person isn't able to fully recover from that stressful experience, and stress symptoms don't go away. In a nutshell, ongoing stress symptoms following a trauma make up PTSD. In other words, the body and mind kind of act like that traumatic stressor is ongoing or could happen again at any time."

Justice: "Yeah, I get that…I definitely feel like that with a lot of things, but mostly with the police in high school thing and with a lot of stuff that happened with my ex."

Julian: "Totally, and that makes sense. What we also know is true for you, Justice, is that you experience regular stress that everyone experiences and stress based on your minoritized identities. We call that minority stress, which you carry with you on a daily basis, and which is on top of all of the other stress you deal with."

Justice: "Yeah, that's true. And, that's why I just shut everything out. I just want to stay away from everyone and everything. I just can't deal with anything."

Julian: 'Yeah, I can understand that. And, at the same time, I can imagine that also has some downsides too?'

Justice: "I mean, yeah, I guess it does."

Julian: "And, what's complicated is that minority stress can also activate or even worsen some of your PTSD symptoms because they share similarities. For example, you have personal experience of being assaulted by a police officer who shouted slurs at you. That's a traumatic stressor. Now, you may be walking down the street one day, and you could overhear someone yelling slurs, even if not even directed at you, and that could trigger your own minority stress and traumatic stress. The reality is, Justice, you may be bombarded with messages and images of minority stress that activate your own trauma history. Our job in this therapy together will be to help you cope most effectively with minority stress while also helping you recover from past trauma."

Justice: "Geez, that sounds like a lot. I'm not sure I can do that…"

Julian: "I know it sounds like a lot. Remember that we're a team. We're going to work together to identify what's bothering you, how to address it within the context of therapy, and how to help you move forward in your life. I'm confident that you can get through this feeling stronger. You willing to give this a shot?"

Justice: "Yeah, I think so. I'm feeling nervous about it, though."

Julian: "Yeah, for sure you do. Why wouldn't you? Look at all you've been through! You've done the hard part by making it through the door. Treatment won't be any harder than what you've been through already, Justice. You ready to talk a bit more about treatment?"

Justice: "Yeah, I think I'm ready."

Treatment

Prolonged Exposure (PE; Foa et al., 2019) is an evidence-based treatment that is based on an emotional processing theory of PTSD and conceptualizes PTSD as a disorder of non-recovery. More specifically, PE theorizes PTSD as manifesting via failure to emotionally process traumatic memories and ongoing behavioral avoidance of situational and other objects, etc., due to trauma-related distress. Key components of PE include psychoeducation about "common reactions" to trauma, a breathing retraining technique to manage distress, in-vivo exposure, imaginal exposure, and trauma processing. Exposure techniques directly target avoidance; imaginal exposure in particular facilitates emotional processing of traumatic memories; in-vivo (i.e., "in real life") exposure involve situations (e.g., people, places, objects, sensory experiences) that clients avoid because they serve as trauma reminders and/or because they cause trauma-related distress. Collectively, exposure techniques function to reduce avoidance, increase sense of mastery and competency, and in turn facilitate recovery from past trauma. Recovery from trauma can also foster resilience through self-empowerment, self-efficacy, and liberation. Further, existing literature (Williams et al., 2014) and related treatment protocols (Harned, 2022) have described modifications to PE when working with minoritized populations, suggesting that it is well-suited to also address racial trauma, traumatic invalidation, and internalized stigma. Relatedly, the in-vivo exposure hierarchy, collaboratively developed by therapist and client in session two of the PE protocol, can be modified to include behavioral activation tasks to address co-occurring depression and situations to address problematic shame (Harned, 2022), an emotion commonly part of internalized stigma and one that interferes with self-affirmation and pride (e.g.,

Hendricks & Testa, 2012). As such, the hierarchy may also include activities to practice identity self-affirmation; with cultural responsiveness, attentiveness, and planning, the hierarchy can include situations that can provide important corrective learning experiences (Craske et al., 2014) regarding safety and self-competency, to be described in more detail below.

Prior to beginning the PE therapy protocol, Julian reviewed literature relevant to making modifications when working with Black and queer clients to increase cultural responsiveness when implementing this protocol with Justice to address PTSD and co-occurring racial trauma and minority stress (Harned, 2022; Williams et al., 2014). When sharing additional psychoeducation related to the treatment during the initial session, Julian described both habituation and inhibitory learning models (Craske et al., 2014). Julian was careful when providing psychoeducation about avoidance, ensuring that he did not inadvertently pathologize Justice's avoidance behavior. Julian aimed to balance communicating that avoidance can be adaptive while also problematic in the maintenance of trauma-related distress:

Julian: "So, here's how avoidance works. Avoidance provides us with relief in the short term, but it actually keeps us stuck and maintains PTSD in the long run. It also blocks us from being able to tell what we're actually capable of. If I go to the store, and I start feeling anxious in the parking lot, and I leave before I even go in, I'll feel better when I get in my car for sure. Now, I'll think that I spared myself by not going in, but the reality is that I don't know. I never went in. Make sense?"

Justice: "Yeah, that makes sense."

Julian: "Now, what's tricky is that avoidance *can* be adaptive, especially for minoritized people who do actually have it harder than other folx. For example, if you see someone who looks angry, who's posturing, and who starts approaching you, you should probably avoid that person. Right?"

Justice: "Yeah, totally!"

Julian: "But, have there ever been times when you *thought* someone might do something, but you later found out that nothing was wrong?"

Justice: "Yes, that's definitely happened before. I had friends in the past joke with me and say 'you always think it's a trans thing'."

Julian: "Well, I'm never going to say that to you, but I do think it's important for us to help you get better at telling the difference between actual threat and what we might call totally reasonable but learned threat. And, again, because you've had your fair share of trauma *and* minority stress, it's probably hard to tell the difference."

Justice: "Yeah, for real it's hard!"

Julian: "What this also means is that you and I will have to put our heads together and find spaces that are affirming of all of your identities in order for you to practice your exposure tasks. I'll do homework for this, and you let me know if you know of any spaces."

Justice: "Okay. Maybe, I can also start reaching out to some of my old friends to ask?"

Julian: "I am in support of this plan, Justice…I think that's great."

At the conclusion of session one, Julian and Justice mutually agreed to first address the incident of physical assault perpetrated by a police officer via imaginal exposure (to be described below), as this was the memory that Justice reported was bothering them the most. Additionally, Julian shared that this procedure could also be used to address intrusive and distressing memories involving minority stressors (e.g., discrimination).

In session two, Julian and Justice first discussed common reactions to trauma. Julian ensured to make this conversational in lieu of a more "lecture-type" of format when providing this psychoeducation to Justice. Throughout, Julian integrated and reviewed minority stress content and invited Justice to talk about their personal experiences with discrimination, racial trauma, and identity-based stigma and integrated these experiences with the psychoeducational content. Next, Julian introduced the principles and function of in-vivo exposures. Julian explained that in-vivo exposures: (1) break the habit of decreasing distress via avoidance; (2) disconfirm the belief that a feared situation will result in harm; (3) result in habituation over time; and (4) increase one's sense of mastery and competency. Julian also revisited the discussion from session one, in which they discussed how objective risk *is* higher for Justice in *some* contexts given their minoritized identities, and as such, careful consideration would be necessary when planning exposures to maximize likelihood of successful implementation. Julian was also careful to distinguish that the purpose of in-vivo exposure would *not* be for Justice to habituate to racial trauma, discrimination, or other external minority stress experiences. Rather, the aim of in-vivo exposure in particular, would be to help Justice distinguish between objectively safe and unsafe spaces, reduce internalized stigma and its impact (and likewise increase gender euphoria and identity-related pride), and increase Justice's sense of competency and ability to cope with unexpected distal minority stressors. Julian explained that "in addition to fear, experiences with stigma also impact our emotions like shame, making us want to hide, which can be protective. At the same time, just like with fear, it can sometimes go into overdrive, and can keep us from learning about safe spaces and from having loving relationships with people who won't actually reject us. So, we'll also want to think about some exposures to what we'll call 'unjustified shame' or 'stigma' to help you learn that you can trust others and allow your shame and internalized stigma to go down on its own in a safe space." Guided by relevant literature (e.g., Williams et al., 2014) Julian demonstrated openness and willingness to directly name and discuss systemic racism, and to talk about Justice's experiences with racism and racial trauma. Likewise, Julian demonstrated openness and willingness to discuss Justice's experiences with invalidation of their nonbinary and pansexual identities, directly naming invalidation stemming from gender binary systems and heteronormativity.

Next, Julian and Justice collaboratively developed the in-vivo exposure hierarchy. Informed by relevant protocols (Foa, et al., 2019; Harned, 2022), categories included: (1) situations that remind Justice of past traumas; (2) situations that Justice perceives to be dangerous, but that are not objectively harmful; (3) activities that

Justice used to enjoy but does not engage in anymore because of depression; and (4) situations that Justice avoids because of internalized stigma and/or unjustified shame. During discussion, Julian was careful to acknowledge systemic racism within law enforcement, and utilized a culturally-responsive, client-centered approach to identify exposure tasks involving law enforcement-related cues. Lower-level hierarchy cues included pictures/images of law enforcement, which allowed Justice opportunity to engage with exposure while at home; this facilitated willingness to engage and also facilitated use and mastery of coping skills. Over time, the images of law enforcement grew in similarity with respect to physical characteristics with Justice's perpetrator. As Justice built more mastery with this particular trauma-related cue, they were more willing to engage with in-person law-enforcement cues; to ensure safety, Julian first accompanied Justice as a coach outside of a local police department. Over time, Justice was able to describe their law enforcement-related distress as tolerable and believed that if they were ever stopped by law enforcement that they would be able to cope effectively. Regarding exposures to reduce internalized stigma, Julian researched and found a community resource center for LGBTQ+ people that hosted a group for trans and nonbinary people. Julian outreached to inquire about the racial and ethnic diversity within the group to ensure inclusivity and learned that the group had many racial and ethnic identities represented; Julian, therefore, believed that this group would be a good opportunity for Justice to practice exposure. Justice attended their first group in very casual clothing and was generally quiet throughout, but was still able to stay for the entire time. When they discussed what they learned with Julian in the subsequent session, they noted that "everybody was super accepting." When Julian asked about their shame, Justice reported that it eventually went down to the point of them being able to enjoy their experience; Justice stated, "I plan to go back even if you don't assign it to me as an exposure!" Subsequent experiences in these affirming spaces helped facilitate Justice to express their gender in ways that fostered more gender euphoria and identity-related pride. Additionally, Justice was increasingly willing and motivated to engage in behavioral activation tasks on the hierarchy, which in turn reduced depressive symptoms.

In session 3, Julian revisited and more thoroughly explained rationale for imaginal exposure; Julian reminded Justice that cognitive avoidance works in the short term, but ultimately maintains symptoms of PTSD. Julian also reiterated that minority stress complicates recovery, particularly because these stressors may be present on a daily basis and can serve as trauma reminders. Julian stated, "when you were physically assaulted by the officer, he also verbally and emotionally harmed you with identity-based slurs. So, when you're out and about in the world, and you overhear these slurs or something similar, even if there's no actual danger and it's just some stupid bigot yelling, your brain understandably associates it with danger, and the memory will get triggered, so you're going to retreat. Of course, hearing a slur could also actually mean danger because some people who use that kind of abusive language may also be likely to engage in aggressive behavior…it's tricky. What we're doing with imaginal exposure is helping you process the trauma and teach your brain that the memory itself is not dangerous and to help your brain not get confused and think that particular trauma is happening again just because something in your current environment is similar to it. Let's talk more about the rationale for imaginal exposure." Julian explained to Justice that the purpose of imaginal exposure and processing is to: (1) learn that confronting a trauma memory and thinking or talking about trauma are safe; (2) organize the trauma memory; (3) promote habituation; (4) build mastery and competency; and (5) gain new meaning and perspective about the trauma. Julian provided explicit instructions to Justice about how to engage in the procedure. After imaginal exposure, Julian and Justice engaged in processing, which focused initially on exploring Justice's experiences with the imaginal exposure and their thoughts and emotions about the trauma. Julian first strongly reinforced Justice's willingness to engage with the exposure, acknowledging their distress and noting their apparent ability to tolerate high distress without avoiding. Next, Julian explored Justice's perceptions regarding the index event:

Julian: "So, Justice, what are your thoughts about why this happened?"

Justice: [long pause] "I don't know…I just keep thinking that if only I had done something differently, this wouldn't have happened."

Julian: "What do you think you could have done differently?"

Justice: "I don't know. Like…maybe… if I wasn't so obvious, you know?"

Julian: "What do you mean by obvious?"

Justice: "Like… so queer looking, I guess? I could have blended more with everybody else. I don't know. Maybe I should have acted more white? Yeah, more white and less queer and maybe I wouldn't have stood out as a target for that cop."

Julian: "So, if I'm hearing you correctly, you're blaming yourself for what happened to you?"

Justice: "Well, shouldn't I? The way I insisted on expressing myself made me a target!"

Julian: "Justice, do you know what emotions you're feeling right now when you say that out loud?"

Justice: "I don't know. [long pause] I guess shame."

Julian: "Do you recall when we talked about minority stress and internalized stigma and where that comes from?"

Justice: "I do remember us talking about that."

Julian: "Do you think it's possible that may have anything to do with how you're thinking and feeling about this?"

Justice: "I don't know…maybe."

Julian: "This week, Justice, when you're listening to the imaginal portion of the tape for your exposure homework, I'd like to ask you to consider that. Would you be willing to do that?"

Justice: "Yeah, I can do that."

In subsequent imaginal sessions, Justice demonstrated habituation to the memory via repeated imaginal exposure. Likewise, they increasingly recalled more sensory and other details, which helped them contextualize their behavior at the time of the event. Julian continued addressing Justice's self-blame, gently highlighting how systemic racism, transphobia, and other distal minority stress factors have contributed to internalized stigma, which in turn led Justice to erroneously assume that aspects of their own identity and expression led to their traumatization. Once Justice was able to make this realization, they reported a decrease in shame, and a subsequent increase in anger. Julian validated Justice's experience of anger and allowed space for Justice to express this emotion openly. Julian also engaged in discussion with Justice about ways in which expressions of anger for Black people may be perceived differently by the larger social environment than expressions of anger from cultural majority individuals (i.e., white people), and asked Justice, "does this resonate with your personal experiences?" Justice agreed and acknowledged that they often feel afraid to be angry, especially in public, due to fear that they will be targeted by police. This discussion then led to Justice endorsing sadness and expressing tearfulness; Julian offered validation. Justice eventually was able to acknowledge a strong sense of powerlessness, both at the time of the index trauma and in general, related to their multiple minoritized identities. Discussions during processing portions of these sessions, as well as when discussing successes with in-vivo exposures, focused on balancing Justice's very real experiences as a multiply-marginalized person with how they can live in ways that are empowering including connecting and having meaningful relationships with affirming others, finding spaces where they can express their authentic self, and engaging in advocacy and other values-based activities. Over time, Justice's sadness decreased and their acceptance that this event occurred increased. Julian and Justice were clear that acceptance does not mean approval, but rather acknowledgement that this event happened, even if painful. Justice was able to identify relevant factors contributing to the index trauma including systemic factors (e.g., oppression) as well as individual factors (i.e., perpetrator racism and transphobia).

In the final session, as consistent with protocol, Justice recalled the trauma memory in full and re-rated distress levels for all in-vivo exposure items on the hierarchy. Relatedly, Julian readministered all measures; Justice endorsed a score of 19 (below cutoff) on the PCL-5 past month symptoms of PTSD, anchored to the police officer assault. Justice endorsed a reduction in racial trauma, as indicated by a score of 51 on the Racial Trauma Scale (Williams et al., 2022; previous score was 91; recommended cutoff is 48), with an elevated score on the Lack of Safety subscale in particular and most significant reductions in the Negative Cognitions and Difficulty Coping subscales. Lastly, Justice endorsed an overall elevated score on the Gender Minority Stress and Resilience Measure (Testa et al., 2015) but notable reductions in subscales of non-affirmation of identity, internalized transphobia, and negative expectations about the future, as well as improvements in sense of pride and community connectedness. Julian and Justice were able to use responses to these questionnaires to facilitate discussion of progress in treatment:

Julian: "What do you make of these scores? Some changed, quite a bit, and some didn't."

Justice: "Well…the way I see it is…I'll always be Black. I'll always be queer. There will always be some risk that comes with that. But, at the same time, that doesn't mean that I'm always in danger. Or, that people are always out to get me. Or, that people won't love me because of that."

Julian: "I love that."

Justice: "Yeah, me too…haha!"

Julian: "So, what else do you think you've learned as part of doing this treatment?"

Justice: "I've also learned that it feels pretty good to not feel *so* threatened *all* the time. That makes it a lot easier to get out and do things. And, when you're not always threatened, you can better tell what's going on. I know I can cope, and that's pretty cool. I've also realized that I can actually do a lot! So, that makes me feel confident that I can do even more. And, even if others don't have confidence in me because of whatever they have going on, that's their deal. I know who I am, and I know I can do things. I'm really proud of what I've accomplished in this therapy."

As part of treatment consolidation, Julian and Justice discussed relapse prevention; Julian reiterated that minority stressors may be present on a daily basis, and therefore, have the potential to activate trauma-related symptoms. Julian normalized fluctuations in trauma-related symptoms over time and discussed the importance of ongoing engagement in exposure and management of avoidance urges. Lastly, Julian reinforced Justice's inherent wisdom, strength, and resilience, as well as learned skills and welcomed Justice to return at any point in future should they believe they would benefit from a refresher/booster.

Conclusion

Gold-standard, evidence-based treatments for PTSD exist (e.g., CPT, Resick et al., 2016; PE; Foa et al., 2019), and these treatments can be effective when treating trauma-related problems experienced by minoritized people including LGBTQ+ people. However, when treating PTSD and trauma-related problems complicated by minority stress (and in the context of ongoing systemic oppression), their utility is less well understood. This is an especially important point considering that no PTSD treatments have been specifically designed for or investigated with exclusively minoritized samples, and minoritized identities have not been adequately represented (e.g., Grau et al., 2022). Does this mean that researchers and clinicians need to reinvent the wheel? No. Does it mean that culturally responsive guidelines and adaptations are needed? Absolutely, and literature has begun attending to this gap (e.g., Berke et al., 2022; Livingston et al., 2020; Williams et al., 2014), thankfully.

For minorized people, minority stress experiences can serve as trauma-related cues (e.g., being called a slur while out in public may be reminiscent of past identity-based assault). And, given that minority stress is likely to be present during the course of trauma-focused treatment, failure to acknowledge would be a disservice and limits cultural responsiveness. Relatedly, failure to attend to dynamics between therapist and client as it relates to identities and lived experiences is also problematic. For example, a white therapist working with a Black client may inadvertently invalidate the very real systemic racism that exists in the larger social environment and run the risk of ineffectively utilizing cognitive restructuring techniques (e.g., challenging negative thoughts based in reality) and/or exposure techniques (e.g., assigning tasks that are objectively risky for Black, but not white people). As such, it is imperative, both from an ethical and effectiveness lens, that minority stress frameworks be integrated within rapport building, assessment (see Chap. 2), case formulations, and treatment planning and implementation. As demonstrated in this chapter, this is entirely possible and doing so in a culturally informed and client-centered way can be highly effective.

Disclaimer The views expressed in this chapter are those of the authors and do not necessarily reflect the official policy or position of the U.S. Department of Veterans Affairs nor the U.S. Government.

References

American Psychiatric Association. (2013). *Diagnostic and statistical manual of mental disorders* (5th ed.). APA. https://doi.org/10.1176/appi.books.9780890425596

Arnett, J. E., III, Frantell, K. A., Miles, J. R., & Fry, K. M. (2019). Anti-bisexual discrimination as insidious trauma and impacts on mental and physical health. *Psychology of Sexual Orientation and Gender Diversity, 6*(4), 475–485. https://doi.org/10.1037/sgd0000344

Berke, S. B., Liautaud, M. M., Chen, D., & Sloan, C. A. (2022). Applying cognitive behavioral principles to promote health in transgender and gender diverse individuals. *Cognitive and Behavioral Practice*. https://doi.org/10.1016/j.cbpra.2022.05.002

Binion, K., & Gray, M. J. (2020). Minority stress theory and internalized homophobia among LGB sexual assault survivors: Implications for posttraumatic adjustment. *Journal of Loss & Trauma, 25*(5), 454–471. https://doi.org/10.1080/15325024.2019.1707987

Blevins, C. A., Weathers, F. W., Davis, M. T., Witte, T. K., & Domino, J. L. (2015). The posttraumatic stress disorder checklist for DSM-5 (PCL-5): Development and initial psychometric evaluation. *Journal of Traumatic Stress, 28*(6), 489–498. https://doi.org/10.1002/jts.22059

Bovin, M. J., & Marx, B. P. (2023). The problem with overreliance on the PCL–5 as a measure of PTSD diagnostic status. *Clinical Psychology: Science and Practice, 30*(1), 122–125. https://doi.org/10.1037/cps0000119

Brewster, M. E., & Moradi, B. (2010). Perceived experiences of anti-bisexual prejudice: Instrument development and evaluation. *Journal of Counseling Psychology, 57*(4), 451–468. https://doi.org/10.1037/a0021116

Brooks, V. R. (1981). *Minority stress and lesbian women*. Lexington Books.

Bumiller, E. (2011). Obama ends 'Don't Ask, Don't Tell' policy. *The New York Times*. Retrieved from: https://www.nytimes.com/2011/07/23/us/23military.html

Burks, D. J. (2011). Lesbian, gay, and bisexual victimization in the military: An unintended consequence of "Don't Ask, Don't Tell"? *American Psychologist, 66*(7), 604–613. https://doi.org/10.1037/a0024609

Craske, M. G., Treanor, M., Conway, C. C., Zbozinek, T., & Vervliet, B. (2014). Maximizing exposure therapy: An inhibitory learning approach. *Behaviour Research and Therapy, 58*, 10–23. https://doi.org/10.1016/j.brat.2014.04.006

Dyar, C., Feinstein, B. A., & Davila, J. (2019). Development and validation of a brief version of the anti-bisexual experiences scale. *Archives of Sexual Behavior, 48*, 175–189. https://doi.org/10.1007/s10508-018-1157-z

Farmer, C. C., Mitchell, K. S., Parker-Guilbert, K., & Galovski, T. E. (2017). Fidelity to the cognitive processing therapy protocol: Evaluation of critical elements. *Behavior Therapy, 48*(2), 195–206. https://doi.org/10.1016/j.beth.2016.02.009

Feinstein, B. A., & Dyar, C. (2017). Bisexuality, minority stress, and health. *Current Sexual Health Reports, 9*, 42–49. https://doi.org/10.1007/s11930-017-0096-3

Foa, E. B., Hembree, E. A., & Rothbaum, B. O. (2019). *Prolonged exposure therapy for PTSD: Emotional processing of traumatic experiences, therapist guide* (2nd ed.). Oxford University Press.

Gonzalez, K. A., Ramirez, J. L., & Galupo, M. P. (2017). "I was and still am": Narratives of bisexual marking in the# StillBisexual campaign. *Sexuality & Culture, 21*, 493–515. https://doi.org/10.1007/s12119-016-9401-y

Grau, P. P., Kusch, M. M., Williams, M. T., Loyo, K. T., Zhang, X., Warner, R. C., & Wetterneck, C. T. (2022). A review of the inclusion of ethnoracial groups in empirically supported posttraumatic stress disorder treatment research. *Psychological Trauma: Theory, Research, Practice, and Policy, 14*(1), 55–65. https://doi.org/10.1037/tra0001108

Gray, M. J., Litz, B. T., Hsu, J. L., & Lombardo, T. W. (2004). Psychometric properties of the life events checklist. *Assessment, 11*(4), 330–341. https://doi.org/10.1177/1073191104269954

Harned, M. S. (2022). *Treating trauma in dialectical behavior therapy: The DBT prolonged exposure protocol (DBT PE)*. Guilford Publications.

Hatzenbuehler, M. L. (2009). How does sexual minority stigma "get under the skin"? A psychological mediation framework. *Psychological Bulletin, 135*(5), 707–730. https://doi.org/10.1037/a0016441

Hendricks, M. L., & Testa, R. J. (2012). A conceptual framework for clinical work with transgender and gender nonconforming clients: An adaptation of the Minority Stress Model. *Professional Psychology: Research and Practice, 43*(5), 460–467. https://doi.org/10.1037/a0029597

Herek, G. M. (1993). Sexual orientation and military service: A social science perspective. *American Psychologist, 48*(5), 538–549. https://doi.org/10.1037/0003-066X.48.5.538

Hook, J. N., Davis, D. E., Owen, J., Worthington, E. L., Jr., & Utsey, S. O. (2013). Cultural humility: Measuring openness to culturally diverse clients. *Journal of Counseling Psychology, 60*(3), 353–366. https://doi.org/10.1037/a0032595

Hope, D. A., Holt, N. R., Woodruff, N., Mocarski, R., Meyer, H. M., Puckett, J. A., Eyer, J., Craig, S., Feldman, J., Irwin, J., Pachankis, J., Rawson, K. J., Sevelius, J., & Butler, S. (2022). Bridging the gap between practice guidelines and the therapy room: Community-derived practice adaptations for psychological services with transgender and gender diverse adults in the central United States. *Professional Psychology: Research and Practice, 53*(4), 351–361. https://doi.org/10.1037/pro0000448

Levenson, J. S., Craig, S. L., & Austin, A. (2023). Trauma-informed and affirmative mental health practices with LGBTQ+ clients. *Psychological Services, 20*(Suppl 1), 134–144. https://doi.org/10.1037/ser0000540

Livingston, N. A., Berke, D., Scholl, J., Ruben, M., & Shipherd, J. C. (2020). Addressing diversity in PTSD treatment: Clinical considerations and guidance for the treatment of PTSD in LGBTQ populations. *Current Treatment Options in Psychiatry, 7*(2), 53–69. https://doi.org/10.1007/s40501-020-00204-0

Marchi, M., Travascio, A., Uberti, D., De Micheli, E., Grenzi, P., Arcolin, E., Pingani, L., Ferrari, S., & Galeazzi, G. M. (2023). Post-traumatic stress disorder among LGBTQ people: A systematic review and meta-analysis. *Epidemiology and Psychiatric Sciences, 32*, e44. https://doi.org/10.1017/S2045796023000586

Meyer, I. H. (2003). Prejudice, social stress, and mental health in lesbian, gay, and bisexual populations: Conceptual issues and research evidence. *Psychological Bulletin, 129*(5), 674–697. https://doi.org/10.1037/0033-2909.129.5.674

Mosher, D. K., Hook, J. N., Captari, L. E., Davis, D. E., DeBlaere, C., & Owen, J. (2017). Cultural humility: A therapeutic framework for engaging diverse clients. *Practice Innovations, 2*(4), 221–233. https://doi.org/10.1037/pri0000055

Nadal, K. L., Whitman, C. N., Davis, L. S., Erazo, T., & Davidoff, K. C. (2016). Microaggressions toward lesbian, gay, bisexual, transgender, queer, and genderqueer people: A review of the literature. *Journal of Sex Research, 53*(4–5), 488–508. https://doi.org/10.1080/00224499.2016.1142495

Posner, K., Brown, G. K., Stanley, B., Brent, D. A., Yershova, K. V., Oquendo, M. A., et al. (2011). The Columbia–Suicide Severity Rating Scale: initial validity and internal consistency findings from three multisite studies with adolescents and adults. *American Journal of Psychiatry, 168*(12), 1266–1277. https://doi.org/10.1176/appi.ajp.2011.10111704

Puckett, J. A. (2019). An ecological approach to therapy with gender minorities. *Cognitive and Behavioral Practice, 26*(4), 647–655. https://doi.org/10.1016/j.cbpra.2019.08.002

Resick, P. A., Monson, C. M., & Chard, K. M. (2016). *Cognitive processing therapy for PTSD: A comprehensive manual*. Guilford Publications.

Root, M. P. P. (1992). Reconstructing the impact of trauma on personality. In L. S. Brown & M. Bailou (Eds.), *Personality and psychopathology: Feminist reappraisals* (pp. 220–265). Guilford Press.

Ross, L. E., Salway, T., Tarasoff, L. A., MacKay, J. M., Hawkins, B. W., & Fehr, C. P. (2018). Prevalence of depression and anxiety among bisexual people compared to gay, lesbian, and heterosexual individuals: A systematic review and meta-analysis. *Journal of Sex Research, 55*(4–5, 435), –456. https://doi.org/10.1080/00224499.2017.1387755

Salomaa, A. C., Livingston, N. A., Bryant, W. T., Herbitter, C., Harper, K., Sloan, C. A., Hinds, Z., Gyuro, L., Valentine, S. E., & Shipherd, J. C. (2023). A bottom-up approach to developing a unified trauma-minority stress model for transgender and gender diverse people. *Psychological Trauma: Theory, Research, Practice, and Policy, 15*(4), 618–627. https://doi.org/10.1037/tra0001373.supp

Salomaa, A. C., Berke, D., Harper, K., Valentine, S. E., Sloan, C. A., Hinds, Z., Gyuro, L., Herbitter, C., Bryant, W. T., Shipherd, J. C., & Livingston, N. A. (2024). A patient-centered model of mental health care for trauma and minority stress in transgender and gender diverse people: A bottom-up network analysis. *Psychology of Sexual Orientation and Gender Diversity*. Advance online publication. https://psycnet.apa.org/doi/10.1037/sgd0000705

Salway, T., Ross, L. E., Fehr, C. P., Burley, J., Asadi, S., Hawkins, B., & Tarasoff, L. A. (2019). A systematic review and meta-analysis of disparities in the prevalence of suicide ideation and attempt among bisexual populations. *Archives of Sexual Behavior, 48*, 89–111. https://doi.org/10.1007/s10508-018-1150-6

Shipherd, J. C., Berke, D., & Livingston, N. A. (2019). Trauma recovery in the transgender and gender diverse community: Extensions of the Minority Stress Model for treatment planning. *Cognitive and Behavioral Practice, 26*(4), 629–646. https://doi.org/10.1016/j.cbpra.2019.06.001

Sue, D. W. (Ed.). (2010). Microaggressions and marginality: Manifestation, dynamics, and impact. John Wiley & Sons.

Testa, R. J., Habarth, J., Peta, J., Balsam, K., & Bockting, W. (2015). Development of the gender minority stress and resilience measure. *Psychology of Sexual Orientation and Gender Diversity, 2*(1), 65–77. https://doi.org/10.1037/sgd0000081

Weathers, F. W., Bovin, M. J., Lee, D. J., Sloan, D. M., Schnurr, P. P., Kaloupek, D. G., Keane, T. M., & Marx, B. P. (2018). The Clinician-Administered PTSD Scale for DSM–5 (CAPS-5): Development and initial psychometric evaluation in military veterans. *Psychological Assessment, 30*(3), 383–395. https://doi.org/10.1037/pas0000486

Williams, M. T., Malcoun, E., Sawyer, B. A., Davis, D. M., Nouri, L. B., & Bruce, S. L. (2014). Cultural adaptations of prolonged exposure therapy for treatment and prevention of posttraumatic stress disorder in African Americans. *Behavioral Sciences (Basel, Switzerland), 4*(2), 102–124. https://doi.org/10.3390/bs4020102

Williams, M. T., Osman, M., Gallo, J., Pereira, D. P., Gran-Ruaz, S., Strauss, D., Lester, L., George, J. R., Edelman, J., & Litman, L. (2022). A clinical scale for the assessment of racial trauma. *Practice Innovations, 7*(3), 223–240. https://doi.org/10.1037/pri0000178.supp

Chapter 5
Helping LGBTQ+ Clients Recover from Conversion Therapy or Non-Affirming Care Experiences

Douglas C. Haldeman

Highlights

- Despite the lack of empirical evidence supporting sexual orientation or gender identity change efforts, or conversion therapy, these efforts have been used and are still used today.
- No existing guidelines are designed to counteract the negative effects of these harmful change efforts
- This chapter summarizes the history and methods used in Sexual Orientation Change Efforts/Gender Identity Change Efforts (SOCE/GICE), clinical issues in working with conversion survivors, and provides case material to illustrate affirming care practices for practitioners working with conversion survivors. Given the relatively more developed literature on SOCE and my own practice, case examples are focused on SOCE.

Positionality

I am an elder, cisgender, white gay male who has been involved in clinical, organizational, and advocacy work on behalf of LGBTQ persons for over 40 years. I was inspired to become a psychologist by my late friend and mentor, the gay rights icon Harvey Milk, whose acquaintance I made in 1978 when he was fighting an initiative to prohibit gay men and lesbians from teaching in the California public schools (I was a high school teacher at the time). I made Harvey a posthumous promise that I would carry on his legacy by serving our community as a clinician and advocate. Since becoming a psychologist, my work has focused on advancing social equity and competent treatment for LGBT persons.

D. C. Haldeman (✉)
John F. Kennedy School of Psychology and Social Sciences at National University, San Diego, CA, USA
e-mail: dhaldeman@nu.edu

N. A. Livingston et al. (eds.), *Addressing Minority Stress and Enhancing Resilience with Diverse LGBTQ+ Clients*, CBT: Science Into Practice,
https://doi.org/10.1007/978-3-031-92836-9_5

Introduction

A recent population-based study shows that 7% of LGB-identified individuals have undergone some kind of effort, therapeutic, religious, or otherwise, to change their same-sex attractions and behaviors (Blosnich et al., 2020). The adverse mental health sequelae to such efforts, for many, include increased suicidal ideation and suicide attempts, depression, and a number of associated concerns (Dehlin et al., 2015; Green et al., 2020; Ryan et al., 2018). As a result, many survivors of conversion efforts seek additional mental health treatment for concerns related to, or exacerbated by, conversion therapy efforts. However, there are no existing guidelines or recommendations for how to conduct treatment designed to counteract the adverse effects of conversion or other non-affirming care experiences. This chapter will offer guidance specific to the needs of conversion survivors for the practitioner facilitating their recovery.

The term "conversion therapy" is commonly understood to refer to efforts by mental health practitioners to change sexual orientation or gender identity, although the term itself is a misnomer. There is no justification for labeling such efforts as "therapy"; a wide range of strategies associated with conversion efforts may be employed in a clinical setting, but there is no standard protocol for conducting such treatments. Furthermore, there is no evidence that sexual orientation is amenable to change, therapeutic or otherwise (APA, 2021c). Thus, we use the less familiar but more accurate terms, "sexual orientation change efforts (SOCE)" or "gender identity change efforts (GICE), in reporting its harmful effects.

This chapter will summarize the history and methods used in SOCE, integrating available content on GICE where relevant, relevant policies and legal regulations, and clinical issues in working with conversion survivors. These are illustrated with case material including examples of clinical dialogue. The chapter concludes with recommendations for practitioners working with conversion survivors. It should be noted at this point that nearly all studies of conversion therapies and the physical and psychological effects thereof are about men. Therefore, almost all of the references in this chapter are about cisgender gay men in conversion therapies. Very few conversion studies are about, or even include women (Spandler & Carr, 2022). The reasons for this have never been clear, although it may have to do with the laws that prohibited sodomy, largely interpreted to mean male sames-sex sexual activity. In England, for example, as well as in many US jurisdictions, the laws prohibiting same-sex behavior were limited to men (Spandler & Carr, 2022). In any case, caution must be exercised in extrapolating the results of conversion therapy studies to women. It should be further noted that the majority of conversion studies focus on sexual orientation change, not gender identity. Therefore, those references to GICE will be included in this chapter when supported by extant research.

History and Methods of SOCE/GICE

SOCE/GICE are predicated on the dangerous and unfounded beliefs that same-sex attraction and transgender/nonbinary identification are wrong and morally inferior to heterosexuality and cisgender identification. Reports of efforts to change unwanted same-sex attractions and behaviors, including quasi-therapeutic, aversive, spiritual, behavioral, and other methods, appeared in the literature as early as the nineteenth century (Murphy, 1992). Long before and after the removal of "homosexuality" from the DSM in 1975, same-sex attractions were stigmatized and viewed as abnormal by many; furthermore, same-sex behavior was criminalized in many US jurisdictions and abroad. The etiology of same-sex attraction has been variously explained by a host of empirically unsubstantiated theories, including childhood sexual trauma, poor parenting, or peer abuse (APA, 2009; Glassgold, 2022; Gonsiorek, 1991; Haldeman, 1994).

Perhaps owing to the increased visibility of LGBTQ persons in our society and the concomitant increase in public acceptance of sexual minorities, some believe that SOCE are a thing of the past. This is incorrect. According to current estimates, SOCE continues to affect thousands each year. The Williams Institute, an LGBTQ think tank affiliated with the UCLA School of Law, provides the following data relative to the prevalence of SOCE (Williams Institute, 2019):

- 698,000 LGBT adults (ages 18–59) in the U.S. have received conversion therapy, including about 350,000 LGBTQ adults who were subjected to the practice as adolescents;
- 16,000 LGBT youth (ages 13–17) will receive conversion therapy from a licensed health care professional before they reach the age of 18 in the 32 states that currently do not ban the practice;
- 10,000 LGBT youth (ages 13–17) live in states that ban conversion therapy and have been protected from receiving conversion therapy from a licensed health care professional before age 18;
- An estimated 57,000 youth (ages 13–17) across all states will receive conversion therapy from religious or spiritual advisors before they reach the age of 18.

Absent a standard methodology for therapists who purport to change same-sex orientation, a variety of methods have been used. The earliest claims of "successful" SOCE appeared in the psychoanalytic literature in the 1960s (Bieber et al., 1962; Socarides, 1968), suggesting that same-sex attractions among gay men were the result of a disrupted attachment to the father and an enmeshed bond with the mother. In so doing, the parents of the same sex attracted individual are also stigmatized and blamed for their bad parenting. In 1991, Nicolosi doubled down on this unsubstantiated theory by recommending a treatment model in which the patient is cured of his same-sex desires and becomes heterosexual, or at least celibate, through an identification with the male therapist in which the bond corrects the paternal "love deficit" that has been motivating the patient to seek out other men for sexual gratification (Nicolosi, 1991).

Behavioral methods have been employed in SOCE, such as masturbatory reconditioning, guided imagery, and forced gender expression (e.g., presentation, behavior) conforming with the norms associated with one's sex assigned in GICE. Cisgender men undergoing SOCE at residential centers or camps are often encouraged to just date women, regardless of the potential for the emotional damage that could accrue from such fraudulent relationships. These strategies are often reinforced in group "therapy" sessions in which members are expected to bond with each other in non-sexual ways (e.g., playing basketball or other sports, engaging in "typical male" activities), and in so doing, generate group support—and pressure—to develop heterosexual behaviors, using the women participants date as conversion experiments.

Most harmful, however, are the aversive conditioning techniques employed to eradicate diverse sexual orientations or non-heterosexual attractions. Methods of this sort rely on the administration of nausea-inducing drugs or delivery of an electrical shock to the male patient's hands and/or genitals while he views homoerotic pictorial material. The cessation of the shock is then accompanied by an image of a nude woman, with the objective being a reconditioning of the individual's sexual response patterns. Needless to say, this method was ineffective and harmful. An early proponent of this method, psychologist Gerald Davison, later recanted and opposed this process in his 1972 Presidential address to the Association for the Advancement of Behavior Therapy following an excoriating confrontation by psychologist and gay activist Charles Silverstein. Davison has written a number of articles focusing on the social forces of heteronormativity that sustain conversion methods (Davison, 1976, 1982). Illustrating this perspective, he cites Begelman (1975, p.180): "The efforts of behavior therapists to reorient homosexuals to heterosexuality by their very existence constitute a significant causal element in reinforcing the social doctrine that homosexuality is bad" (Davison, 1991). To this day, Davison is a vocal critic of conversion methods.

Every major healthcare organization in the United States has condemned aversive conversion methods as cruel and ineffective, yet they persist to this day. The use of electric shock, nausea-inducing drugs, and castration followed by post-mortem transplantation of the testicles of deceased heterosexual men have all been reported (Silverstein, 1991). We do not know how many people have been subjected to these kinds of "therapeutic" torture, but it is reasonable to think that the adverse physical and psychological effects on the individual are substantial.

It should be made clear that the following case material is paraphrased and aggregated, with no identifying information, for the purposes of examination. One patient I (the author) saw who had been through numerous conversion electric shock sessions described it thus: "I didn't become straight by getting shocked, I just became at war with my body. I can't think about sex without feeling awful, like the current is going through my body again. I can't stand to have anyone touch me, especially on my genital area. I can't even shake someone's hand anymore without gritting my teeth. I'm not straight, I'm just hollow. I'm nothing." He was experiencing the effects of his conversion trauma acutely and was suicidal—not uncommon for conversion survivors. Therapy was a long process of gradually reorienting the patient, through mindfulness techniques, to his own body so that he could heal and reclaim his physical self.

Most conversion survivors did not go through "therapy" at all but rather sought religious or spiritual pathways to sexual orientation change. According to Blosnich et al. (2020), nearly 81% of SOCE survivors underwent conversion efforts led by a pastor, priest, pastoral counselor, or other religious leader. However, such religious leaders are notoriously secretive about their methods, the details of which are even more nebulous than those of so-called psychotherapeutic strategies but may involve prayer groups, "laying on of the hands," (a term referring to a clergyperson transferring the "power of the holy spirit" in a healing ceremony; Verrett, 2022), or even exorcism.

Regardless of the methodology, there is no evidence of successful "conversions" to heterosexual orientation. In 2009, APA released a report reviewing nearly 100 studies purporting to demonstrate sexual orientation change and found no empirical basis for their claims. These studies were criticized on a variety of methodological grounds. All relied on self-report and retrospective memory, both of which are influenced by the considerable social desirability demands faced by many conversion survivors. Further, subjects in these studies were improperly classified (including bisexual individuals who already had the capacity for different-gender attractions). Finally, few studies reported any outcome data to demonstrate the stability of treatment effects (APA, 2009).

Organizational Policies and Legal Regulations

Despite "homosexuality" having been dismissed as a mental illness in the 1970s, healthcare organizations were slow to develop policies addressing SOCE. The APA's first SOCE policy, adopted in 1998, focused entirely on ethical admonishments, stopping far short of actually opposing SOCE due to pushback from practitioner groups. Practitioners were concerned that there were insufficient data to oppose SOCE (apart from numerous anecdotal claims of harm from survivors) and that a prohibitive policy would set a dangerous precedent for other therapeutic modalities deemed to have insufficient empirical support, even though SOCE are not a recognized therapeutic modality. APA's policies evolved over time, however; in 2009, the APA Task Force Report on Appropriate Therapeutic Responses to Sexual Orientation included a resolution that admonished psychologists that there was no credible evidence to support SOCE (APA, 2009). Finally, in 2021, the APA adopted a resolution formally opposing SOCE (APA, 2021a). At the same time, the APA adopted its first resolution opposing GICE (APA, 2021b). Other organizations that have adopted policies against SOCE include the American Academy of Child and Adolescent Psychiatry (2012), American Association of Sex Educators, Counselors, and Therapists (2017), the American College of Physicians (2015), the American Counseling Association (2025), the American Psychiatric Association (2021), and the National Association of Social Workers (2000).

In 2012, California became the first state in the nation to ban the use of SOCE with minors by licensed mental health professionals. Since then, as of this writing, 20 other states, the District of Columbia, and over 70 local jurisdictions have followed suit (APA, 2021c). Internationally, SOCE have been totally banned in Belgium, Canada, France, Israel, Spain, the United Kingdom, New Zealand, several European and South American countries, Taiwan, and regions of Spain and Australia (Gerbut et al., 2020). In 2013, the United Nations Human Rights Council's (UNHRC) Special Rapporteur on torture and other cruel, inhuman, or degrading treatment or punishment stated that some SOCE rise to the level of human rights violations, constituting "abuses in health-care settings that may cross a threshold of mistreatment that is tantamount to torture or cruel, inhuman or degrading treatment or punishment" (UNHRC, 2013). After a wide-ranging international exploration, the UN Independent Expert on protection against violence and discrimination based on sexual orientation and gender identity characterized the many efforts under the term "conversion therapy" as "relying on the medically false pathologization of sexual orientation and gender identity, manifested through interventions that inflict severe pain and suffering and result in psychological and physical damage, calling for measures to prevent conversion efforts, which it defines as "degrading, inhuman and cruel" (UNHRC, 2020, p. 21).

It bears repeating that youth are the most vulnerable age group when it comes to SOCE, and that those who are exposed to or forced into SOCE are 2–3 times more likely to attempt suicide (Blosnich et al., 2020; Ryan et al., 2018). Reliable prevalence data about GICE are less available. However, a cross-sectional probability sample of 27,716 transgender persons in the US reports that 13.5% have experienced exposure to GICE (Turban et al., 2019). Reasons for the relative lack of GICE prevalence data are unclear but it is clear that more research is needed.

Clinical Issues with SOCE/GICE Survivors

There is no "one size fits all" protocol for treating SOCE survivors, owing to their unique cultural contexts and experiences. Like everyone else, most SOCE survivors stand at the intersection of several aspects of power and privilege. All early research on SOCE involved White gay men. As noted earlier in this chapter, lesbians' sexuality was ignored or even welcomed, in part because of men's eroticization of female same-sex sexuality or because there were no legal prohibitions against it (Spandler & Carr, 2022). Research with Black, Indigenous, and People of Color (BIPOC) was not even considered, mirroring the trend in general LGBTQ+ research at the time. Changing the identity of trans individuals was primarily limited to treating gender diverse children, forcing them into activities deemed "appropriate" for their sex assigned at birth (Zucker & Bradley, 1995). It is difficult to identify the similarities or differences between survivors of SOCE and GICE, since the vast majority of studies focus on SOCE or group SOCE and GICE together (Fish & Russell, 2020).

A patient seeking to recover from the damages of SOCE may present with one, many, or all of the following issues: suicidality, depression, chronic anxiety, alienation (from self, family, and community), shame, masculinization or feminization, intimacy-avoidance, and sexual dysfunction (Haldeman, 2001). Given the prevalence of suicidal ideation following SOCE, the clinician's first order of business is an assessment of acute suicidality, as well as determining the current emotional and mental state concerning their experiences.

Why do some LGBTQ individuals seek out SOCE in the first place? The answer to this question is key to understanding the patient's unique life circumstances and sociocultural context. Some authors have identified the internalization of negative social attitudes about same-sex attraction as "sexual identity distress" (Dehlin et al., 2015; Shidlo & Schroeder, 2002). With 30 years of clinical experience working with survivors of SOCE, I lay the demand for SOCE on the doorstep of toxic, anti-LGBTQ religions. Judith Glassgold, chair of APA's 2009 Task Force on Appropriate Therapeutic Responses to Sexual Orientation, agrees, identifying anti-gay religion as a primary motivating factor in seeking SOCE. She observes that the incompatibility between a person's same-sex attraction and their conservative religious beliefs can be a great source of distress, one that the individual attempts to relieve through SOCE (Glassgold, 2022).

Guidelines, Policies, and Research

Guidance for practitioners seeking to provide affirmative care to LGBT people is available from several sources. The APA guidelines for psychotherapy with lesbian, gay, and bisexual clients (APA, 2021c) are in their third iteration. Guidelines for transgender individuals were adopted in 2015 (APA, 2015). The Task Force on Appropriate Therapeutic Responses to Sexual Orientation provides a summary of what constitutes affirmative care for LGB individuals, including the following: demonstrating acceptance, conducting a comprehensive assessment, and promoting the development of active coping strategies, social support, and identity exploration and development (APA, 2009). Additionally, several authors have developed modality-specific affirmative care protocols for LGBT individuals, including CBT (Martell et al., 2003) and a variety of multi-modal approaches (Pachankis & Safren, 2019).

A SOCE Case Example

As previously mentioned, adherence to homophobic religions is a significant motivating factor for many who participate in SOCE. The conflict between same-sex attraction and conservative religion creates a variety of related issues for many: fear of God's retribution, loss of identity as a person of faith, rejection by family and community, and lack of familiarity with/aversion to the queer community (APA, 2021c; Fjelstrom, 2013; Flentje et al., 2013). Some SOCE survivors will reject religion, or even any form of spiritual practice, outright. Some will embrace a more tolerant, accepting religious environment as offered by welcoming and affirming denominations. But for others, the internal conflict between sexual orientation and religious identification is painful. The following excerpt from a patient transcript highlights some of the issues that are prominent in the aftermath of SOCE for many individuals who are conflicted about their same-sex attractions or behaviors. The patient is a 22-year-old White cisgender man I saw who came from a rural, low SES environment, with a high school education.

T: How many times have you been to conversion therapy?
P: Five times. Twice with my minister, but it never really took hold because I kept sliding back and having sex with men, so he sent me to a residential treatment center. I went there three times.
T: For how long?
P: The shortest time was about 6 weeks. The last time I was there for 6 months.
T: What was it like there?
P: It was a waste of time. They had us practice visualizing having sex with women when we masturbate, but every time I got close (to ejaculation) the image would turn into a guy.
T: Were you in a group or individual treatment?
P: Both. In the group, we just talked about supporting each other thinking about women, but I don't think anyone really meant it. I think it was just to show the counselors we were changing so that we could get out of there. My individual counselor kept telling me that I was going to burn in hell if I didn't change, but then he would end each session with us jerking off together.
T: That was part of the treatment?
P: Yes, he told me it was what we needed to do so that I could get comfortable with my male sexuality.
T: I'm not following.
P: I think he was just a closet case charlatan pretending to be an ex-gay therapist.
T: Did you think that was abusive?
P: Not at the time. I thought it was what I needed to do to live.
T: What do you mean?
P: I'm from a small town, ok? A small town where most everyone is evangelical Christian. They quote the scripture to fit their purposes. But I'd lived there all my life—my family, my friends, my faith community—if they all rejected me, I'd have nothing. And if I tried to live as a gay man, they would reject me—as the minister said, "You shall be cast out of this community as God will surely cast you out of heaven for your abominable sins."
T: What were you taught about what it means to be gay?
P: That I'd never have a happy relationship because homosexuals can't have them. They can't have families; they can't have regular jobs. They can't ever be happy. They just have random sex with each other, and they all use drugs, ok?

T: What else did you learn?
P: That if I went that route, I would end up dead from AIDS. It was really bad. I didn't have anywhere to turn.
T: How did you end up here?
P: After the last time at the (conversion) program, I just kind of gave up on the idea and went back home. One day, my dad caught me having sex with a buddy. He nearly beat me to death, then he gave me an hour to pack my shit and get out of the house. My mother was hysterical, and she begged my dad to change his mind, so he started to hit her too. As I left, she stuffed some money in my pocket even though she was weeping and bloody. That's the last I ever saw or heard from either of them.
T: That sounds pretty traumatic. What did you do then?
P: I had enough money for a bus ticket here (Seattle) because I thought I'd have an easier time of it in a big city, you know, where there's more gay people, more than in Boise.
T: And was it easier here?
P: Not really. It was just a different kind of hard. I had the freedom to do what I wanted, but I still felt (long pause) awful inside. I hated myself, really. I'd learned to hate my own feelings, my own body. I worked the streets for a while to earn money, but I just ended up hating myself even more.
T: I can understand. That's all you've been taught, so it seems like a normal reaction.
P: Sure hope that can change.
T: Unlearning the lies of conversion efforts takes time and effort before you replace them with an understanding that fits who you are.

The conflict between sexual orientation and religious identity must be handled carefully. The belief that one is condemned to everlasting punishment cannot be easily dismantled through psychoeducation. Attempting to teach the survivor to see themselves differently can sometimes backfire. For instance, and as another patient who admitted to having "homosexual feelings" warned me: "You better not 'turn me into a gay,' because then I'd know you're an agent of the devil." Rather, a thoughtful and deep inquiry into the existential issues surrounding this crisis of the self enables the therapist to meet the survivor where they are. This requires careful probing into the individual's belief system. This is the same patient as above:

T: I'm curious about your beliefs. Can you describe your experience of God?
P: Well, he is everywhere; he sees and knows all. He knows what I've been doing, and he is punishing me.
T: So, God is punitive?
P: Just like everyone else.
T: Is he your Creator?
P: Of course. Man is created in his image and likeness.
T: And that includes you.
P: Yes. But I've let Him down.
T: Help me understand, then: God created you as gay just so he can hate you?

P: (Long pause) No. (another pause) Well, wait. That doesn't…I don't know. It's in the Bible.

T: What is?

P: That homosexuality is wrong. It's an abomination.

T: What else does the Bible say?

P: I don't know what you mean. Lots of things.

T: Oh, I was just thinking about the passages in which people could own slaves, sell their daughters, or stone women to death if they misbehave. Not eating shellfish, or wearing clothing made from different fabrics; other things that we don't follow today. Just wondering why we might still focus on a possibly mistranslated passage from Leviticus, which actually does not address modern same-sex behavior or relationships.

P: I've never thought of it like that. It isn't the way I was taught.

T: I know. But aren't you trying to find a way to reconcile your sexual orientation and your religious beliefs? Doesn't that mean challenging some of what you've been taught?

P: That's gonna be hard. I still feel bad about being gay, and even worse for not being able to change it.

This excerpt shows the disparity between the patient's true self and his belief system. And indeed, this patient's integration of self and belief was difficult; abandoning or modifying a toxic belief system cannot be changed overnight, nor should it be. His shame about being same-sex attracted was exacerbated by his guilt over being unable to change it. In this patient's case, group support was instrumental in helping him integrate the sexual and spiritual aspects of his identity. He found such support in the form of a group called "Evangelicals Concerned" where he met others from similar backgrounds. This group modeled for him the possibility of integrating same-sex identity and conservative religious beliefs and practices. Ultimately, the patient found a social and spiritual home in this group—as well as a partner.

Treatment with BIPOC Survivors

According to data presented by Blosnich et al. (2020) from the population-based Generations study, some BIPOC individuals experience SOCE at greater rates than their White counterparts. Black people experience SOCE at more than twice the rate of White people; for Latinx individuals, the rate is half again as high as for White people. Unfortunately, the Generations study did not include sufficient numbers of Asian American or Native American individuals to provide adequate data for those groups. In any case, the practitioner who works with BIPOC persons in recovery from SOCE must be prepared to understand the unique challenges faced by these groups.

BIPOC queer persons stand at an intersection of race, sexual orientation/gender identity, and religion—as well as SES and ability status for some. This poses potential danger, because at this intersection, the individual can be hit from several directions. Literally, this is the kind of triple- or quadruple-stigmatization that Kimberlee Crenshaw discussed in her early work on the concept of intersectionality (Crenshaw, 1989). It is incumbent on the practitioner to have a clear grasp of each individual's co-varying experience with multiple stigmas and the effect that they may have had.

A SOCE Case: Cultural Considerations

The following are derived from prior clinical case examples. In the previous case example, we see the toxic effects of shame and self-hatred exacerbated by the patient's family as well as the misinformation disseminated by the patient's religious institution. The patient comes to treatment with a history of SOCE failures, misunderstandings about same-sex attraction and behavior from a powerful religious institution, little formal education, and engaging in sex work to survive. He does, however, possess White privilege. But what happens when the cultural contextual variables are changed? In the following case, the patient is "Jason," a single 30-year-old African American gay man from the American Deep South, where he grew up in a middle-class family. He has a college degree in Business and works as a mid-level manager at the headquarters of a large company. Like the previous patient, he was forced into group and individual SOCE as a teenager after he came out to his family, and continued until his exasperated therapist gave up due to the patient's lack of "progress." The first excerpt (edited for meaning) is from the patient's intake session.

T: What brings you here today?
P: I guess I feel…I don't know; I'm not feeling very good about myself. Never have, really.
T: What is that about, do you think?
P: Mostly it's about being gay. It doesn't go over so well where I come from.
T: Tell me about that.
P: My family, my church, my town—it was all against me. I didn't have any…support, nothing like that.
T: For being gay?
P: Yeah, but it started a long time before I even knew what that meant. They all called me a "funny boy," I guess because of the way I acted, and how I liked to look nice and neat. My friends were all girls, I felt more comfortable with them. They didn't beat me up or call me names.
T: Did your family help you?
P: They were the worst of all because I couldn't get away from them. At least I could run away from the bullies. Couldn't run away from my family.
T: Tell me about them.

P: It was just me, my mom, and my aunt—my dad had left before I was born. Ever since I can remember, both of them were on my case.
T: About what?
P: Oh, you know—it was always, "Jason, don't walk that way. You look like a sissy." Or as I got older and got interested in school and would come home to tell them what I'd learned that day, all they would say was stuff like, "Don't talk so *white*. You sound like a faggot. A white faggot. You ain't a faggot, are you?" I didn't even know what that was, but I learned soon enough.
T: Was there any support for you, anywhere?
P: My grandma lived nearby. I took to going over there after school. She was the only one who showed me any love, but she passed when I was 10.

In this excerpt, we see the patient struggling with being isolated and stigmatized because of his gender non-conforming presentation. He learns early on that there is something wrong with him; he can tell just from the tone of his mother's voice. The constant exhortations he receives from his family to "act different," amplified by the verbal abuse and bullying he is subjected to at home and school, just leave him confused. He becomes depressed and withdrawn, avoiding even the girls with whom he had played. Jason's mother and aunt noticed this gradual change in his behavior, even as they continued browbeating him for not trying hard enough to "stop being a sissy and act like a boy." By the time he turned 12, he avoided all social activities and became progressively more tearful in response to the scolding he received from his mother and aunt. Finally, Jason's mother took him to see the pastor of her church.

T: What happened when you went to see the pastor?
P: Oh, he just gave me a bunch of lectures about how I was hurting my mom by "acting" the way I was. But I didn't see it as "acting"—I was just being myself. And the more I tried to be what they all wanted, the worse it got. See, that was the *real* "acting." I couldn't change how I walked or talked…I just felt silly trying.
T: And then?
P: The pastor got very frustrated…one day, he just started yelling at me, told me he was going to slap the devil out of me, and he started hitting me. I cried and ran out of there. But when I got home, he'd already called Mom—and I got the worst beating of my life. But that wasn't even the worst part of it.
T: What was the worst part?
P: My mom came to me later, and brought me some ice for my swollen, bruised face; she put a band-aid on a cut under my eye. Then she looked at me and said, "I'm ashamed of you, boy. You bring shame on this house. You're worthless."

As puberty progresses, Jason realizes that he is attracted to other boys. He feels scared and shamed by this realization, but the power of his attractions is such that he lays awake each night thinking of them. At school, he sees a counselor and admits that he is worried about how he feels toward other boys. The school counselor, feeling that this issue is outside her area of competence, refers him to a licensed therapist.

T: How was your experience with the therapist?

P: (Chuckles) Pretty bad. He was this grumpy old white dude who smelled like cigarettes and sour milk. He looked at me like I was something that had just crawled out of the trash. Told me I just needed to "toughen up," shit like that. He gave me some exercises to do, but I'd already tried that sort of stuff before—you know, walk like a man, lower your voice, talk about girls and sports. Think about girls when you touch yourself. Wasn't anything new. And I think he could tell pretty quickly that I wasn't interested. I don't think he liked me.
T: So, it sounds like a waste of time, and even harmful.
P: Well, I don't know. I did learn one thing. I gave up on anyone being sympathetic, let alone supportive. As mean as my family was, here's someone being paid to help me and not even he gives a shit.
T: For how long did you see him?
P: (Laughs) Too long, although it was only about 6 months or so. He got fed up and said I should go to one of those religious camps where they try and change you, but I told him I'd already had enough of that. I'd prayed to Jesus for years, I told him, but still had these feelings. I asked him, what if God wants me to be gay?
T: How did he respond?
P: He kind of snorted and scoffed—"God doesn't want *anyone* to be gay. It's an aberration," he said. "Maybe I am an aberration, then," I said. I reminded him that I'd been trying for years, on my own, with the pastor, and then with him—to change my feelings, but they only got stronger. Maybe I should just accept that. So, he fired me on the spot; told me not to come back, that I was "hopeless."
T: How did it feel for him to do that?
P: It was a relief, really. (Chuckles) And now I had "hopeless" to add to "worthless" in my self-image.
T: You found that funny?
P: I had to. Otherwise, I'd probably have killed myself.

Jason eventually leaves home for college, where he buries himself in his studies—in part to demonstrate that he isn't "worthless," but also to suppress his sexual feelings. Upon graduation, he is recruited by a large company in the Pacific Northwest, which serves the dual purpose of professional opportunity and getting him as far away from home as possible. He acknowledges that, because of his move, some part of him hopes that he will be able to reinvent himself as self-confident and valuable. However, the reality proved more complicated than he had imagined.

T: How was it for you, moving here?
P: Scary and freeing at the same time…I could get away and be myself, except I didn't know anyone here. And so many white people! Kind of a culture shock, learning how to code-switch and talk to white people.
T: You're talking to one right now.
P: (Laughs) I know. It's just different from how I talk to the folks back home. I feel pretty comfortable with you. Besides, there aren't any Black therapists on my insurance plan (laughs again). No offense, you know.
T: None taken. So how is it for you navigating the world here? Your work colleagues, your social life?

P: I get along fine with everyone at work; I'm the only Black person in my department, but I haven't had any issues. Social life, though…that's a different story.
T: How so?
P: Well, can I be honest about the gay community up here?
T: Please.
P: Biggest bunch of racist fucks I ever did see! I walk into a club and half the room is staring at me like I just escaped from the zoo, and the other half looks away. Oh, and then some of them? Fetishists. "Oooh, Mr. Chocolate!" one of them says to me the other night. And then later someone comes up to me, doesn't say a thing, just grabs my crotch and asks, "Is it true what they say?" I slapped his hand away and told him to fuck off. Then someone else who's watching says, "Well, isn't *she* a touchy thing!" I left angry. I still am. That's just the example from last Friday night. Don't want to hurt your feelings, but man…
T: You aren't here to take care of my feelings, Jason, and besides—I see it and hear it myself. The racism among white gay men. The objectification, the disdain, all of it.
P: Well, I gotta say…this is the first time I've ever talked to a white man about racism.
T: And it won't be the last. I want to invite you to continue this discussion.

It was clear that there had to be space to discuss racism in the gay community in the treatment. It was a part of daily life for Jason, a Black man who lived, worked, and socialized in a predominantly White world. Here he was, far from home and his family and community of origin—attempting to navigate the perimeter of a gay social context that was foreign and unwelcoming. He doesn't have a sense of belonging or inclusion in either place. In checking community resources, the therapist found that there was a support group for Black gay men that met every Sunday evening in the basement of a church. Thinking it would be helpful for Jason to meet other Black gay men, the therapist recommended that Jason consider attending, which he did. Here is an excerpt from the session that followed:

T: How was the group last Sunday?
P: Man, that was some fucked-up shit. I hated it.
T: Oh no—I'm sorry to hear that. What made it so bad?
P: It was so goddam Jesus-y! They all sat up in there praying, swaying with their hands in the air and eyes closed—I was waiting for them to start drooling and rolling around on the fucking floor, talking in tongues.
T: My mistake, Jason—I should have done more research before recommending it to you. A well-intentioned mistake, but a mistake, nonetheless. I am so sorry.
P: Well, wow. That's a first. A white person apologizing! (chuckles) I sure don't hear that every day.

This may seem like a small thing, but it touches on the racial dynamics of this therapeutic relationship. The therapist had made a well-intentioned blunder by neglecting to check on the group to which he was referring the patient. Had he done so, he would have discovered that the focus of the group would likely provoke Jason's as-yet unresolved bitterness and resentment toward his abusive church upbringing.

Further, the therapist acknowledged to Jason that it could have caused a rupture—all because of the many assumptions that well-intentioned White people make on behalf of non-White individuals regarding what they need. This created space for regular conversations about microaggressions and other features of our racist community and society. In turn, this led to work on a heretofore untouched area: his body image.

P: I am going to start a fast this weekend. Actually, it's a "juice cleanse." Oprah is recommending it.
T: What? Why? (the therapist was taken aback, as Jason was a very trim man, appearing to be in excellent shape)
P: I'm trying to get more comfortable with my body, and I thought if I lost a bit of weight it might help.
T: Help with what?
P: Oh, maybe make it easier to meet people.
T: Do you see yourself as overweight?
P: Well, not really—except I can do this (he grabs a small fold of skin around his midsection).
T: Can you recall a time when you did feel comfortable in your body?
P: (long pause) No.
T: Then I wonder if maybe this…discomfort…started a long time ago?
P: I don't know. Maybe.
T: Did you ever get over the feeling that there was something wrong with you?
P: (another long pause) No. I don't think so.
T: So, maybe that's where this is coming from. (Pause). What's going on in your head right now, Jason?
P: (faraway voice) He's a sissy. And he's ugly, too.
T: That's what you're hearing?
P: Yes.
T: And are you ugly?
P: People say I'm attractive…but I'm not sure I trust that.
T: And are you a sissy?
P: I don't know. You tell me.
T: What matters is what you think. Would it be ok if you were a sissy?
P: I'm…not sure…
T: What if I thought I was a sissy?
P: Yeah, but you aren't one.
T: But what if I thought that about myself? Would you think less of me?
P: Of course not.
T: But you're willing to think less of yourself. What makes it different when you look at yourself, as opposed to when you look at me?

A full discussion of the dynamics between White therapists and clients of color is beyond the scope of this chapter. Suffice it to say that in this case, the work to repair and rebuild Jason's self-concept required an exploration beyond mere family dynamics. Every element of his early life—family, community, church, and school—constituted part of an overall cultural experience that formed and deformed his sense of identity. Compounded by these factors was the sense of cultural dissonance he experienced upon leaving the US Deep South and entering an almost entirely White world in the Northwest. Jason's work with a White therapist on his self-concept began with conversations about racism.

Bullied at school and abused at home, it is to be expected that he would have felt traumatized. He was a child with no safe haven. Jason's experiences with the pastor and then a conversion therapist were perhaps, at first glance, minor elements in the genesis of his self-devaluation. However, they served to strongly reinforce the messages he received from family, school, and peers who held the imprimatur of religion and socially acceptable behavior—as delivered by powerful individuals, a pastor, and a therapist. Their insistence that he was broken and needed to change created a plethora of feelings—shame, fear, and sadness—which lodged themselves firmly in Jason's limbic system. Not only did he come to think less of himself for who he was, but he also came to feel discomfort in his own skin, self-hatred. However, this is a case in which SOCE are a significant element in the client's presenting concern because it did more than amplify the messages he was already getting at home, school, and in the world. SOCE, as delivered by people in positions of power, literally screamed at him that he needed to perform an impossible task: change—his sexual orientation, his behavior, and his entire presentation. If only I could, thought Jason—but I cannot, so there is the final confirmation. Worthless and hopeless. Why go on?

But go on Jason did, discovering in the process an internal resilience he didn't know he had. Jason had undergone conversion efforts—first, informally, by a clergyperson; then, more formally and by an actual therapist—as a very vulnerable person. He had little ego strength to defend against what was being done to him in the name of "therapy." His self-esteem was nonexistent, thanks to years of being derided and shunned by the very people who should have embraced and supported him. It was therefore important in Jason's recovery that the therapist disrupts the power differential between them. SOCE transgresses the psychotherapeutic mandate to let the client lead by imposing a *preordained* outcome on the process (i.e., the therapist's preconceived agenda, but not the client's, for conversion therapy), and an impossible one at that. In this way, power is gradually restored to Jason so that he may begin his recovery. Incidentally, though there may have been a racial discordance between Jason and the therapist, their common identities as gay men may have mitigated this difference.

Recovery from Treatment from GICE

Although "homosexuality" was removed from the DSM in 1980, "Gender Dysphoria" still appears in the DSM today, as well as in the ICD-10 (F64.9). This provides a basis for the use of GICE, methods that are used to steer the trans or gender diverse individual to a gender identity and presentation that more closely aligns with the person's assigned sex at birth. APA has opposed GICE as ineffective, harmful, and unethical (APA, 2021b); regardless, such methods persist, particularly with children whose parents force them into treatment out of concern for their atypical gender presentation and identity.

The first such treatments for gender non-conforming boys were developed by Richard Green (1987), who recommended therapists engage their young male clients in traditionally male activities and play (e.g., roughhousing, sports) while shaming and ridiculing them for effeminate behaviors or voicing an interest in "girls play." This attempt at social engineering also included extra time spent with Dad and limited contact with Mom. This method was promoted by Zucker and Bradley (1995), at a time when atypical gender activities and presentation were rarely supported by parents, or for that matter, the profession. As a leader in the movement to redirect the interests and presentation of gender-nonconforming children (Zucker et al., 2012), Zucker's work has evolved to allow such children to develop gender identities on their own. He has recently worked in this area with a Dutch group advocating a "wait and see" approach to gender-variant children. This approach permits children to explore gender-nonconforming behaviors and presentation provided that they only do so in the home and not in public, which is problematic but seemingly based on research indicating that most gender non-conforming children do not go on to adopt a trans identity as adults (Steensma & Cohen-Kettenis, 2011). This study was also the basis for recommending prepubertal hormone blockers with gender variant adolescents.

The current best practice in this area, however, is that the gender-variant child is provided with a safe environment for exploration. Any attempt to interfere with the child's own exploration of activities or presentation is associated with poor mental health outcomes (APA, 2021b; Singh et al., 2022). The incidence of suicide attempts, for instance, is 2–3 times higher among trans individuals who have been through some form of GICE (Ryan et al., 2018). In general, mental health concerns of trans and gender diverse persons are seen as accruing from a hostile social environment (Bockting et al., 2013). Trans youth are regularly subjected to bullying and physical violence at their schools; transgender workers often face abuse on the job. GICE only compounds these harms. Conversely, a study from the University of Washington shows that gender-variant children who were permitted to present socially consistent with their own gender identity were equal to cisgender children on dimensions of cognitive, social, and emotional functioning (Olson et al., 2016).

Fortunately, there are standards of care for trans individuals published by the World Professional Association of Transgender Health (WPATH, 2022; Coleman et al., 2012). These standards provide the practitioner working with trans individuals' information relative to assessment, psychotherapy, and consultation. They do not include any recommended GICE therapies. In addition, APA has published a set of practice guidelines for practitioners working with trans people (APA, 2015).

"Julie," a White 25-year-old trans woman, came to therapy to explore the possibility of engaging in gender transition. She initiated treatment using her dead name (the name given along with one's assigned sex at birth that one no longer uses), as she was still living and presenting as a man. Julie was a computer expert and worked for a large online social media company. She lived alone and would wear traditionally female clothing in her off hours, but not in public. Upon initial presentation, Julie appeared as depressed as she said she was: eyes downcast, stringy blond hair hanging to her shoulders, and wearing androgynous, shapeless clothing.

T: Welcome, (dead name). What brings you here today?
J: Please call me Julie. And I use she/her pronouns.
T: Of course, Julie. What's going on?
J: I…I just hate my life. I've been going through so much…so painful, I don't even know where to start.
T: Take your time; start wherever you like. You are safe here.
J: Well, I heard you see a lot of…transgender people? And I think…I am one. In fact, I know I am. I'm a woman.
T: Well, you are welcome here. Have you been female for a long time?
J: Ever since I can remember. All I wanted to do was put on my mom's dresses, play with other girls, put on makeup—if it was girly, I wanted to do it! It was the only time I felt happy. Mom didn't mind. I hated going to school as a boy; I felt like I was putting on a costume I didn't want to wear.
T: Were you able to dress and play like a girl at home, then?
J: Not after my dad came home early and caught me wearing mom's Rumba dress and her high heels. He beat the crap out of me. He made me go and see this therapist.
T: What was that like?
J: Horrible. The therapist was even worse than my dad. He wanted me to go outside and play football, wrestle with me, that sort of thing. I couldn't stand him touching me and I burst out crying one day. He slapped me to get me to stop but that just made it worse. I didn't care about sports; I just wanted to get away from him. But my dad made me keep going. The therapist never hit me again, but he just kept yelling at me to "act like a boy!" and "You're a wimp! You're a sissy! You're pathetic!" I couldn't stand it anymore, so one night I went into the medicine cabinet and took a bunch of pills. I didn't even know what I took, but it was enough to land me in the hospital.
T: You must have felt so desperate. Did you get some help after that?
J: No, they just locked the pills away. Dad wouldn't even look at me. When I was 16, I ran away. Worked the streets, stayed in a youth shelter. I finished high school online and took some computer classes at the community college. Found I had a real talent for that.
T: Were you feeling better at that point?
J: Yes and no. It was good to be out of the house, but I still thought about suicide every day.
T: Did you make any more attempts?
J: Yes, cutting—but that time, they just sewed me up, kept me for 3 days, and then I left.

After several months of trauma therapy and monitoring of the suicidal feelings, Julie says:

J: There's something I've been meaning to ask you. But it feels risky.
T: Please; take your time.
J: Would you…would you be ok with it if sometime I came to a session dressed (as a woman)? I mean, this is supposed to be my safe place, right?
T: Of course. I would welcome that.

The very next session, Julie appeared in a navy suit with a white silk blouse, and for the first time, she seemed happy. Julie always came "dressed" after that, sometimes in business attire, and sometimes more casually. One day, Julie said that she was ready to go to work as a woman.

J: Well, I went to work dressed, and guess what? Nobody said anything!
T: That's great, Julie. Do you know how happy you seem?
J: (Smiles) I know.

Julie later reported that soon thereafter, her manager took her aside and asked if Julie would like a company-wide diversity training on transgender people's experiences for her co-workers. The therapist congratulated her for her advocacy and encouraged her to continue exploring ways to live authentically. Julie blossomed; she developed a friend network in the trans community, went on hormones, and was in the transition process. Eventually, 2 years into treatment, Julie was ready for gender affirmation surgery:

J: Big news!
T: Tell me.
J: I found a surgeon in Arizona, "Dr. Smith". Do you know him?
T: Yes, I've worked with him for years, consulting and providing support letters for his trans patients. He's excellent. Are you interested in gender-affirming surgery?
J: I want it so bad! I have all my life. And now (thanks to Julie's advocacy) my company's insurance will cover most of it.
T: I'll be happy to write him a letter on your behalf.

Julie was satisfied with her surgery and she was seen periodically for several years afterward. She was in a stable relationship with a woman (a reminder that gender transition does not necessarily affect sexual orientation), she had a supportive friend network, and she was doing well at work. This story demonstrates the importance of supportive environments for trans persons. Trans and gender-nonconforming persons are at elevated risk for suicide attempts (Blosnich et al., 2020; Ryan et al., 2018). Support, both therapeutic and social, saved Julie from becoming a statistic.

Antidotes to SOCE and GICE: The Real "Reparative" Therapy in Summary

Most therapeutic endeavors begin with the therapist forming a working connection with the client. With 40 years of experience working with and advocating via the courts and legislatures for traumatized LGBTQ survivors, I believe that it is important to minimize the power differential with the client. Guidance in this regard is offered by the principles of Therapeutic Assessment (Finn & Tonsager, 2002; See Chap. 2), an approach to psychological assessment that is based on, among other things, collaboration, respect, humility, and compassion. These attributes are key to any therapist hoping to help clients recover from the ill effects of SOCE/GICE. In this way, the therapist facilitates the direction of treatment based on the client's needs. The therapist demonstrates respect for the client as the expert on their own life, and that they decide the direction of therapy in a collaborative process.

Purveyors of SOCE/GICE are often seen as arrogant and all-knowing; such an attitude is probably a prerequisite for being able to conduct oppressive treatments. Humility on the part of the therapist, on the other hand, demonstrates the therapist's understanding of their common humanity. In truth, Jason's therapist—despite having had privileges unavailable to Jason– had some personal understanding of what it means to be marginalized and devalued. Finally, Jason's previous encounters with the pastor and the therapist had been anything but compassionate. Both exacerbated Jason's shame and sense of failure. A therapist who offers compassion to the client in recovery from SOCE or GICE provides an emotionally corrective experience, mitigating the damage of the past while establishing a basis for work in recovery. To feel as if one's therapist cares is central to the success of any therapeutic enterprise, and Jason's therapist demonstrated this by expressions of compassion, but also by his willingness to engage in thoughtful (and sometimes difficult) dialogues about race, racism, and the gay community.

Developing a working relationship is the first step in recovery from SOCE, but it is just the beginning. What comes next depends on a variety of factors, starting with the cultural context. The queer community itself is a microcosm of all aspects of identity: here you find diversity in terms of sexual orientation (gay/lesbian/bisexual/asexual/pansexual, etc.), gender identity, race/ethnicity, age, ability status, SES, religious/spiritual identification, and so on. These must be considered and carefully investigated in order to facilitate healing and recovery, as people in all categories may have been subjected to SOCE.

The course and duration of recovery treatment will depend on the client's level of trauma, and the resultant dysfunction evident in their life. Someone who was subjected to electric shock methods and thrown out of their families may have different needs than someone whose SOCE experience was less traumatizing. However, since the potential for psychological trauma exists for all SOCE/GICE survivors, it is helpful for those working with this population to have a basic understanding of trauma-informed therapy. It is also useful for the therapist to have at least some cultural knowledge of the queer community, given the number of SOCE survivors who want to live authentic lives but are unfamiliar or afraid to make social and romantic connections with other queer people.

Similarly, cultural awareness is required in this work. Most of the literature in LGBT psychology, as is the case in psychology as a whole, is based on research and practice conducted with White men. What works for many White men may not be applicable or may even be harmful in other cultural contexts. Take, for instance, the issue of coming out to family and friends. Historically, gay men were advised that coming out to friends and family members was associated with better mental health than those who did not disclose (Bell & Weinberg, 1978). This advice was not appropriate even for all White gay men, but it certainly ignored the different norms and values held by various cultural groups. Encouraging clients to come out to their families can be risky, given the potential for serious ruptures in both familial and therapeutic relationships. Again, it is the client who is the expert on their life and family.

Future Directions for Research

There are a number of possible directions for future research on how to assist clients recovering from toxic conversion experiences. The overall question to be addressed is what works, and with whom? Typically, survivors of conversion methods have been lumped together as one group. But there may be differences in a variety of factors: why people seek it out voluntarily, what are the circumstances in which people are forced into it, and what the psychological (and sometimes physical) sequelae of conversion experiences might be. Further, we know very little about the differential experiences of those who have undergone SOCE and those who have undergone GICE.

Other questions we might consider have to do with the recovery process itself. What does therapeutic recovery from conversion methods look like? What therapeutic modalities are best suited for the conversion recovery process? Theoretically, the principles suggested in this chapter should be equally applicable across modalities. Existential/humanistic, cognitive-behavioral, psychodynamic, Acceptance and Commitment Therapy (ACT), Dialectical Behavior Therapy (DBT)—all of these potentially lend themselves well toward helping to address client issues such as have been highlighted in this chapter, depending on the therapeutic orientation of the clinician and the unique needs of the client. Lastly, research is the most powerful tool for legislative advocacy about this issue.

Conclusion

Efforts by therapists, pastoral counselors/clergy, and others to change sexual orientation and gender identity have been opposed by major healthcare organizations on the grounds that they are ineffective and potentially harmful. As of this writing, 20 states and 70 local jurisdictions have banned conversion practices with minors and adults. Data show that participation in SOCE/GICE brings an elevated risk of suicidality and other adverse mental health consequences. Despite the practical and ethical concerns about conversion efforts, to date no recommendations have been offered for helping clients recover from these and other non-affirming care practices. This chapter is an initial effort at raising awareness about the needs of conversion survivors through clinical research and observation, as well as laying the groundwork for future research on clinical work with conversion survivors.

The LGBT community is as diverse as the mainstream society in which it is embedded, and diverse clients require diverse healing and recovery strategies. General guidelines for such strategies are offered here with the caveat that much more research is needed to refine treatment approaches for each unique individual. Questions regarding what kinds of treatment strategies work with whom will only be answered with more clinical research.

In the meantime, the many healthcare organizations that have developed policies and guidelines opposing conversion therapy can amend them by including reference to the need for SOCE and GICE survivors' care and a need for further study. In turn, more detailed research will enable organizations to amend their guidelines with specific recommendations for practitioners who are facilitating clients' recovery from SOCE/GICE.

Further research in this area can—and should—be used for political advocacy. Psychologists have historically been notoriously reticent to become political advocates. This position ignores the fact that anti-LGBT social policies and legislative initiatives have a direct, adverse impact on the mental health of LGBT persons residing in the jurisdictions in which they occur (Rostosky et al., 2009). In the current political climate, there is a groundswell of efforts in many conservative states to limit and even prohibit the enactment of safeguards for LGBT individuals. These efforts are not limited to LGBT persons. Emboldened by the US Supreme Court's invalidation of Roe v. Wade, conservative pogroms in many states have implications for a wide range of issues. These efforts include limiting access to reproductive care and gender-affirming treatments, revising school curricula to expunge topics (such as slavery) that reflect poorly on White people, and banning books deemed unsavory by conservative morality police. Such strategies aim to exert systemic control over the individual, potentially jeopardizing the mental health and well-being of all who belong to marginalized groups.

As psychologists who care about public welfare, we have a responsibility to do more than engage in our customary research and practice activities. Our allegiance is not just to the individual, but to use psychological science for the betterment of society. Understanding the dangers of conversion methods, and how to help those who have been harmed by them, is endemic to the public interest.

References

American Academy of Child and Adolescent Psychiatry. (2012). Conversion therapy.

American Association of Sex Educators, Counselors, and Therapists. (2017). Position on reparative therapy. https://www.aasect.org/position-reparative-therapy

American College of Physicians. (2015). Internists offer recommendations and statements on how to achieve health equity for LGBT patients. https://www.acponline.org/acp-newsroom

American Counseling Association (2025). *Conversion therapy statement.* https://www.counseling.org/about/values-statements/conversion-therapy#

American Medical Association. (2019). *Ban conversion therapy.* Retrieved from: https://policysearch.ama-assn.org/policyfinder/detail/%22Ban%20Conversion%20Therapy%20D-515.978%22?uri=%2FAMADoc%2Fdirectives.xml-D-515.978.xml

American Psychiatric Association. (2021). LGBTQ youth face mental health challenges: social support and safe spaces make a difference. https://www.psyciatry.org/news-room

American Psychological Association. (2021a). *APA resolution on sexual orientation change efforts.* Retrieved from: https://www.apa.org/about/policy/resolution-sexual-orientation-change-efforts.pdf, 20 April 2023.

American Psychological Association. (2021b). *APA resolution on gender identity change efforts.* Retrieved from: https://www.apa.org/about/policy/resolution-gender-identity-change-efforts.pdf, 20 April 2023.

American Psychological Association. (2021c). *APA guidelines for practice with sexual minority persons.* Retrieved from: https://www.apa.org/about/policy/psychological-sexual-minority-persons.pdf, 20 April 2023.

American Psychological Association. (2015). Guidelines for psychological practice with transgender and gender nonconforming people. *American Psychologist, 70*(9), 832–846.

American Psychological Association. (2009). *Report of the American Psychological Association task force report on appropriate therapeutic responses to sexual orientation.* https://www.apa.org/pi/lgbt/resources/therapeutic-response.pdf

Begelman, D. A. (1975). Ethical and legal issues of behavior modification. In M. Hersen & R. Eisler (Eds.), *Progress in behavior modification* (pp. 159–189). Academic Press.

Bell, A. P., & Weinberg, M. S. (1978). *Homosexualities: A study of diversity among men and women.* Simon and Schuster.

Bieber, I., Dain, H. J., Dince, P. R., Drellich, M. G., Grand, H. G., & Gundlach, R. H. (1962). *Homosexuality: A psychoanalytic study.* Basic Books.

Blosnich, J. R., Henderson, E. R., Coulter, R. W. S., Goldbach, J. T., & Meyer, I. H. (2020). Sexual orientation change efforts, adverse childhood experiences, and suicide ideation and attempt among sexual minority adults, United States, 2016–2018. *American Journal of Public Health, 110*(7), 1024–1030.

Bockting, W. O., Minter, M. H., Swinburne-Romine, R. E., Hamilton, A., & Coleman, E. (2013). Stigma, mental health, and resilience in an online sample of the US transgender population. *American Journal of Public Health, 103*(5), 943–951.

Coleman, E., Bockting, W., Botzer, M., Cohen-Kettenis, P., DeCuypere, G., Feldman, J., Fraser, L., Green, J., Knudson, G., Meyer, W. J., Monstrey, S., Adler, R. K., Brown, G. R., Devor, A. H., Ehrbar, R., Ettner, R., Eyler, E., Garofalo, R., Karasic, D. H., & Zucker, K. (2012). Standards of care for the health of transsexual, transgender, and gender-nonconforming people, version 7. *International Journal of Transgenderism, 13*(4), 165–232.

Crenshaw, K. (1989). Demarginalizing the intersection of race and sex: A Black feminist critique of antidiscrimination doctrine, feminist theory, and antiracist politics. *University of Chicago Legal Forum, 1989*(1), Article 8.
Davison, G. C. (1976). Homosexuality: The ethical challenge. *Journal of Consulting and Clinical Psychology, 44*(2), 157–162.
Davison, G. C. (1982). Politics, ethics, and therapy for homosexuality. *American Behavioral Scientist, 25*(4), 423–434.
Davison, G. C. (1991). Constructionism and morality in therapy for homosexuality. In J. C. Gonsiorek & J. D. Weinrich (Eds.), *Homosexuality: Research implications for public policy* (pp. 137–148). Sage.
Dehlin, J. P., Galliher, R. V., Bradshaw, W. S., Hyde, D. C., & Crowell, K. A. (2015). Sexual orientation change efforts among current or former LDS church members. *Journal of Counseling Psychology, 62*(2), 95–105.
Finn, S. E., & Tonsager, M. E. (2002). How therapeutic assessment became humanistic. *The Humanistic Psychologist, 30*(Spring/Summer), 10–22.
Fish, J. N., & Russell, S. T. (2020). Sexual orientation and gender identity change efforts are unethical and harmful. *American Journal of Public Health, 110*(8), 1113–1114.
Fjelstrom, J. (2013). Sexual orientation change efforts and the search for authenticity. *Journal of Homosexuality, 60*(6), 801–827.
Flentje, A., Heck, N. C., & Cochran, B. N. (2013). Sexual reorientation therapy interventions: Perspectives of ex-ex-gay individuals. *Journal of Gay & Lesbian Mental Health, 17*(3), 256–277.
Gerbut, V., Karabin, T., Lazur, Y., Mendzhul, M., & Vashkovich, V. (2020). Conversion therapy bans in national legislations around the globe. *Georgian Medical News, 308*, 192–198.
Glassgold, J. M. (2022). Research on sexual orientation change efforts: A summary. In D. C. Haldeman (Ed.), *The case against conversion "therapy:" evidence, ethics, and alternatives* (pp. 19–50). APA Books.
Gonsiorek, J. C. (1991). The empirical basis for the demise of the illness model of homosexuality. In J. C. Gonsiorek & J. D. Weinrich (Eds.), *Homosexuality: Research implications for public policy* (pp. 115–136). Sage.
Green, A. E., Price-Feeney, M., Dorison, S. H., & Pick, C. J. (2020). Self-reported conversion efforts and suicidality among US LGBTQ youth and young adults, 2018. *American Journal of Public Health, 110*(8), 1221–1227.
Green, R. (1987). *The sissy boy syndrome*. Yale University Press.
Haldeman, D. C. (2001). Therapeutic antidotes: Helping gay and bisexual men recover from conversion therapies. *Journal of Gay and Lesbian Psychotherapy, 5*(3–4), 117–130.
Haldeman, D. C. (1994). The practice and ethics of sexual orientation conversion therapy. *Journal of Consulting and Clinical Psychology, 62*(2), 221–227.
Martell, C. R., Safren, S. A., & Prince, S. E. (2003). *Cognitive-behavioral therapies with lesbian, gay and bisexual clients*. Guilford Press.
Murphy, T. F. (1992). Redirecting sexual orientation: Techniques and justifications. *Journal of Sex Research, 29*, 501–523.
National Association of Social Workers. (2000). "Reparative" and conversion "therapies" for lesbians and gay men. https://www.socialworkers.org
Nicolosi, J. (1991). *Reparative therapy of male homosexuality*. Jason Aronson.
Olson, K. R., Durwood, L., DeMeules, M., & McLaughlin, K. A. (2016). Mental health of transgender children who are supported in their identities. *Pediatrics, 137*(3), e20153223.
Pachankis, J. A., & Safren, S. A. (Eds.). (2019). *Handbook of evidence-based mental health practice with sexual and gender minorities*. Oxford University Press.
Rostosky, S. S., Riggle, E. D. B., Horne, S. G., & Miller, A. D. (2009). Marriage amendments and psychological distress in lesbian, gay and bisexual (LGB) adults. *Journal of Counseling Psychology, 59*, 56–66.

Ryan, C., Toomey, R. B., Diaz, R. M., & Russell, S. T. (2018). Parent-initiated sexual orientation change efforts with LGBT adolescents: Implications for young adult mental health and adjustment. *Journal of Homosexuality, 67*(2), 159–173.

Shidlo, A., & Schroeder, M. (2002). Changing sexual orientation: A consumer's report. *Professional Psychology: Research and Practice, 33*, 249–259.

Silverstein, C. (1991). Psychological and medical treatments of homosexuality. In J. C. Gonsiorek & J. D. Weinrich (Eds.), *Homosexuality: Research implications for public policy*. Sage.

Singh, A. A., Cokley, R. K., & Gorritz, F. B. (2022). Using the APA guidelines for psychological practice to develop trans-affirming counseling for trans and gender nonconforming clients. In D. C. Haldeman (Ed.), *The case against conversion "therapy": Evidence, ethics, and alternatives*. APA Books.

Socarides, C. W. (1968). *The overt homosexual*. Grune & Stratton.

Spandler, H., & Carr, S. (2022). Lesbian and bisexual women's experiences of aversion therapy in England. *History of the Human Sciences, 35*(3–4), 218–236. https://doi.org/10.1177/09526951211059422

Steensma, T. D., & Cohen-Kettenis, P. T. (2011). Gender transitioning before puberty? *Archives of Sexual Behavior, 40*(4), 649–650.

Turban, J. L., King, D., Reisner, S. L., & Keuroghlian, A. S. (2019). Psychological attempts to change a person's gender identity from transgender to cisgender: Existing prevalence data across US states, 2015. *American Journal of Public Health, 109*(10), 1452–1454.

United Nations Human Rights Council. (2020). *Report on conversion therapy by independent expert on protection against violence and discrimination based on sexual orientation and gender identity*. https://undocs.org/A/HRC/44/53

United Nations Human Rights Council. (2013). *Report of the Special Rapporteur on torture and other cruel, inhuman or degrading treatment or punishment (A/HRC/22/53).*

Verrett, B. (2022). Why is the laying on of hands so significant? *Bible Study Tools*, https://www.biblestudytools.com/bible-study/topical-studies/why-is-the-laying-on-of-hands-so-significant.html#google_vignette

Williams Institute. (2019). *Conversion Therapy and LGBT Youth*. https://williamsinstitute.law.ucla.edu/publications/conversion-therapy-and-lgbt-youth/

World Professional Association for Transgender Health. (2022). *Standards of Care, Version 8*. https://www.wpath.org/publications/soc

Zucker, K. J., Wood, H., Singh, D., & Bradley, S. J. (2012). A developmental, biopsychosocial model for the treatment of children with gender identity disorder. *Journal of Homosexuality, 59*(3), 369–397.

Zucker, K. J., & Bradley, S. J. (1995). *Gender identity disorder and psychosexual problems in children and adolescents*. Guilford Press.

Part II
Developmental and Lifespan Considerations

Chapter 6
Facilitating Identity Development and Affirmation Among LGBTQ+ Clients

Diana J. Cox, Tara R. Sullivan, and Ethan H. Mereish

Highlights

Practicing elements of affirmative psychotherapy for LGBTQ+ clients is not merely a provider preference; rather, pursuing fair and equitable treatment is a foundational part of providing ethical psychotherapeutic care to any client population. This chapter is designed to help clinicians become more comfortable with practicing identity affirmation with LGBTQ+ clients, and this goal is intertwined with the objective of empowering clients to self-affirm, explore, and develop their gender and sexual identities. Identity affirming care is paramount for promoting positive mental health outcomes in LGBTQ+ populations. Clinicians are also bound by an ethical duty to provide affirmative care for LGBTQ+ clients. The overarching goals of this chapter are as follows:

- Review the theory, research, and clinical applications of identity development and affirmation.
- Discuss specific existing interventions and empirical factors that promote LGBTQ+ affirmation and highlight considerations for marginalized subgroups.
- Apply theory by illustrating what affirmation and identity development may look like in a clinical setting through a case study.

D. J. Cox
Department of Psychology, American University, Washington, DC, USA

VA Boston Healthcare System, Boston, MA, USA

Department of Psychiatry, Boston University Chobanian & Avedisian School of Medicine, Boston, MA, USA

T. R. Sullivan · E. H. Mereish (✉)
Lavender Lab, Department of Psychology, University of Maryland, College Park, MD, USA
e-mail: emereish@umd.edu

N. A. Livingston et al. (eds.), *Addressing Minority Stress and Enhancing Resilience with Diverse LGBTQ+ Clients*, CBT: Science Into Practice,
https://doi.org/10.1007/978-3-031-92836-9_6

Positionality

We are a group of psychology researchers, educators, and clinicians at various stages in our careers. We represent a range of sexual and gender identities (queer and bisexual; genderqueer, cisgender woman, cisgender man) and racial/ethnic identities (Black, Multiracial, Biracial, Middle Eastern). Our intention for collaborating on this chapter was to provide theoretical background and clinical guidelines for clinicians who are facilitating identity development and identity affirmation for LGBTQ+ clients. Two authors are trained in several therapeutic modalities, such as Cognitive Behavioral Therapy (CBT), Acceptance and Commitment Therapy (ACT), and Dialectical Behavioral Therapy (DBT). One author is a licensed psychologist and has extensive experience working with racially and ethnically diverse LGBTQ+ individuals and couples with mood and anxiety disorders, substance use, and stress. Another author will be working towards licensure after completion of her doctoral degree and has experience working with LGBTQ+ individuals in medical settings. All authors have expertise in conducting research that investigates the health outcomes of LGBTQ+ populations. We collectively share a professional and personal commitment to support the LGBTQ+ community through clinical practice, research, and advocacy.

Influential Theories of Sexual Identity Development

During the late twentieth century, researchers created stage theories to operationalize a universal progression of sexual identity development. Vivienne Cass proposed a stage model of development, based on the idea that identity formation occurs through the interactions between a sexual minority individual and their environment in six discrete *stages*: confusion, comparison, tolerance, acceptance, pride, and synthesis (Cass, 1979). Addressing the limitations of Cass's model, McCarn and Fassinger (1996) developed a model of sexual identity development focused on *phases,* which better demonstrated the lifelong continuity of development, illustrated a flexible and dynamic understanding of developmental pathways, and accounted for the fact that development can be nonlinear or circular. They differentiated between the development of individual sexual identity and group membership identity (processes are explained in Table 6.1).

Scholars recommend that the concepts outlined in these stage/phase models can help clinicians generate questions to guide conversations with clients and support their identity development (Goodrich & Brammer, 2021; Kenneady & Oswalt, 2014). For example, within the *exploration phase* of McCarn and Fassinger's model, the clinician can help the client explore what it would mean to them to be a sexual minority and how this may impact their lives. Identity exploration with the client may also involve helping them to connect with LGBTQ+ resources, peers, and organizations where they can explore their identity outside of therapy. It is not recommended to present the model information in a linear format, so as to not make clients feel pressured to conform to the linearity of the models (Goodrich & Brammer, 2021). Additional identity development facilitation examples are provided in Table 6.1.

Table 6.1 Sample questions to facilitate sexual and gender identity development*

McCarn & Fassinger's (1996) Stages of Individual Sexual Identity Development	McCarn & Fassinger's (1996) Stages of Group Sexual Identity Development	Bockting & Coleman's (2007) Stages of Gender Identity Development	Example Questions for Individual/Group Sexual/Gender Identity Development	Skills/Interventions that Clinician can use for Individual/Group Sexual/Gender Identity Development
Awareness (i.e., recognition of sexual attractions)	**Awareness** (i.e. recognition that different sexual orientations exist, as well as recognition of heterosexism)	**Pre-Coming Out** (i.e., awareness of gender incongruence)	-When did you first become aware of your sexual attractions/gender identity? -What is it like for you to be aware of your sexuality/gender now? -What feelings and thoughts do you have about your sexual orientation/gender? -What does it mean to you to be a part of the LGBTQ+ community? -In what ways do you think LGBTQ+ people are treated differently in your community/society? -Have others assumed you are heterosexual and/or cisgender? -If so, how has that influenced you?	-Engage client in affective exploration (e.g., feelings wheel) to identify emotions related to client's awareness of sexuality/gender -Validate client's feelings, experiences, and thoughts through verbal and nonverbal behavior (e.g., open body language, using reflective listening) -Provide psychoeducation on common LGBTQ+ terms and identity processes -Address potential internalized stigma and/or negative attitude towards LGBTQ+ identity and communities through empathic confrontation with client
		Coming Out (i.e., disclosure of gender identity to self and others)	-How do you define your sexuality/gender identity? -What would it mean to you if you told others about your sexuality/gender identity? -Have you told anyone about your sexual/gender identities before? How did the conversation(s) go?	-Express appreciation and positive regard for client when they disclose their identity -Role play coming out with client so they can practice telling others about their identity -Provide psychoeducation on considerations for coming out to others (e.g., safety) -Assess both affirming and safe spaces and individuals -Identify skills to help clients cope with experiences of stigma and discrimination (e.g., thought challenging, assertiveness training, emotion regulation strategies)

(continued)

Table 6.1 (continued)

McCarn & Fassinger's (1996) Stages of Individual Sexual Identity Development	McCarn & Fassinger's (1996) Stages of Group Sexual Identity Development	Bockting & Coleman's (2007) Stages of Gender Identity Development	Example Questions for Individual/Group Sexual/Gender Identity Development	Skills/Interventions that Clinician can use for Individual/Group Sexual/Gender Identity Development
Exploration (i.e., active examination of sexual identity)	**Exploration** (i.e., pursuit of experiential knowledge of sexual minority people and communities)	**Exploration** (i.e., learning more about gender identity and experimentation with gender expression)	-How would your life be different and/or the same if you were LGBTQ+ [use term that client uses]? -What would you like to learn about your sexuality/gender and what it means to you? -What are your attitudes towards other LGBTQ+ people? -What would it mean to you if you identified as part of a greater LGBTQ+ community? -In which ways would you like to explore, experiment with, or express your sexuality/gender?	-Provide resources for client to learn more about their identity (e.g., affirmative books, community organizations, popular media, support groups) -Help client connect with other LGBTQ+ individuals either online or in-person -Reflective listening to client experiences related to identity exploration -Use motivational interviewing to explore any ambivalence a client might have about exploring their identity -Provide psychoeducation on positives and strengths of LGBTQ+ identity and communities (e.g., queer and transgender joy) -Provide psychoeducation on experiences of minority stress
Deepening/ Commitment (i.e., selection of a sexual identity label)	**Deepening/ Commitment** (i.e., creation of personal relationships with other sexual minority people)	**Intimacy** (i.e., development of emotional connections and sense of belongingness)	-What sexual identity label do you think fits your own understanding of your sexuality? -What does this identity mean to you? -What is important for you about this identity? -What do you think you need to feel belonging with other [insert gender label the client is using; e.g., nonbinary] and other gender diverse people and/or communities? -What would it mean to you to be accepted by other [insert gender label] and gender diverse people? -How connected are you to other LGBTQ+ people or communities? -What is it about your connections with other LGBTQ+ people that you find meaningful?	-Engage in reflections about LGBTQ+ peers, role models, and greater community -Explore reactions to different LGBTQ+ relationships and connections client has -Collaborate with client to help them find LGBTQ+ connections and community -Define challenges and strengths of identity development -Use problem-solving skills to navigate obstacles that impede identity development (e.g., contextual factors)

Internalization/ Synthesis (i.e., self-acceptance of sexual minority identity)	**Internalization/ Synthesis** (i.e., clear identification of sexual minority group membership and how it fits into self-concept)	**Identity Integration** (i.e., self-acceptance of new gender identity)	-How have you been able to accept your sexuality/gender? -How does being a [insert identity label that client uses; e.g., bisexual, agender] person influence who you are? -What about being [insert identity label] makes you proud? What brings you joy about being [insert identity label]? -What does it mean to you to be a part of the LGBTQ+ community? How does being a part of the LGBTQ+ community influence how you see yourself?	-Use values clarification exercise where client connects important values to their LGBTQ+ identity and how it connects to their other identities (e.g., race/ethnicity) -Engage client in reflection on identity development journey (e.g., positives and negatives) -Explore emotions related to identity development -Use mindfulness exercises to help client imagine their future identity development

*The information presented in this table are suggestions for questions and interventions that clinicians can use in their work with LGBTQ+ clients. We do not recommend asking all of these questions or using every skill in a session, as intensely focusing on identity in this manner can be harmful (e.g., microaggressive) to the client. We encourage the clinician to reflect upon the therapeutic usefulness of employing any of these questions or skills, and how they may harm or benefit the client. As such, we recommend considering asking one of these questions or using an intervention only when clinically relevant to each client. Additionally, while these questions and interventions focus on sexual and gender identity, it is important for clinicians to consider how they work in tandem with other identities (e.g., racial and ethnic identity) and related developmental processes

These sexual identity development models were primarily developed with a limited focus on lesbian and gay individuals, which limits their generalizability to individuals who are attracted to more than one gender (Kenneady & Oswalt, 2014). These models often do not acknowledge the interconnectedness of sexual and gender identity development processes (Kenneady & Oswalt, 2014). Additionally, these developmental models do not consider how other social identities, such as race/ethnicity, influence sexual identity development.

Influential Theories of Gender Identity Development

Several models have been created to understand gender identity development among transgender and gender diverse (TGD) individuals. Bockting and Coleman (2007) proposed that transgender identity development occurs over five different stages, which TGD individuals may cycle through in any order. These stages are detailed in Table 6.1. A strength of this model is its recognition that biopsychosocial factors influence both identity development and the achievement of developmental tasks.

Several critiques of other gender identity stage models are worth noting. A general limitation is the fact that many of these models were adapted from sexual identity development theories for gay or lesbian individuals (Katz-Wise et al., 2017). While sexual and gender identity development processes are interrelated, it is important not to conflate the two; both processes have unique effects on an individual. Some models specifically assume that all TGD individuals wish to seek medical gender affirmation, which is not the experience of all TGD people (Fiani & Han, 2018). Additionally, these models are often more applicable for binary transgender identity formation than for nonbinary identity formation (Katz-Wise et al., 2017). Addressing these limitations, Matsuno and Budge (2017) summarize recent research on nonbinary identity development models, which reject the linearity and rigidity of prior gender identity development models and encourage an expansive view of gender beyond binary conceptualizations. Nonbinary gender identity development can include exploration and self-definition of one's nonbinary identity, navigation of cissexism-related stressors, continual identity affirmation, and acceptance of the self (Matsuno & Budge, 2017).

Milestone Approaches to Sexual and Gender Identity Development

Moving away from the limitations of stage models, identity development has been reconceptualized through a focus on *milestones* that LGBTQ+ individuals experience as they form their identities (Hall et al., 2021). Milestones are important events within an individual's lifespan that represent a significant point of development, achievement, or life change (Hall et al., 2021). In contrast to other models, milestone events are more discrete experiences rather than continuous periods of time. Some milestones, such as disclosure, are not one-time events, but rather, a series of realizations and disclosures across the lifespan (Martos et al., 2015).

Several important sexual orientation identity development milestones have been documented in a recent systematic review of the literature (Hall et al., 2021). Among sexual minority individuals, the most common milestones are: first awareness of attractions, sexual minority self-identification, engagement in sexual activity, and coming out. Notably, the researchers suggested that for some individuals, milestones can happen consecutively or concurrently (e.g., the awareness of attraction milestone can occur simultaneously with first sexual activity). Milestones may also be understood as a cascade in which early experiences of milestones influence future identity development experiences across the lifespan (e.g., awareness of sexual attraction can become a foundational milestone that may then lead to engaging in sexual behavior, or vice versa). Moreover, there is some evidence indicating that milestone timing varies among different sexual minority groups (Hall et al., 2021; Martos et al., 2015). Bisexual individuals tend to reach milestones later than gay and lesbian individuals (Hall et al., 2021; Martos et al., 2015). For more information about these group differences, we recommend reviewing the articles published by Hall et al. (2021) and Martos et al. (2015).

Milestones provide a more nuanced understanding of identity development because they do not suggest a singular pathway of identity development. While there are often patterns in the timing and sequence of certain milestones, they can occur at different points depending on the individual (e.g., coming out as a sexual minority can occur before or after engagement in sexual behavior). Alternatively, some individuals may not experience certain milestones within their lifetime, but this does not make their identity development any less legitimate or dynamic (e.g., a pansexual person does not need to have sexual or romantic experiences with people of varying genders to know they are pansexual). Milestones also consider the historical contexts that influence LGBTQ+ people across birth cohorts and their developmental trajectories (Bishop et al., 2020). Milestones may also account for differences in development for people with intersectional identities, such as LGBTQ+ people of color (Hall et al., 2021). Experiences of minority stress can also delay reaching certain milestones and may limit the opportunity an individual has to explore their identity in affirming environments (Martos et al., 2015).

There are several developmental milestones that exist for TGD people. One of the first milestones a TGD person may experience is gender awareness and gender incongruence (i.e., the feeling that one's sex assigned at birth does not match how they view themselves or feel in their body; Doyle, 2022). Some TGD individuals also experience gender dysphoria, or the distress caused by experiencing gender incongruence. While gender dysphoria is an experience that many TGD individuals face, we caution clinicians not to assume that gender dysphoria is a developmental milestone for all TGD people. Doing so may insinuate that pathology is intrinsic to gender identity development, which is an inaccurate and harmful assumption. Self-identification of being TGD and coming out as TGD are other important milestones during gender identity development. TGD individuals sometimes experience dual coming out milestones related to their gender and sexual identities, though not all TGD individuals identify as sexual minorities. These coming out milestones can occur one before the other (i.e., coming out as LGBQ+ before TGD, or vice versa) or simultaneously.

Gender affirmation is an important TGD developmental process that can lead to gender identity milestones. Gender affirmation refers to the process by which TGD people experience validation of their gender through psychological, social, medical, or legal means (Matsuno & Israel, 2018). Some TGD individuals may elect for gender affirming care (e.g., hormone therapy, gender-affirming surgeries) depending on age, gender identity, insurance coverage, and availability of care (Lane et al., 2018). It is important to note group differences of gender affirmation. A survey of TGD adults indicated that nonbinary individuals reported taking fewer gender-affirming steps (e.g., undergoing medical, social, legal, or psychological gender affirmation changes) as compared to their binary transgender peers (Breslow et al., 2021). Nonbinary people also tend to report later ages for all gender identity milestones compared to individuals with binary transgender identities (Tatum et al., 2020). This may be due to the lack of resources available regarding nonbinary identity awareness, gender norms, and transition processes as compared to binary transgender identities (Fiani & Han, 2018). Another explanation may be that nonbinary individuals exist on a spectrum that is inherently more fluid in nature and do not conform to the same milestones as those who identify with the gender binary.

While the findings from these systematic reviews of LGBTQ+ milestones can help inform clinicians of common patterns in gender and sexual identity development, it is important for clinicians to take an individualized approach with clients. Understanding a client's milestones, including progression, affirmation, or disruptions, will enable clinicians to better understand the context of the client's identity development. Clinicians should first become familiar with common milestones of LGBTQ+ identity development by reviewing the milestones mentioned in the Hall et al. (2021) and Tatum et al. (2020) articles. When applying the milestone approach during therapeutic sessions, clinicians may consider requesting a client's permission to ask them questions about their identities. Clinicians should provide a rationale for why they would like to know this information about the client and how it may benefit the therapeutic work, particularly as it relates to the presenting concerns. The therapist may say something like, "You've mentioned that you want to explore your gender identity in therapy. Would it be alright if I asked you some questions to get a better sense of what this means to you and how we can explore this together?" When permission is granted, clinicians may invite clients to discuss the developmental milestones that they have reached, how they have reached them, and the importance and meaning they associate to them, if any. However, it is important to note that examining these milestones is not relevant for all LGBTQ+ clients' presenting concerns; thus, clinicians should consider them for conceptualizing their client's concerns when appropriate.

Sexual and Gender Identity Development Alongside Racial/Ethnic Identity Development

LGBTQ+ Black, Indigenous, and People of Color (QTBIPOC) experience converging oppressive systems of structural racism, heterosexism, and cissexism (Cerezo et al., 2020), which can impact identity development and inflict stress and harm. These intersectional stressors are associated with negative mental health outcomes for QTBIPOC populations (Mereish et al., 2022). Identity formation among QTBIPOC is shaped by the negotiation of insider/outsider status in different social settings (e.g., family, school, communities; Cerezo et al., 2020). Familial and cultural expectations strongly influence identity expressions, decisions to come out, and pressures to adhere to gender norms within one's racial/ethnic community of origin (Cerezo et al., 2020). In one study, heterosexism and cissexism in QTBIPOC participants' racial/ethnic communities meant that openly living as LGBTQ+ could lead to exclusion from immediate and extended family members, as well as one's broader racial/ethnic community (Cerezo et al., 2020).

Existing at the intersections of minoritized racial/ethnic and sexual and/or gender identities may lead to the development of conflicts in allegiances, theorized by Morales as a relevant factor within QTBIPOC identity development (Morales, 1989). Morales (1989) proposed that QTBIPOC individuals can experience anxiety in relation to betraying their sexual identity, their gender identity, or their racial/ethnic identity, when one is forced to prioritize one aspect of their identity over another. Conflicts in allegiances can arise in situations where the individual faces competing forces that undermine integration of racial/ethnic and sexual and/or gender identities. Conflicts in allegiances can be resolved through identity integration, a process that involves developing a positive self-concept as an act of resilience and empowerment. In this regard, resilience can be characterized as the acknowledgement of social pressure to conform and active resistance to marginalization by embracing QTBIPOC identity and community (Cerezo et al., 2020). Clinicians working with QTBIPOC clients should aim to assess the salience of their clients' intersecting identities (e.g., "What does it mean to you to be Black, queer, and transgender?") and promote their QTBIPOC clients' journeys of identity integration.

Identity Affirmation

Identity affirmation refers to how an individual develops positive feelings, self-acceptance, and a sense of belongingness for their ingroups (Busby et al., 2020). Feelings of pride and connectedness to one's LGBTQ+ identity may help buffer against some of the negative effects of victimization and other types of bias-related social threats (Busby et al., 2020; Stock et al., 2018). Furthermore, strong and positive connections to others with shared or similar identities may help individuals bolster their sense of belonging to their group and reframe discriminatory events (i.e., minority stressors) as a shared experience instead of a personal threat (Stock et al., 2018). Identity affirmation for LGBTQ+ individuals is essential for promoting positive health outcomes and imperative for enhancing resilience and conceptualizing LGBTQ+ identity concerns from a strengths-based perspective. For this reason, it is important for the clinician to model and practice identity affirmation with LGBTQ+ clients, so that they can learn to be identity affirming outside of therapy. Identity affirmation may look different across identity development, particularly when considering what milestones a client has or has not reached, and what the client's goals are in terms of understanding their identity.

Interventions and Empirical Factors that Promote Identity Development and Affirmation

Interventions

Researchers and clinicians have incorporated identity affirmation into interventions for LGBTQ+ individuals, though few interventions exist that solely focus on identity affirmation as the main goal of treatment. The majority of these interventions are based on cognitive-behavioral therapy (CBT), which were adapted to address how experiences of minority stress impact mental health and used to help LGBTQ+ individuals cope with these stressors (Austin et al., 2017; Craig & Austin, 2016; Pachankis et al., 2015). Dialectical-behavior therapy protocols have also been adapted for affirmation by explaining how to use certain behavioral and emotional regulation strategies for minority stressors (Skerven et al., 2019).

Most of these interventions have been designed for LGBTQ+ adults (Austin et al., 2017; Pachankis et al., 2015, 2020), though there are some interventions that are specifically intended for LGBTQ+ youth (Craig, 2012, 2013; Craig & Austin, 2016; Lucassen et al., 2015). A limited number of interventions have also addressed promoting affirmation for LGBTQ+ individuals while considering other intersectional identities, such as individuals with minoritized racial/ethnic identities or individuals living with HIV (Craig, 2012; Flentje, 2020). Brief LGBTQ+ identity affirmation interventions (e.g., 20 min per day for 3 days) often involve the use of expressive writing activities to engage LGBTQ+ individuals in reflections on the strengths of their identity (Pachankis et al., 2020). Note, expressive writing in this context is centered on the positives of being LGBTQ+, rather than stress-related narratives.

Themes of Affirmative Practice

Identity affirmation-focused clinical treatments and interventions have several common themes that are worth noting for clinical practice. Many of these interventions include modules centered on validating LGBTQ+ identity (Austin et al., 2017;

Craig & Austin, 2016; Pachankis et al., 2015). Validation can take many different forms and can be tailored to specific LGBTQ+ identity development milestones (see Table 6.1 for specific interventions). Validation can be an especially important skill to use with clients who are questioning or becoming aware of their LGBTQ+ identity. Expressing empathy and using reflective listening are techniques that the clinician can use to help the client become more accepting of their identity development experiences (e.g., "It sounds like your experiences of being queer and the messages you've received from others about queerness are sometimes conflicting. It makes sense why you might feel confused right now, and it's okay that you feel that way."). The clinician sharing their knowledge about common LGBTQ+ identity development milestones can also help normalize the process of LGBTQ+ identity development.

Providing psychoeducation is another meaningful identity affirmation technique for LGBTQ+ clients. Specifically, psychoeducation can create an opportunity for clients to learn healthy identity development processes and recognize that LGBTQ+ identity is not pathological. Additionally, providing relevant information for LGBTQ+ identity development can be instrumental for clients to explore what their identity-related experiences mean to them. Interventions, like the ESTEEM protocol (Pachankis et al., 2015), use psychoeducation to explain the effects of minority stress on overall health and wellbeing. The ESTEEM intervention specifically teaches LGBTQ+ adult clients about how experiences of stigma and discrimination can impact their thoughts, feelings, and behaviors. Psychoeducation can also include examining different types of minority stressors (e.g., heterosexism, cissexism, binegativity) at the individual (e.g., harassment), cultural (e.g., conflicts in allegiances), and institutional (e.g., policies banning gender-affirming care) levels. AFFIRM (Craig & Austin, 2016) and Rainbow SPARX (Lucassen et al., 2015) are other similar psychoeducation focused interventions that were designed for LGBTQ+ adolescents. Psychoeducation may also involve helping clients find resources that help them inform their decisions around developmental milestones (e.g., a client who is deciding on how to come out and disclose their identity to others may benefit from comprehensive and affirming resources such as the Trevor Project's "The Coming Out Handbook"; https://www.thetrevorproject.org/resources/guide/the-coming-out-handbook/). See Table 6.1 for more examples of psychoeducation for clients with different identity development needs.

Identifying skills is another common component of identity-affirming interventions. Identity affirmation underlies teaching coping skills by empowering the client to realize that being LGBTQ+ is not the problem (i.e., externalization of discrimination) and that they have a choice in how they can respond to stigma. The motivation behind identifying and using certain behavioral skills depends upon the milestones that a client has reached and what they would stand to gain from learning and applying these skills. The therapist should take a personalized approach with a client and consider which behavioral skills are most appropriate. For clients who are approaching milestones of coming out to others, the use of behavioral exercises, such as role plays, can help them practice interpersonal effectiveness in what they would like to communicate. Part of identity affirmation work with clients may also involve helping clients identify effective coping methods for encountering minority stressors, especially if they are related to developmental milestones. The ESTEEM protocol developed modules that help clients address experiences of minority stress using common CBT skills, like cognitive restructuring and mindfulness (Pachankis et al., 2015). Interventions like AFFIRM, ASSET, and Rainbow Sparx have also been designed to help LGBTQ+ youth to recognize unhelpful and shaming thinking patterns, use problem-solving skills, engage in mindfulness, and practice effective interpersonal skills related to their identity (Craig, 2013; Craig & Austin, 2016; Lucassen et al., 2015). There are also ESTEEM modules that help LGBTQ+ clients develop assertiveness skills and responses to discrimination in non-life-threatening social situations, which can help reduce the negative effects of stigma and facilitate self-efficacy and autonomy (Pachankis et al., 2015). Moving beyond coping, resistance skills and practices (e.g., advocacy) are also important to consider when navigating oppression and can be self-affirming practices.

Another common practice in affirming treatment involves helping clients elicit their own affirmation through identity affirming activities in their lives (Austin et al., 2017; Craig, 2012; Craig & Austin, 2016; Li et al., 2023). This can be especially useful for clients who are looking to explore their LGBTQ+ identity. The therapist and client may discuss ways in which they wish to learn about their LGBTQ+ identity and what they hope to gain through identity exploration. This could involve collaboratively creating a list of identity affirming activities to try within and outside of therapy (e.g., trying gender affirming pronouns, engaging with LGBTQ+ media content, searching for in-person and online LGBTQ+ communities). Encouraging clients to behaviorally explore their identities may help facilitate affirmation through helping them experience a sense of pride and connectedness with their identities. The therapist can also draw upon creative interventions, like Pachankis and colleagues' (2020) writing task, and assign the client homework to engage in reflective writing about themselves and how they feel about their identities when they engage in identity-affirming activities. This type of reflection is important for LGBTQ+ clients to draw connections between their own identity-affirmation efforts and its respective positive mental health benefits. Helping clients generate their own identity affirmation is broadly useful for LGBTQ+ clients at all milestones, but this may be especially important for those who have limited opportunities to be affirmed by their external environments.

Additional Affirmation Considerations for Minoritized Subgroups of LGBTQ+ People

Despite broad affirmation strategies for LGBTQ+ clients, LGBTQ+ experiences are not homogeneous; specifically, clinicians must contextualize their clients' experiences within intersecting systems of oppression and explore special considerations for the affirmation of TGD, bisexual+, and QTBIPOC clients.

Affirmation Considerations for Transgender and Gender Diverse Clients

While working with TGD clients, clinicians should recognize the overall importance of gender affirmative processes in impacting TGD clients' psychosocial well-being. In recent years, research within TGD communities has recognized the powerful psychosocial benefits that can arise from the experiences of being affirmed and validated in one's gender–known as gender euphoria (Tebbe & Budge, 2022). Notably, gender euphoria is not the absence of gender dysphoria; rather, it refers to feelings of joy, rightness, and authenticity for TGD individuals following experiences of gender affirmation (Austin et al., 2022). While further operationalization of gender euphoria is needed, preliminary evidence suggests that this concept is linked to subjective well-being in TGD communities (Bradford et al., 2021).

Theories of gender affirmation and gender euphoria can help clinicians affirm their TGD clients. Similar to general affirmation approaches for LGBTQ+ clients, clinicians can work to dismantle their own biases about gender diversity (Matsuno & Israel, 2018; Matsuno, 2019). Part of this unlearning process can also include therapists learning how to correctly inquire about client pronouns and how to discuss gender identity appropriately with clients (Budge et al., 2020; Matsuno & Israel, 2018; Matsuno, 2019). These TGD affirmative therapeutic elements, when combined with psychoeducation on the impact of cissexism-based stressors, have demonstrated initial efficacy in reducing distress, internalized cissexism, and non-affirmation for TGD clients in a randomized controlled pilot trial (Budge et al., 2020; Tebbe & Budge, 2022).

Several frameworks exist to help clinicians in affirming care with TGD clients. The Transgender Resilience Intervention Model provides a synthesized, multi-level framework for promoting transgender identity affirmation and resilience (Matsuno & Israel, 2018). Individual-level interventions can take the form of helping clients build hope, pride, self-acceptance, and self-definition of their TGD identities (Matsuno & Israel, 2018). Group-level interventions, which help build clients' social support networks and overall connectedness to the TGD community, include encouraging clients to find and serve as positive TGD role models, and can include group and family therapy opportunities (Matsuno & Israel, 2018). Finally, at the structural and community levels, clinicians can engage in advocacy to dismantle cissexist policies and institutions (e.g., advocate for workplace protections, gender-neutral bathrooms, and reduced barriers to gender affirming care; Matsuno & Israel, 2018).

Clinicians can also incorporate principles from the Gender Affirmative Lifespan Approach (GALA) into their clinical care with TGD clients. GALA is a developmentally tailored psychotherapeutic framework that provides guidance for affirming TGD clients (Spencer et al., 2021). Components of GALA include: (1) working with the client to build their gender literacy (e.g., supporting the client in defining their gender identity and their experiences of gender identity development in their respective social contexts), (2) helping the client develop resiliency against experiences of stigma (e.g., exploring coping mechanisms against cissexist minority stressors), (3) moving beyond binary conceptualizations of gender (e.g., affirming and validating all forms of gender expressions and gender identities), (4) discussing pleasure-oriented positive sexuality in therapy to disrupt cisnormative ideas about sexual health and promote TGD body autonomy (e.g., providing the client with psychoeducation on safe sexual health practices for TGD individuals), and (5) facilitating connections for the client to access gender affirming medical care (e.g. providing referrals for gender affirming surgery; Spencer et al., 2021). Though empirical validation is needed to understand the clinical efficacy of the GALA model (Spencer et al., 2021), the framework provides a grounded starting point for affirming care with TGD clients.

Despite being unified under the 'TGD' umbrella, it is important for clinicians to recognize that the experiences of binary transgender (e.g., transgender men and transgender women) and nonbinary transgender (e.g., nonbinary and genderqueer) individuals can differ in identity development, gender affirmation, and well-being. Ideas of gender affirmation that are rooted only in binary ideas of gender (e.g., transitioning from man to woman or vice versa) can lead to the perpetuation of transnormativity–a societal overemphasis on the experiences of binary transgender individuals, leaving the experiences of nonbinary and gender diverse individuals as invisible (Tatum et al., 2020). Thus, clinicians must recognize and work to dismantle the insidious ways in which transnormativity influences their interactions with gender diverse clients. Moreover, throughout the therapeutic relationship building process, clinicians should allow ample space for TGD clients to self-define their gender identity labels and explore what these labels mean to the client personally and how they may shift over time (Matsuno & Budge, 2017). If gender affirmation and transition are important therapeutic goals for a TGD client, clinicians should discuss with the client their expectations and desired outcomes for their affirmation journey (Matsuno & Budge, 2017; Matsuno, 2019). For example, the clinician should not automatically assume that a TGD client would feel most affirmed with medical gender affirmation processes.

Affirmation Considerations for Bi+ Clients

Bisexual+ (bi+) clients–those who experience emotional, romantic, and/or sexual attractions to more than one gender (e.g., bisexual, pansexual, queer)–experience unique health disparities (Feinstein & Dyar, 2017) in comparison to their monosexual counterparts (e.g., heterosexual, lesbian, and gay individuals), which necessitates affirmation strategies which recognize these differences. Such disparities are theorized to be a result of a unique form of stigma impacting those who identify under the bi+ umbrella (Brewster & Moradi, 2010). This stigma is categorized under three domains: (1) sexual orientation instability, known as viewing bi+ identities as transient and unstable sexual identities, (2) sexual irresponsibility, defined as viewing bi+ people as hypersexual and unfaithful partners, and (3) interpersonal hostility, described as the social alienation and dislike that bi+ people experience (Brewster & Moradi, 2010). As a result of these multiple stigma domains, bi+ individuals are vulnerable to experiences of stigma and discrimination from both within, and outside, of the LGBTQ+ community. Bi+ individuals can internalize stigmatizing messaging they receive from the external world, known as internalized binegativity (Israel et al., 2019). Internalized binegativity involves a process of adopting both heterosexist and monosexist beliefs, which can insidiously impact the identity development and affirmation of bi+ people (Israel et al., 2019).

One intervention aimed at reducing such internalized binegativity was adapted from the Releasing Internalized Stigma for Empowerment intervention model (Lin et al., 2019). This online intervention consists of four modules tailored for bi+ populations: (1) combatting stereotypes surrounding bi+ identities, (2) identification and rejection of binegative messaging, (3) reinforcement of rejection of binegative messaging, and (4) enhancing self-affirmation of bi+ identities (Israel et al., 2019). Initial results suggested that this intervention was efficacious in reducing internalized binegativity. While further research is needed to support the use of this intervention in a clinical context, this framework could serve as a starting point for clinicians to inform their work to reduce clients' internalized binegativity (Israel et al., 2019). Clinicians can work with their clients to create a therapeutic plan which involves an affirmation progression: moving from the client's recognition and rejection of binegative messaging, to individual reflection and affirmation of positive dimensions of bi+ identity. These positive dimensions can include: freedom to live and love authentically and honestly, heightened self-awareness, freedom from societal constraints and labels, and community belonging (Rostosky et al., 2010).

Research is also beginning to recognize the powerful, affirmative impacts of bi+ positive-identity related experiences and bi+ visibility. Bipositive events–experiences of positivity related to one's bi+ identity (Flanders et al., 2017)–have been linked to increases in identity strength and affirmation, and decreases in depression and anxiety symptoms, in a sample of solely bisexual cisgender women (Dyar & London, 2018). Clinicians can utilize bipositive events as a source of resilience and identity affirmation for their bi+ clients, which can include thinking of the benefits and unique perspectives that bi+ identity can bring to a client's life (Dyar & London, 2018; Flanders et al., 2017). Additionally, clinicians can facilitate interpersonal bipositive events by allowing their client's identity to be seen and validated in the therapeutic setting.

Affirmation Considerations for QTBIPOC Clients

Promoting identity integration, alongside identity affirmation, can be particularly beneficial for QTBIPOC clients. Throughout the intake and relationship building process, clinicians can utilize scales such as the Queer People of Color Identity Affirmation Scale to assess the integration of a client's QTBIPOC identities and identity-based growth and resilience (Ghabrial & Andersen, 2021). Clinicians can also rely on theoretical frameworks, such as the Racial Queer Identity Framework (Adames & Chavez-Dueñas, 2021), to better understand how their client conceptualizes their racial/ethnic identity in relation to their queer identity. Within this framework, Adames and Chavez-Dueñas (2021) propose that interpersonal and systemic messaging surrounding one's racial/ethnic and queer identities can contribute to the development of racial-queer schemas, ranging from an advanced integration of one's identities as a queer person of color, to a non-advanced denial of both one's racial and queer identities. In working with QTBIPOC clients, clinicians should seek to identify their client's schemas surrounding their racial/ethnic and queer identities and should tailor affirmation approaches accordingly.

Unfortunately, few empirically validated interventions exist that have been specifically designed to promote the identity affirmation of QTBIPOC clients. Despite this dearth of research, several factors are associated with QTBIPOC affirmation and community resilience at large. For example, critical social justice advocacy (engaging in efforts to advance social justice) and community power building (building networks of activism within one's community) are additional methods through which QTBIPOC clients can be encouraged to build their identity affirmation and connectedness to one's community (Hudson & Romanelli, 2020). To this end, clinicians can share resources for engagement in QTBIPOC organizations, and they can encourage QTBIPOC clients to connect to their community through finding positive role models. QTBIPOC clients can also be encouraged to connect in intersectional ways with their ancestral histories and practices of their racial/ethnic communities (Adames et al., 2021). This can take the form of encouraging clients to explore their families' intergenerational memories, discussing visiting sites with ancestral and cultural significance, or encouraging learning about how sexual orientation and gender identity have been expressed in one's racial/ethnic community across history. Ultimately, further research is needed to establish psychotherapeutic frameworks that center the affirmation and resilience of QTBIPOC communities (Table 6.2).

Table 6.2 National organizations and resources for QTBIPOC

The National Queer And Trans Therapists Of Color Network (nqttcn.com)	**Trans People of Color Coalition** (transpocc.org)
Trans Women of Color Collective (twocc.org)	**Rest For Resistance By QTPOC Mental Health** (restforresistance.com)
Trans Latina Coalition (translatinacoalition.org)	**Familia: Trans Queer Liberation Movement** (familiatqlm.org)
Black Trans Advocacy Coalition (blacktrans.org)	**Center for Black Equity - Black Prides** (centerforblackequity.org/black-lgbtq-prides)
The Rooted Collective (bemorerooted.org)	**National Queer Asian Pacific Islander Alliance** (nqapia.org)

Case Study

The following case study was developed to integrate theory, research, and clinical practice, by illustrating clinical recommendations to facilitate identity development and affirmation for QTBIPOC clients. Jordan is a 19-year-old, Biracial, Jamaican, and White North American queer transgender man, who uses he/him pronouns. His presenting concerns are related to his experiences of loneliness and isolation on his college campus, specifically as they relate to his LGBTQ+ identities. Jordan reported being initially excited to move away from his hometown, where he experienced heterosexist and cissexist bullying, to an urban university where he thought he would have more opportunities to meet other LGBTQ+ peers. However, he has experienced difficulty finding LGBTQ+ community because of his university's social climate, and there are not many LGBTQ+ or BIPOC spaces on campus. Given that he did not have LGBTQ+ connections when he was at home, and thought his social life would improve at college, he has been feeling very depressed about his current circumstances. Additionally, Jordan has experienced racist and cissexist incidents at school that cause him to feel even more lonely and unsupported by his environment. His family is outwardly accepting of his sexual and gender identities, but they avoid talking about his identities and struggle to affirm him. Jordan is questioning his sexuality because of recent sexual encounters. For this case, the therapist, Evan, is a 37-year-old White North American, gay, cisgender man, who uses he/him pronouns.

Clinician Considerations Prior to Treatment

Before meeting with Jordan, there are several steps the therapist takes to begin affirmative care from the outset. Consistent with the APA's guidelines of affirmative care and practices of cultural competence and humility, Evan regularly reflects on his own identities and privileges, reads scholarly articles about White privilege, and journals about his own biases and growth edges as a therapist. He is part of consultation groups, seeks clinical supervision with other providers, and is a member of professional organizations that offer resources and continuing education for clinicians who work with LGBTQ+ clients.

Clinician Approach to Identity Affirmation

Clinicians who have more independence in their practice are encouraged to create affirming spaces for clients (e.g., eliminating heterosexist and cissexist language from paperwork, decorating office spaces with LGBTQ+ artwork). For clinicians who have less autonomy to change their work environments, we propose several suggestions. We recommend that the clinician advocate for organizational changes, so that LGBTQ+ clients can feel more comfortable in the therapy space. This could entail creating more culturally informed paperwork or leading organization-wide trainings to increase LGBTQ+ cultural humility. If the clinician is knowledgeable about workplace barriers for LGBTQ+ clients, they should inform the clients of such barriers (e.g., giving advance notice that the therapy office has no gender neutral bathrooms). Additionally, if it feels authentic to the individual, the clinician may consider physically portraying their affirmation of LGBTQ+ identity (e.g., hanging LGBTQ+ affirming flags in the office, wearing a pin on their clothing to designate LGBTQ+ community affiliation).

Identity Affirmation at the Beginning of Treatment

Identity affirmation is a crucial process for affirming the client, alleviating a client's mental health concerns, and building and strengthening the therapeutic relationship. Within the first few sessions and/or as part of the intake session, the clinician is encouraged to call awareness to their and the client's social identities and related socialization experiences. Raising this topic acknowledges the existence of the client's identities and can also signal that therapy is a safe and affirming space to discuss their identities. The therapist may want to broach the subject by asking permission from the client, which is a common therapeutic technique. Evan asked Jordan in their second session, "On your intake form, I noticed that you described yourself as a Biracial, queer transgender man. Would it be okay if I asked you some questions about your identity-related experiences, so I can get a better understanding of how they relate to what brings you into therapy?". Asking for permission and providing a rationale for why this topic is being brought up also gives Jordan the autonomy to choose whether he would like to talk about his identities. This is especially important for clients who have experienced oppression-based trauma and stress. These processes are done in addition to the general therapeutic practices of assessing symptoms, such as the depression and loneliness that Jordan reported.

Milestone Approach

The clinician employs a milestone approach for their discussion about identities (Hall et al., 2021). Evan asks Jordan about when he first became aware of his LGBTQ+ identities and his experiences related to his sexual, gender, and racial/ethnic identities. Jordan first describes his experiences of realizing he was transgender at 13 years old and how he navigated the development of his gender identity. He mentions that he has engaged in social gender affirmation, but has yet to start his medical gender affirmation. Evan inquires what, if any, medical gender affirmation is important to Jordan, as this is consistent with a milestone approach and assumes medical affirmation is not the ultimate outcome for TGD people (Matsuno & Budge, 2017). The clinician also assesses Jordan's experiences of gender euphoria (e.g., "What brings you joy as a transgender man?") rather than solely focusing on his experiences of gender dysphoria (Tebbe & Budge, 2022). The clinician may also use the opportunity to ask Jordan about his perceived successes and challenges of his gender identity development milestones. Successes and challenges in this regard may entail the level of support Jordan received from others and his own self-acceptance of his identity at different development timepoints. These outcomes represent how affirmed Jordan has felt, and currently feels, in his LGBTQ+ identity. They also reveal his connection to others and environments that affirm him.

During treatment, Jordan also raises that he is questioning his sexuality, which prompts Evan to use Goodrich and Brammer's (2021) recommendations and draw upon concepts found in McCarn and Fassinger's (1996) sexual identity development model (see Table 6.1 for example prompts) and overall milestone approaches to guide their discussion of identity exploration. Evan allows Jordan to describe his identities in his own words, which normalizes identity uncertainty and fluidity throughout their discussion (Mereish et al., 2018). For example, Evan begins by asking Jordan what being queer means to him, and about his romantic desires and attractions. Jordan describes his initial awareness that he had same-sex sexual fantasies at an early age and subsequently considered himself gay, but also how he has become aware of his attraction to multiple genders in later adolescence. Evan validates Jordan's experiences and normalizes the dynamic nature of sexual orientation. Evan also prompts Jordan to reflect upon what it would mean to him to explore his sexuality more.

When discussing his sexual identity, Jordan expresses self-judgment and confusion about his sexual identity and how it has been more emotionally difficult than exploring his gender identity. Evan uses empathy and reflective listening to validate Jordan. Evan also uses psychoeducation to point out that, while sexual and gender identity development can influence one another, they are often different processes for each person. He engages Jordan in self reflections on what has made his gender identity development different than his sexual identity exploration. This helps Jordan think about how his approach to gender identity milestones and sexual identity milestones are inherently different for him and cannot be equally compared.

Identity Affirmation During Treatment

Alongside Jordan's feelings of isolation, Jordan reports experiencing microaggressions from one of his professors and classmates. When Jordan describes how his experiences of cissexism and racism affect him, the clinician may intervene by using the structure of LGBTQ+ affirming therapy (Austin et al., 2017; Pachankis et al., 2015). Evan knows that it is important to validate the client's experiences with oppression, and his cognitive, emotional, behavioral, and interpersonal reactions to such events. Challenging the client on whether an event was an act of discrimination can be a microaggression that can minimize and invalidate the client's lived experience (Skerven et al., 2019). Evan assesses Jordan's familiarity with the concept of minority stress and explains how experiences of stigma and oppression influence mental health. Evan provides psychoeducation related to oppression-based reactions and identifies existing strengths and resilience factors that have worked for Jordan and that he feels efficacious in using; and, if warranted, Evan suggests additional skills and techniques to navigate these stressors.

Evan also acknowledges how intersectionality may play a role in Jordan's experiences of oppression. Using the Racial Queer Identity Framework with Jordan also helps him to understand how he conceptualizes his racial, sexual, and gender identities (Adames et al., 2021). When Jordan shares information about his identity-related and oppression-based experiences, Evan is careful to follow clinical recommendations and refrains from pathologizing the client's LGBTQ+ identities or experiences (Mereish et al., 2018). Evan emphasizes that it is not the existence of Jordan's identities that is causing distress, but society's negative and misinformed reactions to him, and the interlocking systems that perpetuate and maintain his experiences of oppression. This method of identity affirmation helps the client depersonalize experiences of minority stress (Cohen, 2006). Evan also explores assertiveness and self-advocacy skills with Jordan to help him navigate his experiences with his professors and peers, and he helps Jordan find resources for reporting bias incidents at his university.

Continuing his effort to affirm Jordan, the therapist starts to help Jordan build his own identity affirmation practices. Evan continues to use psychoeducation to explain how feelings of pride and connectedness to one's identity and community can help buffer against the negative effects of minority stress (Busby et al., 2020). The therapist discovers that Jordan enjoys creative writing and assigns him homework to write reflections on the strengths of being queer, transgender, and biracial, which is inspired by a brief expressive writing intervention for LGBTQ+ young adults (Pachankis et al., 2020). Evan also encourages Jordan to engage in activities that help promote his gender euphoria. Evan may do this by sharing reflections on how Jordan's mental health symptoms seem to improve when he engages in activities that affirm his gender identity. Jordan can then use this insight to engage in more identity affirmation outside of therapy. Evan may use this opportunity to assign Jordan homework to find in-person and online support groups for other LGBTQ+, BIPOC, and QTBIPOC young adults. Through the therapist's encouragement and modeling of identity affirmation, Jordan begins to seek out engagement with LGBTQ+, BIPOC, and QTBIPOC community events and organizations. This not only affirms Jordan, but also addresses his symptoms of loneliness and depression.

Evan uses treatment progress check-ins to ask Jordan about his experiences of identity affirmation inside and outside of therapy. Evan typically asks Jordan about his feelings related to the level of identity-related supports he is receiving across multiple sources. At the start of therapy, Jordan expressed low support from others, and consequently more negative feelings towards himself and his LGBTQ+ identity. After Jordan has been able to regularly use skills he has learned to affirm himself, he expresses that he is more confident in exploring his sexuality and that he is more connected to supportive LGBTQ+, BIPOC, and QTBIPOC peers. Evan reflects that Jordan seems to be feeling more affirmed in his identity and feeling accomplished by all the changes he has been making in his life. Evan might use the opportunity to ask Jordan about how his LGBTQ+ identity is integrated with his holistic identity. Some identity development models would refer to this as internalization or synthesis of identity, which entails self-acceptance of LGBTQ+ identity and how LGBTQ+ group membership fits into a person's self-concept. The clinician approaches this by asking Jordan about his sense of pride and connectedness to the greater LGBTQ+ community. Evan might then use a values clarification exercise to prompt Jordan to reflect upon how his values are connected to being LGBTQ+.

As Jordan's symptoms of depression and isolation are consistently below clinical threshold, Evan and Jordan plan for termination. Within the last several sessions, they discuss Jordan's progress and review useful concepts (e.g., minority stress) and coping strategies (e.g., identity affirmation) that he learned throughout treatment. They identify obstacles that could affect Jordan's maintenance of his mental health and signals that would suggest returning to therapy. Evan celebrates Jordan's personal strengths and achievements in therapy. Evan prompts Jordan to reflect upon how he hopes to continue exploring his identity in the future. Evan also provides a list of appropriate referrals to QTBIPOC-affirming resources at discharge.

In summary, Evan used multiple approaches to affirm Jordan's identity in treatment. He effectively tailored his identity affirmation approach based on Jordan's needs and developmental milestones. Using techniques such as validation, psychoeducation, skills training, reflection, and values clarification helped Evan model identity affirmation to Jordan. At the end of treatment, Jordan was spontaneously using identity affirmation within and outside the therapy room.

Disclaimer The views expressed in this chapter are those of the authors and do not necessarily reflect the official policy or position of the U.S. Department of Veterans Affairs nor the U.S. Government.

References

Adames, H. Y., & Chavez-Dueñas, N. Y. (2021). Reclaiming all of me: The racial queer identity framework. In K. L. Nadal & M. R. Scharrón-del Río (Eds.), *Queer psychology*. Springer.

Adames, H.Y., Chavez-Dueñas, N.Y., Cruz, X., & Mchabcheb, R. (2021). *Our collective healing: A toolkit for queer and trans people of color (QTPOC)*. www.icrace.org.

Austin, A., Craig, S. L., & Alessi, E. J. (2017). Affirmative cognitive behavior therapy with transgender and gender nonconforming adults. *The Psychiatric Clinics of North America, 40*(1), 141–156. https://doi.org/10.1016/j.psc.2016.10.003

Austin, A., Papciak, R., & Lovins, L. (2022). Gender euphoria: A grounded theory exploration of experiencing gender affirmation. *Psychology & Sexuality, 13*(5), 1406–1426.

Bishop, M. D., Fish, J. N., Hammack, P. L., & Russell, S. T. (2020). Sexual identity development milestones in three generations of sexual minority people: A national probability sample. *Developmental Psychology, 56*, 2177–2193.

Bockting, W., & Coleman, E. (2007). Developmental stages of the transgender coming-out process: Toward an integrated identity. In *Principles of transgender medicine and surgery* (pp. 137–158). Routledge.

Bradford, N. J., Rider, G. N., & Spencer, K. G. (2021). Hair removal and psychological well-being in transfeminine adults: Associations with gender dysphoria and gender euphoria. *Journal of Dermatological Treatment, 32*(6), 635–642.

Breslow, A. S., Wojcik, H., Cox, R., Tran, N. M., & Brewster, M. E. (2021). Toward nonbinary nuance in research and care: Mapping differences in gender affirmation and transgender congruence in an Online National US Survey. *Transgender Health, 6*(3), 156–163.

Brewster, M. E., & Moradi, B. (2010). Perceived experiences of anti-bisexual prejudice: Instrument development and evaluation. *Journal of Counseling Psychology, 57*(4), 451–468.

Budge, S. L., Sinnard, M. T., & Hoyt, W. T. (2020). Longitudinal effects of psychotherapy with transgender and nonbinary clients: A randomized controlled pilot trial. *Psychotherapy: Theory, Research, & Practice.* https://doi.org/10.1037/pst0000310

Busby, D. R., Horwitz, A. G., Zheng, K., Eisenberg, D., Harper, G. W., Albucher, R. C., Roberts, L. W., Coryell, W., Pistorello, J., & King, C. A. (2020). Suicide risk among gender and sexual minority college students: The roles of victimization, discrimination, connectedness, and identity affirmation. *Journal of Psychiatric Research, 121*, 182–188.

Cass, V. C. (1979). Homosexual identity formation. *Journal of Homosexuality, 4*(3), 219–235.

Cerezo, A., Cummings, M., Holmes, M., & Williams, C. (2020). Identity as resistance: Identity formation at the intersection of race, gender identity, and sexual orientation. *Psychology of Women Quarterly, 44*(1), 67–83.

Cohen, G. L. (2006). Reducing the racial achievement gap: A social-psychological intervention. *Science, 313*(5791), 1307–1310. https://doi.org/10.1126/science.1128317

Craig, S. L. (2012). Strengths first: An empowering case management model for multiethnic sexual minority youth. *Journal of Gay & Lesbian Social Services, 24*(3), 274–288.

Craig, S. L. (2013). Affirmative Supportive Safe and Empowering Talk (ASSET): Leveraging the strengths and resiliencies of sexual minority youth in school-based groups. *Journal of LGBT Issues in Counseling, 7*(4), 372–386.

Craig, S. L., & Austin, A. (2016). The AFFIRM open pilot feasibility study: A brief affirmative cognitive behavioral coping skills group intervention for sexual and gender minority youth. *Children and Youth Services Review, 64*, 136–144.

Doyle, D. M. (2022). Transgender identity: Development, management and affirmation. *Current Opinion in Psychology, 48*, 101467. https://doi.org/10.1016/j.copsyc.2022.101467

Dyar, C., & London, B. (2018). Bipositive events: Associations with proximal stressors, bisexual identity, and mental health among bisexual cisgender women. *Psychology of Sexual Orientation and Gender Diversity, 5*(2), 204–219.

Feinstein, B. A., & Dyar, C. (2017). Bisexuality, minority stress, and health. *Current Sexual Health Reports, 9*, 42–49. https://doi.org/10.1007/s11930-017-0096-3

Fiani, C. N., & Han, H. J. (2018). Navigating identity: Experiences of binary and non-binary transgender and gender non-conforming (TGNC) adults. *The International Journal of Transgenderism, 20*(2–3), 181–194. https://doi.org/10.1080/15532739.2018.1426074

Flanders, C. E., Tarasoff, L. A., Legge, M. M., Robinson, M., & Gos, G. (2017). Positive identity experiences of young bisexual and other nonmonosexual people: A qualitative inquiry. *Journal of Homosexuality, 64*(8), 1014–1032.

Flentje, A. (2020). AWARENESS: Development of a cognitive–behavioral intervention to address intersectional minority stress for sexual minority men living with HIV who use substances. *Psychotherapy, 57*(1), 35. https://doi.org/10.1037/pst0000243

Ghabrial, M. A., & Andersen, J. P. (2021). Development and initial validation of the queer people of color identity affirmation scale. *Journal of Counseling Psychology, 68*(1), 38–53.

Goodrich, K. M., & Brammer, M. K. (2021). Cass's homosexual identity formation: A critical analysis. *Journal of Multicultural Counseling and Development, 49*(4), 239–253.

Hall, W. J., Dawes, H. C., & Plocek, N. (2021). Sexual orientation identity development milestones among lesbian, gay, bisexual, and queer people: A systematic review and meta-analysis. *Frontiers in Psychology, 12*.
Hudson, K. D., & Romanelli, M. (2020). "We are powerful people": Health-promoting strengths of LGBTQ communities of color. *Qualitative Health Research, 30*(8), 1156–1170.
Israel, T., Choi, A. Y., Goodman, J. A., Matsuno, E., Lin, Y. J., Kary, K. G., & Merrill, C. R. (2019). Reducing internalized binegativity: Development and efficacy of an online intervention. *Psychology of Sexual Orientation and Gender Diversity, 6*(2), 149–159.
Katz-Wise, S. L., Budge, S. L., Fugate, E., Flanagan, K., Touloumtzis, C., Rood, B., Perez-Brumer, A., & Leibowitz, S. (2017). Transactional pathways of transgender identity development in transgender and gender nonconforming youth and caregivers from the trans youth family study. *The International Journal of Transgenderism, 18*, 243–263.
Kenneady, D. A., & Oswalt, S. B. (2014). Is Cass's model of homosexual identity formation relevant to today's society? *American Journal of Sexuality Education, 9*(2), 229–246.
Lane, M., Ives, G. C., Sluiter, E. C., Waljee, J. F., Yao, T. H., Hu, H. M., & Kuzon, W. M. (2018). Trends in gender-affirming surgery in insured patients in the United States. *Plastic and Reconstructive Surgery. Global Open, 6*(4), e1738.
Li, G., Archer Lee, Y., Lin, X., Krampitz, E., Atilla, G., Nguyen, K. C., Rosen, H. R., Tham, C. Z. E., & Chen, F. S. (2023). Self-affirmation reduces internalized heterosexism in sexual minority people. *Psychology of Sexual Orientation and Gender Diversity*.
Lin, Y. J., Israel, T., & Ryan, W. S. (2019). Releasing internalized stigma for empowerment: Development of theory-driven interventions for sexual and gender minorities. *Journal of LGBT Issues in Counseling, 13*(4), 276–292.
Lucassen, M. F., Merry, S. N., Hatcher, S., & Frampton, C. M. (2015). Rainbow SPARX: A novel approach to addressing depression in sexual minority youth. *Cognitive and Behavioral Practice, 22*(2), 203–216. https://doi.org/10.1016/j.cbpra.2013.12.008
Martos, A., Nezhad, S., & Meyer, I. H. (2015). Variations in sexual identity milestones among lesbians, gay men and bisexuals. *Sexuality Research & Social Policy, 12*(1), 24–33.
Matsuno, E. (2019). Nonbinary-affirming psychological interventions. *Cognitive and Behavioral Practice, 26*(4), 617–628.
Matsuno, E., & Budge, S. L. (2017). Non-binary/Genderqueer identities: A critical review of the literature. *Current Sexual Health Reports, 9*, 116–120.
Matsuno, E., & Israel, T. (2018). Psychological interventions promoting resilience among transgender individuals: Transgender Resilience Intervention Model (TRIM). *The Counseling Psychologist, 46*(5), 632–655. https://doi.org/10.1177/0011000018787261
McCarn, S., & Fassinger, R. (1996). Revisioning sexual minority identity formation: A new model of lesbian identity and its implications for counseling and research. *The Counseling Psychologist, 24*, 508–534.
Mereish, E. H., Gamarel, K. E., & Operario, D. (2018). Understanding and addressing alcohol and substance use in sexual and gender minority youth. In P. M. Monti, S. M. Colby, & T. O. Tevyaw (Eds.), *Brief interventions for adolescent alcohol and substance abuse* (pp. 305–327). The Guilford Press.
Mereish, E. H., Parra, L. A., Watson, R. J., & Fish, J. N. (2022). Subtle and intersectional minority stress and depressive symptoms among sexual and gender minority adolescents of color: Mediating role of self-Esteem and sense of mastery. *Prevention Science, 23*(1), 142–153.
Morales, E. S. (1989). Ethnic minority families and minority gays and lesbians. *Marriage & Family Review, 14*(3–4), 217–239. https://doi.org/10.1300/J002v14n03_11
Pachankis, J. E., Hatzenbuehler, M. L., Rendina, H. J., Safren, S. A., & Parsons, J. T. (2015). LGB-affirmative cognitive-behavioral therapy for young adult gay and bisexual men: A randomized controlled trial of a transdiagnostic minority stress approach. *Journal of Consulting and Clinical Psychology, 83*(5), 875–889. https://doi.org/10.1037/ccp0000037
Pachankis, J. E., Williams, S. L., Behari, K., Job, S., McConocha, E. M., & Chaudoir, S. R. (2020). Brief online interventions for LGBTQ young adult mental and behavioral health: A random-

ized controlled trial in a high-stigma, low-resource context. *Journal of Consulting and Clinical Psychology, 88*(5), 429–444. https://doi.org/10.1037/ccp0000497

Rostosky, S., Riggle, E. D., Pascale-Hague, D., & McCants, L. E. (2010). The positive aspects of a bisexual self-identification. *Psychology & Sexuality, 1*(2), 131–144.

Skerven, K., Whicker, D. R., & LeMaire, K. L. (2019). Applying dialectical behaviour therapy to structural and internalized stigma with LGBTQ+ clients. *The Cognitive Behaviour Therapist, 12*, e9. https://doi.org/10.1017/S1754470X18000235

Spencer, K. G., Berg, D. R., Bradford, N. J., Vencill, J. A., Tellawi, G., & Rider, G. N. (2021). The gender-affirmative life span approach: A developmental model for clinical work with transgender and gender-diverse children, adolescents, and adults. *Psychotherapy, 58*, 37–49.

Stock, M. L., Gibbons, F. X., Beekman, J. B., Williams, K. D., Richman, L. S., & Gerrard, M. (2018). Racial (versus self) affirmation as a protective mechanism against the effects of racial exclusion on negative affect and substance use vulnerability among black young adults. *Journal of Behavioral Medicine, 41*(2), 195–207.

Tatum, A. K., Catalpa, J., Bradford, N. J., Kovic, A., & Berg, D. R. (2020). Examining identity development and transition differences among binary transgender and genderqueer nonbinary individuals. *Psychology of Sexual Orientation and Gender Diversity, 7*, 379–385.

Tebbe, E. A., & Budge, S. L. (2022). Factors that drive mental health disparities and promote well-being in transgender and nonbinary people. *Nature Reviews Psychology, 1*, 694–707.

Chapter 7
Doing Affirmative Cognitive Behavioral Therapy with LGBTQ+ Youth and Their Families

Jenny Shen, Ilana Seager van Dyk, and Jeffrey M. Cohen

Highlights

- This chapter overviews the mental health needs of LGBTQ+ youth and their families.
- Interventions for LGBTQ+ youth and their families are reviewed, with an emphasis on gender-affirming mental healthcare.
- An illustrative case vignette is provided, as well as guidance on how to integrate advocacy.

Positionality

We are three clinicians, educators, and researchers trained as clinical psychologists at various stages in our careers. We represent a range of gender and sexual identities (nonbinary, cisgender man, cisgender woman, queer, bisexual, gay, pansexual), ethnicities (Chinese, Jewish, Caucasian, White, indigenous), and national origins (Canada, USA, New Zealand), and have lived experiences of mental health challenges, as well as psychotherapy and medication trials. Our intention with this work is to provide a resource to support the needs of LGBTQ+ youth and their families. All authors are clinically trained, one of whom currently works with LGBTQ+ patients and their families and supervises clinical trainees in a psychiatry

J. Shen (✉)
Department of Psychology, Stony Brook University, Stony Brook, NY, USA
e-mail: jennyshen@mednet.ucla.edu

I. S. van Dyk
School of Psychology, Massey University, Palmerston North, New Zealand

J. M. Cohen
Department of Psychiatry, Columbia University Irving Medical Center, New York, NY, USA

N. A. Livingston et al. (eds.), *Addressing Minority Stress and Enhancing Resilience with Diverse LGBTQ+ Clients*, CBT: Science Into Practice,
https://doi.org/10.1007/978-3-031-92836-9_7

department at an academic medical center; one of whom is a psychology doctoral candidate and incoming postdoctoral fellow at an academic medical center providing trauma-informed care to minoritized youth and families, with an emphasis on serving LGBTQ+ patients; and one of whom is a researcher and faculty in a clinical psychology department with expertise in LGBTQ+ youth mental health. All authors are trained in a range of cognitive-behavioral approaches, including traditional and newer iterations (e.g., Acceptance and Commitment Therapy, Dialectical Behavior Therapy), specialize in the treatment of mood and anxiety disorders, borderline personality disorder, OCD, and PTSD, and have expertise in working with LGBTQ+ youth. Collectively, all authors share a professional and personal commitment to supporting the health and wellbeing of LGBTQ+ people through practice, advocacy, and research.

Introduction

More youth are coming out as LGBTQ+ than ever before (Worthen, 2023). However, anti-LGBTQ+ stigma places LGBTQ+ youth at increased risk for mental health problems compared to cisgender and heterosexual youth (Chodzen et al., 2019; Plöderl & Tremblay, 2015). Growing research in the past two decades shows that these disparities can be attributed to anti-LGBTQ+ experiences (Guz et al., 2021). These minority stressors include anti-LGBTQ+ discrimination at the institutional and interpersonal levels, such as anti-LGBTQ+ bullying from peers (Cyrus, 2017) and environments rejecting of LGBTQ+ identities (e.g., laws blocking access to gender-affirming care; Kline et al., 2022), as well as internalized anti-LGBTQ+ stigma (Williams et al., 2023). These effects may also be particularly heightened in the face of multiple minoritization; increasing work suggests that LGBTQ+ youth, particularly youth of color, are at increased risk for reduced healthcare access, alienation from peers, homelessness, school dropout, and greater rates of involvement in the juvenile justice system (Dank et al., 2015).

Affirmative care, which asserts that all sexual and gender identities are valid and acknowledges the impact of anti-LGBTQ+ stigma, is imperative to reduce these health disparities, and aligns with guidelines for pediatric care (Rafferty et al., 2018) and American Psychological Association (APA) guidelines (APA, 2015; APA Task Force on Psychological Practice with Sexual Minority Persons, 2021). Clinicians may feel anxious about working with LGBTQ+ youth and their families given the complex issues they face, like legislative efforts to ban gender-affirming healthcare and threaten families seeking these services with prosecution (Gordon, 2022), and those limiting classroom discussions on sexual orientation and gender (e.g., House Bill 1557). However, clinicians can be trained to implement LGBTQ+ affirming therapies (Pachankis et al., 2022). Thus, this chapter offers guidance on delivering affirmative mental healthcare for LGBTQ+ youth and their families.

Current Treatments for Youth

Cognitive behavioral therapies (CBTs) are effective in treating a wide range of psychological concerns in youth (Nakao et al., 2021). Similarly, most intervention research with LGBTQ+ youth so far has used a CBT foundation to address minority stress and bolster coping. However, affirmative, empirically tested treatments for LGBTQ+ youth remain nascent. Preliminary interventions for youth have included school-based interventions for LGBTQ+ youth, where clinicians have collaborated with school staff to provide psychoeducation on minority stress and coping strategies (Cohen et al., 2015; Goldbach et al., 2021, 2023; Heck, 2015); CBT interventions administered by clinicians and tested in non-clinical samples of LGBTQ+ youth (Craig & Austin, 2016); and adaptations of adult-oriented LGBTQ+ affirmative CBT interventions (Pachankis et al., 2019, 2020) for teens in a telehealth group format (Seager van Dyk et al., 2022b). Compared to interventions for LGBTQ+ adults, interventions for LGBTQ+ youth must often involve caregiver and/or school collaboration, which may lead to access barriers. As such, there are increasing efforts to make treatments accessible digitally for LGBTQ+ youth, including CBT and single-session interventions targeting minority stress (Craig et al., 2021; Lucassen et al., 2015; Shen et al., 2023). Such digital interventions may serve as adjunctive supports and provide access for those who are in undertreated communities, are hesitant about initiating therapy, or are on clinic waitlists (Cohen et al., 2022).

Current Interventions for Caregivers and Family Members of Youth

Family rejection, a predictor of negative outcomes, can be addressed within caregiver support (Ryan et al., 2009). Fortunately, parents with negative responses towards their child's LGBTQ+ identity report interest in learning to cope with their feelings about their child's identity and improving their relationship with their child (Seager van Dyk et al., 2022a). Work with caregivers is a critical part of treatment, which can include family therapy, caregiver sessions, and group therapy for caregivers (Cohen, 2023). It is also important to tailor caregiver-oriented interventions, given the variety of reactions and challenges caregivers may experience with accepting their LGBTQ+ child. Such work may include psychoeducational interventions (Goodman & Israel, 2019; Huebner et al., 2013; Matsuno & Israel, 2021; Ryan, 2010) and family therapy (Diamond et al., 2012).

Gender Affirmative Model of Care for Youth and Families

Given the lack of resources on providing affirmative CBT for gender diverse youth, our discussion and vignette focus more on gender identity than sexual orientation, although similar principles may be used with cisgender LGBQ+ youth. LGBTQ+

youth have reported needs around: receiving emotional support from caregivers for their LGBTQ+ identity, feeling safe in sharing their identity with mental healthcare providers, seeing inclusive questions used on sexual orientation and gender identity, having symbols of safety and inclusivity in healthcare providers' offices (e.g., a rainbow pride flag), and collaborating around confidentiality for their identity (Zullo et al., 2021). When working with gender diverse youth, clinicians can address these needs by adopting a gender affirmative care model. This includes: (a) continuous collaboration across youth, family, and other healthcare providers; (b) options for consultation services without requiring therapy or psychometric testing; (c) conceptualization of social and medical transitions as stages rather than specific ages; (d) ongoing follow-up for support around puberty blockers and hormone therapy; and (e) alleviating effects of minority stress and building resilience (Ehrensaft, 2017). As such, we conceptualize gender affirmation across multiple domains including, but not limited to: (1) social (e.g., changes related to one's name, pronouns, gender expression); (2) psychological (e.g., supporting individuals in living according to their values); (3) legal (e.g., changes of gender markers); and (4) advocacy and support for medical (e.g., hormones, reproductive options) and surgical needs (e.g., affirming surgeries).

The World Professional Association for Transgender Health Standards of Care Version 8 (WPATH SOC-8) provides guidance for health professionals working with gender diverse youth (Coleman et al., 2022). In line with the WPATH SOC-8, mental healthcare providers supporting prepubescent children integrate information from multiple sources and consider factors that constrain accurate reporting of the child's gender identity or expression. Providers offer developmentally appropriate education to the child and their family on the importance of addressing the child by their desired name and pronouns; potential gender-affirming medical interventions for later when the child approaches puberty, as well as the effects of these treatments on future fertility and options for fertility preservation; and benefits and risks related to social and medical transitions. Mental healthcare providers working with adolescents collaborate with them and their caregivers to provide education and connect them to referrals and resources if gender-affirming medical treatment is indicated, and should be prepared to provide health education to youth, including evaluation of benefits and risks of medical procedures, as well as chest binding, genital tucking, and menstrual suppression agents.

Below, we illustrate an affirmative CBT approach to care, which integrates the gender affirmative model with CBT case conceptualization and techniques. This vignette is not an exhaustive overview of all concerns LGBTQ+ youth present with, but rather an illustrative example of working with a transgender, pansexual youth and his family. The vignette and clinical dialogues are not from an actual patient, but reflect common presentations in practice.

Vignette: Dylan

Case Description

Dylan (he/him), a 14-year-old, Chinese American, transgender, pansexual adolescent boy, met DSM-5-TR diagnostic criteria for gender dysphoria,[1] obsessive-compulsive disorder (OCD), social anxiety, and presented with school avoidance. His school avoidance manifested as him asking to stay home from school, which was accommodated by both parents (i.e., allowing school absences) and the school (i.e., when at school, Dylan spent most of the day in the nurse's office). In this vignette, Dylan works with a clinical psychologist, Dr. Li (she/her), a Chinese American, heterosexual, cisgender woman.

Call from Parent

Dylan's pediatrician recommended his parents seek out mental health treatment for him. Dylan's mother called the clinic expressing concerns about Dylan wearing gloves and that he identifies as transgender; she wondered if the two were related. Although Dylan's mother used his chosen name, she referred to him as her "daughter" and used she/her pronouns to describe him. From this call, the clinician may plan to assess the function of wearing gloves with Dylan, and could hypothesize that Dylan's mother may benefit from psychoeducation around what it means to be transgender, and how being transgender may be unrelated to wearing gloves. The clinician may also plan to check in with Dylan about pronouns, clarify whether these differ from the pronouns his mother used, and use the pronouns Dylan would like the clinician to use.

---

[1] Of note, gender dysphoria is a controversial diagnosis that pathologizes gender diversity, reinforces the social construction of gender roles, and increases minority stress experiences for many transgender and gender diverse people (Davies & Davies, 2020). The conceptualization of gender dysphoria is also often framed in binary ways that may not capture the experiences and embodiment goals of nonbinary individuals (Galupo et al., 2021). We acknowledge that, given the current state of the American healthcare system, receiving a gender dysphoria diagnosis is often, unfortunately, a prerequisite for gaining access to medically necessary gender-affirming care. Thus, it can be helpful for clinicians to communicate these realities around the gender dysphoria diagnosis with patients when discussing gender-affirming care. Notably, the ICD-11 uses "gender incongruence," which individuals may find less stigmatizing while still indicating a need for affirming care (Davies & Davies, 2020).

Intake Session

Dr. Li scheduled an intake with Dylan and his parents to assess for OCD and other psychiatric symptoms and collect gender history. Measures for evaluating potential anxiety disorders and OCD were included based on chief complaints described in the referral (i.e., to assess if wearing gloves at school was related to OCD-related contamination fears or other forms of anxiety). For gender, Dr. Li asked questions related to gender history, gender identity, and embodiment goals (i.e., the bodily changes a person might like to have to feel more aligned with their gender). Additionally, she asked about sexual orientation, intersecting identities, level of disclosure of identities with family members and others, experiences around minority stress and resilience, and identity centrality. She utilized identity-related questions (e.g., from the ADDRESSING framework; Hays, 1996) for Dylan to share identities important to him. Example intake questions around gender identity, expression, and history; sexual orientation; minority stress and resilience; other identities and identity centrality; and embodiment goals are provided in Table 7.1. To signal therapy as a safe space for Dylan, Dr. Li had a pride flag prominently displayed in her office and also selectively self-disclosed identities to acknowledge how she and Dylan might have some shared lived experiences, while being mindful not to generalize her experiences to Dylan's. Such selective self-disclosure can also convey to minoritized youth that they can be successful adults. The results of this intake were incorporated into a case conceptualization provided below.

Below is an example of Dr. Li going through these questions. Dylan expressed wanting to start masculinizing hormones. He also shared considering top surgery (i.e., surgery that removes or augments breast tissue to create a more masculine or feminine appearance) for the future. Dylan immediately wanted to communicate to his parents his correct name and pronouns, and that wearing gloves was related to fears of contamination. Dr. Li asked Dylan how he would like this information to be communicated to his parents.

Dialogue Example #1: Intake with Youth

Therapist: My name is Dr. Li, and I use she/her pronouns. I have some questions today to get to know you and how I can support you. What name and pronouns would you like me to use for you?

Dylan: Dylan and he/him.

Therapist: Okay. How can I be most helpful?

Dylan: Well, I know my mom is worried about me being trans, and she thinks me wearing gloves is related to that. I just want her to use my name and pronouns correctly!

Therapist: Okay, it makes sense you want your mom to use your name and pronouns and I'm happy to support you with that.

Dylan: She keeps dead-naming me. I already told her to use Dylan and he/him but she just doesn't listen. My dad has been using Dylan though at least. Can you talk to them?

(continued)

Therapist: That's really frustrating. Maybe we can work on having that conversation together with them at the end of today's session. *(Dylan nods.)* How did you first come to understand your gender as it is now?

Dylan: I always knew I didn't really feel like a "girl." In fifth grade, I started watching a trans YouTuber, and he gave me words to describe how I always felt.

Therapist: Got it. What steps have you taken to feel more comfortable in your gender?

Dylan: My friends let me wear their masc clothes. I also wear baggy clothes and a binder.

Therapist: That's great to hear you've been able to take steps to feel more comfortable and that your friends helped you with that. Are there other steps you would like to take?

Dylan: I'd like to have a deeper voice, get more muscle, and have a sharper jawline. I want clothes to fit better. I want to start hormones and probably get top surgery at some point later on. It would be great if you could get my parents to make appointments.

Therapist: I'm hearing you would really like to start hormone therapy and have a deeper voice, get more muscular, have a sharper jawline, and have clothes fit better. It sounds like top surgery is something you could be interested in at some point too. And it sounds like you would like your parents to be on board with these. I'm open to supporting you in discussing these goals you have with them. Do you have any concerns or questions with potentially moving towards these goals?[2]

Dylan: I guess I'm kind of worried about any side effects and how long the process might be. I really want to look like a boy by the time I start school next year after summer. Also, with all the laws recently, I want to get this started in case I'm not able to anymore.

Therapist: Makes sense, and I can understand why you feel urgency and how recent anti-trans legislation is scary. Just so you know where I stand, I believe this is a conversation for teens, caregivers, and their healthcare providers. It'll be important for us to speak with your parents and I'm happy to support that conversation to see what's possible for your goals. We also want to ensure you have all the information you need to make a fully informed decision about any interventions. If we start therapy together, we can talk about realistic expectations and timelines. (*Dylan nods.*) I also want to ask about identities that might be important to you such as race or

(continued)

[2] The timing of conversations addressing embodiment goals may vary, and may occur across multiple sessions as needed.

ethnicity, gender, sexual orientation, religion, disability status, or others. Do you have any identities you are open to sharing with me?

Dylan: Being trans for sure. I'm also pan and I'm neurodivergent. And I guess being Chinese American — my culture is really important to me.

Therapist: Thanks for sharing with me. To be transparent, I'm a Chinese American, straight, cisgender woman. I want to acknowledge that while we may have some shared lived experiences with our Chinese American identities, not everyone's experiences are the same within communities, and my experiences as a cisgender, straight person may also differ from yours as a pansexual, trans boy. I'm committed to understanding your experiences and making sure I'm not generalizing my experiences to yours. If there are ever moments where I'm misunderstanding your experiences, please let me know.

Dylan: Okay, sounds good.

(*Given Dylan reported using a binder, therapist also checks in on if he follows safe binding practices and reviews these with Dylan [*Fenway Health, 2022]*).*

Therapist: Could you tell me what being neurodivergent means to you?

Dylan: I just think my brain works differently and sometimes I don't know what to say in social situations.

Therapist: Okay, we can talk more about this in a bit if you'd like. (*Dylan nods.*)

Therapist: You mentioned the anti-trans legislation, and I'm wondering if there is anything else you find stressful about being trans, pan, or Chinese American?

Dylan: Sometimes I wish I wasn't trans and Chinese American. You hear so much anti-trans and anti-Asian sentiment sometimes; it's just hard combined. And how many people you have to explain it to just so they'll use your name and pronouns!

Therapist: I hear that. That can be really tough. (*Dylan nods.*) Would you say there are any things that you enjoy about being trans, pan, or Chinese American?

Dylan: I guess it's cool meeting other people who are LGBTQ+ or Chinese American or both, or like other LGBTQ-POC [people of color]. It just feels like you get each other in a way where others just can't. Just having other kids to talk to who are like me feels nice.

Therapist: For sure. It sounds like having a community of folks who share your identities — trans, pan, Chinese American, and the intersections of these identities — can be really connecting. Where have you been meeting these people?

Dylan: Mostly online. I also started going to the LGBTQ+ Spectrum Club at my school.

Therapist: That's great to hear you've been connecting with people online and in-person.

(*Therapist proceeds with diagnostic questions, including assessment of OCD, social anxiety, and gender dysphoria. Dylan endorsed symptoms for all of*

(continued)

these, noting that he has obsessions around cleanliness, particularly at school; some "just right" compulsions around doing homework; as well as social anxiety around speaking in class and speaking to peers for as long as he can remember.)

Therapist: Coming back to gloves for a moment — may I ask why you wear gloves?

Dylan: School is gross and I don't want to touch everything everyone else has touched. And I don't want to be there. It's just gross.

Therapist: Got it. Some people say it can also be hard to be at school if it feels like they can't go to the bathroom. They may also then try not to drink water or eat to avoid using it. Does that resonate with you?

Dylan: Yeah, I avoid drinking water so I don't have to use the school bathroom.

Therapist: Are there all-gender bathrooms at your school?

Dylan: Yeah, but it's hard to find the teacher who has the key to unlock it.

Therapist: I see. It makes a lot of sense that it would be hard to be at school because of how gross it feels and the steps for accessing all-gender bathrooms. Maybe that's something we can problem-solve together.

Dylan: That would be good.

Therapist: Okay. How about wearing gloves at school or feeling like school is gross? Is there anything you'd want to be different about those experiences, if we could snap our fingers and make it happen?

Dylan: I guess I'd like to not have to feel like I always have to wear gloves or that places with a lot of people, like school, are so gross. I don't know how to change that though.

Therapist: Luckily, we actually have strategies for those situations, so if you're interested in working on that we could do that work together.

Dylan: Okay, I'm down to do that.

Therapist: Great. Thanks for sharing all this with me today. To sum up what we've talked about, you'd really like your parents to use your name and pronouns and to start having discussions with them about moving towards hormone therapy and potentially top surgery at some point. It sounds like you want your mom to know that wearing gloves is unrelated to being trans; it's actually related to feeling gross in places with a lot of people, like school, and you want to work on that as a separate treatment target.

Dylan: Yeah.

Therapist: I also want to share some additional options we can consider if they feel aligned with your goals. Some transmasc folks find voice therapy helpful as another option or supplementary way to lower their voice, as it can be a less invasive option to start with compared to hormone therapy, and some parents may agree to this more readily. Also, some transmasc teens who are assigned female at birth mention heightened dysphoria related to their period, which birth control may be able to help reduce.

(continued)

Dylan: Oh, I might be interested in those, too.

Therapist: Okay, and definitely happy to support you in discussing those as well. We can bring your parents back in. Are there any pieces you would like to update them on versus what you would like me to update them on?

Dylan: I guess I can tell them about my name and pronouns. Could you tell them about the school stuff?

Therapist: Sure. Let's bring them in.

Table 7.1 Example intake questions including gender identity and sexual orientation topics

Introduction
What name and pronouns would you like me to use for you? (How about with your parent(s)/caregiver(s)/family member(s)?)
Gender identity (*Note*: These questions may also be adapted for sexual orientation.)
How would you describe your gender? How did you first come to understand your gender as it is now? Do your parent(s)/caregiver(s)/family member(s) have a different understanding of your gender? What steps have you taken to feel more comfortable in your gender? Are there any other steps you would like to take? (*refer to Embodiment Goals below*) Is there anything related to your gender that you would like me to advocate for with your parent(s)/caregiver(s)/family member(s)/school? Is there anything related to your gender that you would like me to keep private from your parent(s)/caregiver(s)/family member(s)?
Sexual orientation (in addition to the above questions, as adapted for sexual orientation)
Are you dating or in a relationship? Are there any goals you have related to dating or relationships? Are you sexually active (*if age-appropriate*)?
Minority stress, resilience, other identities, and identity centrality
What are some things that you find stressful about being (*insert LGBTQ+ identity/identities patient shared*)? What are some things that are cool/awesome about being (*insert LGBTQ+ identity/identities patient shared*)? How would you describe your race or ethnicity? Do you consider yourself religious or spiritual? What does this look like for you? Are there any other identities we haven't discussed that are important to you or that you think would be helpful for me to know about? Which of your identities are particularly important to who you are? How does your (*cultural/religious/spiritual*) group view (*insert LGBTQ+ identity/identities patient shared*) people? What is it like to be both (*cultural/religious/spiritual identity*) and (*LGBTQ+ identity*)?
Embodiment goals (Hastings et al., 2021)
Think about your body as it is right now: (a) What do you like? What would you like to stay the same? (b) What would you like to change? Are there changes you have already made? Is there anything else you would like to do to feel like you're living in your body as the most authentic version of yourself? When a youth has questions about medical or surgical treatments: (a) Is this something you are interested in? (b) What are you looking forward to? (c) What are your concerns and/or questions? (d) Is there anything that you are not excited about?

Note: These questions should be used in conjunction with clinicians' standard questions about presenting problems.

Dr. Li met with Dylan and his parents, where Dylan communicated his name, pronouns, and desire to start masculinizing hormones to them. He also clarified the function of his wearing gloves. Dylan's mother expressed concerns regarding how psychiatric diagnoses may relate to Dylan's gender identity. Dr. Li clarified current diagnoses (i.e., OCD, social anxiety, and gender dysphoria) as well as Dylan's self-identification as neurodivergent. She provided psychoeducation and explained that a neuropsychological evaluation would best assess Dylan's social communication concerns. Dylan's mother also expressed concerns that Dylan's gender identity may cause his younger sister to question her gender. Dr. Li incorporated validation, psychoeducation, and support for Dylan throughout the conversation.

Dialogue Example #2: Intake Feedback with Youth and Parents

Therapist: I talked with Dylan and we would like to give you an update.

Dylan: I just want you to know I'm actually a boy, and I'm going by the name Dylan and he/him pronouns. And me wearing gloves isn't because I'm trans; it's just because places with lots of germs are really gross places to be. I also want to start hormone therapy.

Mother: Wait … I don't believe in transgender. This sounds like one of those American things that are popular now, but we're Chinese and you know we don't do that. I already tried to understand you saying you're pansexual, and now there's something else you want to change? I'm definitely not ready for hormone therapy.

Father: Well, I just want you to be happy. Will this make you happy, Dylan?

Mother: How does she know what will make her happy at 14-years-old!?

Therapist: Just jumping in; Mom, I appreciate you being willing to hear Dylan out, and it makes sense it will take some time to take in this information. I'm wondering if we can take a moment; it sounds like it's important for Dylan for you to use he/him pronouns and to know that you're hearing him right now. Is there a way to let him know that right now?

Mother: Okay. I can try—I'm trying to hear you. Again, I don't believe in this transgender stuff and I am not agreeing to hormones.

Therapist: We hear you on not being on board with hormones, and I know this might be a lot of new information to take in. Would you be willing to try to use the name Dylan and he/him pronouns? I know this is a change, and it sounds like it's important to Dylan.

Mother: I can try calling him Dylan. I don't know if I can suddenly change to he/him pronouns, and honestly I don't want to encourage this.

Therapist: Okay, I understand this feels like a sudden change and parents understandably experience feelings in reaction to this. I would like to do a parent session to provide more support for you. In the interim, may I ask you to try using Dylan and he/him pronouns?

Mother: Okay, I will give it some thought.

Dylan: Thanks.

(continued)

Therapist: I appreciate everyone being open to this conversation. Mom and Dad, I'm also hearing understandable concerns and I'd be grateful to have the opportunity to discuss more together in a parent session.

Mother: That would be fine, but I'm not sure how it would help. Really I just want to know — are there any psychiatric diagnoses? Do they cause this transgender stuff?

Therapist: It appears that Dylan is experiencing symptoms consistent with OCD and social anxiety, and this contributes to making it challenging for Dylan to go to school or stay in classes. These are separate from Dylan being trans. In therapy, we will continue to collect data, and can revise our diagnoses if the new data points to something else.

Mother: Okay, but I am worried about how her being transgender is going to affect her –

Therapist: (*Gently interrupts*)—his –

Mother: *(Shakes her head and continues)* – sister, and how she thinks of her own gender. She's so young; what if this is going to make her confused about her gender?

Therapist: I completely understand you are concerned and have questions. What we know about gender identity from research is that learning that someone is trans doesn't make someone else more likely to be trans. And many younger kids are understanding of trans and gender identities that are different from "male" or "female".

Mother: I don't agree with that.

Father: Why not? I do.

Therapist: It's a lot to take in and there can be different reactions. Let's plan to continue discussing this in our next sessions, and we can also plan separate parent sessions to ensure you have the support you need and answers to your questions. I can also provide you with some written resources now if you would like (*provides resources in* Table 7.2).

Affirmative CBT Case Conceptualization

Following the intake interview, Dr. Li used an affirmative CBT approach to case conceptualization. An affirmative CBT case conceptualization builds upon a traditional CBT conceptualization, including presenting problems and symptoms, causal factors, maintaining factors, historical and contextual factors, family member-related considerations, patient strengths, core beliefs, and barriers to therapy. Further, an affirmative CBT case conceptualization additionally accounts for intersectional and cultural considerations, as well as minority stress and resilience factors. We review each of these components below, illustrating specific ways of adapting the CBT framework to be LGBTQ+ affirmative.

Presenting Problems and Symptoms

Dylan's presenting problems included OCD, social anxiety, school avoidance, and distress around his current gender expression, such as his physical being not aligning with his embodiment goals. He also requested support with starting masculinizing hormones because he felt distress and urges to avoid school when reminded that his body and gender expression were not fully how he would like them to be. Dylan's obsessions included "The door handles at school are covered in germs that will make me sick," and his compulsions included wearing gloves to avoid contamination, avoiding the school bathroom, avoiding drinking water to minimize bathroom use at school, and checking his bag 4 or 5 times in the morning to make sure he had hand sanitizer and an extra pair of gloves. He also reported repeatedly wiping door handles at home after others had used them, as well as a ritual of taking off his gloves, sanitizing his hands, and putting his gloves back on, which occurred 8 to 9 times per day. He reported that his intrusive thoughts occurred continuously and estimated spending a total of 2 to 3 hours engaging in compulsions per day. OCD impaired his ability to complete homework, due to writing and rewriting his answers, and made it challenging for him to leave his room and spend time with friends and family. Notably, Dylan avoided the school bathroom due to both fears of contamination and discomfort with using binary multi-stall bathrooms; he voiced that having access to an all-gender bathroom at school may be particularly helpful with the latter concern. Social anxiety difficulties included speaking in class and joining conversations with peers due to fears of negative evaluation. He reported that these symptoms impaired his ability to initiate and maintain friendships, and he noted that he would like to make more friends. For school avoidance, he reported difficulties with attending school, and leaving classes a few times a day to stay in the wellness center. He also reported missing school about 1 to 2 days per week, and the school had contacted Dylan's parents about this as well.

Causal Factors

Dylan's school avoidance began at the start of the school year 8 months ago, when Dylan started at a new school with no access to all-gender bathrooms, although his social anxiety had been present for as long as he could remember. Dylan reported fears of contamination in the past year and that these fears intensified at the start of the school year. He described finding it challenging to make friends and feeling isolated. These factors led to him staying home on school days, such that he was missing 1 to 2 days of school per week. When he told his parents he felt too anxious to attend school, they let him stay home.

Maintaining Factors

Dylan's OCD and social anxiety, as well as the lack of all-gender bathroom access and discomfort with his current gender expression (e.g., difficulties getting dressed or looking in mirrors when getting ready for school) contributed to his school avoidance. His parents also accommodated his school avoidance by agreeing to let him stay home at times. Additionally, Dylan reported that when he went to the wellness center, he was allowed to listen to music and watch videos on his smartphone, which was reinforcing. With his OCD, Dylan's compulsions around wearing gloves reinforced his obsessions around cleanliness, which also manifested often at school.

Historical and Contextual Factors

Dylan reported that he started questioning his gender at age 6, and at age 10 he started seeing transgender and gender diverse representation on media that provided some language for his experiences. He had been wearing some of his friends' more traditionally masculine clothing since then. However, he also recalled hearing negative messages about LGBTQ+ people from family members and school peers.

Parent Considerations

Dylan's mother was born in China and moved to the US with her mother a couple decades ago. Dylan's father and his family had been living in the US for several generations, and were also of Chinese descent. Dylan's mother and father were married, and Dylan lived with his mother, father, grandmother, and younger sister. Dylan's mother and father were most involved in treatment, and his grandmother also participated in some family sessions, such as when Dylan invited her to a session to come out to her.

Patient Strengths

Dylan demonstrated insight into his symptoms and needs, and articulated these effectively in-session. He read about gender identity online (e.g., on The Trevor Project's website). Dylan also reported having social support through some friends from his old school, and having some pride related to being transgender through his participation in online gender diverse communities (e.g., TikTok and Reddit).

Core Fears and Maladaptive Beliefs

Dylan's obsessions included "People at school carry germs that could kill me" and "If I touch something dirty, I'm going to get sick and won't be able to do things I want to do." He also endorsed a core fear of negative evaluation which manifested as socially anxious thoughts such as "People at school probably think I'm weird and don't want to talk to me" and "If I ask for what I want or need, I'm always going to be told no and people will be angry that I asked". He also reported unhelpful beliefs about his gender, including, "I'm never going to look like a guy," and "Everyone will always assume I'm a girl."

Barriers to Therapy

These included Dylan's mother experiencing difficulties understanding and supporting Dylan in his gender identity and embodiment goals, as well as difficulties arriving to therapy on time due to his parents' work schedules and his after-school activities. Dylan's mother expressed fears that Dylan being transgender and receiving psychiatric diagnoses of any kind meant that he was "not normal" and "crazy."

Intersectional and Cultural Considerations

Dylan and his mother reported stigma around treatment-seeking in their family, and attributed this to cultural stigma about mental health in their Chinese American family and communities. Dylan's mother and grandmother also reported feeling influenced by anti-LGBTQ+ sentiments from China. Dylan's grandmother also lived with the family, which contributed to his mother's concerns around him coming out, as his grandmother stopped speaking to his adult cousin after they came out as transgender.

Minority Stress and Resilience Factors

Dylan described facing minority stressors that contributed to his presenting problems, including rejection sensitivity that contributed to his social anxiety, concealment of his gender identity and sexual orientation from loved ones, and internalized transphobia and monosexism. He also named community connectedness with LGBTQ+ friends as a source of resilience that helped him get through these minority stressors.

Treatment Plan

Overall, an idiographic, CBT-based treatment plan was formulated with Dylan involving: exposure and response prevention (ExRP; Foa et al., 2012) and medication referrals for his OCD and anxiety symptoms; exposure therapy for his social anxiety; gender-affirming practice involving space in therapy for Dylan to explore options for gender expression and medical interventions; as well as referrals and advocacy for Dylan (e.g., hormone therapy referrals, working with Dylan's family to request all-gender bathrooms at school). Distress tolerance and emotion regulation skills were integrated into treatment involving his social supports and building on his identity pride (e.g., connecting with social supports through text and FaceTime, watching a TV show or streaming channel that he found affirming).

Guidance for Practitioners Conducting Therapy Sessions

When working with LGBTQ+ youth, we recommend offering evidence-based treatments for the relevant psychological conditions while remaining minority stress-informed and providing psychoeducation to caregivers about LGBTQ+ topics as needed. As such, it is important to collaborate with the youth in setting the agendas for individual sessions and integrating identity-related topics. Clinicians can use CBT strategies including validation, behavioral experiments, exposures, and/or problem-solving when identity-related topics arise (e.g., coming out to a family member). Illustrating this, below is an example of how an individual therapy session might have proceeded following case conceptualization. Given that Dr. Li and Dylan had been doing ExRP for his OCD, the session opened with setting an agenda that incorporated this. Dylan also brought up wanting to come out to his 6-year-old sister, Lucy, which was added to the session agenda. Dr. Li worked with Dylan to role-play this using an age-appropriate children's book on gender diversity.

Dialogue Example #3: Session with Youth

Therapist: Good to see you, Dylan. How about we start by setting an agenda together? We usually start by checking in on your anxiety and OCD over the past week. We can discuss any updates from the week and do homework review, including if you've been engaging in or resisting compulsions and checking in on how things have been going with exposures. Anything you'd like to add?

Dylan: I know we were talking about my coming out to my sister, and I'd like to talk about that again. She uses the wrong pronouns and doesn't know my real name. *(Sighs)*

Therapist: Sure thing, I am adding that to the agenda. What level have your anxiety and OCD symptoms been this past week, each out of 10?

Dylan: Anxiety has been like a 4 or 5, and OCD at like a 6.

(*Therapist and Dylan discuss anxiety symptoms and review tracking of obsessions and compulsions [including resisting or engaging in these] over the past week and then conduct an in-vivo exposure from Dylan's exposure hierarchy. Since Dylan reported compulsions to wear gloves to avoid getting his hands dirty, Dr. Li conducted an exposure with Dylan involving touching the floor, and eventually sitting on the floor together with Dylan in-session, and Dylan resisted engaging in the response/compulsion of wearing gloves and washing his hands. Therapist checked in with Dylan on his distress before, during, and after the in-session exposure.*)

Therapist: Tell me about wanting to come out to your sister.

(continued)

Dylan: I want her to use my name and pronouns. My parents got the book you recommended, "Jack (Not Jackie)[3]," and it could be a good way to come out to Lucy, since she's six. I talked to my Mom and Dad about reading it to her, and you're right; they're on board.

Therapist: Great. How were you thinking of using the book?

Dylan: Well, I read to her maybe a few times a week when we're waiting for dinner or sometimes after. I could read it to her then, and see if she has questions.

Therapist: That sounds like an effective plan — you have thought about when you're going to do it, and how you can raise the topic in a way that she can understand given her age. Is there anything you're feeling worried about?

Dylan: Yeah, I guess I'm worried about her not getting it or asking me a lot of questions. Or not wanting to call me by my name and pronouns.

Therapist: Would you want to role-play this, and we can practice together how you might navigate that? You could choose if I'm you and you're Lucy, or vice versa.

Dylan: Sure. I can be Lucy.

Therapist (as Dylan): Okay. (*Reads book aloud.*) So, Lucy, just like the person in this book, I want you to know that I'm actually your brother instead of your sister, and my name is actually Dylan.

Dylan (as Lucy): I don't get it. You're not my sister anymore?

Therapist (as Dylan): You know how your friend Sarah has a brother and a sister?

Dylan (as Lucy): Yeah …

Therapist (as Dylan): Well, what do you think the difference is between a brother and a sister?

Dylan (as Lucy): One's a boy and one's a girl.

Therapist (as Dylan): Right. Sarah's brother and sister both love Sarah and care about her; the only difference is that one's a boy and one's a girl. It turns out that even though some people thought I was a girl, I'm actually a boy, so instead of a sister, you have a brother. I'm still the same person and care about you, and we'll still do the same things we always do together. I just want you to know my name is Dylan and I'm your brother.

Dylan (as Lucy): Okay.

Therapist: How was that?

Dylan: I think that works. I think I can do it.

Therapist: Great. When would you do this?

(continued)

[3] (Silverman, 2018)

Dylan: Maybe next week on Friday after dinner, since we will have more time then in case Lucy has questions.
Therapist: Would it be helpful to also go over what to do if Lucy does not react in a way you would like?
Dylan: Yes, definitely.
(*Therapist and Dylan discuss strategies to cope ahead for a possible negative reaction from his sister, including expressing appreciation to Lucy for hearing him out even if she does not like hearing what he said, practicing acceptance of the situation and mindfulness of his own emotions and thoughts, reminding himself that a negative reaction likely reflects how his sister was socialized and does not take away his worth as a person, and planning a call with his friends for support after the conversation.*)

Throughout treatment, Dr. Li also met with Dylan's parents as needed to provide support and psychoeducation, including discussing the book mentioned above. Below is an example of a session between Dr. Li and Dylan's mother discussing concerns she had about when and how to use Dylan's pronouns, as well as feelings of losing a daughter.

Dialogue Example #4: Session with Dylan's Mother
(*Therapist collaboratively sets an agenda with Dylan's mother.*)
Therapist: Thank you for meeting with me. I want to make sure we have space to discuss when and how to use Dylan's pronouns, as well as feelings around losing your daughter.
Mother: I think you wanted to discuss pronouns and I'm not really sure how this will help. I'm just not very good at pronouns, and actually, I don't like this at all.
Therapist: I appreciate your openness in discussing this, and I understand that adjusting to new pronouns can be challenging. I'd like to understand the emotions you're experiencing. Can you say what you mean when you say you don't like this at all?
Mother: I don't know. This just isn't what I pictured for my child, you know? First she says she's pansexual, and now she's transgender. Why is this happening to us? I feel confused.
Therapist: I hear that this is a significant shift from what you had envisioned for your child, and it's completely normal to feel a sense of loss or confusion during this change. It's okay to grieve the image you had in your mind, and I want you to know that your feelings are valid. Exploring these emotions can help us understand and navigate this together. Can you share more about the specific aspects that are challenging for you, or any fears you might have about what this means for your child and your relationship?

(continued)

Mother: It just seems like everything is changing so quickly, and that I can't understand or support my child. I never expected this, and it's hard to wrap my head around it.

Therapist: I can imagine that the pace of change can be overwhelming, and it's natural to have the emotions you are feeling. You mentioned feeling confused; maybe you're feeling scared and a bit sad or angry, too. *(Mother nods.)* It's okay to take the time you need to experience these emotions. No emotion lasts forever, and I'm here to give you the space to feel and process these emotions. *(Mother nods again.)* It also might be helpful for you and Dylan to have open conversations about your respective experiences and concerns. How would you feel about initiating a conversation with Dylan about your feelings and concerns, emphasizing your desire to be there for him?

Mother: I guess I could try, but I don't even know where to start. What if I say the wrong thing or accidentally hurt her?

Therapist: Having concerns about the conversation shows how much you care! *(Mother smiles.)* You might consider expressing your genuine intentions to Dylan, letting him know that you're navigating your own emotions and that you want to understand his experience better. You could say something like, "I've been reflecting on the changes, and I want you to know that I love and support you. I may not fully understand everything right now, but I'm trying to learn and be here for you the best I can. Can we talk about how you've been feeling and how I can best support you during this time?" How does that approach feel to you?

Mother: I guess I could try that. But I don't know if I can just suddenly use he/him pronouns. It feels so unnatural.

Therapist: I appreciate your willingness, and using new pronouns is unnatural at first. Getting used to new pronouns takes time—just like I imagine it may have taken time to try to understand Dylan saying he's pansexual. (*Mother nods.*) It's a process we can navigate together. It might be helpful to start by practicing in more private settings, such as when you're alone or with your husband. Gradually incorporating the new pronouns into your conversations can make the transition feel more organic. If you find yourself struggling, don't hesitate to reach out, and we can practice it together. It's about finding a pace that feels comfortable for you while also supporting Dylan. How do you feel about that?

Mother: Okay, I'll try but I'm not promising anything. When do I use he/him, and who do I use it with? Do I use he/him with everyone?

Therapist: That's a great question. Ultimately, it's Dylan's decision, but it sounds like for now he asked you to refer to him as he/him at home. As for other people, how do you feel about checking in with him on who he would like you to use he/him with?

(continued)

Mother: I guess I could do that. It just feels like so much to get used to and to remember. What if I just refer to Dylan as Dylan or "the teenager"?

Therapist: That could be a starting point. And over time, perhaps we can practice pronouns together in our sessions.

Mother: Fine. (*Sighs.*) This is all so much. It just feels like I'm losing my daughter.

Therapist: Many parents say this can feel like a loss. What emotions are coming up for you now?

Mother: Sadness, grief. I feel bad for having these feelings but I can't help it.

Therapist: Then maybe shame or guilt, too?

Mother: Yes, those too.

Therapist: Of course, I can see how much you care for Dylan and want the best for him — and we can also hold space for your feelings too in all this, and the experience you're having of losing a daughter. I wonder if another part of this is that you might also be gaining a son.

(*Mother nods, and Dr. Li creates space for her to continue sharing emotions. Dr. Li collaborates with her to brainstorm sources of support, such as individual therapy or a group for parents of transgender youth.*)

In addition to individual-level support, Dr. Li integrated advocacy into treatment with Dylan. Structural changes that ensure LGBTQ+ youths have equal opportunities and access, such as in school settings, are needed to effectively address the impacts of minority stress on LGBTQ+ youth's mental health in the long-term (Hatzenbuehler, 2011). When working with youth, this can include collaborating with families and advocating in schools, particularly as related to obtaining access to bathrooms or sports teams that align with one's gender and making school dances inclusive of clothing choices and partners. Providers can support youth by contacting the school and offering to provide education on these topics, and to brainstorm with school staff on how to increase inclusivity (e.g., making trainings on inclusivity available to all staff) and how to signal safety to LGBTQ+ youth (e.g., using pride flags and pronoun pins) when anti-LGBTQ+ state legislation has made school settings non-affirming. The therapist can also advocate by joining organizational efforts to protest and challenge anti-LGBTQ+ legislation and/or contact their elected officials. Additionally, given the history of pathologization and exclusion of LGBTQ+ communities within the medical and mental healthcare fields, there can be mistrust for the mental healthcare system among LGBTQ+ communities, and more so for LGBTQ+ communities with multiple minoritized identities, such as LGBTQ+ communities of color and LGBTQ+ communities with disabilities. Thus, it is imperative to be mindful of intersecting minoritized identities an LGBTQ+ youth may hold, including working with youth to understand language they may use to describe their identities, and to collaborate with each youth closely to understand their personal needs and how to most effectively advocate for them with families, schools, extracurriculars, and state legislatures.

For Dylan's case, after he reported discomfort using the binary multi-stall bathrooms at school and wanting advocacy around this, Dr. Li obtained his and his parents' permission to set up a meeting with the school and provide education on the importance of access to all-gender bathrooms. A release of information (ROI) was completed for this. The school noted that there was a single-use, all-gender bathroom that was locked to students, but which teachers and staff could access with a key. Dr. Li worked with the school to ensure this bathroom was not locked. Given Dylan's anxiety about asking school staff for access to the bathroom, Dr. Li also worked with Dylan to come up with an interpersonally effective script to ask to use this all-gender bathroom as needed and roleplayed this in session.

Additionally, Dylan reported wanting to join the boys' basketball team while having concerns that he would not be allowed to. Dr. Li worked with Dylan to check the facts around this, and Dr. Li also discussed this with the school, providing education as needed. The school noted they would allow Dylan to join the boys' basketball team, and Dr. Li worked with Dylan to use interpersonal effectiveness skills to directly ask to join the team, which he did. At the same time, Dr. Li provided support to Dylan's parents, who had concerns about him joining the boys' basketball team due to fears of Dylan experiencing derogatory remarks from others. Dr. Li supported the parents in clarifying that the coach was supportive and that a pathway of parental support could be expressing their support for Dylan to him, rather than blocking him from joining. The parents supported this plan after a couple of parent sessions devoted to this issue.

Treatment Summary

Following the treatment plan described above, Dylan practiced coming out to his sister with his friends and came out to his sister the week afterwards. He reported feeling that his sister was receptive, which was a relief, and that he felt happy about being out with her. Sessions continued for 1 year with both Dylan and his parents to address Dylan's OCD, social anxiety, and school avoidance. Dylan also completed a neuropsychological evaluation which suggested that his concerns with communication difficulties were best explained by social anxiety. A diagnosis of a social communication disorder was not supported. Although Dr. Li and Dylan had several sessions of psychoeducation and discussions together with his parents about medical interventions, and his father agreed to it, Dylan's mother did not agree to allow Dylan to start masculinizing hormones. Later, when Dylan reached the age of 18, Dylan's parents reached back out, expressing that they had agreed to allow him to start hormone therapy, upon which Dr. Li connected Dylan and his parents to an endocrinologist referral.

Parent sessions included psychoeducation around gender identity, support with grief around feeling like they lost a daughter and practicing the use of Dylan's name and pronouns. Dr. Li also worked with Dylan's mother, per her request, to write a script apologizing to Dylan about her initial reaction to his coming out (i.e., "I know I had some big feelings when you first came out to me. I was confused, but I am continuing to learn and I love you."). Dylan's mother communicated this to Dylan, who received this positively. Parent sessions also included setting up a reward system for Dylan's completion of exposures targeting his OCD and social anxiety. At the outset of treatment, Dylan's parents suggested using his correct name and pronouns as a reward for him completing exposures and going to school. Later in treatment, his parents suggested using hormone therapy as a reward. In both instances, Dr. Li clarified that gender affirmation is necessary, and is a right, and therefore not an appropriate reward. Dr. Li clarified rights versus rewards, and worked with Dylan and his parents to identify rewards for completing exposures, which included a meal at Dylan's favorite restaurant and a video game. This is consistent with evidence-based principles of behavioral parent training and gender-affirming practice that reduces rejection and cultivates support (Johnson et al., 2020).

As treatment continued, Dylan and his parents reported partial remission of his OCD and social anxiety symptoms and a decrease in school avoidance. They also reported that interference with daily functioning was significantly reduced. Dylan attended classes regularly even with occasional urges to go to the wellness center, and no longer wore gloves as a means to neutralize obsessions with being clean. He did continue to occasionally write and rewrite his homework, despite this symptom being targeted in treatment. However, he spent less time overall engaging in this compulsion, which caused less interference in his life.

Although Dylan continued to endorse gender dysphoria during treatment, he reported feeling more supported by his family in using his name and pronouns over time, and feeling proud of himself for advocating for his desire to join the boys' basketball team. After his parents reached back out for hormone therapy, Dylan started masculinizing hormones, which was associated with decreased gender dysphoria, and he reported that this felt like a helpful step towards his embodiment goals.

Throughout treatment, Dr. Li used a culturally humble approach to create space for Dylan and his family to share identities and lived experiences, including acknowledgment of cultural norms and beliefs (e.g., cultural stigma around transgender identities and mental health treatment). Dr. Li used these discussions, including planful self-disclosure of her own identities, to encourage Dylan and his family to share any feelings and reactions they had regarding Dr. Li and her identities throughout treatment, and to validate that each person's perspectives came from an understandable lived experience even if they differed from one another. This practice encouraged Dylan and his parents to work towards validating each other's emotions while collaborating on Dylan's treatment goals.

Conclusion

This case demonstrates how clinicians can collaborate with youth and family members while practicing cultural humility and advocacy throughout therapy. Continued research is needed on the design and dissemination of interventions (e.g., digital adaptations, single-session interventions) providing effective, affirmative care for LGBTQ+ youth and their families. Advocacy is also needed for legislation that decrease anti-LGBTQ+ stigma and increase accessibility of care for LGBTQ+ youth. Additional resources are provided in Table 7.2.

Table 7.2 Additional resources for working with LGBTQ+ youth and families

General resources
The Trevor Project: https://www.thetrevorproject.org/
Human Rights Campaign: https://www.hrc.org/
The WPATH Standards of Care 8, particularly the child and adolescent chapters (Coleman et al., 2022)
The Audre Lorde Project: https://alp.org/
National Center for Transgender Equality: https://transequality.org/
American Civil Liberties Union – Mapping Attacks on LGBTQ Rights in U.S. State Legislatures: https://www.aclu.org/legislative-attacks-on-lgbtq-rights
Resources for LGBTQ+ youth
The Gender Identity Workbook for Kids: A Guide to Exploring Who You Are (Storck, 2018)
The Gender Quest Workbook: A Guide for Teens and Young Adults Exploring Gender Identity (Testa et al., 2015)
Genders & Sexualities Alliances (GSA) Network: https://gsanetwork.org
Safe Schools Coalition: http://www.safeschoolscoalition.org/
The Queer and Transgender Resilience Workbook: Skills for Navigating Sexual Orientation and Gender Expression (Singh, 2018), particularly appropriate for teens or older teens transitioning into adulthood
Resources for caregivers of LGBTQ+ youth
The Transgender Teen (Brill & Kenney, 2016)
The Transgender Child: A Handbook for Families and Professionals (Brill & Pepper, 2008)
Unconditional: A Guide to Loving and Supporting Your LGBTQ Child (Eriksen, 2022)
This is a Book for Parents of Gay Kids: A Question & Answer Guide to Everyday Life (Owens-Reid & Russo, 2014)
PFLAG: https://pflag.org/
Gender Spectrum: https://www.genderspectrum.org

References

American Psychological Association. (2015). Guidelines for psychological practice with transgender and gender nonconforming people. *American Psychologist, 70*(9), 832–864. https://doi.org/10.1037/a0039906

APA Task Force on Psychological Practice with Sexual Minority Persons. (2021). *Guidelines for Psychological Practice with Sexual Minority Persons*. American Psychological Association.

Brill, S., & Kenney, L. (2016). *The transgender teen*. Cleis Press.

Brill, S., & Pepper, R. (2008). *The transgender child: A handbook for families and professionals*. Cleis Press.

Chodzen, G., Hidalgo, M. A., Chen, D., & Garofalo, R. (2019). Minority stress factors associated with depression and anxiety among transgender and gender-nonconforming youth. *Journal of Adolescent Health, 64*(4), 467–471. https://doi.org/10.1016/j.jadohealth.2018.07.006

Cohen, J. M. (2023). *Doing affirmative cognitive behavior therapy with LGBTQ+ youth and their families*.

Cohen, J., Woicicki, K., Lui, M., & Wilson, H. (2015). *The development and implementation of a CBT informed group for sexual minority adolescents*.

Cohen, J. M., Feinstein, B. A., & Fox, K. (2022). The promise of digital mental Health for LGBTQ+ youths. *Psychiatric Services, 73*(9), 1069–1072. https://doi.org/10.1176/appi.ps.202100569

Coleman, E., Radix, A. E., Bouman, W. P., Brown, G. R., de Vries, A. L. C., Deutsch, M. B., Ettner, R., Fraser, L., Goodman, M., Green, J., Hancock, A. B., Johnson, T. W., Karasic, D. H., Knudson, G. A., Leibowitz, S. F., Meyer-Bahlburg, H. F. L., Monstrey, S. J., Motmans, J.,

Nahata, L., et al. (2022). Standards of Care for the Health of transgender and gender diverse people, version 8. *International Journal of Transgender Health, 23*(sup1), S1–S259. https://doi.org/10.1080/26895269.2022.2100644

Craig, S. L., & Austin, A. (2016). The AFFIRM open pilot feasibility study: A brief affirmative cognitive behavioral coping skills group intervention for sexual and gender minority youth. *Children and Youth Services Review, 64*, 136–144. https://doi.org/10.1016/j.childyouth.2016.02.022

Craig, S. L., Iacono, G., Pascoe, R., & Austin, A. (2021). Adapting clinical skills to telehealth: Applications of affirmative cognitive-behavioral therapy with LGBTQ+ youth. *Clinical Social Work Journal, 49*(4), 471–483. https://doi.org/10.1007/s10615-021-00796-x

Cyrus, K. (2017). Multiple minorities as multiply marginalized: Applying the minority stress theory to LGBTQ people of color. *Journal of Gay & Lesbian Mental Health, 21*(3), 194–202. https://doi.org/10.1080/19359705.2017.1320739

Dank, M., Yu, L., Yahner, J., Pelletier, E., & Mora, M. (2015). *Locked in: Interactions with the criminal justice and child welfare systems for LGBTQ youth, YMSM, and YWSW who engage in survival sex*. William & Mary Law School Scholarship Repository.

Davies, R., & Davies, M. (2020). The (slow) Depathologizing of gender incongruence. *The Journal of Nervous and Mental Disease, 208*, 152–154. https://doi.org/10.1097/NMD.0000000000001119

Diamond, G. M., Diamond, G. S., Levy, S., Closs, C., Ladipo, T., & Siqueland, L. (2012). Attachment-based family therapy for suicidal lesbian, gay, and bisexual adolescents: A treatment development study and open trial with preliminary findings. *Psychotherapy, 49*(1), 62–71. https://doi.org/10.1037/a0026247

Ehrensaft, D. (2017). Gender nonconforming youth: Current perspectives. *Adolescent Health, Medicine and Therapeutics, 8*, 57–67. https://doi.org/10.2147/AHMT.S110859

Eriksen, T. M. (2022). *Unconditional: A guide to loving and supporting your LGBTQ child*. Mango Media.

Fenway Health. (2022). *Binding resources*.

Foa, E. B., Yadin, E., & Lichner, T. K. (2012). *Exposure and response (ritual) prevention for obsessive compulsive disorder: Therapist guide*. Oxford University Press.

Galupo, M. P., Pulice-Farrow, L., & Pehl, E. (2021). "There is nothing to do about it": Nonbinary individuals' experience of gender dysphoria. *Transgender Health, 6*(2), 101–110. https://doi.org/10.1089/trgh.2020.0041

Goldbach, J. T., Rhoades, H., Mamey, M. R., Senese, J., Karys, P., & Marsiglia, F. F. (2021). Reducing behavioral health symptoms by addressing minority stressors in LGBTQ adolescents: A randomized controlled trial of proud & empowered. *BMC Public Health, 21*(1), 2315. https://doi.org/10.1186/s12889-021-12357-5

Goldbach, J. T., Rhoades, H., Rusow, J., & Karys, P. (2023). The development of proud & empowered: An intervention for promoting LGBTQ adolescent mental health. *Child Psychiatry & Human Development, 54*(2), 481–492. https://doi.org/10.1007/s10578-021-01250-2

Goodman, J., & Israel, T. (2019). An online intervention to promote predictors of supportive parenting for sexual minority youth. *Journal of Family Psychology, 34*. https://doi.org/10.1037/fam0000614

Gordon, C. M. (2022). Caught in the middle: The care of transgender youth in Texas. *Pediatrics, 149*(6), e2022057475. https://doi.org/10.1542/peds.2022-057475

Guz, S., Kattari, S. K., Atteberry-Ash, B., Klemmer, C. L., Call, J., & Kattari, L. (2021). Depression and suicide risk at the cross-section of sexual orientation and gender identity for youth. *Journal of Adolescent Health, 68*(2), 317–323. https://doi.org/10.1016/j.jadohealth.2020.06.008

Hastings, J., Bobb, C., Wolfe, M., Amaro, J. Z., & Amand, C. S. (2021). Medical care for nonbinary youth: Individualized gender care beyond a binary framework. *Pediatric Annals, 50*(9), e384–e390. https://doi.org/10.3928/19382359-20210818-03

Hatzenbuehler, M. L. (2011). The social environment and suicide attempts in lesbian, gay, and bisexual youth. *Pediatrics, 127*(5), 896–903. https://doi.org/10.1542/peds.2010-3020

Hays, P. A. (1996). Addressing the complexities of culture and gender in counseling. *Journal of Counseling & Development, 74*(4), 332–338. https://doi.org/10.1002/j.1556-6676.1996.tb01876.x

Heck, N. C. (2015). The potential to promote resilience: Piloting a minority stress-informed, GSA-based, mental health promotion program for LGBTQ youth. *Psychology of Sexual Orientation and Gender Diversity, 2*, 225–231. https://doi.org/10.1037/sgd0000110

Huebner, D. M., Rullo, J. E., Thoma, B. C., McGarrity, L. A., & Mackenzie, J. (2013). Piloting Lead with love: A film-based intervention to improve parents' responses to their lesbian, gay, and bisexual children. *The Journal of Primary Prevention, 34*(5), 359–369. https://doi.org/10.1007/s10935-013-0319-y

Johnson, K. C., LeBlanc, A. J., Sterzing, P. R., Deardorff, J., Antin, T., & Bockting, W. O. (2020). Trans adolescents' perceptions and experiences of their parents' supportive and rejecting behaviors. *Journal of Counseling Psychology, 67*(2), 156–170. https://doi.org/10.1037/cou0000419.supp

Kline, N. S., Griner, S. B., Neelamegam, M., Webb, N. J., Morales, J. J., & Rhodes, S. D. (2022). Responding to "Don't say gay" Laws in the US: Research priorities and considerations for Health equity. *Sexuality Research and Social Policy, 19*(4), 1397–1402. https://doi.org/10.1007/s13178-022-00773-0

Lucassen, M. F. G., Merry, S. N., Hatcher, S., & Frampton, C. M. A. (2015). Rainbow SPARX: A novel approach to addressing depression in Sexual Minority youth. *Cognitive and Behavioral Practice, 22*(2), 203–216. https://doi.org/10.1016/j.cbpra.2013.12.008

Matsuno, E., & Israel, T. (2021). The parent support program: Development and acceptability of an online intervention aimed at increasing supportive behaviors among parents of trans youth. *Journal of GLBT Family Studies, 17*(5), 413–431. https://doi.org/10.1080/1550428X.2020.1868369

Nakao, M., Shirotsuki, K., & Sugaya, N. (2021). Cognitive–behavioral therapy for management of mental health and stress-related disorders: Recent advances in techniques and technologies. *BioPsychoSocial Medicine, 15*(1), 16. https://doi.org/10.1186/s13030-021-00219-w

Owens-Reid, D., & Russo, K. (2014). *This is a book for parents of gay kids: A question & answer guide to everyday life*. Chronicle Books.

Pachankis, J. E., McConocha, E. M., Reynolds, J. S., Winston, R., Adeyinka, O., Harkness, A., Burton, C. L., Behari, K., Sullivan, T. J., Eldahan, A. I., Esserman, D. A., Hatzenbuehler, M. L., & Safren, S. A. (2019). Project ESTEEM protocol: A randomized controlled trial of an LGBTQ-affirmative treatment for young adult sexual minority men's mental and sexual health. *BMC Public Health, 19*(1), 1086. https://doi.org/10.1186/s12889-019-7346-4

Pachankis, J. E., McConocha, E. M., Clark, K. A., Wang, K., Behari, K., Fetzner, B. K., Brisbin, C. D., Scheer, J. R., & Lehavot, K. (2020). A Transdiagnostic Minority stress intervention for gender diverse Sexual Minority women's depression, anxiety, and unhealthy alcohol use: A randomized controlled trial. *Journal of Consulting and Clinical Psychology, 88*(7), 613–630. https://doi.org/10.1037/ccp0000508

Pachankis, J. E., Soulliard, Z. A., Seager van Dyk, I., Layland, E. K., Clark, K. A., Levine, D. S., & Jackson, S. D. (2022). Training in LGBTQ-affirmative cognitive behavioral therapy: A randomized controlled trial across LGBTQ community centers. *Journal of Consulting and Clinical Psychology, 90*, 582–599. https://doi.org/10.1037/ccp0000745

Plöderl, M., & Tremblay, P. (2015). Mental health of sexual minorities. A systematic review. *International Review of Psychiatry (Abingdon, England), 27*, 1–19. https://doi.org/10.3109/09540261.2015.1083949

Rafferty, J., Yogman, M., Baum, R., Gambon, T. B., Lavin, A., Mattson, G., Wissow, L. S., Breuner, C., Alderman, E. M., Grubb, L. K., Powers, M. E., Upadhya, K., Wallace, S. B., Hunt, L., Gearhart, A. T., Harris, C., Lowe, K. M., Rodgers, C. T., & Sherer, I. M. (2018). Ensuring comprehensive care and support for transgender and gender-diverse children and adolescents. *Pediatrics, 142*(4), e20182162. https://doi.org/10.1542/peds.2018-2162

Ryan, C. (2010). Engaging families to support lesbian, gay, bisexual, and transgender youth: The family acceptance project: Part of a special issue: Creating supportive environments for lesbian, gay, bisexual, and transgender youth. *Prevention Researcher, 17*(4), 11–13.

Ryan, C., Huebner, D., Diaz, R. M., & Sanchez, J. (2009). Family rejection as a predictor of negative Health outcomes in white and Latino lesbian, gay, and bisexual young adults. *Pediatrics, 123*(1), 346–352. https://doi.org/10.1542/peds.2007-3524

Seager van Dyk, I., Clark, K. A., Dougherty, L. R., & Pachankis, J. E. (2022a). Parent responses to their sexual and gender minority children: Implications for parent-focused supportive interventions. *Psychology of Sexual Orientation and Gender Diversity*. https://doi.org/10.1037/sgd0000589

Seager van Dyk, I., Layland, E. K., Soulliard, Z. A., & Pachankis, J. E. (2022b). *Piloting LGBTQ+-affirmative cognitive behavioral therapy for youth*. New Zealand Psychological Society.

Shen, J., Rubin, A., Cohen, K., Hart, E. A., Sung, J., McDanal, R., Roulston, C., Sotomayor, I., Fox, K. R., & Schleider, J. L. (2023). Randomized evaluation of an online single-session intervention for minority stress in LGBTQ+ adolescents. *Internet Interventions, 33*, 100633. https://doi.org/10.1016/j.invent.2023.100633

Silverman, E. (2018). *Jack (not Jackie)*. Little Bee Books.

Singh, A. A. (2018). *The queer and transgender resilience workbook: Skills for navigating Sexual orientation and gender expression*. New Harbinger Publications.

Storck, K. (2018). *The gender identity workbook for kids: A guide to exploring who you are*. New Harbinger Publications.

Testa, R. J., Coolhart, D., & Peta, J. (2015). *The gender quest workbook: A guide for teens and young adults exploring gender identity*. New Harbinger Publications.

Williams, D. Y., Hall, W. J., Dawes, H. C., Srivastava, A., Radtke, S. R., Ramon, M., Bouchard, D., Chen, W.-T., & Goldbach, J. T. (2023). Relationships between internalized stigma and depression and suicide risk among queer youth in the United States: A systematic review and meta-analysis. *Frontiers in Psychiatry, 14*, 1205581. https://doi.org/10.3389/fpsyt.2023.1205581

Worthen, M. G. F. (2023). Queer identities in the 21st century: Reclamation and stigma. *Current Opinion in Psychology, 49*, 101512. https://doi.org/10.1016/j.copsyc.2022.101512

Zullo, L., Seager van Dyk, I., Ollen, E., Ramos, N., Asarnow, J., & Miranda, J. (2021). Treatment recommendations and barriers to care for suicidal LGBTQ youth: A quality improvement study. *Evidence-Based Practice in Child and Adolescent Mental Health, 6*(3), 393–409. https://doi.org/10.1080/23794925.2021.1950079

Chapter 8
Addressing Ageism Among LGBTQ+ Older Adults

Kate L. M. Hinrichs, Hannah M. Bashian, Katie C. Mendoza, Anthony N. Correro II, and Mark Brennan Ing

Highlights

- This chapter provides background about the unique lived experiences of LGBTQ+ older adults utilizing a life course perspective to examine how coming of age in various socio-historical contexts can impact development.
- Readers will understand the impact of intersecting forms of oppression on LGBTQ+ older adults' health and well-being using Minority Stress and Iridescent Life Course frameworks.
- We provide information on the intersecting effects of social stigmas and internalized self-stigmas such as ageism, heterosexism, cissexism, and homophobia, and discuss approaches to treating these in a psychotherapy context.
- Attention is given to the value of affirmative therapies and treatments that bolster resilience among LGBTQ+ older adults.
- We present a case example of an older bisexual cisgender man who is experiencing bereavement, loss, and adjustment to aging, demonstrating how internalized ageism and heterosexism can present in treatment.

K. L. M. Hinrichs (✉) · H. M. Bashian
VA Boston Healthcare System, Boston, MA, USA

Harvard Medical School, Boston, MA, USA
e-mail: Kate.Hinrichs@va.gov

K. C. Mendoza
VA Boston Healthcare System, Boston, MA, USA

A. N. Correro II
Department of Neurology, Division of Neuropsychology, Medical College of Wisconsin, Milwaukee, WI, USA

M. Brennan Ing
Brookdale Center for Healthy Aging at Hunter College, The City University of New York, New York, NY, USA

N. A. Livingston et al. (eds.), *Addressing Minority Stress and Enhancing Resilience with Diverse LGBTQ+ Clients*, CBT: Science Into Practice,
https://doi.org/10.1007/978-3-031-92836-9_8

Positionality

We are a group of clinicians, educators, and researchers in psychology at various stages in our careers. We represent a range of gender and sexual identities (cisgender, nonbinary, bisexual, gay, heterosexual, pansexual, queer) and racial/ethnic identities (Latinx, white). Our goal is to produce a resource that can support the diverse needs of LGBTQ+ older adults. Four of the authors are clinicians: three in Geropsychology who practice and supervise in a VA Medical Center and one in Neuropsychology who supervises in an assessment clinic affiliated with a medical school. One author directs a research center on healthy aging. Our lived and professional identities inform our approach to this chapter through use of sociohistorical and biopsychosocial approaches to aging and application of intersectionality through a queer framework for understanding LGBTQ+ older adults in a more nuanced way. Collectively the authors share a commitment to supporting the health and wellbeing of LGBTQ+ older adults through practice, advocacy, and research.

Introduction

The population of LGBTQ+ older adults (age 65+) in the United States (U.S.) is growing. It is estimated that 1.75–4 million LGBTQ+ older adults are living in the U.S. with an expected growth to over 7 million by 2030 (Fredriksen-Goldsen et al., 2011; SAGE, 2021). The older LGBTQ+ community is also diverse. Approximately one in five LGBTQ+ older adults are people of color, a proportion expected to double by 2050 (Choi & Meyer, 2016). There are many unique challenges faced by LGBTQ+ older adults including increased discrimination and violence, lower rates of health insurance coverage, financial barriers, and reduced access to formal social systems of care compared to heterosexual, cisgender older adults (Fredriksen-Goldsen et al., 2011). Additionally, LGBTQ+ older adults of color experience disenfranchisement, inequities, and invisibility, leading to complex experiences of oppression and resilience (Chen et al., 2022; Kum, 2017). For example, African American LGBTQ+ older adults report higher levels of LGBT-related discrimination compared to white LGBTQ+ older adults over their lifespan (Fredriksen-Goldsen et al., 2011).

When thinking of the older LGBTQ+ population, it is essential to take a lifespan perspective given the dynamic social, cultural, political, and economic revolutions of the twentieth century that directly impacted LGBTQ+ people and cultures. Given the wide range of ages included in older adulthood, it is helpful to be aware of the differences that may come up when working clinically with LGBTQ+ older adults who came of age in different historical periods; for example, consider the differences in the lived experiences between a 65-year-old and a 90-year-old. Fredriksen-Goldsen's (2018) report on the social-generational contexts of LGBTQ+ older adults demarcated three distinct generations: the Invisible, the Silenced, and the Pride. Table 8.1 highlights the social and historical contexts for each generation within the U.S. and describes generation-specific considerations.

Table 8.1 Social-generational contexts of LGBTQ+ older adults

	Invisible Generation	Silenced Generation	Pride Generation	Post-Pride Generation
Year Age ranges	1934 or earlier 90+	1935–1949 89–75	1950–1964 74–60	1965–present <60
Historical/ social context	Great depression, WWII, prohibition sodomy laws criminalized sexual behavior outside of male and female interactions Pansy craze was part of entertainment culture and normalized drag performance for entertainment purposes[a] The Society for Human Rights was the first gay rights organization and magazine described publicly as a group focusing on oppressed minorities	Post-WWII Sodomy laws continued	APA DSM-I (1952) listed homosexuality as a "sociopathic personality disturbance" Executive Order 10450 banned homosexuals from working for the federal government Illinois (1962) becomes the first state to decriminalize sexual acts between two consenting adults of the same sex in private	Stonewall Riots (1969) First gay pride marches (1970) Rainbow flag created (1978) AIDS epidemic identified (1981) and HIV identified (1984) APA DSM-III-R (1987) homosexuality removed Don't Ask Don't Tell (1993) repealed in 2010; allows LGB to serve openly in the military Pentagon ban lifted (2016); allows transgender individuals to serve Same-sex marriage legalized nationwide (2015) Pulse nightclub shooting (2016) Supreme court rules title VII of the civil rights act protects LGBTQ+ workers from discrimination (2020)

(continued)

Table 8.1 (continued)

	Invisible Generation	Silenced Generation	Pride Generation	Post-Pride Generation
Considerations[b]	Gay was often used to describe individuals with any LGBTQ+ identity Lowest rates of identity affirmation and outness More likely to never have been married Least likely to experience depression	Higher average age of identity awareness than the Invisible and Pride generations Lowest rates of identity-related stigma	More likely to experience all forms of discrimination and victimization Reclaimed presence and identity in society	Lower rates of health insurance coverage Continue to face significant barriers when accessing health care Support systems and caregiving relationships formed through partners and/or families of choice

Note: [a]Pruitt (2019), [b]Fredriksen-Goldsen (2018), Shiu et al. (2016), Anderson et al. (2022)

Contextualizing Minority Stress in the Lives of LGBTQ+ Older Adults

The Iridescent Life Course framework is a queer adaptation of life course theory that focuses on the ways in which historical and social contexts, intersecting identities, and systems of power and oppression interact to shape an individual's unique life course (Fredriksen-Goldsen et al., 2019). For example, when the Stonewall Riots occurred in 1969, members of the Invisible Generation were approaching midlife, the Silenced Generation were young adults, and the Pride Generation were children and adolescents. Historical contexts likely influenced the timing of key life events, such as LGBTQ+ identity development.

A growing body of research has documented the presence of physical and mental health disparities (e.g., higher rates of depression, disability, HIV/AIDS, tobacco use, substance misuse, cardiovascular disease, and chronic health conditions) among LGBTQ+ older adult populations (Fredriksen-Goldsen et al., 2011, 2013, 2019; Wight et al., 2015). To date, researchers have primarily framed LGBTQ+ health disparities, including those present among older adults, within the theory of minority stress (Brooks, 1981) and the minority stress model (Meyer, 2003). In contrast to younger adults, the deleterious effects of minority stress, especially expectations of rejection, on health and wellbeing may be magnified in middle-aged and older adults, and this relationship may be driven by changes in historical and social contexts (e.g., Frost et al., 2022). Yet, there are important differences in the minority stress experiences, aging trajectories, and health outcomes of the Invisible, Silenced, and Pride Generations (Fredriksen-Goldsen et al., 2022a, b, 2023). As such, joint consideration of the Iridescent Life Course framework and the minority stress model allows for a more nuanced understanding of the experiences of LGBTQ+ older adults.

Ageism and Its Impact on Health and Well-Being

In examining the unique experience of older LGBTQ+ adults, it is vital to understand the impact of ageism and its role in health and well-being. Ageism is a bias against an individual due to their age (Butler, 1969). Ageism is prevalent throughout society and across many, particularly individualistic, cultures, and is often overlooked. Ageism is experienced across the lifespan but occurs most often in later life. In one study, 93% of adults aged 50–80 reported experiencing at least one form of ageism in their daily life (Allen et al., 2022). Ageism often overlaps with ableism and both can cause individuals to be excluded, or exclude themselves, from society.

Ageism presents as either explicit or implicit (Cary et al., 2017). Explicit, or hostile ageism, is an overt form of ageism and includes prejudices (e.g., older adults are worth less and drain the economy). In contrast, implicit, or benevolent, ageism is a more pervasive and accepted form of discrimination and includes infantilization, and assumptions of incompetence and disability (Cary et al., 2017). A common form of benevolent ageism is when an individual speaks to an older adult with the assumption that they are either hard of hearing, cognitively impaired, or incapable of taking care of themselves by speaking loudly or slowly.

Ageism is unique in that all people can experience the negative effects at some point in their lives as they age into a minoritized group. This contrasts with other prejudices in which social marginalization is lifelong and/or group assignment is based on static traits. Thus, ageism can present both in how individuals treat older adults at large but also how older adults view themselves and their own group memberships. This is known as internalized ageism. Internalized ageism is a negative bias a person holds towards their own aging process, and it is associated with worse physical and mental health outcomes and higher risk of mortality (Levy et al., 2009).

Both internalized ageism and external experiences of ageism negatively impact older adults' well-being and experiences of ageism are associated with higher rates of depression, anxiety, and stress (Han & Richardson, 2015; Lyons et al., 2018). In fact, psychologists' ageist beliefs relate to worse treatment outcomes for older adults. Psychologists may believe older people are more rigid in their thinking and less likely to benefit from therapy (Lederman & Shefler, 2023). There is a common misconception that depression is a normal part of aging when in fact depression rates tend to decrease with age (Reynolds et al., 2015). Further, numerous studies have demonstrated the efficacy of therapy for older adults, and the notion that you "can't teach an old dog new tricks" is not supported in the literature (APA, 2014; Karel et al., 2012).

Ageism and Intersectionality

When considering the negative impact of ageism on LGBTQ+ older adults' well-being, it is useful to apply the Iridescent Life Course Framework to consider the intersections of age, generation, and stigmatized identities or experiences. Older LGBTQ+ folks report higher rates of depression and anxiety compared to their cisgender heterosexual peers (Fredriksen-Goldsen et al., 2013). Although minority stress theory provides some rationale for this difference, it does not account for how significant this difference is. To better understand, Feinstein et al., (2023) examined how experiences of age discrimination in older LGBTQ+ older adults differed from cisgender heterosexual older adults and whether this accounted for the difference in depression and anxiety rates among these populations. The study indeed found that LGBTQ+ older adults reported significantly more age discrimination than their cisgender heterosexual peers and that this accounted for the higher rates of depression and anxiety. This study begs the question: what accounts for the higher rates of age discrimination among LGBTQ+ older adults? One possible explanation is the unique experience of discrimination that older LGBTQ+ adults face in the health care setting such as fear of discrimination from healthcare providers due to their sexual or gender identity and/or need to conceal their identity from care staff or residents in nursing homes for fear of discrimination (Feinstein et al., 2023).

Ageism is also present within LGBTQ+ communities (Hoy-Ellis et al., 2016). Many of these communities are youth-focused, offering resources for younger LGBTQ+ folks while ignoring older individuals (Emlet, 2006). This age bias may lead to social isolation for older LGBTQ+ individuals and make it harder for them to find support and access resources. Although there is burgeoning discussion about ageism within LGBTQ+ communities, empirical work on this topic has been limited. Grant et al. (2010) described how ageism within LGBTQ+ communities marginalizes older adults, rendering them invisible, and contributes to internalized ageism. Wight et al. (2015) examined the association of internalized gay ageism (a confluence of ageism and homophobia) and depressive symptoms among older gay and bisexual men and found ageism within the LGBTQ+ community and homophobia in society at-large accelerate subjective aging (one's internal sense of one's age). However, positive perceptions about oneself (cognitions such as "I matter," or "I am needed") moderated the association, thereby reducing depressive symptoms. In contrast, Brennan-Ing et al. (2022) found that psychological and emotional connections to the gay community among older gay and bisexual men were protective against internalized ageism and body image dissatisfaction and promoted healthy behaviors. However, these associations were weaker for those who were HIV-positive, suggestive of the impact of HIV stigma in the LGBTQ+ community.

Chen et al. (2022) conducted a systematic review that revealed the unique experiences of LGBTQ+ ethnic minority older adults. Both ethnic minority and majority LGBTQ+ older adults deal with the ramifications of sexual orientation and gender identity-based discrimination and stigma. However, ethnic minority LGBTQ+ older adults experience more isolation and discrimination within LGBTQ+ spaces due to pervasive racism, which is particularly impactful for older Black gay and bisexual men (Haile et al., 2014). Spirituality is also a more salient aspect of lived experience for ethnic minority LGBTQ+ older people in comparison to ethnic majorities (Chen et al., 2022). And while gay and bisexual men and transgender women regardless of age are disproportionately affected by HIV, HIV is particularly prevalent in communities of color in the U.S. (Centers for Disease Control and Prevention, 2018), and HIV stigma represents an additional aspect of intersectional stigma. Haile et al. (2011) addressed intersectional stigma related to age, sexual orientation, race, socioeconomic status, and HIV status. They found that Black, HIV-positive men who reported difficulty meeting the costs of living and being unemployed felt dehumanized by health care, law enforcement, and religious institutions.

LGBTQ+ older adults may be hesitant to seek out medical or mental health support, due to very real concerns of experiencing stigma and discrimination when disclosing their sexual and gender identities to health care providers (Adams, 2016), leading to poorer health outcomes and leading some to "recloset" in medical settings (Porter et al., 2016). This highlights the importance of intersectionality when developing policy and programmatic responses to address the needs of older LGBTQ+ adults to mitigate the impact of structural power and oppression. Adams (2016) recommended aging service providers take a holistic approach in developing programs for diverse older LGBTQ+ populations, including tailored programming that addresses the needs of specific subgroups, and increasing access by locating services in the communities where these older adults live rather than concentrating them in areas dominated by white gay and bisexual men which is typically the case. Ultimately, psychologists must be mindful of how experiences with intersectional stigma may impact their clients' current presentation and past mental health history and approach their practice with this population with cultural humility.

Resilience and Aging

When considering the impact of age across diverse communities of LGBTQ+ older adults, we must also recognize the unique strengths and resources available to sexual and gender minorities who have a great deal of lived experience. Resilience is defined as the capacity to recover or grow from adverse life experiences. Some of the most pivotal work on personal resilience in the context of LGBTQ+ aging is Kimmel's (1978) work on "crisis competence." Kimmel posited that the crisis experienced by LGBTQ+ youth and young adults when coming to terms with the implications of their sexual identities, including family disruption and alienation, provided an important perspective and built a competence for managing other crises across the life course. This perspective has been supported by empirical work. For example, as compared to older heterosexual men living with HIV, older gay and bisexual men living with HIV are impacted less by HIV stigma and are better able to marshal personal resources to mitigate HIV stigma (Emlet et al., 2013; Porter et al., 2019), suggesting successfully coping with sexual orientation-related stigma may confer competency in coping with HIV stigma.

Religion and spirituality may also serve as important sources of resilience among older LGBTQ+ adults. On a personal level, religious and spiritual beliefs can support coping and adaptation to life challenges. Yet, in the face of homophobic religious environments, older LGBTQ+ adults may undergo a series of intrinsic and extrinsic adaptations to retain a connection to these personal resources. These adaptations include rejecting mainstream religious beliefs that conflict with their sexual identities or being involved with LGBTQ+ affirming congregations (Bower et al. 2021; Brennan-Ing et al., 2013). Religious participation can also serve as an important source of community resilience via increased interaction, social contacts, and provision of social support (Ferraro & Koch, 1994).

Informal Social Networks

Families, friends, neighbors, and communities are often critical external sources of resilience. Having access to these resources is associated with better physical and emotional well-being in later life (Brennan-Ing et al., 2022; Cantor & Brennan, 2000). The informal social networks of older LGBTQ+ adults are shaped by the sociohistorical contexts they experienced (Breder & Bockting, 2023; Fredriksen-Goldsen, 2018). It was common in prior generations for LGBTQ+ people to be ostracized from their families of origin, with many moving away to more accepting communities (Barker et al., 2006; Croghan et al., 2014). Many older LGBTQ+ people formed families of choice (non-kin friends, neighbors, and other social contacts), many of whom were also sexual and gender minorities, providing them with the companionship, social interaction, and support that they could not receive from families of origin (de Vries & Hoctel, 2007; Shippy et al., 2004). However, it would be an overgeneralization to state that all older LGBTQ+ adults lack connections with their families of origin. There is evidence of a reactivation or strengthening of family ties in circumstances of need, such as following a diagnosis of HIV (Brennan-Ing et al., 2017). Nonetheless, older LGBTQ+ adults (as compared to their heterosexual and cisgender peers) have had less access to social support resources from their families of origin and fewer have a partner, spouse, or children as their primary sources of support and caregiving in later life (Brennan-Ing et al., 2017; Fredriksen-Goldsen et al., 2011).

One concern with a lack of connection with families of origin is that they tend to provide the bulk of support for older adults requiring assistance (e.g., meal preparation, shopping, housekeeping, financial support, personal care tasks). When it comes to instrumental support, older LGBTQ+ adults with the most diverse networks (comprised of families of choice and families of origin) have the most support available and are most likely to have caregiving needs met (Brennan-Ing et al., 2017; Breder & Bockting, 2023). In contrast, non-kin social supports (friends or families of choice) are primarily relied upon to provide emotional support and advice (Barker et al., 2006; Breder & Bockting, 2023; Cantor & Brennan, 2000; Shippy et al., 2004). While families of choice are critical to successful aging for LGBTQ+ older adults, the level of assistance they provide does not entirely compensate for the lack of family support.

Given the physical and mental health disparities experienced by older LGBTQ+ adults, many will require care in their later years and rely on their partner or spouse or will turn to friends to be their caregivers (Barker et al., 2006). However, there are several challenges when non-related or unmarried individuals step into a caregiving role, including lack of legal recognition of caregiving status as well as potential conflicts with the family of origin concerning legal matters, care plans, need for institutionalized care, etc. (Cantor et al., 2004; Croghan et al., 2014). In these situations, it is important that legal documentation (e.g., durable power of attorney, health care proxies) be executed in line with the preferences of the care recipient so that they may exercise some control at a time of increased vulnerability due to incapacity.

Finally, because of high levels of unmet needs among older LGBTQ+ adults, many will need formal community-based services to meet their support and caregiving needs in later life. Cantor's *Hierarchical Compensatory Model* of social support posits that older adults prefer to receive support from close family such as partner/spouse and children. When such support is not available, they will turn to more distant relatives, then friends and neighbors, and lastly to formal sources of support such as government and community-based health and social services in a hierarchal manner (Cantor & Brennan, 2000). Given available data, the current generation of LGBTQ+ older adults will increasingly turn to the formal service sector to meet their support needs (Brennan-Ing et al., 2014). Thus, it is imperative that providers who support this population have adequate training to serve older LGBTQ+ adults in a culturally humble and competent manner to support their well-being in their later years.

Psychological Interventions

Addressing Internalized Stigma

Internalized stigma of all sorts is known to be harmful to one's mental and physical health and would benefit from treatment with psychological approaches. Some research has shown mindfulness and acceptance-based practices can be beneficial for reducing stereotypes and self-stigma (Murphy et al., 2023) and acceptance and commitment therapy (ACT) has been shown to promote flexibility in response to societal stigma (Luoma et al., 2008). There is also emerging evidence that these techniques work with specific sexual minority populations. One study using an ACT-based intervention showed a reduction in internalized homophobia, depression, anxiety, and stress (Yadavaia & Hayes, 2012). Another pilot study combining ACT with compassion-focused therapy showed promise in reducing self-stigma for gay and bisexual men living with HIV (Skinta et al., 2015). Although there is limited research around reducing aging self-stigma in psychotherapy, these acceptance based therapies may also be useful in reducing internalized ageist attitudes. Helping LGBTQ+ older adults become aware of what ageism is and how it may impact their health and well-being may be one way to start challenging internalized ageism. Further, providing psychoeducation around normal aging and exploring with older adults how their views of their own aging may be getting in the way of living their values may also improve their mental health. In addition to interventions for internalized stigma at the individual level, there has been some acknowledgement of the need for structural, societal, and policy-level interventions as well (Steward, 2022).

Resilience

Kimmel's 1978 seminal work on personal resilience in the context of LGBTQ+ aging, referred to as "crisis competence" suggests that the challenges experienced by LGBTQ+ youth when coming to terms with the implications of their sexual identities provides an important perspective and a competence for managing other challenges throughout the life course and has been supported by empirical work. Leveraging this crisis competence by recognizing and building on the psychological strengths and skills acquired by LGBTQ+ older adults over their lifetimes has been recommended when delivering mental health services to LGBTQ+ older adults (Hinrichs & Donaldson, 2017). Clinically, this can be accomplished by exploring how one survived past challenges, rallying the resources they have used in the past, and applying those skills to current struggles. For example, LGBTQ+ older adults likely have developed strategies to manage homophobia and/or cissexism directed at them from others and may leverage these skills to help cope with experiences of ageism later in life.

Affirmative Psychotherapy

Rather than serving as a specific technique or set of techniques, affirmative psychotherapy refers to a set of attitudes or approaches utilized with LGBTQ+ clients. Affirmative therapy is grounded in humanistic principles of empathy and unconditional positive regard for clients through use of overt acceptance of sexual and gender minority clients, and affirmation that their feelings, sexuality, and relationships are normal, healthy expressions of their humanity; affirmative psychotherapy is recommended for use with LGBTQ+ older adults (Hinrichs & Donaldson, 2017). Papers and guidelines outlining ways of applying affirmative psychotherapy principles to work with LGBTQ+ older adults all emphasize acknowledging, emphasizing, and strengthening resiliency and adaptability (Crisp et al., 2008; APA, 2014; APA, 2021). There is also encouragement for practitioners to consider how they might adapt various psychotherapy modalities to meet the unique needs to LGBTQ+ older adults (Crisp et al., 2008). Adaptations might include taking more time to build rapport, conducting therapy at a slower pace, and accommodating any sensory deficits such as vision or hearing.

Case Illustration

This clinical case was crafted to provide insight into the unique vulnerabilities, stressors, and resiliency factors that LGBTQ+ older adults experience. We demonstrate life span and intersectional approaches to psychological practice with LGBTQ+ older adults.

Therapist and Client Descriptions and Presenting Problem

In this case, the therapist Jane is an English-speaking, middle-aged, white, heterosexual, cisgender woman who uses she/her pronouns and identifies as an ally. Luis, the client, is a 73-year-old, bilingual (Spanish/English), cisgender man who was referred for therapy after he became tearful in a Primary Care appointment, sharing that he recently lost his partner. The stated reason for referral was bereavement. Luis is a retired electrician who lives alone in the house he and his partner shared. He considers himself widowed and middle class. He did not require an interpreter. Notably, on his intake form he omits reporting his sexual orientation. Luis uses hearing aides and reading glasses, but is otherwise in very good health. He has no known psychiatric history. He is unsure if he "really needs" therapy but agreed to an intake session to discuss how it might help.

Luis arrived to his appointment and was a bit reserved when meeting his therapist. Jane introduced herself and her pronouns and offered space for Luis to share how he would like to be addressed. She reduced background noise in the office and spoke clearly to ensure Luis could hear her well. Throughout the first session he began to seem more comfortable, even commenting on the rainbow lanyard worn by Jane which she wears to show support for LGBTQ+ individuals. Luis shared he was born in the U.S. to parents who moved from Puerto Rico. He has three siblings, and they were raised in an urban working-class family with some extended family living nearby. They have additional extended family in Puerto Rico. As a child his parents reinforced strict gender roles and when Luis tried to express emotions or show affection his father responded by saying things like "stop being queer, man up". His parents were devout Catholics and the family was involved in their church community. Luis said he believes in God, but no longer belongs to a Catholic church. For many years now he has been a member of an Episcopalian congregation and his siblings sometimes "give him shit" for leaving the Catholic church, however he notes he feels comfort in the rituals of church and "feels more comfortable" at this church.

When asked about his marital and relationship history, Luis said that he was married once, for about 10 years, before he and his wife divorced. They have two children together who are now in their 40's. He said he had "some other relationships" in the years afterward but did not go into detail. Jane asked if he dated women, men, or people of other genders, and Luis paused. "Both," he said. "I guess I'm what they call bisexual now, but I just went with people I liked. I loved my wife, and later I loved Gary, but that was always confusing to people." When asked who Gary was, Luis became tearful and said Gary had been his partner for 32 years. "He was like my husband, but we weren't technically married, you know?" Luis shared that 4 months ago Gary died following a long illness during which Luis served as Gary's primary caregiver. "It was so hard, and I miss him so much. He was my whole world." Jane expressed condolences for Luis' loss and stated her appreciation for him being willing to share his sexuality with her, acknowledging how this can be challenging in new spaces.

When asked about other supports in his life, Luis notes he has some regular contact with his siblings and children, and tries to maintain ties with them as much as he can, but that those relationships are strained due to them having a hard time understanding his relationship with Gary. Jane asked who in his life he was "out" to and what the coming out process had been like. Luis admitted he had not formally come out to very many people. Within his family Gary had always been referred to as his "roommate" and it was never really talked about beyond that, although he believes his family members all know and understand that Gary was actually a partner and someone he loved. Luis has a few friends and acquaintances, mostly from his former place of employment but he rarely discussed his personal life with them and none knew Gary had been his partner. He attends church regularly but is not involved beyond attending Sunday services; the church he attends is LGBTQ+ affirming though Luis admits he does not participate frequently and shares that Gary was "always the more social one" in their relationship and that Gary had been more "out" with a stronger connection to the LGBTQ+ community in their town. Luis indicated he was not very connected with other bisexual or gay men or the larger LGBTQ+ community. He had always preferred to focus on work, church, and his relationship with Gary.

Without Gary, Luis admits he has been feeling sad, lonely, "a bit lost," and unsure of himself. For the first time he is "feeling old" and does not have a plan for his life at this stage, stating "I had expected to get old with Gary. Without him here it feels like I am just an old man without much left to look forward to." Jane made a mental note of this internalized aging stereotype but did not challenge this belief yet, instead focusing on rapport. When asked about his goals for therapy, Luis replied, "I'm not sure I even need this, but my doctor was worried when I started crying at my last appointment. He thinks I'm depressed. I'm not sure I am, but I feel so lonely." He agreed to try therapy starting with a focus on the sadness and loneliness he has been feeling since Gary died.

Case Formulation

Luis' case illustrates many issues that can arise when working with older LGBTQ+ people. One must consider the intersections of this client's age, ethnicity, family background, religious background, significant life events, cohort experiences, sexual orientation, and gender identity. Luis grew up in a Catholic, Puerto Rican, immigrant family which imparted strict belief systems regarding gender roles and expression, as well as heteronormative values. His family's strong Catholic faith was intolerant of diverse sexual orientations and genders and may have provided him with beliefs about gender and sexuality that left him feeling excluded from the Catholic community and even from God's love. This is important as we know that growing up in more conservative environments with little support for LGBTQ+ people, and few LGBTQ+ people who are out, can lead to internalized sexual stigma (Lee & Quam, 2013).

Following his 10-year marriage to a woman Luis engaged in sexual and romantic relationships with both men and women before settling into a long-term relationship with Gary. Given he found joy and pleasure in these varied relationships, he expresses that he is bisexual, but he does not think of bisexuality as an identity. Instead, he views it as a category that others use to describe his relationships and behaviors. Despite his many years with Gary, Luis never immersed himself in the LGBTQ+ community (which he refers to as "the gay community") or connected with other LGBTQ+ people. Instead he focused on his relationship with Gary, career, and faith. As a group, bisexual older adults report more internalized stigma, greater identity concealment, and less social support and community belongingness than lesbian and gay older adults, which may be due to many factors, including biphobia within lesbian and gay communities (Fredriksen-Goldsen et al., 2022b).

Clinicians cannot underestimate the impact that generational cohort experiences likely had on Luis' life experiences and mental health. He is of the Pride Generation, wherein his early life was shaped by society's pathologizing and criminalization of "homosexuality" and gender diversity. Over his life course these behaviors became decriminalized and LGBTQ+ people have been increasingly open and accepted in their identities. His parents' generation suppressed and silenced LGBTQ+ people. Given Luis' age, it is important to consider how these larger, shared experiences shaped and impacted his life course and identity development. Luis' lack of connection to the larger LGBTQ+ community may also impact his ability to explore some of these issues within himself and likely further contribute to internalized sexual stigma. Overall, Luis appears to be a man who has not had a consistent means with which to deeply explore his sense of self as a sexual being and as a part of multiple marginalized groups. He has had limited affirmative relationships or environments in his life, and it appears that his entry into a mental health setting is not due to his concerns about his sexual identity, but rather to bereavement. We don't yet know Luis' view of aging or what it means to him to be older, but based on comments made during the initial session, Jane has begun to theorize that Luis also holds some internalized negative views of aging. Luis would likely benefit from an affirmative approach using interpersonal and relational methods exploring grief, past and current relationships, role transitions, belongingness, and internalized ageism and stigma. It will also be important to clarify whether it is grief or depression that might be fueling his sadness.

Course of Treatment

Early in treatment Jane focused on developing an open and safe relationship with Luis. She accomplished this by listening attentively, validating Luis' feelings, and by showing no discomfort in talking about sexuality as it relates to family, faith, and relationships. She made use of affirmative therapy practices throughout their work together. Jane had an opportunity to do this early in the therapeutic relationship when Luis disclosed his relationship history and the fact that his siblings and children do not "understand" his relationship with Gary. In learning his history, the therapist overtly conveyed a nonjudgmental and affirmative stance both with environmental cues in her office (e.g. wearing a rainbow lanyard, a SafeZone poster, the Advocate magazine in her waiting room) and through verbal cues (e.g. asking open questions about sexuality, relationships, and family without making assumptions, expressing warmth and interest in hearing about his relationship with Gary, and asking what terms to use to describe his sexuality and his relationships). This fostered trust in the relationship and set the groundwork for insight-oriented psychotherapy. They spent some time engaged specifically on bereavement work to address sadness and grief while using interpersonal and relational approaches to explore past and current relationships and to work toward a corrective relational experience wherein Luis could be accepted for his true and full self. Often when a client is referred for bereavement it is important for the therapist to consider whether the client is suffering from depression versus bereavement. For Luis, based on the timing of his loss (less than 6 months), it was determined that bereavement was the more appropriate diagnosis. However, Jane continued to assess for depression throughout with the Geriatric Depression scale, which is an appropriate scale for older adults with symptoms of depression.

As treatment continued, Luis appeared more comfortable discussing his views of himself as "abnormal" because of his same-sex relationships, as well as his sense of disconnection from the LGBTQ+ community. Jane highlighted that Luis does not feel fully part of either the LGBTQ+ community or cis-heteronormative society. Together, they explored the meaning of "normal" as it relates to being bisexual considering topics such as who gets to define what is considered normal, challenging some core beliefs about what makes one normal or good, and engaging in acceptance work around it not being his job to change others' thoughts about him. Jane incorporated homework throughout therapy to help Luis become more aware of his automatic negative thoughts about his sexual identity and work to challenge these thoughts or beliefs as appropriate. Luis responded well to homework and reported that it helped him practice outside of therapy and feel more in control of his life.

Over time Luis became more flexible in his beliefs about sexuality in general as well as his own past sexual behaviors and relationships.

As therapy continued, the focus shifted to reconstructing his life without Gary. Socratic questioning was used to help Luis explore his beliefs about what it means to be a single bisexual older adult. Luis gradually expressed curiosity about engaging in LGBTQ+ community programming as a way to meet other people with similar experiences. He and Jane looked up local resources and groups with age-inclusive programming, but when it came time to attend one, Luis found himself feeling anxious and self-conscious. His fears were primarily focused on his age, suggesting internalized ageism. He asked, "Won't I be the oldest person there? When Gary talked about events they always sounded like they were for young people, and no one wants to hang out with an old guy." As rapport was firmly established, Jane took time to point out this automatic thought and explore the accuracy of it, providing psychoeducation about internalized ageism and its impact on one's health and well-being. Luis had never heard this term before but acknowledged that it fit his current experience. Jane encouraged him to think about other times in his life when he has done something he was initially apprehensive about. Luis shared about a time he attended a holiday party at work alone, even though he was worried about what others would think. This memory provided the structure to look back on how he had overcome fear and engaged in the activity, and then apply a similar process of rallying his internal resources to the current concern about being 'too old' for these social events.

While thinking about possible LGBTQ+ social outlets, Luis unexpectedly found himself facing a health problem of his own. He fractured a hip, and because he did not have a caregiver in the home with him, he went to a subacute rehabilitation facility for a few weeks for post-surgical treatments, including physical therapy for mobility. Here, he interacted with many other older people, as well as the staff, but struggled to open up to them. He initially shared that he was widowed, but when people responded by mentioning how much he must miss his wife, he felt uncomfortable and was unsure if he should correct them. He did not like to be dishonest (honesty was prioritized in his family and faith), but he worried others might treat him differently if they knew his deceased partner was a man. This brought new fears about aging without a partner and wondering if he would be able to trust hired caregivers someday. Thankfully Luis was able to engage in telehealth visits with Jane while in rehab where he shared these experiences and, using a combination of cognitive-behavioral and acceptance strategies was able to begin processing these new challenges. For example, they discussed the automatic thoughts he was experiencing, how accurate these thoughts were, and what thoughts could be challenged versus accepted. Through this, it was acknowledged that some of these thoughts such as "people may treat me differently because of my age and sexuality" were accurate and when these types of thoughts were identified, acceptance work was the focus rather than challenging these thoughts.

Additionally, Luis shared disappointment that his children did not offer to help him during this time. He shared that within Puerto Rican culture it is often expected that family members care for each other, especially in times of sickness or injury.

He expected his children to help him and felt let down that they did not. He suspected part of the reason they were not helping was because they saw him as a burden (i.e., internalized ageism) and would be unsure of how to talk to him about Gary's death. He also noted their disconnect from Puerto Rican culture. These themes of internalized and societal ageism and sexual stigma, and Eurocentrism became regular topics to explore in therapy. Cognitive and behavioral techniques of thought records, cognitive restructuring, and reframing continued to be used to challenge ageist, heterosexist, and biphobic thoughts and attitudes. Specifically, Jane and Luis continued to identify negative automatic thoughts about getting older (e.g., "What's the point in trying, it's too late for me?") and bisexuality (e.g., "I don't fit in anywhere") and how these thoughts were impacting his behaviors and emotions. The therapist also continued to infuse acceptance to acknowledge that there are some realities in our society that we cannot individually change.

When Luis returned home from physical rehabilitation Jane suggested implementing activity scheduling and behavior activation (using behaviors to impact one's emotions) to keep his mobility up and to address his sadness and anxiety. He found that scheduling daily walks and weekly calls with his children and sharing his stories with them reduced his isolation and he became more open to trying social activities. Luis found he was now open to exploring the local LGBTQ+ community and began attending a coffee group for LGBTQ+ older adults at a nearby senior center. He also began getting involved in his church community by joining the choir and volunteering with the church's soup kitchen. As he increased his social activities his sadness improved, but he remained anxious about making new friends, deepening his connection to his children, coming out to new people in his life, and dating, which made sense as these had been long-held concerns. His continued engagement in affirmative psychotherapy was a real strength and allowed him to eventually explore many areas of his life. As treatment progressed, he began to adjust his concept of family to include not just his family of origin, but also his faith community, new friends, and the larger LGBTQ+ community. He had not previously considered family a group you could build or choose, and this concept was a revelation to him. Reconceptualizing family was helpful as he worked to rebuild a life and a retirement that felt safe and authentic for him. Luis eventually decided to terminate therapy saying he felt he had learned a lot and now has a life he felt engaged in rather than anxious about.

Clinical Practices and Summary

Luis was in psychotherapy for about 10 months, and over that time went from being bereaved, isolated, and unsure of himself, to being more socially engaged, open, and positive about himself and his sexual identity. The use of affirmative therapy was appropriate as it targeted Luis' long-standing insecurity and lack of belonging that stemmed from the surrounding culture and difficulty finding a place where he "belonged". Jane created a safe place for Luis to discuss his sexuality more openly and process his grief without judgment. By examining his past and current relationships, Luis and Jane were able to identify an underlying interpersonal theme of isolation and "otherness". As treatment went on, the addition of new health issues added a layer that commonly occurs when working with older adults. This health issue was something Luis had not dealt with before and revealed new concerns about identity disclosure and internalized ageist attitudes. Use of interpersonal, cognitive behavioral, and acceptance strategies helped Luis reframe and gain comfort with many aspects of his life. Further, the health challenge demonstrated to Luis that he needed more support in his life, which prompted him to explore LGBTQ+ spaces and re-engage in his relationships with his children and church community. Throughout this course, the therapist worked with Luis as he learned to identify and confront his negative thoughts and to acknowledge when automatic thoughts or old learning might be at play. It was important to acknowledge the challenges he has faced as a bisexual older adult and the many sources of resilience he carried with him. It was also useful to highlight the challenges that can come from societal responses to a sexual minority identity to not only validate Luis' lived experience but to also demonstrate awareness of larger societal issues. Over time Luis was able to challenge his thoughts on his own and increase his engagement with others. It is expected that Luis would continue to improve by continuing to participate in social activities with people who understand him and who can directly relate to his experience. Once he became more aware of the barriers that were keeping him from interacting with those groups of people, he spontaneously began to seek out the experiences he needed to feel socially fulfilled.

Conclusion

There is great diversity among LGBTQ+ older adults and the current medical and mental health systems are unlikely to be prepared to meet the needs of increasingly diverse older populations. Thus, it is imperative that providers who work with this population have adequate training to serve older LGBTQ+ adults in a culturally humble and competent manner to support their health and well-being as they age. As both ageism and sexual stigma are widely seen in society, thus often unconsciously internalized by many, it is vital that therapists take time to acknowledge their own assumptions and biases prior to working with LGBTQ+ older adults so as to not unconsciously affirm internalized beliefs these individuals may have about themselves. Use of intersectional, life course, and affirmative approaches can set the stage to build overt and safe places to explore all facets of oneself. In doing this work, cognitive and behavioral techniques can be used to challenge internalized thoughts and attitudes related to ageism and sexual stigma. Relational therapies and ACT principles of acceptance can be utilized when facing societal or systemic issues that are beyond individual change efforts. Therapists would do well to acknowledge, and lean into, the great resilience found within LGBTQ+ older adults. By tapping into their lived experiences and crisis competency, affirmative health care professionals and therapists can promote the well-being of LGBTQ+ older adults as they navigate this phase of life.

Disclaimer The views expressed in this chapter are those of the authors and do not necessarily reflect the official policy or position of the U.S. Department of Veterans Affairs nor the U.S. Government.

References

Adams, M. (2016). An intersectional approach to services and care for LGBT elders. *Generations, 40*(2), 94–100.

Allen, J. O., Solway, E., Kirch, M., Singer, D., Kullgren, J. T., Moïse, V., & Malani, P. N. (2022). Experiences of everyday ageism and the health of older US adults. *JAMA Network Open, 5*(6), e2217240. https://doi.org/10.1001/jamanetworkopen.2022.17240

American Psychological Association (APA). (2014). Guidelines for psychological practice with older adults. *American Psychologist, 69*(1), 34–65. https://doi.org/10.1037/a0035063

American Psychological Association (APA), APA Task Force on Psychological Practice with Sexual Minority Persons. (2021). *Guidelines for psychological practice with sexual minority persons*. Retrieved from www.apa.org/about/policy/psychological-practice-sexual-minority-persons.pdf

Anderson, J. G., Flatt, J. D., Cicero, E. C., Kittle, K., Myers, C. R., Rose, K. M., & Wharton, W. (2022). Inclusive care practices and policies among sexual and gender minority older adults. *Journal of Gerontological Nursing, 48*(12), 6–15. https://doi.org/10.3928/00989134-20221107-03

Barker, J. C., Herdt, G., & De Vries, B. (2006). Social support in the lives of lesbians and gay men at midlife and later. *Sexuality Research & Social Policy, 3*, 1–23. https://doi.org/10.1525/srsp.2006.3.2.1

Bower, K. L., Lewis, D. C., Bermúdez, J. M., & Singh, A. A. (2021). Narratives of generativity and resilience among LGBT older adults: Leaving positive legacies despite social stigma and collective trauma. *Journal of Homosexuality, 68*(2), 230–251. https://doi.org/10.1080/00918369.2019.1648082

Breder, K., & Bockting, W. (2023). Social networks of LGBT older adults: An integrative review. *Psychology of Sexual Orientation and Gender Diversity, 10*(3), 473–489. https://doi.org/10.1037/sgd0000552

Brennan-Ing, M., Seidel, L., Larson, B., & Karpiak, S. E. (2013). "I'm created in god's image, and god don't create junk": Religious participation and support among older GLBT adults. *Journal of Religion, Spirituality & Aging, 25*(2), 70–92. https://doi.org/10.1080/15528030.2013.746629

Brennan-Ing, M., Seidel, L., Larson, B., & Karpiak, S. E. (2014). Social care networks and older LGBT adults: Challenges for the future. *Journal of Homosexuality, 61*(1), 21–52. https://doi.org/10.1080/00918369.2013.835235

Brennan-Ing, M., Seidel, L., Larson, B., & Karpiak, S. E. (2017). Social networks and supports among older gay and bisexual men: The impact of HIV. In *Later-life social support and service provision in diverse and vulnerable populations* (pp. 54–76). Routledge.

Brennan-Ing, M., Haberlen, S., Ware, D., Egan, J. E., Brown, A. L., Meanley, S., et al. (2022). Psychological connection to the gay community and negative self-appraisals in middle-aged and older men who have sex with men: The mediating effects of fitness engagement. *The Journals of Gerontology. Series B, Psychological Sciences and Social Sciences, 77*(1), 39–49. https://doi.org/10.1093/geronb/gbab076

Brooks, V. R. (1981). *Minority stress and lesbian women*. Lexington Books.

Butler, R. N. (1969). Age-ism: Another form of bigotry. *Gerontologist, 9*(4), 243–246. https://doi.org/10.1093/geront/9.4_part_1.243

Cantor, M. H., & Brennan, M. (2000). *Social care of the elderly: The effects of ethnicity, class and culture*. Springer.

Cantor, M. H., Brennan, M., & Shippy, R. A. (2004). Caregiving among older lesbian, gay, bisexual, and transgender New Yorkers. Final report. New York: National Gay and Lesbian Task Force Policy Institute.

Cary, L. A., Chasteen, A. L., & Remedios, J. (2017). The ambivalent ageism scale: Developing and validating a scale to measure benevolent and hostile ageism. *Gerontologist, 57*(2), e27–e36. https://doi.org/10.1093/geront/gnw118

Centers for Disease Control and Prevention. (2018). *Diagnoses of HIV infection among adults aged 50 years and older in the United States and dependent areas, 2011–2016*. http://www.cdc.gov/hiv/library/reports/hiv-surveillance.html

Chen, J., McLaren, H., Jones, M., & Shams, L. (2022). The aging experiences of LGBTQ ethnic minority older adults: A systematic review. *Gerontologist, 62*(3), e162–e177. https://doi.org/10.1093/geront/gnaa134

Choi, S. K., & Meyer, I. H. (2016). *LGBT aging: A review of research findings, needs, and policy implications*. Retrieved from https://www.jstor.org/stable/resrep34905

Crisp, C., Wayland, S., & Gordon, T. (2008). Older gay, lesbian, and bisexual adults: Tools for age-competent and gay affirmative practice. *Journal of Gay and Lesbian Social Services, 20*(1–2), 5–29. https://doi.org/10.1080/10538720802178890

Croghan, C. F., Moone, R. P., & Olson, A. M. (2014). Friends, family, and caregiving among midlife and older lesbian, gay, bisexual, and transgender adults. In B. de Vries & C. Croghan (Eds.), *Community-based research on LGBT aging* (pp. 79–102). Routledge.

de Vries, B., & Hoctel, P. (2007). The family-friends of older gay men and lesbians. In *Sexual inequalities and social justice* (pp. 213–232). University of California Press.

Emlet, C. A. (2006). "You're awfully old to have this disease": Experiences of stigma and ageism in adults 50 years and older living with HIV/AIDS. *Gerontologist, 46*(6), 781–790. https://doi.org/10.1093/geront/46.6.781

Emlet, C. A., Brennan, D. J., Brennenstuhl, S., Rueda, S., Hart, T. A., Rourke, S. B., & Team, O. C. S. (2013). Protective and risk factors associated with stigma in a population of older adults living with HIV in Ontario, Canada. *AIDS Care, 25*(10), 1330–1339. https://doi.org/10.1080/09540121.2013.774317

Feinstein, B. A., Katz, B. W., Benjamin, I., Macaulay, T., Dyar, C., & Morgan, E. (2023). Disparities in depression and anxiety related to sexual orientation and gender identity among older adults: The role of age discrimination. *Stigma and Health*. Advance online publication. https://psycnet.apa.org/doi/10.1037/sah0000462

Ferraro, K. F., & Koch, J. R. (1994). Religion and health among black and white adults: Examining social support and consolation. *Journal for the Scientific Study of Religion, 33*(4), 362–375. https://doi.org/10.2307/1386495

Fredriksen-Goldsen, K. I. (2018). Shifting social context in the lives of LGBTQ older adults. *Public Policy & Aging Report, 28*(1), 24–28. https://doi.org/10.1093/ppar/pry003

Fredriksen-Goldsen, K. I., Kim, H. J., Emlet, C. A., Muraco, A., Erosheva, E. A., Hoy-Ellis, C. P., et al. (2011). *The aging and health report*. Institute for Multigenerational Health.

Fredriksen-Goldsen, K. I., Emlet, C. A., Kim, H. J., Muraco, A., Erosheva, E. A., Goldsen, J., & Hoy-Ellis, C. P. (2013). The physical and mental health of lesbian, gay male, and bisexual (LGB) older adults: The role of key health indicators and risk and protective factors. *Gerontologist, 53*(4), 664–675. https://doi.org/10.1093/geront/gns123

Fredriksen-Goldsen, K. I., Jen, S., & Muraco, A. (2019). Iridescent life course: LGBTQ aging research and blueprint for the future—A systematic review. *Gerontology, 65*, 253–274. https://doi.org/10.1159/000493559

Fredriksen-Goldsen, K. I., Emlet, C. A., Fabbre, V. D., Kim, H.-J., Lerner, J., Jung, H. H., Harner, V., & Goldsen, J. (2022a). Historical and social forces in the iridescent life course: Key life events and experiences of transgender older adults. *Ageing & Society*. Advance online publication. https://doi.org/10.1017/S0144686X22000563

Fredriksen-Goldsen, K. I., Jen, S., Clark, T., Kim, H.-J., Jung, H. H., & Goldsen, J. (2022b). Historical and generational forces in the iridescent life course of bisexual women, men, and gender diverse older adults. *Sexualities, 25*(1–2, 132), –156. https://doi.org/10.1177/1363460720947313

Fredriksen-Goldsen, K., Hoy-Ellis, C., Kim, H. J., Jung, H. H., Emlet, C. A., Johnson, I., & Goldsen, J. (2023). Generational and social forces in the life events and experiences of lesbian and gay midlife and older adults across the iridescent life course. *Journal of Aging and Health, 35*(3–4), 265–281. https://doi.org/10.1177/08982643221125517

Frost, D. M., Meyer, I. H., Lin, A., Wilson, B. D. M., Lightfoot, M., Russell, S. T., & Hammack, P. L. (2022). Social change and the health of sexual minority individuals: Do the effects of minority stress and community connectedness vary by age cohort? *Archives of Sexual Behavior, 51*, 2299–2316. https://doi.org/10.1007/s10508-022-02288-6

Grant, J., Koskovich, G., Frazer, M., & Bjerk, S. (2010). *Outing age 2010. Public policy issues affecting gay, lesbian, bisexual and transgender elders, 2010*. National Gay and Lesbian Task Force. Retrieved from: https://www.lgbtagingcenter.org/resources/pdfs/OutingAge2010.pdf

Haile, R., Padilla, M. B., & Parker, E. A. (2011). 'Stuck in the quagmire of an HIV ghetto': The meaning of stigma in the lives of older black gay and bisexual men living with HIV in New York City. *Culture, Health & Sexuality, 13*(4), 429–442. https://doi.org/10.1080/13691058.2010.537769

Haile, R., Rowell-Cunsolo, T. L., Parker, E. A., Padilla, M. B., & Hansen, N. B. (2014). An empirical test of racial/ethnic differences in perceived racism and affiliation with the gay community: Implications for HIV risk. *Journal of Social Issues, 70*(2), 342–359. https://doi.org/10.1111/josi.12063

Han, J., & Richardson, V. E. (2015). The relationships among perceived discrimination, self-perceptions of aging, and depressive symptoms: A longitudinal examination of age discrimination. *Aging & Mental Health, 19*(8), 747–755. https://doi.org/10.1080/13607863.2014.962007

Hinrichs, K. L. M., & Donaldson, W. (2017). Recommendations for use of affirmative psychotherapy with LGBT older adults. *Journal of Clinical Psychology, 73*(8), 945–953. https://doi.org/10.1002/jclp.22505

Hoy-Ellis, C. P., Ator, M., Kerr, C., & Milford, J. (2016). Innovative approaches address aging and mental health needs in LGBTQ communities. *Generations, 40*(2), 56–62.

Karel, M. J., Gatz, M., & Smyer, M. A. (2012). Aging and mental health in the decade ahead: What psychologists need to know. *The American Psychologist, 67*(3), 184–198. https://doi.org/10.1037/a0025393

Kimmel, D. C. (1978). Adult development and aging: A gay perspective. *Journal of Social Issues, 34*(3), 113–130. https://doi.org/10.1111/j.1540-4560.1978.tb02618.x

Kum, S. (2017). Gay, gray, black, and blue: An examination of some of the challenges faced by older LGBTQ people of color. *Journal of Gay & Lesbian Mental Health, 21*(3), 228–239. https://doi.org/10.1080/19359705.2017.1320742

Lederman, S., & Shefler, G. (2023). Psychotherapy with older adults: Ageism and the therapeutic process. *Psychotherapy Research, 33*(3), 350–361. https://doi.org/10.1080/10503307.2022.2094298

Lee, M. G., & Quam, J. K. (2013). Comparing supports for LGBT aging in rural versus urban areas. *Journal of Gerontological Social Work, 56*(2), 112–126. https://doi.org/10.1080/01634372.2012.747580

Levy, B. R., Zonderman, A. B., Slade, M. D., & Ferrucci, L. (2009). Age stereotypes held earlier in life predict cardiovascular events in later life. *Psychological Science, 20*(3), 296–298. https://doi.org/10.1111/j.1467-9280.2009.02298.x

Luoma, J. B., Kohlenberg, B. S., Hayes, S. C., Bunting, K., & Rye, A. K. (2008). Reducing self-stigma in substance abuse through acceptance and commitment therapy: Model, manual development, and pilot outcomes. *Addiction Research and Theory, 16*(2), 149–165. https://doi.org/10.1080/16066350701850295

Lyons, A., Alba, B., Heywood, W., Fileborn, B., Minichiello, V., Barrett, C., et al. (2018). Experiences of ageism and the mental health of older adults. *Aging & Mental Health, 22*(11), 1456–1464. https://doi.org/10.1080/13607863.2017.1364347

Meyer, I. H. (2003). Prejudice, social stress, and mental health in lesbian, gay, and bisexual populations: Conceptual issues and research evidence. *Psychological Bulletin, 129*, 674–697. https://doi.org/10.1037/0033-2909.129.5.674

Murphy, D. J., Mackenzie, C.S., Porter, M.M., & Chipperfield, J.G. (2023). *Effectiveness of a process based intervention in decreasing internalized ageism* [Unpublished thesis]. University of Manitoba.

Porter, K. E., Brennan-Ing, M., Chang, S. C., Dickey, L. M., Singh, A. A., Bower, K. L., & Witten, T. M. (2016). Providing competent and affirming services for transgender and gender nonconforming older adults. *Clinical Gerontologist, 39*(5), 366–388. https://doi.org/10.1080/07317115.2016.1203383

Porter, K. E., Brennan-Ing, M., Burr, J. A., Dugan, E., & Karpiak, S. E. (2019). HIV stigma and older men's psychological well-being: Do coping resources differ for gay/bisexual and straight men? *The Journals of Gerontology. Series B, Psychological Sciences and Social Sciences, 74*(4), 685–693. https://doi.org/10.1093/geronb/gbx101

Pruitt, S. (2019). *How gay culture blossomed during the roaring twenties. HISTORY. A&E television networks.* https://www.history.com/news/gay-culture-roaring-twenties-prohibition. Accessed April 5, 2023.

Reynolds, K., Pietrzak, R. H., El-Gabalawy, R., Mackenzie, C. S., & Sareen, J. (2015). Prevalence of psychiatric disorders in U.S. older adults: Findings from a nationally representative survey. *World Psychiatry, 14*(1), 74–81. https://doi.org/10.1002/wps.20193

SAGE & National Resource Center on LGBT Aging (2021). *Facts on LGBT aging*. https://www.sageusa.org/wp-content/uploads/2021/03/sage-lgbt-aging-facts-final.pdf

Shippy, R. A., Cantor, M. H., & Brennan, M. (2004). Social networks of aging gay men. *The Journal of Men's Studies, 13*(1), 107–120. https://doi.org/10.3149/jms.1301.107

Shiu, C., Muraco, A., & Fredriksen-Goldsen, K. (2016). Invisible care: Friend and partner care among older lesbian, gay, bisexual, and transgender (LGBT) adults. *Journal of the Society for Social Work & Research, 7*(3), 527–546. https://doi.org/10.1086/687325

Skinta, L., Matthew, M. D., Wells, G., & Dilley, J. W. (2015). Acceptance and compassion-based group therapy to reduce HIV stigma. *Cognitive and Behavioral Practice, 22*(4), 481–490. https://doi.org/10.1016/j.cbpra.2014.05.006

Steward, A. (2022). Toward interventions to reduce internalized ageism. *Journal of Human Behavior in the Social Environment, 32*(3), 336–355. https://doi.org/10.1080/10911359.2021.1898516

Wight, R. G., LeBlanc, A. J., Meyer, I. H., & Harig, F. A. (2015). Internalized gay ageism, mattering, and depressive symptoms among midlife and older gay-identified men. *Social Science & Medicine, 147*, 200–208. https://doi.org/10.1016/j.socscimed.2015.10.066

Yadavaia, J. E., & Hayes, S. C. (2012). Acceptance and commitment therapy for self-stigma around sexual orientation: A multiple baseline evaluation. *Cognitive and Behavioral Practice, 19*(4), 545–559. https://doi.org/10.1016/j.cbpra.2011.09.002

Chapter 9
Addressing Ableism to Promote the Mental Health of LGBTQ+ Persons with Disabilities

Franco Dispenza, Jordan B. Westcott, and Mary Chase Breedlove Mize

Highlights

This chapter provides readers with an overview of the psychosocial nuances surrounding the intersections of LGBTQ+ identity and disability, offering practical insights for mental health professionals primed to provide affirmative psychological care. Recognizing the scarcity of empirical research on LGBTQ+ individuals with disabilities, we have intentionally drawn from the existing body of scholarship that examines the lives and psychosocial needs of this population. In this chapter, we focus on:

- Heightened vulnerability to ableism, microaggressions, and minority stressors, and how these factors contribute to an increased risk of mental health symptoms, such as depression and anxiety.
- Counseling and psychological strategies, including implications for conceptualizing social justice in clinical practice.
- The importance of centering resilience and strength in treatment/intervention approaches to affirm and empower LGBTQ+ individuals with disabilities.

The chapter includes two distinct case examples that reveal the diversity of psychological care and practice that can be applied with LGBTQ+ persons with disabilities. We provide these case studies as a means of demonstrating clinical

F. Dispenza (✉)
Georgia State University, Atlanta, GA, USA
e-mail: fdispenza1@gsu.edu

J. B. Westcott
University of Tennessee, Knoxville, Knoxville, TN, USA

M. C. B. Mize
Agnes Scott College and Seek and Find Counseling and Consulting, Decatur, GA, USA

N. A. Livingston et al. (eds.), *Addressing Minority Stress and Enhancing Resilience with Diverse LGBTQ+ Clients*, CBT: Science Into Practice,
https://doi.org/10.1007/978-3-031-92836-9_9

decision-making heuristics and clinical practices grounded in psychological theory and evidence.

Positionality
We approach this chapter from several shared identities. We are cisgender individuals who identify as White/European American, share diverse sexual orientations, and we each have our own personal histories of living with chronic medical illnesses and disabilities. Professionally, we bring a diverse range of expertise to this chapter, grounded in our clinical and research experiences with LGBTQ+ persons living with chronic illnesses and disabilities across the lifespan. Our team includes early- and mid-career professionals with doctorates in counselor education and counseling psychology. Each of us is also certified as a counselor, with two independently licensed to provide counseling and psychological care in our respective states. We each work at institutions of higher education, conducting multicultural and lifespan development research, and training mental health and rehabilitation professionals. We acknowledge the privileges and limitations inherent in our perspectives and strive to approach our work with humility, recognizing the importance of centering the voices and experiences of those we serve.

Introduction

LGBTQ+ persons live with a variety of disabilities, including physical (e.g., mobility impairment because of injury, limb loss), sensory (e.g., blindness, deafness), cognitive (e.g., cerebrovascular diagnoses, dementia), intellectual or developmental (e.g., autism, cerebral palsy), chronic illnesses (e.g., HIV/AIDS, cancer, diabetes), and psychiatric/behavioral conditions (e.g., bipolar disorder, schizophrenia, post-traumatic stress disorder; Fredriksen-Goldsen et al., 2012; Human Rights Campaign [HRC], 2022; Substance Abuse and Mental Health Services Administration [SAMHSA], 2023; Surfus, 2023). Disability scholars similarly position people without known disabilities as *temporarily able-bodied* or *temporarily able-minded* to reflect that any individual, including persons living with other disabilities, may acquire a first or new disability at any point during their lifespan (e.g., Breckenridge & Vogler, 2001). Relatedly, LGBTQ+ persons living with disabilities can present with mental health concerns related to and distinct from their disabilities. It is therefore imperative that mental health providers (MHPs; e.g., psychologists, counselors, marriage and family therapists, social workers) understand the unique mental health needs and psychosocial contexts of LGBTQ+ persons living with disabilities, especially their experiences with ableism.

Ableism includes the beliefs, institutional and interpersonal processes, and practices that cast disability as a lesser state of physical and psychological being when compared to able-bodied, able-minded individuals (see disability guidelines written by the American Psychological Association [APA], 2022). Ableism also constitutes marginalization, othering, and invisibility of people with disabilities at both individual- and society-level power structures (APA, 2022), and can present at any point of one's lifespan (e.g., acquired disability through accident or injury). Further, ableist attitudes, stereotypes, and prejudices can be psychologically absorbed by an individual, leading to internalized ableism (Dispenza & DeBlaere, 2017). LGBTQ+ persons with disabilities often encounter ableism, and internalize instances of ableism, through daily microaggressions. Microaggressions subsequently increase the risk of depressive symptoms and lower one's satisfaction with social supports among LGBTQ+ persons living with disabilities (Conover & Israel, 2019). In a qualitative study with LGBTQ+ college students living with disabilities, Miller and Smith (2021) found that common microaggressions included denial of disability experiences, denial of personal identity (inclusive of both LGBTQ+ and disability identities), being treated as a second-class citizen due to disability, and minimization of mental health. Those sampled in the study also avoided public community spaces to evade LGBTQ+ and disability related microaggressions, and participants highlighted how structural ableism, inaccessible resources (e.g., physical access to ramps), and exclusionary services were experienced as daily occurrences of environmental microaggressions (Miller & Smith, 2021).

Experiences with ableism and ableist microaggressions have negative effects on mental health, including increased somatic symptoms and negative affect (Kattari, 2020). The addition of ableism appears to elevate risk of poorer mental health outcomes among LGBTQ+ persons above and beyond sexual and gender minority stress experiences. Using national survey data from the U.S. Census Bureau's Household Pulse Survey, Brucker et al. (2023) reported that LGBT adults with disabilities were more likely to report mental health issues, more likely to have received mental health treatment, and more likely to report unmet mental health needs when compared to their non-disabled or non-LGBT counterparts.

Sexual and disability-related proximal minority stress (e.g., internalized heterosexism, internalized ableism, stigma consciousness) also impacts the lives of LGBTQ+ persons with disabilities, particularly in the way LGBTQ+ persons adjust and adapt to their disabilities. Dispenza (2023) reported that internalized stigma and stigma consciousness predicted reactions to disability impairment, specifically denial, externalized hostility, internalized anger, and anxiety in a sample of LGBTQ+ persons living with disabilities. Similarly, proximal minority stress was associated with poorer ratings of quality of life functioning for LGBTQ+ persons with disabilities (Dispenza, 2023).

Identity disclosure is another area of concern, since LGBTQ+ persons with disabilities expend additional energy managing disclosure of their LGBTQ+ identity as well as their disability, which may be complicated by requiring formal accommodations or external supports (Miller & Smith, 2021). Like LGBTQ+ identities, some disabilities may be invisible or concealable, whereas others may be visible or apparent to others. LGBTQ+ persons with disabilities therefore navigate decision-making about identity disclosure in the context of concealing LGBTQ+ identity and/or disability experiences. These and other processes are impactful in the daily lives of LGBTQ+ persons with disabilities, as well as in the context of service delivery, explored in greater depth below.

Counseling and Psychological Care with LGBTQ+ Persons with Disabilities

LGBTQ+ persons with disabilities will access mental health services (Brucker et al., 2023; The Trevor Project, 2023), including individual, couples, family, group, and career counseling services across a wide range of foci (Dispenza et al., 2017). But few evidence-based approaches exist for LGBTQ+ persons with disabilities given the limited empirical research and scholarship. Regardless, several concepts and themes do emerge in the extant scholarship, providing some useful guidance for clinical practice with LGBTQ+ persons with disabilities. In this section, we provide an overview of themes from empirical scholarship and highlight important clinical considerations for working with LGBTQ+ persons with disabilities. These considerations are also informed by our own personal and professional experiences.

Perhaps the most important recommendation is that MHPs acquire disability-specific knowledge and skills (e.g., medical aspects of disability, psychosocial adaptation and adjustment to acquired disabilities, family and caregiving, disability law, education, and employment) to work competently with persons with disabilities (APA, 2022; Chapin et al., 2018). When MHPs have knowledge related to disabilities, they are better equipped to address disability concerns with clients, helping them to increase self-acceptance, develop positive disability identities, and ultimately manage their symptoms with greater autonomy (Conner et al., 2023). For example, an MHP might explicitly explore how a client identifies their disability, if a client uses person-first or disability-first language (APA, 2022), and how disability impacts their client's life in positive ways. An MHP might also disclose their own disability identities to process how similarities and differences in disability status impact the helping relationship. These approaches to broaching disability, whether taken together or employed individually, demonstrate acceptance of disability and curiosity to understand clients' unique experiences of their disabilities, which is tied to best practice. In a qualitative study of 24 clients with physical disabilities, two-thirds of whom identified as LGBTQ+, participants indicated that MHPs' understanding and acceptance of their disabilities were key to developing a positive therapeutic relationship (Conner et al., 2023).

Knowledge of disability can also impact clinical outcomes. For example, LGBTQ+ youth with disabilities who believed their MHP understood their disability were less likely to consider and attempt suicide compared with those who felt their MHP misunderstood their disabilities (The Trevor Project, 2023). Alternatively, MHPs who avoid discussing disability can potentially invalidate and pathologize their clients by communicating that disability is an unacceptable topic to discuss or demonstrating discomfort with disability as the MHP (Conner et al., 2023).

Although MHPs need to develop knowledge specific to disabilities (APA, 2022; Chapin et al., 2018; Conner et al., 2023), knowledge alone is insufficient to provide affirmative counseling and psychological care (e.g., assessment, psychotherapy). It is important to develop an intersectional understanding of LGBTQ+ identity and disability (Dispenza, 2023; Dispenza et al., 2016a, b), and ensure that aspects of these intersecting identities (e.g., interlocking systems of oppression and privilege) are factored into clinical assessment and intervention. Intersectionality competence requires MHPs to have knowledge and awareness of sociocultural identity development, psychosocial stigma, and minority stressors related to LGBTQ+ identity, disability identity, and other privileged and marginalized social positions held by clients (Dispenza et al., 2017, 2016a, b). Additionally, Dispenza et al. (2017) found that MHPs working with LGBTQ+ persons with disabilities identified affirmative consciousness (i.e., conscious resistance of negative stereotypes of LGBTQ+ persons with disabilities alongside intentionally incorporating strengths) as being critical to care. Specific MHP skills that might enhance practice include resisting stereotypes or assumptions and upholding affirmative attitudes. Although these practices address one's own implicit bias, MHPs may also explore and even challenge how ableist, heterosexist, and intersecting stereotypes impact clients' experiences and worldviews, thereby disrupting internalized stigma.

Social justice and advocacy are central to addressing ableism in counseling and psychological care with LGBTQ+ clients with disabilities (Dispenza et al., 2016a, b, 2017). MHPs need to consider systems-based approaches—and a person's history within systems—when conceptualizing clients and treatment planning. It is important for MHPs to recognize the importance of empowering their clients to obtain necessary accommodations (e.g., academic or work accommodations, assistive devices) and navigate school, employment, and healthcare systems that are not always affirming or safe (Conner et al., 2023; Dispenza et al., 2017). Thus, collaborative empowerment and nurturing autonomy are essential to supporting LGBTQ+ clients with disabilities (Dispenza et al., 2016a, b). MHPs also need to consider the personal, social, and community supports their LGBTQ+ clients with disabilities need to function optimally in their respective environments, and they need to tailor connections to outside resources that are affirming to all intersecting identities.

Accommodations are another specific example of social justice praxis that can help combat ableism (Dispenza et al., 2016a, b). In one study, LGBTQ+ clients with physical disabilities reported that many of their negative experiences with MHPs involved inflexibility, particularly when they needed accommodations to meaningfully participate in mental health services (Conner et al., 2023). MHPs should explore what accommodations clients may need to participate in services prior to and throughout treatment, particularly when their clients have a dynamic disability. For example, a client whose use of mobility aids changes based on symptom severity might need different accommodations at different times (e.g., wheelchair access some weeks, while they may use a cane other weeks; or the need to change session format to telehealth some weeks versus an in-person office visit during other weeks). Beneficial accommodations include ensuring accessibility or holding meetings in different and more accessible locations, providing sliding scale fees, rearranging office furniture, and rescheduling appointments without a fee when disability symptoms prevent attendance (Conner et al., 2023).

Although there is less evidence supporting concrete interventions and approaches compared with the general practice guidelines offered by professional practice associations (e.g., APA, American Counseling Association), some scholarship provides insight into specific actions MHPs can employ to support LGBTQ+ clients with disabilities and combat the impact of ableism. For example, Conner et al. (2023) highlighted several disability-LGBTQ+ affirming interventions in their qualitative study, including tracking and logging disability-related symptoms, identifying triggers of ableism and minority stress, and educating clients on how to cope and emotionally regulate in times of identity-related stress. Focusing counseling and psychological interventions on psychosocial adaptation—or how an individual integrates disability into their social identities and psychological functioning—can also prove beneficial when aiming to help clients arrive at a psychological state of acceptance or adjustment to their disability (Conner et al., 2023; Dispenza, 2023).

Creative approaches also appear to be beneficial for this population. A qualitative study exploring the impacts of a narrative therapy group led by psychologists for LGBTQ+ persons with learning disabilities evaluated participants' perspectives on the group (Elderton et al., 2014). Participants indicated that they felt empowered by the group and sharing their own stories, as well as positively impacted by hearing the stories of other LGBTQ+ persons with learning disabilities (Elderton et al., 2014). MHPs also believe queer music therapy holds promise for facilitating change among LGBTQ+ clients with disabilities, highlighting experiences where LGBTQ+ clients have been able to explore the intersectionality of their identities through lyric analysis (Boggan et al., 2017). Participants in this qualitative study specifically named that queer music therapy models should integrate disability and empower clients to embrace fluidity both in how they identify (i.e., related to disability and LGBTQ+ identity) as well as functioning (i.e., the impact of their disability; Boggan et al., 2017).

Clinical Perspectives on Resilience and Strength

Resilience and strength are key to affirmative counseling and psychological care with LGBTQ+ persons with disabilities, even as MHPs acknowledge disparities and challenges (Chapin et al., 2018; Fredriksen-Goldsen et al., 2014). Possessing a sense of control and autonomy over one's life and disability (Dispenza et al., 2016a) and emotional coping with disability limitations and symptoms (Conner et al., 2023; Dispenza et al., 2016a) are especially worth exploring during a clinical assessment. For instance, MHPs may consider exploring how clients have coped with stigma, minority stress, disability, and mental health symptoms up to this point to identify effective strategies for resilience as part of a treatment plan. Additionally, MHPs may consider intentionally exploring the emotional impact of disabilities without pathologizing those emotions or implying that the disability symptoms have psychological causes (Conner et al., 2023). Processing disability experiences while acknowledging what has been effective in coping can help LGBTQ+ clients with disabilities generalize that coping to other areas of their life, as well as to new challenges that emerge.

Advocacy for social change is also part of resilience for LGBTQ+ clients with disabilities. Collaborative empowerment is one way to help clients develop the skills they need to advocate for themselves in a variety of contexts, involving a joint relationship that focuses on co-constructing a sense of power, dignity, and autonomy in clients' lives (Dispenza et al., 2016a, b). Using collaborative empowerment, such as by identifying ways clients can use existing strengths to address challenges in their lives or by working together to explore ways of having more autonomy in one's life, can ultimately promote resilience that can be generalized to other situations. When clients identify a barrier or challenge, MHPs might collaborate with the client to identify concrete advocacy steps that the client can implement in their life to address any encountered adversity. For example, for a client experiencing disability discrimination at work, MHPs might help them identify reporting procedures for ADA violations, role play conversations the client could have with their employer, and proactively connect them to disability legal supports in the community. It is beneficial for MHPs to engage in advocacy (Conner et al., 2023; Dispenza et al., 2017), yet it is equally important for LGBTQ+ clients with disabilities to develop skills to advocate for their own needs.

Social engagement is another key element of health, wellbeing, and strength for LGBTQ+ persons with disabilities (Dispenza et al., 2016a, b). Meaningful inclusion is especially important in social engagement, particularly given that some disabilities may limit energy or ability to engage in certain life activities. MHPs should explore what meaningful engagement looks like for each LGBTQ+ client living with a disability, considering the unique context of their disability symptoms, coping strategies, and social networks. Many people with disabilities form community in creative ways, such as in online spaces (Dispenza et al., 2019) and maintaining social connections through phone calls, video chats, or texts. Rather than viewing these types of social engagement as inferior to in-person interactions, MHPs might explore how these creative social contacts meet clients' social engagement needs and what needs remain unmet. Openness and flexibility in how clients meet their needs may allow them to leverage strengths specific to their lived experience with a disability, ultimately enhancing their quality of life. At the same time, where possible, MHPs may consider strategies for enhancing social and participation in clients' local communities while attending to ways that these opportunities may be inaccessible.

Although it is important to attend to strengths, it is equally important to acknowledge challenges experienced by LGBTQ+ persons with disabilities. For example, we have heard some MHPs try to reframe experiences with diagnoses such as autism spectrum disorder or Attention Deficit/Hyperactivity Disorder as "superpowers." While it can be beneficial to reframe some components of a disability experience to identify its strengths, some individuals with disabilities may encounter these euphemisms or tropes as minimizing or invalidating their experience with the disability. Balancing explorations of strengths through the client's perspective with acknowledging and processing the very real challenges they face is key to demonstrating an affirmative understanding and sensitivity to the realities of their disability.

Addressing Ableism and Cissexism in Therapy: A Case Study

Our experiences have taught us that MHPs frequently emphasize sensory, physical, or mobility related issues when asked to contemplate disability among LGBTQ+ individuals. However, they sometimes overlook developmental disabilities (including cognitive and intellectual variations of functioning, such as autism)—especially among gender diverse individuals (Strang et al., 2021; Maroney et al., 2023). Furthermore, persons with developmental disabilities (e.g., autism) may present with co-occurring mental health concerns, which MHPs are well equipped to address alongside needs related to disability. To illustrate the intersections of autism, gender diversity, ableism, and mental health, we present a clinical case study. All names utilized in the case are pseudonyms. Additional identity demographics are included to enrich the case study. Lastly, many of the details of the case have been fictionalized.

Case Background

Alex Hall Carter (he/him pronouns) presented to a university counseling center during the spring semester at the encouragement of his mother and father. Alex was 19-years old at the time of his initial consultation session, and identified as a biracial, queer, transgender man. Alex also identified as autistic and preferred use of identity-first language. As part of his vocational rehabilitation school-to-work transition plan, Alex was attending a post-secondary inclusive education program[1] at a university in the southeast United States. The goal of the program was to prepare Alex for a career in digital media productions.

During his initial consultation with Sarah Davis (European American, cisgender, she/her pronouns, heterosexual, neurodivergent with ADHD, LGBTQ+ ally), a predoctoral psychology intern, Alex reported some depressed mood and difficulty concentrating on his program and academics. He also reported profound anxiety, including increased feelings of irritability, general worry and unease, as well as heart palpitations and sweating during social situations. He stated these feelings had been getting worse over the past 6 months. He denied any history of trauma, abuse, or any history of suicide ideation or attempts. He said to Sarah, “I feel like a failure. I can’t connect with other people, and I think it’s because I’m autistic and trans.” Alex was not out to many of his classmates about his transgender and autistic

[1] Under Section 504 of the *Rehabilitation Act of 1973* and Title II of the *Americans with Disabilities Act* of 1990, students with disabilities are protected from being discriminated against in entry to postsecondary educational institutions. Post-secondary inclusive education programs are designed to empower individuals with intellectual and developmental disabilities to succeed on college campuses and prepare them for competitive and integrated employment opportunities.

identities and had difficulty deciding if he should ever disclose his identities given some negative past experiences with disclosure.

Later, during the consultation session, Alex stated "I know the stuff with my program is meant to get me to work, but I want to do more school. I wasn't always the best in school, and I needed a lot of support growing up. School can be really hard for me, but I want to try. I want to push through it, but I'm scared I can't do it. I know work is important, and I want to be able to make it on my own one day." Sarah recognized several intersecting factors that added both nuances and complexities to Alex's presentation of depression and anxiety. Alex also presented with proximal gender minority stress, such as internalized cissexism, and internalized ableism. When the consultation session ended, Alex provided Sarah with documentation from previous psychoeducational evaluations and clinical notes from his childhood psychologist. Below is a summary of that documentation.

Alex's Disability and Educational History

Documentation revealed that Alex was diagnosed with autism spectrum disorder (ASD) when he was 5 years old by pediatric psychologist, Dr. Isabel Torres-Ortiz (a board certified and licensed psychologist in Clinical Child and Adolescent Psychology; Latin American, cisgender woman, she/her pronouns, bisexual and neurotypical). Alex had difficulty grasping social and emotional cues, fixated on household objects, had a preference for solitude, and presented with sensitivity to sunlight and certain noises (e.g., clicking sounds, doors closing). Alex also presented with both externalizing (e.g., impulsivity, aggression, issues with attention) and internalizing behaviors (e.g., social anxiety, depression), along with delays in verbal fluency. Periodically tested throughout his childhood and adolescence by both school psychologists and Dr. Torres-Ortiz, Alex's Full Scale Intelligence Quotient (FSIQ) scores ranged between 86 and 89 on the Wechsler Intelligence Scales—psychological tests commonly used to assess intellectual and cognitive functioning. Alex's IQ scores fell within the low average range, placing his cognitive functioning between the 16th and 23rd percentiles compared to same-age peers. Concurrent academic achievement testing demonstrated commensurate performance, with composite scores falling between the 16th and 20th percentiles across standardized measures.

Alex's mother and father, both employed as corporate attorneys with sufficient financial resources, were able to secure many early developmental and educational interventions and services for Alex. In addition to having a pediatrician who specialized in children with developmental disabilities, Alex received applied behavior analysis (ABA) on the recommendation of the school district, occupational therapy, speech therapy, and participated in a therapeutic after-school community program to support his socioemotional development throughout elementary, middle, and high school. He also received ongoing mental and behavioral health care from Dr. Torres-Ortiz. Dr. Torres-Ortiz noted in her documentation that Alex struggled with

ABA[2] as he matriculated into high school. Alex described feeling that ABA "forced me to fit in by hiding that I'm autistic." He stopped ABA in 9th grade, and preferred participating in inclusive high school educational classroom experiences where he felt he could interact with others with more authenticity. He was later connected to a state vocational rehabilitation counselor to begin planning career and work opportunities when he turned 15 years old. As he grew into his adolescence Alex displayed a moderate to high level of adaptive and independent functioning.

Alex's Gender Development History

Dr. Isabel Torres-Ortiz, who had both expertise in developmental disabilities and LGBTQ+ affirming care with youth, also worked with Alex therapeutically. She completed Alex's last psychoeducation evaluation prior to beginning his postsecondary college program, and she detailed her prior clinical work with Alex. Dr. Torres-Ortiz first began working with Alex after he had verbalized feelings of depression, anxiety, and some persistent gender dysphoria that became more intense when he turned 13. At the time, Alex's parents were concerned that his "obsession" with his gender was a new symptom of his autism. Alex participated in 12 months of individual counseling with Dr. Torres-Ortiz, and family counseling sessions (with another MHP). Alex's family moved toward affirming their transgender son and worked through their own fears and internalized stigma to actively support him. When Alex entered high school at age 14, he encountered resistance from school administrators and struggled to make friends. He also encountered some bullying because of his gender presentation and autism. This lack of acceptance contributed to feelings of isolation and distress, at which point Alex's parents moved him into a private high school that provided more affirming support for youth with autism. However, supports for his transgender identity were still lacking. They struggled to connect with gender diverse youth despite living in a large metropolitan city. At the age of 18, Alex began his medical transition with testosterone hormone therapy with a gender affirming healthcare provider. He experienced positive changes, such as a deeper voice, increased muscle mass, and the growth of facial hair, which aligned more closely with his affirmed gender.

[2] Critics have raised concerns about long-term adverse psychological consequences related to ABA. Supporters point out that modern ABA approaches have evolved and are more focused on fostering autonomy. The ongoing debate underscores the need for ethical practices and respect for neurodiversity. See Leaf et al. (2022) for a review.

Clinical Approach

To prepare a formal treatment plan for Alex, Sarah reviewed the *Guidelines for Assessment and Intervention with Persons with Disabilities* (APA, 2022), *Disability-Related Counseling Competencies* (Chapin et al., 2018 and endorsed by the American Rehabilitation Counseling Association), *Guidelines for Psychological Practice with Transgender and Gender Nonconforming People* (APA, 2015), *Guidelines for Psychological Practice with Sexual Minority Persons* (APA, 2021), and the *Multicultural Guidelines: An Ecological Approach to Context, Identity, and Intersectionality* (APA, 2017). Together, these guidelines provided Sarah with some of the necessary knowledge and insight to conceptualize, design, and implement fair and ethical psychological interventions, while responsively considering how to integrate Alex's gender, race, culture, sexuality, and disability into his psychological care.

Clinical Assessment

As part of her treatment plan, Sarah engaged Alex in a formal assessment prior to beginning any counseling or psychotherapy. Gender diverse individuals, and persons with disabilities, consistently report microaggressions, significant stressors, traumas, and other adverse encounters when navigating disability, medical/health, and educational systems (Faccini & Allely, 2021; Hall & Delaney, 2021). Although Alex denied any significant abuse or trauma histories, he did have some adverse experiences navigating his education as a result of how people treated him because of his identities. Thus, borrowing from general rehabilitation clinical practices, she conducted an ecological assessment of stigma. This is a multilevel, informal, qualitative assessment interview that requires an in-depth exploration of stigma and minority stress across structural, interpersonal, and intrapersonal system levels.

At the structural level, Sarah assessed for significant histories in which laws, institutional policies, and sociocultural norms discriminated, restricted access, failed to protect, or reinforced stigmatization because of Alex's disability, gender, race, or sexual orientation (e.g., *Describe any barriers at school or work you have encountered because of your disability, gender, race, or sexual orientation*). The interpersonal level assessed for direct experiences of discrimination, harassment, bullying, violence, microaggressions, micro- or macro-invalidations, and general lack of support (e.g., *Have you ever been the target of bullying or violence because of your identity? Have you ever felt that your experiences or identity were invalidated or dismissed by others? How did you respond to these situations?*). The intrapersonal level assessment is a focused assessment of proximal minority stressors, including internalized stigma, negative self-beliefs, or intrapersonal devaluation as they relate to disability, gender, race, and sexual orientation (e.g., *Have there been moments when you felt devalued or felt lesser than because of your identity? How have those feelings shaped your interactions or decisions?*). This was also the time in which Sarah inquired about Alex's anxiety of being rejected and concealing his identities to avoid being stigmatized.

Sarah also made the decision to formally screen and track Alex for anxiety and depression. It was important to utilize assessment tools that had reliable and valid psychometric properties for young adults living with autism. Sarah used the *Patient Health Questionnaire* (PHQ-9) to assess depression, since Arnold et al. (2020) concluded that the PHQ-9 was a valid and reliable tool to assess depressive symptoms among adults with autism. However, Sarah was cautious with the tool since Robeson et al. (2024) reported evidence that the PHQ-9 does not measure suicidality in college students with autism in the same way it does for students without autism. Alex denied any suicidality during their work together. Sarah also used the *Anxiety Scale for Autism-Adult* (ASA-A; Rodgers et al., 2020), which assesses the unique ways in which anxiety presents for persons with autism, including social phobia, anxious arousal, and feelings of uncertainty. Rodgers et al. (2020) reported the measure being useful in both research and clinical contexts. Sarah used both the PHQ-9 and the ASA-A to track symptomology throughout their work together, noting a gradual decline in anxiety and depression over the course of their work together in the spring semester.

Counseling and Psychological Care

Individual counseling was limited to 12 sessions at the university counseling center. To secure a trusting, empowering, and safe therapeutic alliance with Alex, Sarah remained attentive to her tone, body language, and choice of words during counseling sessions. Sarah worked collaboratively with Alex to establish mutually agreed upon treatment goals to address Alex's depression and anxiety, and together they identified the following aims: (1) work toward recognizing and challenging internalized ableism and transphobia to cultivate a more positive self-image; (2) process past experiences related to identity disclosure and develop strategies for confidently sharing identities; and (3) develop strategies and skills to manage minority and oppressive stress while also recognizing and utilizing available support systems.

Sarah found it essential to empower Alex's capacity for self-determination regarding the intersection of his transgender and disability identities. Empowering gender diverse persons with disabilities to make decisions about their gender-and disability-affirming care enhances their sense of agency and well-being (Strang et al., 2021). During their sessions, she consistently encouraged Alex to make his own decisions regarding his care and life choices. Sarah used open-ended questions to explore Alex's feelings and thoughts, allowing him to take the lead in discussions about how to self-affirm his gender and disability, while reinforcing his personal sense of agency and autonomy. Relatedly, Maroney and Horne (2022) found that transgender persons on the autism spectrum reported several unique aspects of having multiple intersecting identities, including capacity to engage with unique perspectives, greater empathy, and freedom from traditional gender role expectations. By focusing on Alex's personal strengths, life achievements, and the positive aspects of his identities, Sarah helped him build confidence and a stronger sense of self. Sarah intentionally reflected and amplified the positive components of Alex's identities, including ways of bolstering the resiliencies he had developed throughout his life. This shift helped build self-esteem and resilience against internalized negative beliefs.

Minority stress theory highlights how mental health concerns (e.g., depression, anxiety) for autistic and gender-diverse individuals are largely influenced by systemic cissexism, heterosexism, and ableism (Maroney & Horne, 2022). Oppression and minority stressors were evident when Sarah conducted an ecological assessment of stigma. Sarah dedicated several sessions to explore how harmful systemic cissexism, heterosexism, and ableism impacted his daily life, including his fears of failure, self-worth, and tension between his career ambitions and disability. She also connected those systems of stigma to Alex's own experiences of depression and anxiety. To resist these oppressive and stigmatizing stressors, Sarah introduced Alex to mindfulness and self-compassion practices to help manage negative emotions. She also worked with Alex to develop a plan on when and how to practice mindfulness and self-compassion outside of individual counseling sessions.

A significant adaptation for transgender individuals with disabilities may include concealing, or selectively disclosing their identities to ensure safety (Hunter et al., 2020; Maroney & Horne, 2022), as was the case with Alex. Counseling sessions were also used to assist Alex in managing when and how to disclose, while also balancing authenticity with safety. Sarah also supported Alex in identifying situations where selective disclosure might be necessary to protect his well-being. In these sessions, Sarah used role-playing exercises to help Alex practice conversations where he might need to assert his identity or set boundaries. They discussed potential scenarios and outcomes, allowing Alex to feel more prepared and confident in navigating these challenges.

Opportunities to connect with other gender diverse people with disabilities can help build connections, lessen feelings of isolation, and foster a sense of belonging (Hunter et al., 2020; Strang et al., 2021). Online communities are especially valuable for autistic transgender individuals, providing a platform for peer feedback, identity exploration, and community. Sarah and Alex used several counseling sessions to explore various autistic and transgender online communities and support groups that matched his interests, and specifically explored the benefits and challenges of engaging in these spaces. She reflectively assisted Alex to navigate the complexities of fitting into both online and in-person communities, addressing the overlapping forms of discrimination or bullying he might encounter (see Maroney et al., 2023). She also strategized with Alex how to interact with online communities (e.g., respectfully asking questions, listening, sharing one's experiences, offering emotional encouragement), and provided Alex with feedback on effective and ineffective communication.

Relatedly, connecting to gender diverse and neurodiverse role models can offer hope, inspiration, and empower individuals by showing how others have successfully navigated life challenges (Strang et al., 2021). Although 12 individual counseling sessions was a short time to select a specific mentor, Sarah guided Alex in identifying traits and characteristics of potential role models who could provide him guidance. By connecting with others who had successfully navigated similar challenges, Alex began to feel less isolated and more supported in his journey.

Addressing Ableism, Heterosexism, and Ageism in Therapy: A Case Study

MHPs must scrutinize any conscious or unconscious biases regarding diverse sexual orientations, recognizing that people with disabilities also identify as lesbian, gay, bisexual/plurisexual, queer, or asexual (APA, 2021, 2022; Dispenza et al., 2017; Hunter et al., 2020). MHPs need to be aware that disability extends across the lifespan, including older adulthood, which means the intersections of ableism, disability, sexual orientation, and age become important clinical considerations. Older adults in the United States are the fastest growing proportion of the population (Administration for Community Living, 2022), and up to 3.4% of older people identify as LGBTQ+ (Jones, 2022). LGB older adults also have a high likelihood of living with a disability, and they are more likely than heterosexual older adults to report mental health disorder diagnoses and serious psychological distress (Masa et al., 2024). To illustrate intersections between older adulthood, sexual orientation, and disability, we present the case of June Newman. Only pseudonyms are used, and case details have been significantly altered for purposes of this clinical illustration.

Case Background

At the time of treatment, June Newman (she/her) was a 68-year-old Black, bisexual, cisgender woman living with several chronic illnesses and disability conditions. June had been recently discharged from the hospital after a short-term stay for stabilization after expressing desire and intent for suicide. Upon her discharge, her psychiatrist referred her for individual therapy to a community-based mental health agency to process her most recent experience of wanting to die by suicide. June had a history of psychiatric hospitalizations for her bipolar I disorder and past suicide attempts.

June married her ex-husband Roger when she was 30 years of age, and they divorced after 10 years of marriage when she turned 40. They had no children. Roger filed for divorce after June had a manic episode (i.e., mixture of irritable mood and euphoria), and charged over $50,000 on their credit cards in the span of 2 days. Roger is now completely estranged from June. After her divorce from Roger, June quit her job as a medical transcriptionist and moved in with her parents, who both died when June was 59 years of age. June was raised in a very religiously conservative environment, with largely negative beliefs toward the LGBTQ+ community (i.e., "it's a sin") and significant negativity toward people with mental illness (i.e., it's a punishment for sin).

June had tumultuous relationships with her two siblings throughout her childhood and young adult years. They often blamed and judged June for her bipolar diagnosis, ignored her when she cycled through periods of severe mania and depression, and resented her when she later asked for their support after her manic episodes. However, after her parents died, she maintained a friendly but distant relationship with her siblings; she reported mostly positive interactions, but she did not have close relationships or friendships with them. June also reported feeling resentful of her siblings. She managed to provide care for their parents despite her mental health, and she has never been able to disclose her sexual orientation to her family—"because I know they'd really cut me out for good if they knew who I really was." June dated a few men and a few women privately in the years since her divorce, but never felt like she could move forward in another relationship. At the time of counseling, she had only disclosed her bisexual identity to her long-time psychiatrist. After the death of her parents, she moved into an apartment and began working at a department retail store.

Several months following June's 65th birthday, she had to go to the emergency room for severe back pain, which was caused by a large tumor on her spine. She was later diagnosed with metastatic breast cancer (which had spread to her spine), and underwent intensive chemotherapy, radiation, surgery to remove the tumor, and a double mastectomy. June is now in remission from cancer, but after these procedures, she now lives with chronic nerve pain. June's pain makes it difficult to stand or sit for extended periods of time. She often wakes up throughout the night due to the pain and has difficulty concentrating and focusing when the pain is intense. A year and a half into her remission, June had to cut her hours from full-time to part-time at the department store due to her pain and the physical toll of her job. This loss of income meant June could no longer afford her apartment and had to move. Through the help of a family friend, she now lives in subsidized senior housing. The counselor assigned to June, Dara Lee, was a 46-year-old cisgender, heterosexual, Asian American, clinical rehabilitation counselor with 20 years of clinical experience.

Intersection of Physical and Psychiatric Disabilities

June had been living with bipolar I disorder for her entire life, but only had a formal diagnosis when she turned 40. Both prior to and after her diagnosis, she encountered interpersonal and structural ableism from nearly every system in her life. June reported constantly being told as a child by her parents, siblings, teachers, grandparents, and church members statements such as "get it together," "stop being lazy," and "stop acting crazy." This led to internalized ableist attitudes toward mental health disorders even prior to June's diagnosis. A lifetime of these microaggressions exacerbated her stress, mental health struggles, and desire for suicide. June's young adult life was marked by instability regarding her education and career opportunities. For example, she attempted to enroll in night courses after high school to become a medical transcriptionist but dropped out after one semester during a manic episode. Her employment was largely impacted by the frequency and duration of the (then unrecognized) mania and depression across her lifespan. However, despite these cycles, she worked hard to maintain employment. The chronic, painful neuropathy she experienced after her cancer treatment has now limited many instrumental activities and activities of daily living, including her capacity to work. During a time when her mental health was more stable (and she was able to maintain her jobs for longer periods of time), her cancer diagnosis and resulting disability had once again severely impacted her career opportunities.

Clinical Approach

Conceptualizing Suicide

Older adults (Lutz & Fiske, 2018), LGBTQ+ persons (Rogers et al., 2021), and persons with disabilities (Marlow et al., 2021) each experience heightened risk for suicide. June had expressed suicide desire for many years. According to her documentation, she had a severe suicide attempt and hospitalization when she was 40 after a prolonged manic episode. Her recent hospitalization was a result of her voluntary admission to inpatient treatment. She reported, "I don't see the point of living anymore. I'm going to die alone and sometimes I just want to get it over with. I'm afraid to be at home alone right now."

For MHPs, the Interpersonal Theory of Suicide (IPTS; Joiner, 2005; Van Orden et al., 2010) may be a useful framework for understanding June's suicide risk in the context of her experiences as a Black, bisexual, cisgender woman living with multiple disabilities. The IPTS posits that individuals are most at risk of suicide when they have both the desire and capability for suicide (Van Orden et al., 2010). Desire for suicide includes two major risk factors: thwarted belongingness and perceived burdensomeness.

June experienced thwarted belongingness, where fundamental needs to belong were unmet, as evidenced by her identity concealment as a bisexual woman. June's parents never knew she was bisexual, and she was fearful to disclose this aspect of her identity to her siblings so as not to be cut out of their lives, largely due to their beliefs that "being gay is wrong." Due to her family of origin and other societal influences, June experienced internalized binegativity (negative attitudes toward and stereotypes about bisexual people; Dyar & Feinstein, 2018). June's fundamental need to belong with others (Joiner, 2005), specifically, to be known and accepted for her full identity by her family, went unmet. June's feelings of thwarted belongingness were likely a compounding combination of feeling like she did not belong in her family, and feeling as if she was unable to accept a core part of her identity.

June experienced perceived burdensomeness, or one's perceptions that others/society would benefit from one's own death (Joiner, 2005), as evidenced by her recent hospitalization (particularly because it happened a few months after she cut hours at her job and moved into senior housing). Perceived burdensomeness consists of two aspects: feeling like one is a liability, and feeling hatred toward oneself (Van Orden et al., 2010). Experiences with ableism and internalized ableism can also contribute to feelings of perceived burdensomeness, which exacerbated June's suicide risk by enhancing perceptions of liability and self-hatred. June's physical and psychiatric disabilities may be categorized as invisible disabilities; they are not visible to the outside (i.e., she does not have visible equipment such as a wheelchair). An example of how ableism impacts her perception of burdensomeness can be found in her documentation history: prior to reducing her hours from full-time to part-time, she asked her manager at the department store if she could sit in a chair behind the register, and the request was denied. Her manager said, "we don't want folks to think our staff are old, incapable, and lazy." This experience not only exemplified the negative impact of ableism, but of ageism as well, and the impact contributed to her feelings of perceived burdensomeness. June did not seek further accommodations for fear of losing her job and struggles to manage her pain daily. Due to her pain and employment stress, she has isolated herself from neighbors, friends, acquaintances, and family; this profound social isolation resulted in worsening mental health outcomes that led to her most recent hospitalization. For older adults, loneliness and low perceived social support are risk factors for suicide desire (Mize et al., 2024).

Conceptualizing Aging, Ableism, and Minority Stress

June's experience illustrates how ableism includes systemic removal of individuals living with disability from public spaces—in her case, having to reduce her hours at work from full time to part time. In a similar way, ageism can also contribute to the erasure of older adults from public view; oftentimes, conceptualizations of the aging process are based in ableist biases (Langmann & Weßel, 2023). These intersections are especially salient in June's case: her psychiatric disability (one she has experienced throughout her life), her physical disability (chronic pain recently acquired because of cancer treatment), her bisexuality, and her age are aspects of her identity that include unique and interacting experiences of minority stress. LGBTQ+ older adults living with chronic minority stress may be at higher risk for premature cognitive aging (Correro 2nd & Nielson, 2020). However, despite this risk and accumulation effects of continued exposure to minority stressors across the lifespan, researchers have also found resilience and self-esteem increase with age among LGBTQ+ older adults (Koziara et al., 2022), perhaps as they develop increasingly adaptive coping processes to navigate these stressors.

Counseling and Psychological Care

June's counselor, Dara, initiated counseling with a thorough suicide risk assessment and safety planning. Dara co-constructed a safety plan with June: she assessed for sources of strength and support, identification of June's warning signs and access to lethal means and provided interdisciplinary collaboration with her psychiatrist to assist with medication management. Once the safety plan was established, Dara began to explore and discuss June's suicide feelings and behaviors as if they were symptoms of a lifetime of concealing her minoritized identities as a bisexual woman with disabilities. Using the IPTS as a guiding framework to begin therapy, she helped June process her feelings of loneliness, isolation, thwarted belongingness, and the inherent ableism in her perceptions of feeling like a liability (perceived burdensomeness). During this process, June identified feeling disconnected to her family, herself, and the world because of, in her words, "hiding and hating a part of me that I want to accept before I die." After a few sessions of processing the origins of her feelings of thwarted belongingness and perceived burdensomeness, Dara decided to utilize Internal Family Systems therapy (IFS; Schwartz, 2013) to help June process the disconnection she felt, alongside unlearning her internalized ableism and binegativity.

IFS is an evidence-based approach that conceptualizes the human psyche as comprising multiple distinct parts, all coordinated by what is termed "the Self." IFS recognizes two primary categories of parts: protective parts that serve defensive functions, and wounded parts that carry emotional pain from past experiences (also called exiles). The ultimate therapeutic goal in IFS is to achieve internal harmony through self-leadership, where the client's core Self—characterized by qualities such as compassion, curiosity, and clarity—guides these internal parts effectively (Schwartz, 2013). IFS differs fundamentally from other modalities, such as cognitive behavioral therapy (CBT), in both philosophy and practice. Whereas CBT employs directive interventions aimed at modifying problematic thoughts and behaviors, IFS takes a more exploratory stance. Rather than attempting to change or correct thoughts directly, IFS practitioners help clients understand the purpose and origins of these thoughts, viewing them as expressions of protective parts trying to maintain psychological safety. This approach emphasizes curiosity and compassion over correction (Haragutchi & Fuller, 2023).

In clinical practice, IFS practitioners utilize a structured process known as the *6Fs* (e.g., find, focus, flesh out, feel, befriend, and fear) to help clients differentiate their protective parts from their Self. To illustrate, Dara first worked to **find** the protective parts by asking June, *"What inside needs your attention now?"* Next, Dara supported June to **focus** on the sensation she identified. With the sensation in focus, Dara processed ways for June to **flesh out** the part she was countering (e.g., asking questions such as, *"How do you experience this sensation? What does it look like? What does it sound like?"*). Next, Dara asked June how she **feels** toward this part. This portion of the process involves balancing emotional safety and therapeutic challenges, depending on the intensity of the part. After processing how June felt toward the part, Dara worked to be**friend** the part by learning more about its role and function. Finally, Dara explored what this part **feared**, asking questions such as, "*What would happen if this part stopped doing its job?*" (Anderson et al., 2017). Using the 6Fs, Dara encouraged June to speak directly to the two basic categories of parts: her exiles (e.g., parts that carry the burden of past trauma, shame, and painful memories) and protectors (e.g., parts that developed to protect against difficult situations; Schwartz, 2013). June's bisexual part was an exile: when she was younger, she learned from her family system and cultural context that bisexuality was not accepted. In fact, to live authentically as bisexual would be potentially life-threatening. To protect June from rejection from her family, June's bisexual part became an exile of her mind. Similarly, the part of June who lives with bipolar I disorder was also exiled; June's symptoms (which were misunderstood for most of her life) were often accompanied by feelings of shame and fear. June's protector parts stepped in to ensure these exiles would never emerge. Though the intention of June's protectors was to ensure survival, the impact was internalized biphobia and ableism: to keep the bisexual and disabled parts of herself away, she embodied those beliefs about herself, which were often reinforced within her cultural and systemic context. From Dara's IFS perspective, her protector parts may have been the ones behind her suicidal thoughts—as a last-ditch effort to control her exiled parts.

Throughout treatment, June was able to identify, understand, and compassionately integrate these parts into her full self. The results of June's hard work with Dara's support were overwhelmingly positive: June reported less mental health distress, no more desire for suicide, and less physical pain. These outcomes were congruent with several IFS studies that have found a reduction in symptoms of depression, PTSD, and physical pain following IFS treatment (Hodgdon et al., 2021 Shadick et al., 2013).

Conclusion

The psychosocial experiences of ableism, heterosexism, cissexism, and other intersecting oppressive forces can significantly impact the mental health of LGBTQ+ individuals living with disabilities. Ableism, conceptualized as stigma and discrimination against people with disabilities (APA, 2022), has the propensity to contribute to poor mental health for all persons. However, the compounded and intersecting stress from navigating ableism, cissexism, and heteronormative societal norms can increase symptoms of anxiety, depression, and other mental health conditions. To effectively support LGBTQ+ persons with disabilities, MHPs must develop competencies that include an understanding of the unique experiences of this group. This involves comprehensive training in cultural competence, awareness of intersectional identities, and the adoption of inclusive practices that affirm disability, gender, and sexual orientation. By fostering an environment of empathy and inclusivity, MHPs can better address the complex mental health needs of LGBTQ+ individuals with disabilities, promoting holistic well-being and resilience across the lifespan.

References

Administration for Community Living. (2022). *2021 profile of older Americans*. https://acl.gov/sites/default/files/Profile%20of%20OA/2021%20Profile%20of%20OA/2021ProfileOlderAmericans_508.pdf.

American Psychological Association. (2015). Guidelines for psychological practice with transgender and gender nonconforming people. *The American Psychologist, 70*(9), 832–864. https://doi.org/10.1037/a0039906

American Psychological Association. (2017). *Multicultural guidelines: An ecological approach to context, identity, and intersectionality*. Retrieved from: http://www.apa.org/about/policy/multicultural-guidelines.pdf

American Psychological Association, APA Task Force on Guidelines for Assessment and Intervention with Persons with Disabilities. (2022). *Guidelines for assessment and intervention with persons with disabilities*. Retrieved from https://www.apa.org/about/policy/guidelines-assessment-intervention-disabilities.pdf

American Psychological Association, APA Task Force on Psychological Practice with Sexual Minority Persons. (2021). *Guidelines for psychological practice with sexual minority persons*. Retrieved from www.apa.org/about/policy/psychological-practice-sexual-minority-persons.pdf

Anderson, F. G., Sweezy, M., & Schwartz, R. C. (2017). *Internal family systems skills training manual: Trauma-informed treatment for anxiety, depression, PTSD & substance abuse*. PESI Publishing & Media.

Arnold, S. R. C., Uljarević, M., Hwang, Y. I., Richdale, A. L., Trollor, J. N., & Lawson, L. P. (2020). Brief report: Psychometric properties of the patient health questionaire-9 (PHQ-9) in autistic adults. *Journal of Autism and Developmental Disorders, 50*, 2217–2225. https://doi.org/10.1007/s10803-019-03947-9

Boggan, C. E., Grzanka, P. R., & Bain, C. L. (2017). Perspectives on queer music therapy: A qualitative analysis of music therapists' reactions to radically inclusive practice. *Journal of Music Therapy, 54*(4), 375–404. https://doi.org/10.1093/jmt/thx016

Breckenridge, C. A., & Vogler, C. A. (2001). The critical limits of embodiment: Disability's criticism. *Public Culture, 13*(3), 349–357. https://muse.jhu.edu/pub/4/article/26251/summary?casa_token=9Bk_B8GCirkAAAAA:56Nr3x8oFtyJcxlKN6aJfwCIgBmvYMFJ4igj-2y6U4yCqa8GT-GfZ_69p9_1oJRp6_I-pu4dIN8

Brucker, D. L., Surfus, C., & Henly, M. (2023). Mental health experiences in 2021 for adults with disabilities who are lesbian, gay, bisexual, or transgender. *Rehabilitation Psychology, 68*(4), 374–384. https://doi.org/10.1037/rep0000511

Chapin, M., McCarthy, H., Shaw, L., Bradham-Cousar, M., Chapman, R., Nosek, M., Peterson, S., Yilmaz, Z., & Ysasi, N. (2018). *Disability-related counseling competencies*. American Rehabilitation Counseling Association, a division of ACA. https://www.counseling.org/docs/default-source/competencies/arca-disability-related-counseling-competencies-v51519.pdf?sfvrsn=984f4bd0_1

Conner, K. J., Acosta, V. M., Nouri, R., Tyler von Wrangel, M., Gramillo, E., & Conner, A. (2023). Psychotherapy experiences of U.S. adults with physical disabilities: Recommendations for affirmative practice. *The Counseling Psychologist, 51*(7), 970–1004. https://doi.org/10.1177/00110000231186824

Conover, K. J., & Israel, T. (2019). Microaggressions and social support among sexual minorities with physical disabilities. *Rehabilitation Psychology, 64*(2), 167–178. https://doi.org/10.1037/rep0000250

Correro, A. N., 2nd, & Nielson, K. A. (2020). A review of minority stress as a risk factor for cognitive decline in lesbian, gay, bisexual, and transgender (LGBT) elders. *Journal of Gay & Lesbian Mental Health, 24*(1), 2–19. https://doi.org/10.1080/19359705.2019.1644570

Dispenza, F., Brennaman, C., Harper, L. S., Harrigan, M. A., Chastain, T. E., & Procter, J. E. (2019). Career development of sexual and gender minority persons living with disabilities *The Counseling Psychologist, 47*(1), 98–128. https://doi.org/10.1177/0011000018819425

Dispenza, F. (2023). Chronic illness and disability among sexual minority persons: Exploring the roles of proximal minority stress, adaptation, and quality of life. *Psychology of Sexual Orientation and Gender Diversity*. https://doi.org/10.1037/sgd0000642

Dispenza, F., & DeBlaere, C. (2017). Ability status and sexual orientation. In *The SAGE encyclopedia of psychology and gender* (Vol. 4, pp. 6–9). SAGE Publications, Inc.. https://doi.org/10.4135/9781483384269

Dispenza, F., Harper, L. S., & Harrigan, M. A. (2016a). Subjective health among LGBT persons living with disabilities: A qualitative content analysis. *Rehabilitation Psychology, 61*(3), 251–259. https://doi.org/10.1037/rep0000086

Dispenza, F., Viehl, C., Sewell, M. H., Burke, M. A., & Gaudet, M. M. (2016b). A model of affirmative intersectional rehabilitation counseling with sexual minorities: A grounded theory study. *Rehabilitation Counseling Bulletin, 59*(3), 143–157. https://doi.org/10.1177/0034355215579916

Dispenza, F., Varney, M., & Golubovic, N. (2017). Psychological and counseling practices with sexual and gender minority persons living with chronic illnesses and disabilities (CID). *Psychology of Sexual Orientation and Gender Diversity, 4*(1), 137–142. https://doi.org/10.1037/sgd0000212

Dyar, C., & Feinstein, B. A. (2018). Binegativity: Attitudes toward and stereotypes about bisexual individuals. In D. J. Swan & S. Habibi (Eds.), *Bisexuality: Theories, research, and recommendations for the invisible sexuality* (pp. 95–111). Springer/Springer Nature. https://doi.org/10.1007/978-3-319-71535-3_6

Elderton, A., Clarke, S., Jones, C., & Stacey, J. (2014). Telling our story: A narrative therapy approach to helping lesbian, gay, bisexual and transgender people with a learning disability identify and strengthen positive self-identity stories. *British Journal of Learning Disabilities, 42*(4), 251–336. https://doi.org/10.1111/bld.12075

Faccini, L., & Allely, C. S. (2021). Dealing with trauma in individuals with autism spectrum disorders: Trauma informed care, treatment, and forensic implications. *Journal of Aggression, Maltreatment & Trauma, 30*(8), 1082–1092. https://doi.org/10.1080/10926771.2020.1853295

Fredriksen-Goldsen, K. I., Kim, H.-J., & Barkan, S. E. (2012). Disability among lesbian, gay, and bisexual adults: Disparities in prevalence and risk. *American Journal of Public Health, 102*(1), e16–e21. https://doi.org/10.2105/AJPH.2011.300379

Fredriksen-Goldsen, K. I., Simoni, J. M., Kim, H., Lehavot, K., Walters, K. L., Yang, J., Hoy-Ellis, C. P., & Muraco, A. (2014). The health equity promotion model: Reconceptualization of lesbian, gay, bisexual, and transgender (LGBT) health disparities. *American Journal of Orthopsychiatry, 84*(6), 653–663. https://doi.org/10.1037/ort0000030

Hall, S. F., & DeLaney, M. J. (2021). A Trauma-Informed Exploration of the Mental Health and Community Support Experiences of Transgender and Gender-Expansive Adults. *Journal of homosexuality, 68*(8), 1278–1297. https://doi.org/10.1080/00918369.2019.1696104

Haragutchi, A. H. & Fuller, K. (2023). *Internal family systems therapy: How it works & what to expect.* Retrieved from ChoosingTherapy.com

Hodgdon, H. B., Anderson, F. G., Southwell, E., Hrubec, W., & Schwartz, R. (2021). Internal Family Systems (IFS) Therapy for Posttraumatic Stress Disorder (PTSD) among Survivors of Multiple Childhood Trauma: A Pilot Effectiveness Study. *Journal of Aggression, Maltreatment & Trauma, 31*(1), 22–43. https://doi.org/10.1080/10926771.2021.2013375

Human Rights Campaign. (2022). *Understanding disability in the LGBTQ+ community*. https://www.hrc.org/resources/understanding-disabled-lgbtq-people.

Hunter, T., Dispenza, F., Huffstead, M., Suttles, M., & Bradley, Z. (2020). Queering disability: Exploring resilience of sexual and gender minority persons living with disabilities. *Rehabilitation Counseling Bulletin, 64*(1), 31–41. https://doi.org/10.1177/0034355219895813

Joiner, T. E. (2005). *Why people die by suicide*. Harvard University Press.

Jones, J. M. (2022, February 17). *LGBT identification in U.S. ticks up to 7.1%.* Gallup. https://news.gallup.com/poll/389792/lgbt-identification-ticks-up.aspx

Kattari, S. K. (2020). Ableist microaggressions and the mental health of disabled adults. *Community Mental Health Journal, 56*, 1170–1179. https://doi.org/10.1007/s10597-020-00615-6

Koziara, K., Mijas, M. E., Galbarczyk, A., Wycisk, J., Pliczko, M. P., Krzych-Miłkowska, K., & Grabski, B. (2022). It gets better with age: Resilience, stigma, and mental health among lesbian, gay, bisexual, transgender and queer persons from Poland. *Frontiers in Psychology, 13*, 958601. https://doi.org/10.3389/fpsyg.2022.958601

Langmann, E., & Weßel, M. (2023). Leaving no one behind: Successful ageing at the intersection of ageism and ableism. *Philosophy, Ethics, and Humanities in Medicine: PEHM, 18*(1), 22. https://doi.org/10.1186/s13010-023-00150-8

Leaf, J. B., Cihon, J. H., Leaf, R., McEachin, J., Liu, N., Russell, N., Unumb, L., Shapiro, S., & Khosrowshahi, D. (2022). Concerns about ABA-based intervention: An evaluation and recommendations. *Journal of Autism and Developmental Disorders, 52*(6), 2838–2853. https://doi.org/10.1007/s10803-021-05137-y

Lutz, J., & Fiske, A. (2018). Functional disability and suicidal behavior in middle-aged and older adults: A systematic critical review. *Journal of Affective Disorders, 227*, 260–271. https://doi.org/10.1016/j.jad.2017.10.043

Marlow, N. M., Xie, Z., Tanner, R., Jo, A., & Kirby, A. V. (2021). Association between disability and suicide-related outcomes among U.S. adults. *American Journal of Preventive Medicine, 61*(6), 852–862. https://doi.org/10.1016/j.amepre.2021.05.035

Maroney, M. R., & Horne, S. G. (2022). "Tuned into a different channel": Autistic transgender adults' experiences of intersectional stigma. *Journal of Counseling Psychology, 69*(6), 761–774. https://doi.org/10.1037/cou0000639.supp

Maroney, M. R., Levitt, H. M., & Horne, S. G. (2023). Exploring the efficacy of an online intervention in processing experiences of heterosexism among autistic-LGBTQ+ individuals. *Journal of Autism and Developmental Disorders*. https://doi.org/10.1007/s10803-023-06027-1

Masa, R., Inoue, M., Prieto, L., Baruah, D., Nosrat, S., Mehak, S., & Operario, D. (2024). Mental health of older adults by sexual minority status: Evidence from the 2021 National Health Interview Survey. *Journal of Applied Gerontology, 43*(3), 276–286. https://doi.org/10.1177/07334648231203838

Miller, R. A., & Smith, A. C. (2021). Microaggressions experienced by LGBTQ students with disabilities. *Journal of Student Affairs Research and Practice, 58*(5), 491–506. https://doi.org/10.1080/19496591.2020.1835669

Mize, M. C., Shannonhouse, L., Minton, C. B., Fullen, M., Shaikh, A., & Westcott, J. (2024). Suicide risk factors among older adults: Implications for counselors as Medicare providers. *Journal of Counseling & Development*. https://doi.org/10.1002/jcad.12512

Robeson, M., Brasil, K. M., Adams, H. C., & Zlomke, K. R. (2024). Measuring depression and anxiety in autistic college students: A psychometric evaluation of the PHQ-9 and GAD-7. *Autism*. https://doi.org/10.1177/13623613241240183

Rodgers, J., Farquhar, K., Mason, D., Brice, S., Wigham, S., Ingham, B., Freeston, M., & Parr, J. R. (2020). Development and initial evaluation of the anxiety scale for autism-adults. *Autism in Adulthood, 2*(1), 24–33. https://doi.org/10.1089/aut.2019.0044

Rogers, M. L., Hom, M. A., Janakiraman, R., & Joiner, T. E. (2021). Examination of minority stress pathways to suicidal ideation among sexual minority adults: The moderating role of LGBT community connectedness. *Psychology of Sexual Orientation and Gender Diversity, 8*(1), 38–47. https://doi.org/10.1037/sgd0000409

Schwartz R. C. (2013). Moving from acceptance toward transformation with Internal Family Systems Therapy (IFS). *Journal of Clinical Psychology, 69*(8), 805–816. https://doi.org/10.1002/jclp.22016

Shadick, N. A., Sowell, N. F., Frits, M. L., Hoffman, S. M., Hartz, S. A., Booth, F. D., Sweezy, M., Rogers, P. R., Dubin, R. L., Atkinson, J. C., Friedman, A. L., Augusto, F., Iannaccone, C. K., Fossel, A. H., Quinn, G., Cui, J., Losina, E., & Schwartz, R. C. (2013). A randomized controlled trial of an internal family systems-based psychotherapeutic intervention on outcomes in rheumatoid arthritis: a proof-of-concept study. *The Journal of rheumatology, 40*(11), 1831–1841. https://doi.org/10.3899/jrheum.121465

Strang, J. F., Knauss, M., van der Miesen, A., McGuire, J. K., Kenworthy, L., Caplan, R., Freeman, A., Sadikova, E., Zaks, Z., Pervez, N., Balleur, A., Rowlands, D. W., Sibarium, E., Willing, L., McCool, M. A., Ehrbar, R. D., Wyss, S. E., Wimms, H., Tobing, J., et al. (2021). A clinical program for transgender and gender-diverse neurodiverse/autistic adolescents developed through community-based participatory design. *Journal of Clinical Child and Adolescent Psychology, 50*(6), 730–745. https://doi.org/10.1080/15374416.2020.1731817

Substance Abuse and Mental Health Services Administration. (2023). *Lesbian, gay, and bisexual behavioral health: Results from the 2021 and 2022 National surveys on drug use and health* (SAMHSA Publication No. PEP23-07-01-001). Center for Behavioral Health Statistics and Quality, Substance Abuse and Mental Health Services Administration. https://www.samhsa.gov/data/report/LGB-Behavioral-Health-Report-2021-2022

Surfus, C. R. (2023). A statistical understanding of disability in the LGBT community. *Statistics and Public Policy, 10*(1) Advance online publication. https://doi.org/10.1080/2330443X.2023.2188056

The Trevor Project. (2023). *Research brief: The mental health of LGBTQ+ young people with disabilities.* https://www.thetrevorproject.org/wp-content/uploads/2023/11/The-Trevor-Project-Mental-Health-of-LGBTQ-Young-People-with-Disabilities-Report-Dec-2023.pdf

Van Orden, K. A., Witte, T. K., Cukrowicz, K. C., Braithwaite, S. R., Selby, E. A., & Joiner, T. E., Jr. (2010). The interpersonal theory of suicide. *Psychological Review, 117*(2), 575–600. https://doi.org/10.1037/a0018697

Part III
Underrepresented Groups and Intersectionality

Chapter 10
Addressing Interlocking Systems of Oppression and the Need for Radical Hope and Healing for LGBTQ+ BIPOC Clients

Koree S. Badio, Julio A. Martin, and Roberto L. Abreu

Highlights

In this chapter, we invite readers to think about how intersectional systems of oppression impact the experiences of LGBTQ+ BIPOC communities. We provide the readers tangible steps for working with LGBTQ+ BIPOC clients in a manner that goes beyond coping, with a focus on thriving and liberation. Specifically, we provide the following:

- An overview about the experiences of oppression and trauma among LGBTQ+ BIPOC communities.
- Theoretical underpinnings that go beyond psychology's traditional, deficit-based frameworks for conceptualizing presenting concerns among LGBTQ+ BIPOC clients:
  - Liberation Psychology (Comas-Díaz, 2007; Martín-Baró, 1994)
  - Radical Hope (Mosley et al., 2020)
  - Radical Healing (French et al., 2020)
- A case study that illustrates a liberatory, racial hope, and radical healing lens of working with LGBTQ+ BIPOC clients
  - Focuses on how the therapist's approach not only facilitates their client's liberation, but also their own.

K. S. Badio · J. A. Martin · R. L. Abreu (✉)
Department of Psychology, University of Florida, Gainesville, FL, USA
e-mail: rabreu26@ufl.edu

N. A. Livingston et al. (eds.), *Addressing Minority Stress and Enhancing Resilience with Diverse LGBTQ+ Clients*, CBT: Science Into Practice,
https://doi.org/10.1007/978-3-031-92836-9_10

Positionality
The authors of this book chapter represent a range of racial, ethnic, gender, and sexual identities. The first author, Koree S. Badio, is a doctoral candidate majoring in Counseling Psychology and self-identifies as a Black, Afro-Caribbean, heterosexual, and cisgender woman. Pulling inspiration from healing paradigms such as Black Liberation Psychology, Radical Hope, and Restorative Justice, Koree is passionate about utilizing science and practice to engender psychological, spiritual, and political wellness for marginalized communities. Koree has provided culturally affirming and trauma-responsive mental health support for youth and adults navigating interlocking system of oppression, including African and African-descent refugees, sexual and gender minorities, and women of color. Thus, Koree's contribution to this text is grounded in her pursuit of liberation and loving wellness for LGBTQ+ BIPOC.

The second author, Julio A. Martin, is a doctoral candidate in the Counseling Psychology Ph.D. program at the University of Florida and identifies as a first-generation, Cuban, cisgender gay man. Julio has conducted various clinical practicum experiences working with undocumented Latinx communities and young people and adults with marginalized identities whose experiences of oppression directly impacted their mental health as conceptualized from a Liberation Psychology framework. From this lens, Julio has gone through the process of decolonizing his approach and engaging in aspects of spirituality, radical humility, and *acompañamiento* to therapy, which informs his contributions to this text.

The third author, Roberto L. Abreu, is an Associate Professor in Counseling Psychology at the University of Florida. They identify as a non-Black, Latine, bilingual, cisgender, queer presenting, man. Roberto's clinical experiences include college students at counseling centers, incarcerated people in both state and federal prisons, veterans with several mental illness and addictions, and community mental health. Across these clinical experiences, Roberto has witnessed the impact that multiple systems of oppression have on clients, but also how healing can transform clients when they are allowed to claim their whole humanity.

Key Terms

Critical reflection: The analysis of one's social situation (Adames et al., 2022).
Critical consciousness: How marginalized individuals learn to critically analyze their social conditions and act to change them (Watts et al., 2011).
Cultural authenticity: The honoring and appreciation for ancestral wisdom and cultural knowledge (Adames et al., 2022).

Introduction

In the United States, minoritized communities are disproportionately affected by different systems of oppression. Specifically, Lesbian, Gay, Bisexual, Trans, and Queer (LGBTQ+) communities and Black and Indigenous People of Color (BIPOC) experience oppression due to interlocking systems of oppression (Mallory et al., 2015). Social justice scholars and trailblazers such as Crenshaw (1989) and the Combahee

River Collective (1977) have explored the ways in which historically marginalized groups, such as individuals who identify as both LGBTQ+ and BIPOC exist within multiple systems of oppression (Carbado et al., 2013). Given the oppressive systems that LGBTQ+ BIPOC navigate (White supremacy, colonialism, racism, cissexism, heterosexism, monosexism; Meyer et al., 2012; Mosley et al., 2021), it is imperative for mental health professionals to be culturally competent in ways to serve these communities. According to the American Psychological Association (APA, 2021), practitioners and trainees have an ethical obligation to understand the influence of oppression and how it impacts their clients' psychological, social, and occupational functioning. Moreso, psychologists are required to provide services that are anti-oppressive. For example, APA's ethical Principle D (Justice) states that psychologists ought to recognize that fairness and justice are human rights and that all persons are entitled to access and benefit from psychological services. In addition, APA ethical code 2.01(b) (Boundaries of Competence) establishes that when working with culturally diverse populations, psychologists strive to understand cultural factors through consultation, training, education, or supervision. This chapter focuses on the application of strategies that are consistent with these ethics and that empower LGBTQ+ BIPOC clients.

Culturally responsive psychotherapeutic practices require providers to build awareness about ways in which their marginalized clients are impacted by systems of oppression (Adames et al., 2018). When considering the distress that occurs when contending with oppressive environments, systems, and beliefs, it is crucial that mental health providers center the principles of justice and liberation for their LGBTQ+ BIPOC clients (Adames et al., 2018; Mosley et al., 2021). The purpose of this chapter is trifold: (1) present an overview about the experiences of oppression and trauma among LGBTQ+ BIPOC communities, (2) explore the theoretical underpinnings of liberation psychology, radical hope, and radical healing (see Table 10.1) as they relate to the wellness of LGBTQ+ BIPOC communities, and (3) illustrate how clinicians might use liberating and radical approaches when working with LGBTQ+ BIPOC clients.

Table 10.1 Theoretical Approaches

Approach	Definition	Examples
Culturally Responsive Therapy	An approach to psychotherapy that emphasizes the therapist's understanding and responsiveness to a client's cultural identities and beliefs, to include age, cultural values, gender, language, race, and sexual orientation among others (Cabassa & Baumann, 2013).	Consideration of cultural factors throughout case conceptualization (Benuto et al., 2021). Integrate client's cultural practices into treatment plan (Huey et al., 2023).
Radical Hope	The belief in the collective healing and thriving of communities of Color, and other marginalized communities, in spite of systems of oppression (Mosley et al., 2020).	Holding an awareness of the reality of oppression, coupled with the belief that positive change for LGBTQ+ BIPOC communities is possible (Cherrington, 2018). Envisioning possibilities for the wellness of LGBTQ+ BIPOC communities (Mosley et al., 2020).

(continued)

Table 10.1 (continued)

Approach	Definition	Examples
Radical Healing	A theoretical framework that attends to how BIPOC communities, and other marginalized communities, heal from oppression-related stress and trauma (French et al., 2020).	Considering how systems of oppression and privilege shape a client's life (French et al., 2020). Moving beyond traditional modalities of treatment; prioritize healing rather than coping with marginalization (French et al., 2020).
Liberation Psychology	A decolonial approach to understanding and addressing psychological distress related to the oppression of individuals and groups (French et al., 2020; Martín-Baró, 1994).	Supporting clients with recovering their historical memory (Neville et al., 2021). Challenging dominant ideologies that blame people for their identity-based oppression (Neville et al., 2021).

Experiences of Oppression and Resilience Among LGBTQ+ BIPOC Communities

The United States is one of the most multicultural nations in the world and continues to grow in diversity. Despite the growing presence of BIPOC and LGBTQ+ communities in the nation, many people coming from marginalized backgrounds must contend with the omnipresent existence of oppression (French et al., 2020). Due to the longstanding history of racism, sexism, and cis-heteronormativity in the United States, LGBTQ+ individuals with minoritized racial and ethnic identities are often subject to personal, relational, structural, and intergenerational oppression and trauma related to their multiple identities (French et al., 2020; Parker-Barnes et al., 2022). Specifically, research has shown that LGBTQ+ BIPOC communities experience higher rates of victimization and familial and peer rejection in comparison to their white and cisgender and heterosexual peers, leading to internalized feelings of shame, as well as barriers to care (e.g., Abreu et al., 2021; Katz-Wise & Hyde, 2012; Wirtz et al., 2020).

Victimization

Research shows that LGBTQ+ BIPOC communities experience high rates of victimization (e.g., violent crimes) and sexual exploitation (e.g., Russell et al., 2014; Mosley et al., 2021). For example, LGBTQ+ people are nearly four times more likely than heterosexual and cisgender individuals to be victims of violent crimes (Flores et al., 2020). Moreover, Black people are more likely to be victims of homicide, and violent crimes against Black and Latinx people are less likely to be solved

(Quandt & Jones, 2021). Notably, a study of 454 Black and Latinx sexual minority cisgender men and transgender women found that participants were at increased risk for experiencing sexual and physical violence and discrimination related to their racial, ethnic, and gender identity and expression (Arrington-Sanders et al., 2022). Additionally, a recent study of 3352 Latinx LGBTQ+ high school students found that approximately 42% of participants experienced victimization at the intersection of their sexual orientation, gender identity, and their race and ethnicity (Zongrone et al., 2020). These findings demonstrate that LGBTQ+ BIPOC communities are at increased risk of experiencing victimization related to their multiple marginalized identities.

Internalized Oppression

Internalized oppression, or believing and enacting oppressive and negative messages from the dominant group regarding attributes about one's own marginalized group, is related to a range of adverse health outcomes among marginalized individuals (Gale et al., 2020). Specifically, there is a wealth of research documenting the negative impacts that internalized oppression has on LGBTQ+ BIPOC communities, including a reduction in feelings of self-worth, psychological well-being, and life satisfaction (e.g., Adames et al., 2018). Because LGBTQ+ BIPOC people carry multiple marginalized identities, they are susceptible to experiencing internalized oppression related to racial, ethnic, sexual, and gender discrimination (Drazdowski et al., 2016). Ultimately, research shows that internalized oppression often contributes to feelings of powerlessness, hopelessness, low self-esteem, shame, and psychological distress among LGBTQ+ BIPOC communities, which in turn may lead to limiting one's expectations for one's own ability to engage in health-promoting behaviors (Gale et al., 2020; Jackson et al., 2020; Mereish et al., 2019).

Family and Peer Rejection

Research also demonstrates that family and parental acceptance promotes psychological well-being among LGBTQ+ individuals (Dickenson & Huebner, 2016). Family rejection refers to behaviors that are opposite of love, affection, and support (e.g., neglect, abuse; see review in Abreu et al., 2021). In terms of family relations, research shows that BIPOC people are less likely to be out to their family as a sexual minority compared to their white counterparts (e.g., Abreu et al., 2022). For example, Mosleyand colleagues (2021) note that Black queer individuals face familial and/or peer rejection and negative experiences in religious communities. Moreso, concealing one's LGBTQ+ identity, which one may utilize for self-protection against threat, can keep one apart from culturally affirming communities (Pachankis et al., 2020).

Barriers to Care

Although LGBTQ+ BIPOC communities are increasingly vulnerable to experiencing emotional distress and mental health challenges (Noyola et al., 2020; Toomey et al., 2018), research shows that LGBTQ+ BIPOC communities are less likely to receive quality and culturally responsive healthcare (Mosley et al., 2021; Romanelli & Hudson, 2017). Additionally, BIPOC and LGBTQ+ youth from lower socioeconomic backgrounds face additional healthcare access barriers related to their intersecting identities, such as challenges accessing affordable gender-affirming care (Salerno et al., 2020). Access to effective services is imperative to address the physical and mental health disparities that LGBTQ+ BIPOC communities disproportionately face.

Experiences of Resilience and Resistance Among LGBTQ+ BIPOC Communities

According to French et al. (2020), cultivating radical hope requires the will or strength to resist oppression. As mentioned previously, radical hope refers to the belief in the collective healing and thriving in communities of color in spite of systems of oppression (Mosley et al., 2020). Moreover, resilience is described as one's ability to use available resources to overcome adversities or adapt to social and psychological stressors (Matsuno & Israel, 2018; Richaud, 2013). Although resilience is typically referenced through a white, Eurocentric lens focusing primarily on individual-level processes, radical healing conceptualizes resilience and resistance as transformative collective processes. Specifically, LGBTQ+ BIPOC communities demonstrate resilience and resistance through their commitment to experience joy and pleasure despite the awareness of oppression (French et al., 2020; Parmenter & Galliher, 2024; Parmenter et al., 2024; Singh et al., 2020). For example, research shows that LGBTQ+ BIPOC communities engage in collectivist practices, such as leaning into supportive communities that affirm their social identities (Hailey et al., 2020; Mosley et al., 2021; Parmenter & Galliher, 2024; Parmenter et al., 2024).

A recurrent finding in the literature is that LGBTQ+ community spaces are largely white, cisgender, young, and monosexual (Barrett & Pollack, 2005; Parmenter et al., 2020; Stone et al., 2020). In response to predominantly white LGBTQ+ spaces, LGBTQ+ BIPOC people often form micro-identity communities (Abreu et al., 2021). For example, in a study by Cerezo and colleagues (2014), Latina transgender women relied on and valued social support from their "family of choice," which typically involved other Latina transgender women. Additionally, Mosley et al. (2021) name the interconnectedness between self-acceptance and community building for Black queer individuals, such that creating supportive networks is "critical for survival and personal liberation" (p. 293). Engagement in activism is also a recurrent theme in resilience research among LGBTQ+ BIPOC communities (see review in Sostre et al., 2024). Lastly, research shows that the utilization of faith and spiritual practices could be associated with positive mental health outcomes for some LGBTQ+ BIPOC communities (see review in Lockett et al., 2023). Spirituality fosters self-awareness and self-acceptance among LGBTQ+ people (Wood & Conley, 2014). For example, in a qualitative study with 37 Black gay and bisexual men, the researchers found that Black gay and bisexual men coped with homophobic and biphobic messages by remaining close to a higher power and engaging in self-love and self-acceptance practices (Della et al., 2002). According to Lockett and colleagues (2023), LGBTQ+ BIPOC participants were more likely to report identifying with a higher power rather than subscribing to religious practices due to negative experiences from religious communities.

Liberation Psychology, Radical Hope, and Radical Healing

In Latin America, Ignacio Martín-Baró began to conceptualize Liberation Psychology as he worked with farm workers in El Salvador. While treating people for PTSD, anxiety, and paranoia, Martín-Baró observed that people were being robbed, kidnapped, raped, and expelled violently from their land. Thus, he concluded that their responses of fear, worry, and paranoia were not a source of pathology but instead a result of the stressors in their environments (Comas-Díaz, 2007; Martín-Baró, 1994).

Acknowledging that psychology is largely influence by Western ideologies, which does not account for the role of systems of oppressions in the well-being of people, Martín-Baró took on the task to develop a new psychology praxis that centers the people's subjective experiences as a way to empower them to change their oppressive contexts rather than adapt to them. In the new praxis of psychology proposed by Martín-Baró (1994), people are not removed from their social and political contexts, and the histories of how people came to experience their context are constantly in conversation with their experiences. To promote psychological wellness, Liberation Psychology aims to help people question their conditions and what has led to these conditions as they recover ancestral knowledge about the truth of who they are and what serves them best. The following descriptions are what Martín-Baró identified as the three essential theoretical and practical components of Libcration Psychology (Martín-Baró, 1994).

First, Liberation Psychology aims to recovery the historical memory of clients, to include (1) Helping people recover their sense of identity, (2) Allowing themselves to rely on their culture, and (3) Rescuing aspects of identity that served in the past and can be utilized in the present for liberation. The three components of the recovery of historical memory aim to help the individual integrate parts of themselves that enable the development of their identity. The ultimate goal of this practical piece is for people to gain the confidence to trust their understanding of what is real amidst the distortions of systems of oppression.

Second, he urged for the need to de-colonize our consciousness given that most of what we call commonsense is based primarily on Western ideology (Martín-Baró, 1994). De-colonizing is not only the responsibility of the client. The practitioner must simultaneously deconstruct their often victimizing and pathologizing Western approaches as they work with clients. Thus, the practice of de-colonizing is aimed at aiding both the practitioner and the client with the goal of both being liberated from oppressive ideologies (Barratt, 2011).

Third, Martín-Baró points out the importance of empowering people to change their environment by allowing them to use their own knowledge and experiences, their collective histories, and their collective values. Theoretically, Martín-Baró (1994) had an unwavering faith in the capacity for humans to change the world. In the practical sense, through a lens of Liberation Psychology, peoples' virtues are alive in their traditions, religious practices, and social structures. The identification and use of virtues of the people is the driving force toward healthy development, as it makes people aware of the strengths and tools that they can utilize to make the changes necessary to improve their experiences.

These central tenets of Liberation Psychology have inspired therapists to conceptualize frameworks and approaches to facilitate the healing of LGBTQ+ BIPOC communities. Below, we unpack therapeutic strategies such as liberation psychotherapy, spirituality, radical humility, and *acompañamiento* related to Liberation Psychology aimed at LGBTQ+ BIPOC communities to understand their collective power and liberation. We also provide an overview of how radical hope and radical healing, developed explicitly for oppressed and marginalized communities in the U.S., promote these communities' collective liberation. Finally, we provide a case example to illustrate the application of these approaches in the therapeutic context.

Decolonizing the Therapist Through Liberation Psychotherapy

Therapists who want to take on a Liberation Psychology approach in psychotherapy must liberate themselves from colonized, Western thinking as described by Martín-Baró. To this end, the therapist needs to question their assumptions as they are, in nature, driven by attitudes from Western approaches (Comas-Díaz, 2020). Through this process, the therapist removes the automatic practice of pathologizing and blaming the client for their difficulties. Instead, the therapist identifies oppressive environments that influence the client's presenting concerns, conceptualizes oppression as inherently traumatic, and works to target oppression trauma that has been experienced by the client. According to Comas-Díaz and colleagues (2019), oppression trauma refers to any form of trauma related to historical, socioeconomic, and geopolitical oppression, including victimization related to one's racial-ethnic identity, gender identity, and sexual orientation. Moreover, persons who experience intersecting, or multiple forms of oppression are at increased risk for developing trauma-related mental health challenges, and are often diagnosed with post-traumatic stress disorder (PTSD) (Bryant-Davis, 2019).

Notably, psychological distress related to oppression trauma is seen as a natural reaction and, thus, the need to pathologize the client is removed (Comas-Díaz, 2007). From this end, therapists must see their work with clients from a social justice perspective, where there is a balance between therapist and client. Only when therapists decolonize their approach they can help their clients address their internalized oppression by deconstructing their colonizing stories, reformulating their personal and collective identities, developing a sociopolitical consciousness, and enacting radical change (Comas-Díaz, 2007; Comas-Díaz et al., 2019; Harrell, 2000). Then, the therapist is able to formulate a treatment plan to alleviate the presenting symptomology from an understanding that is rooted in oppressive systems.

While decolonizing their approach, Liberation Psychology therapists need to recognize how individuals who hold historically minoritized identities, including LGBTQ+ BIPOC peole, are susceptible to experiencing oppression trauma as they are exposed to victimization on a sporadic, acute, and chronic basis (Comas-Díaz et al. 2019; Harrell, 2000). They must understand that the impact of oppression trauma is a subjective experience that cannot be captured through a formal diagnosis, such as PTSD, because the experiences of oppressed individuals is not isolated to a set of symptoms from one single event but to the accumulation of historical and ongoing oppressive experiences (Comas-Díaz et al. 2019). That is, while clients may meet DSM criteria for a formal diagnosis, pathologizing their experiences does not capture the historical and contextual symptoms that produce their reactions. Instead of diagnosing the client, the Liberation Psychology therapist and client analyze and diagnose the environment together.

Spirituality

The Liberation Psychology therapist must acknowledge and utilize the virtues of the people. Spirituality has been a long-standing healing power for oppressed communities. During the Atlantic slave trade, enslaved African people across Latin America used religion and spirituality as empowerment tools that provided crucial pathways to survival (Sweet, 2009). Therefore, Liberation Psychology therapists recognize that spirituality is a powerful tool within oppressed communities and should consider how omitting this tool is part of a colonized approach that strips oppressed communities of internal resources that have the power to enact change and disrupt control. Consequently, spirituality is a crucial component of Liberation Psychology work that includes interconnectedness, communality, holism, solidarity, and transformational values (Comas-Díaz, 2016). Indeed, Martín-Baró (1994) described how spirituality empowers the oppressed to believe that the divine works through them in achieving liberation.

Spiritual activism in Liberation Psychology works to help clients connect with different aspects of their world, including ancestral knowledge. For example,

Keating (2006) describes how oppressed people build *conocimiento,* or conscious awareness, that draws knowledge from several sources, including experiences, dreams, intuition, and inner voices through spiritual activism. Therefore, the therapist encourages clients to use their imagination and empowers them to connect their inner and outer worlds. Connecting BIPOC communities to their spiritual senses has led to new forms of resistance, as seen in Women of Color in the United States (e.g., conceptualizing their experiences as a result of systemic oppression and not a personal flaw; Keating, 2006). From this perspective, spirituality in Liberation work operates as a portal for the client to tap into internal resources. Although the practice is at the individual level, the process leads to an outward-directed source of compassionate acts designed to bring about change (e.g., realizing that rest is an important factor in healing). Thus, the Liberation Psychology therapist works with a collective as they work with the individual and their divine cultural ancestry.

Radical Humility and Acompañamiento

An essential component of Liberation work is the psychotherapeutic relationship and the ability of therapists to let go of their sense of expertise and join the client in their pain. The term radical is typically used in a political context to highlight a critical attitude or ideology that promotes the understanding that complete change is necessary to reduce a social problem (Collin, 2004). Radical humility refers to the total shift in the therapist's stance, leading to an equal power balance. It allows the therapist to embody the client's suffering to reflect on their experience and, through radical empathy, feel the client's pain (Koss-Chioino, 2007). When therapists can accompany clients in their pain through radical humility and empathy, they can exemplify principles of interconnectivity- *tú eres mi otro yo* (you are my other me)- and see themselves in their clients (Comas-Díaz, 2020). Ultimately, using radical humility and empathy anchors the therapist in a indigenous concept of All Our Relations, in which the therapist represents not only a counselor but also a teacher, mentor, advocate, witness, and sibling, among other roles, as they demonstrate the integration of the four constructs of indigenous healing: spirituality, community, environment, and self (Portman & Garrett, 2006).

While radical humility allows the Liberation Psychology therapist to join the client's pain, *acompañamiento* helps the therapist be aware of their role in *accompanying* the client in their journey. One way to accomplish this is to point out therapy power imbalances within the therapist-client relationship and society (Comas-Díaz, 2020). In this process, the therapist provides an example of how power imbalances show up in spaces and models how to address power in relationships, creating the space for clients to practice autonomy and awareness of themselves and others. It is important to note that Liberation Psychology therapists do not abandon the understanding of mental illness's biological underpinnings and how they impact clients. For instance, the therapist maintains awareness of the functions of the nervous system, as well as the neurological differences across neurodevelopmental disorders.

Yet, the Liberation Psychology therapist's primary focus is to understand the sociocultural factors that provoke the outcomes of these underlying mechanisms and empower their clients to address these external factors to alleviate any internal conflict (Watkins, 2012).

Radical Hope

We recognize that some clients are uninterested or not ready to explore their religious and/or spiritual connection in healing. For example, as described above, LGBTQ+ people have a complicated history with religion and spirituality given that these have served as both an oppressive and affirming practice (see review in Lockett et al., 2023). Therefore, exploring the client's hope for a different future can provide an alternative pathway from religious and spiritual beliefs in guiding clients toward change. BIPOC communities in the United States have shown the ability to increase hope for a better future even in the face of ongoing trauma (Chang & Banks, 2007). Mosley and colleagues (2020) described four components of radical hope and proposed a framework to introduce how these components work with others necessary for achieving radical healing.

The first two components of radical hope include understanding the history of oppression and resistance and embracing ancestral pride. As clients learn of the history of oppression, they also learn how their ancestors have resisted oppression throughout centuries. This exploration aims to guide the client in building pride in their ancestry and feeling empowered by their resistance. The two additional components are envisioning new opportunities for the future and helping the client create meaning and purpose to move them forward. To this end, the framework specifies that the client must possess the first two components of collective memory and agency while orienting their collective and individual toward the future to exhibit the characteristics of radical hope that can serve radical healing.

Radical Healing

Radical healing is in line with the tenets of Liberation Psychology and Radical Hope in that oppressed communities must be conscious of their oppression to resist further trauma. In their Radical Healing framework, French et al. (2020) share characteristics necessary to move collectives toward radical healing. First, oppressed communities need to build critical consciousness of their experience by engaging in reflection and developing critical action (Watts et al., 2011). The framework unpacks how the development of critical consciousness of oppressive systems through critical reflection and questioning of these systems leads to political efficacy or confidence in being an activist in social change (Diemer & Blustein, 2006; Watts et al., 2011).

Envisioning possibilities, collectivism, cultural authenticity, and self-knowledge are crucial components for radical healing. Presenting authentically or with cultural authenticity is an act of resistance against forces that undermine personal and collective worth and are, therefore, crucial in moving oppressed people toward action. In the process, individuals build knowledge about themselves, their ancestors, and the histories that have shaped their experiences. The radical healing framework complements the tenets of Liberation Psychology to guide therapists' conceptualization of radical healing. The following sections consider how Liberation Psychology, Radical Hope, and Radical Healing provide a path for the liberation of LGBTQ+ BIPOC communities from oppression.

Case Study

The following case study illustrates a dual process between the client and the therapist, both striving for liberation from oppression. The client is seeking liberation from the oppressive contextual settings impacting their well-being. The therapist seeks liberation from a colonized, Western psychological lens that can further perpetuate oppression rather than liberation for the client. The therapist must decolonize their approach by continuously interrogating their conceptualization of the client from a liberatory, racial hope, and radical healing lens. Through this process, the therapist needs to recognize that their common sense and theoretical approach is informed by a colonized worldview. Therefore, the following case analysis focuses on the therapist's approach to decolonize their interaction with the client while facilitating the client's own liberation.

Setting, Client, and Therapist

The setting is a community mental health center in Orlando, Florida. The center typically sees low-income clients who cannot afford mental health services. Therefore, the clinic operates within a sliding scale, and clients pay as little as $1 for services. The clinic is directed by a licensed psychologist who oversees master's and doctoral-level training.

The client in this case, Lurde, 22 years old, is an Afro-Caribbean (Haitian) transgender woman who is a 2nd generation immigrant seeking services for depressive symptoms and ongoing anxiety about her future. Lurde self-referred to the clinic after learning about the community services offered on a sliding scale that could allow her to afford the services. Lurde recently completed a bachelor's degree in Sociology. Lurde began her transition shortly after her 18th birthday, given that her parents would not allow her to transition earlier. Lurde is currently living with her parents and describes their relationship as "fine", but shares not feeling fully supported by them. Lurde has a dark skin complexion and expressed that others typically perceive her to be African American. Lurde shared an extensive history of depression and passive suicide ideation, with no history of attempting to die by suicide. Currently, Lurde is hopeless about being able to find work suitable for her education level and feels anxiety about her future, her ability to become independent from her parents, and her ability to experience wellness.

The therapist assigned to work with Lurde, Angel, is a doctoral-level trainee who identifies as an Afro-Latino, cisgender man, and who is a 1st generation immigrant. Angel has about 9 months to work with Lurde, meeting weekly for 50 min, and has approval from the clinic supervisor to pursue a radical healing and liberation approach with his clients. However, the clinic supervisor does not use a radical healing or liberation orientation and has minimal knowledge of the approach. Angel has previous clinical experience and has explained his approach sufficiently to receive approval and autonomy to use radical healing and liberation as his theoretical grounding of understanding his client's concerns.

Therapeutic Exchange

In the following exchange between the client and the therapist during their fifth session, Lurde shares with Angel about how a recent dream has brought up to the surface painful memories about past and current oppressive experiences, as well as pleasurable memories about her ancestors. As Lurde's memories unfolded in the here-and-now, Angel is able to accompany Lurde in her pain and make a series of observations that allows her to explore her experiences within the systems of oppression that she is being forced to navigate. Angel uses therapeutic skills grounded in liberation psychology, radical hope, and radical healing to facilitate the client's empowerment.

Lurde: *Last night I dreamt of being hired as an instructor at my old middle school... *chuckles* I don't miss that time of my life. I was bullied so much!*

Angel: *Tell me more about what came up for you during your dream.*

Lurde: *My memory of the dream is a little spotty, but I remember this one moment when my students and I sat around in a circle and talked about the meaning of love and community. We talked about the importance of practicing kindness and acceptance of one another. One of the students even cried and was embraced by his peers...*

Angel: *It sounds like you facilitated a really loving environment for the students in your dream... What was it like for you to visit the place that was so unloving to 11-year-old you?*

Lurde: (pauses) *In Haiti, we have this saying "Sa ki pa touye ou, li angrese ou", which means "What does not kill you is an opportunity to become stronger". Even though that time of my life was difficult, I wouldn't be who I am today if it wasn't for those experiences. I think I'm stronger for it... It's just, I don't wake up feeling strong... Lately I've been feeling tired.*

Angel: *What does "feeling strong" look like for you?*

Lurde: *I was raised to believe that strength is the will to fight through every obstacle. My parents fought through oppressive immigration policies to get us settled in America. My grandparents fought through a dictatorship. They didn't have the luxury to feel distressed or depressed.*

Angel: *You and your family have persevered through devastating and dehumanizing circumstances.*

Lurde: *Yes! And now it's strange because I feel like the fight in me is gone... I don't know how to get it back.*

The clinical exchange above illustrates the therapist building rapport with the client through compassionate curiosity, reflective listening, and cultural sensitivity. We echo Adames and colleagues' (2018) assertion that to make psychotherapy a healing space for minoritized clients, therapy must be conscious of interlocking systems of oppression. Gradually, the therapist and Lurde explore her social, cultural, and political background. This process refers to *critical reflection,* otherwise known as the analysis of one's social situation. *Critical reflection* was also essential in facilitating *critical consciousness* in the interaction between Lurde and the therapist. From this exchange, we understand that Lurde seeks to reconnect with her intergenerational strengths (e.g., resilience). In the context of radical healing, resilience is an important ingredient for liberation. Ultimately, radical healing calls for practitioners and clients to become curious together about the client's cultural knowledge, history, and resources.

Angel: *Lurde, you mentioned that lately you've been feeling tired and have been experiencing some difficulty with motivation. Do you remember when those feelings started?*

Lurde: (sigh and a few seconds of silence) *I think it was shortly after I graduated from college and moved back home with my parents. It's been hard finding a job I'm qualified for and passionate about. I've interviewed with a few organizations for project coordinator positions and have been turned down each time. It's really disheartening.*

Angel: *It's really difficult to put yourself out there and be met with rejection from prospective employers.*

Lurde: (nods, looks down, remains silent, and appears increasingly sad)

Angel: *I'm curious about what's going on for you in this moment Lurde.*

Lurde: *Makes me think about how my extended family wanted nothing to do with me once I decided to transition... it feels like every time I put myself out there, I'm disregarded... I've always felt rejected.*

Angel: *Rejection is an isolating and, oftentimes, soul-wounding experience. If I'm hearing you correctly, it sounds like throughout your life, you've experienced abandonment rather than acceptance for who you are.*

Lurde: (begins to cry)... *It's so hard not being seen as who I am. My parents still call me by my birth name even when I correct them... Because I'm Black, people treat me as African American and do not acknowledge my Haitian culture or flat-out vilify Haitian culture and ask me if Voodoo is demonic. I'm tired of having to explain myself to the world constantly.*

Angel: *Explaining your humanity to people who insist on seeing important parts of your humanity as trivial due to transphobia and anti-Black racism is exhausting.*

Lurde: (releases a big sigh of relief) *Exactly! Maybe that's why I've been feeling tired lately, because I've been reliving experiences of having to explain myself to employers and putting my passion and interests out there, only to be met with a "No."*

Within this therapeutic process, the therapist continues to provide emotional support to the client and help her build her critical consciousness as a second generation Haitian trans woman. Together, the client and counselor identify that Lurde is experiencing psychological distress related to internalized and externalized transphobia and anti-Blackness. These interlocking systems of oppression have left Lurde to internalize oppression as a result of experiencing rejection and isolation due to her trans and Haitian identity. The therapist offers emotional support by recognizing how Lurde's lived experiences with oppression (e.g., transphobia and anti-Black racism) are disruptive and are impacting her well-being. Specifically, the therapist helps name that Lurde is contending with the chronic erasure of her identities by being called her birth name rather than her chosen name and by navigating macroaggressions as it relates to her culture (e.g., contending with the demonization of Haitian culture). Moreso, the therapist frequently inquiries about Lurde's experience (e.g., *"I'm curious about what's going on for you in this moment")* and validates her experience (e.g., *"Explaining your humanity to people who insist on seeing important parts of your humanity as trivial due to transphobia and anti-Black racism is exhausting"*). In concert with radical healing, clinicians must humanize the client by validating their feelings of distress related to oppression.

Angel: *As we've been talking today, I've learned that you're an incredibly resourceful and resilient individual and that you care deeply about your community. In the dream that you shared with me earlier, you were empowering your students. Is advocacy something that means a lot to you?*

Lurde: *I love it. When I was in undergrad, I used to volunteer as a crisis counselor for a local crisis center, and it was an experience that I really enjoyed. It changed my life.*

Angel: *How so?*

Lurde: (Releasing a deep sigh) *It gave me a reason to keep going. For a while, I thought life was meaningless and fleeting. But being there for people who felt alone gave me a desire to keep going.*

Angel: *Being a crisis counselor gave you a radical hope and a life-giving purpose bigger than yourself. Is that correct?*

Lurde: *Precisely... It would be nice to pick it back up. I had stopped volunteering my senior year to focus on applying to jobs and studying for the GRE.*

Angel: (nods) *It's clear how passionate you are about helping people. That's a wonderful strength, especially since our society normalizes individualism and self-centeredness.*

Lurde: (smiles softly) *Thank you! My mom always says I have the same care-taking spirit as my Grandmother. She was always housing people, cooking for people in the community, and volunteering at church every Sunday. I feel like her spirit is protecting me and guiding me.*

Angel: *What advice do you think she would give you as you're navigating this season of your life?*

Lurde: (chuckles) *Her favorite saying is "Chita pa bay", which means one must work to receive the things one wants in life. Her wisdom was to the point, but always delivered with a sweetness to it. So, yeah, that's probably what she would tell me.*

Angel: *How does it feel to connect with your grandmother's wisdom?*

Lurde: *It feels great! It reminds me that I have the strength of my ancestors, and with them, I can face it all.*

Radical healing calls for therapists to help clients resist oppression by reconnecting with their cultural authenticity. Utilizing a strengths-based approach (e.g., *"As we've been talking today, I've learned that you're an incredibly resourceful and resilient human being and that you care deeply about your community"*), the therapist and Lurde discuss how her cultural worldview inspires her to cultivate resistance to oppression and radical hope. With the therapist's support, Lurde identifies that engaging in advocacy ameliorates her hopelessness. Moreso, in creating an empathetic and culturally responsive space for Lurde, her recollection of her grandmother's wisdom empowered the client to lean into her ancestral knowledge for strength.

The exchange above focused primarily on supporting Lurde with internalizing, developing, and nurturing critical anchors of liberation and radical healing such as critical consciousness, strength and resistance, collectivism, and radical hope. We encourage therapists to connect the content that LGBTQ+ BIPOC clients bring into the session with the radical healing principles that are salient to the client's presenting concerns (Adames et al., 2022). In concert with the egalitarian nature of radical healing, the therapist is not only supporting the client in their liberation but is also simultaneously pursuing their own liberation from systems of oppression. Thus, it's crucial that therapists constantly deepen their cultural awareness and critical consciousness by considering how structural issues manifest in the client and themselves.

Conclusion

This chapter explores the tenets of Liberation Psychology, radical hope, and radical healing in the context of LGBTQ+ BIPOC communities. Given the increased attention to systemic racism and anti-LGBTQ+ legislation sweeping the nation, clinicians need to develop awareness as it relates to interlocking systems of oppression and internalized oppression and trauma. The clinical exchange in the chapter highlights the benefit of utilizing these psychological frameworks when working with a

Haitian Black trans woman who is experiencing psychological trauma related to transphobia and anti-Black racism. In maintaining a Liberation Psychology and radical healing approach, the therapist assisted Lurde with building critical consciousness about how oppression has impacted her well-being while creating space for Lurde to connect with her intergenerational strengths and experience radical hope. Liberation Psychology, radical hope, and radical healing provide LGBTQ+ BIPOC clients with tools to resist, heal, and thrive in the wake of sociopolitical oppression by developing, nurturing, and internalizing critical consciousness, hope, and joy (Brondolo et al., 2009; Conway-Phillips et al., 2020).

References

Abreu, R. L., Gonzalez, K. A., Capielo Rosario, C., Lockett, G. M., Lindley, L., & Lane, S. (2021). "We are our own community": Immigrant Latinx transgender people community experiences. *Journal of Counseling Psychology, 68*(4), 390–403. https://doi.org/10.1037/cou0000546

Abreu, R. L., Hernandez, M., Ramos, I., Badio, K. S., & Gonzalez, K. A. (2022). Latinx bi+/plurisexual individuals' disclosure of sexual orientation to family and the role of Latinx cultural values, beliefs, and traditions. *Journal of Bisexuality*. 23(1), 1–26. https://doi.org/10.1080/15299716.2022.2116516

Adames, H. Y., Chavez-Dueñas, N. Y., Lewis, J. A., Neville, H. A., French, B. H., Chen, G. A., & Mosley, D. V. (2022). Radical healing in psychotherapy: Addressing the wounds of racism-related stress and trauma. *Psychotherapy, 60*(1), 39–50. https://doi.org/10.1037/pst0000435

Adames, H. Y., Chavez-Dueñas, N. Y., Sharma, S., & La Roche, M. J. (2018). Intersectionality in psychotherapy: The experiences of an AfroLatinx queer immigrant. *Psychotherapy, 55*(1), 73–79. https://doi.org/10.1037/pst0000152

American Psychological Association. (2021). *Ethical principles of psychologists and code of conduct*. https://www.apa.org/ethics/code

Arrington-Sanders, R., Alvarenga, A., Galai, N., Arscott, J., Wirtz, A., Carr, R., Lopez, A., Beyrer, C., Nessen, R., & Celentano, D. (2022). Social determinants of transactional sex in a sample of young Black and Latinx sexual minority cisgender men and transgender women. *Journal of Adolescent Health, 70*(2), 275–281.

Barratt, B. B. (2011). Ignacio Martín-Baró's 'Writings for a Liberation Psychology': forum: Inspiring psychoanalytic writing. *Psycho-analytic Psychotherapy in South Africa, 19*(2), 121–134.

Barrett, D. C., & Pollack, L. M. (2005). Whose gay community? Social class, sexual self-expression, and gay community involvement. *The Sociological Quarterly, 46*(3), 437–456. https://doi.org/10.1111/j.15338525.2005.00021.x

Benuto, L. T., Newlands, R., Singer, J., Casas, J., & Cummings, C. (2021). Culturally sensitive clinical practices: A mixed methods study. *Psychological Services, 18*(4), 632–642. https://doi.org/10.1037/ser0000493

Brondolo, E., Brady Ver Halen, N., Pencille, M., Beatty, D., & Contrada, R. J. (2009). Coping with racism: A selective review of the literature and a theoretical and methodological critique. *Journal of Behavioral Medicine, 32*, 64–88. https://doi.org/10.1007/s10865-008-9193-0

Bryant-Davis, T. (2019). The cultural context of trauma recovery: Considering the posttraumatic stress disorder practice guideline and intersectionality. *Psychotherapy, 56*(3), 400–408. https://doi.org/10.1037/pst0000241

Cabassa, L. J., & Baumann, A. A. (2013). A two-way street: Bridging implementation science and cultural adaptations of mental health treatments. *Implementation Science, 8*, 1–14. https://doi.org/10.1186/1748-5908-8-90

Carbado, D. W. (2013). Colorblind intersectionality. Signs: *Journal of Women in Culture and Society, 38*(4), 811–845. https://doi.org/10.1086/669666

Cerezo, A., Morales, A., Quintero, D., & Rothman, S. (2014). Trans migrations: Exploring life at the intersection of transgender identity and immigration. Psychology of Sexual Orientation and Gender Diversity, 1(2), 170–180. https://doi.org/10.1037/sgd0000031

Chang, E. C., & Banks, K. H. (2007). The color and texture of hope: Some preliminary findings and implications for hope theory and counseling among diverse racial/ethnic groups. *Cultural Diversity & Ethnic Minority Psychology, 13*(2), 94–103. https://doi.org/10.1037/1099-9809.13.2.94

Cherrington, A. M. (2018). Research as hope-intervention: Mobilising hope in a South African higher education context. *South African Journal of Education, 38*(4), 1–9. https://hdl.handle.net/10520/EJC-13f729a98e

Collin, P. H. (2004). Dictionary of politics and government. Retrieved from https://cir.nii.ac.jp/crid/1970023484896710295

Comas-Díaz, L. (2007). Ethnopolitical psychology: Healing and transformation. In E. Aldarondo (Ed.), *Advancing social justice through clinical practice* (pp. 91–118). Lawrence Erlbaum Associates Publishers.

Comas-Díaz, L. (2016). Racial trauma recovery: A race-informed therapeutic approach to racial wounds. In A. N. Alvarez, C. T. H. Liang, & H. A. Neville (Eds.), *The cost of racism for people of color: Contextualizing experiences of discrimination* (pp. 249–272). American Psychological Association. https://doi.org/10.1037/14852-012

Comas-Díaz, L. (2020). Liberation psychotherapy. In L. Comas-Díaz & E. Torres Rivera (Eds.), *Liberation psychology: Theory, method, practice, and social justice* (pp. 169–185). American Psychological Association. https://doi.org/10.1037/0000198-010

Comas-Díaz, L., Hall, G. N., & Neville, H. A. (2019). Racial trauma: Theory, research, and healing: Introduction to the special issue. *American Psychologist, 74*(1), 1. https://doi.org/10.1037/amp0000442

Combahee River Collective. (1977). The Combahee River Collective Statement. https://americanstudies.yale.edu/sites/default/files/files/KeywordCoalition_Readings.pdf

Conway-Phillips, R., Dagadu, H., Motley, D., Shawahin, L., Janusek, L. W., Klonowski, S., & Saban, K. L. (2020). Qualitative evidence for resilience, stress, and ethnicity (RiSE):A program to address race-based stress among Black women at risk for cardiovascular disease. *Complementary Therapies in Medicine, 48*, Article 102277. https://doi.org/10.1016/j.ctim.2019.102277

Crenshaw, K. (1989). Demarginalizing the intersection of race and sex: A black feminist critique of antidiscrimination doctrine, feminist theory and antiracist politics. *The University of Chicago Legal Forum, 1*, 139–167.

Della, B., Wilson, M., & Miller, R. L. (2002). Strategies for managing heterosexism used among African American gay and bisexual men. *Journal of Black Psychology, 28*(4), 371–391. https://doi.org/10.1177/009579802237543

Dickenson, J. A., & Huebner, D. M. (2016). The relationship between sexual activity and depressive symptoms in lesbian, gay, and bisexual youth: Effects of gender and family support. *Archives of sexual behavior, 45*(3), 671–681. https://doi.org/10.1007/s10508-015-0571-8

Diemer, M. A., & Blustein, D. L. (2006). Critical consciousness and career development among urban youth. *Journal of vocational behavior, 68*(2), 220–232. https://doi.org/10.1016/j.jvb.2005.07.001

Drazdowski, T. K., Perrin, P. B., Trujillo, M., Sutter, M., Benotsch, E. G., & Snipes, D. J. (2016). Structural equation modeling of the effects of racism, LGBTQ discrimination, and internalized oppression on illicit drug use in LGBTQ people of color. *Drug and Alcohol Dependence, 159*, 255–262. https://doi.org/10.1016/j.drugalcdep.2015.12.029

Flores, A. R., Langton, L., Meyer, I. H., & Romero, A. P. (2020). Victimization rates and traits of sexual and gender minorities in the United States: Results from the National Crime Victimization Survey, 2017. *Science Advances, 6*(40), eaba6910.

French, B. H., Lewis, J. A., Mosley, D. V., Adames, H. Y., Chavez-Dueñas, N. Y., Chen, G. A., & Neville, H. A. (2020). Toward a psychological framework of radical healing in communities of color. *The Counseling Psychologist, 48*(1), 14–46.

Gale, M. M., Pieterse, A. L., Lee, D. L., Huynh, K., Powell, S., & Kirkinis, K. (2020). A Meta-Analysis of the Relationship Between Internalized Racial Oppression and Health-Related Outcomes. *The Counseling Psychologist, 48*(4), 498–525. https://doi.org/10.1177/0011000020904454

Hailey, J., Burton, W., & Arscott, J. (2020). We are family: Chosen and created families as a protective factor against racialized trauma and anti-LGBTQ oppression among African American sexual and gender minority youth. *Journal of GLBT Family Studies, 16*(2), 176–191. https://doi.org/10.1080/1550428X.2020.1724133

Harrell, S. P. (2000). A multidimensional conceptualization of racism-related stress: Implications for the well-being of people of color. *American Journal of Orthopsychiatry, 70*(1), 42–57. https://doi.org/10.1037/h0087722

Huey Jr, S. J., Park, A. L., Galán, C. A., & Wang, C. X. (2023). Culturally responsive cognitive behavioral therapy for ethnically diverse populations. *Annual Review of Clinical Psychology, 19*, 51–78. https://doi.org/10.1146/annurevclinpsy-080921-072750

Jackson, S. D., Mohr, J. J., Sarno, E. L., Kindahl, A. M., & Jones, I. L. (2020). Intersectional experiences, stigmarelated stress, and psychological health among Black LGBQ individuals. *Journal of Consulting and Clinical Psychology, 88*(5), 416–428. https://doi.org/10.1037/ccp0000489

Katz-Wise, S. L., & Hyde, J. S. (2012). Victimization experiences of lesbian, gay, and bisexual individuals: A metaanalysis. *Journal of sex research, 49*(2-3), 142–167.

Keating, A. (2006). From borderlands and new mestizas to nepantlas and nepantleras. *Human Architecture: Journal of the Sociology of Self-knowledge, 4*, 5–16.

Koss-Chioino, J. D. (2007). Whose broad experience? How great the audience? Zygon: *Journal of Religion and Science, 42*(2). 273–276.

Lockett, G. M., Brooks, J. E., Abreu, R. L., & Sostre, J. P. (2023). "I want to go to a place that's openly talking about the experiences of people of color who also identify as LGBTQ+": Cultural, religious, and spiritual experiences of LGBTQ people of color. *Spirituality in Clinical Practice, 10*(3), 261–270. https://doi.org/10.1037/scp0000288

Mallory, C., Hasenbush, A., & Sears, B. (2015). Discrimination and harassment by law enforcement officers in the LGBT community. Retrieved from https://escholarship.org/uc/item/5663q0w1

Martín-Baró, I. (1994). *Writings for a liberation psychology* (A. Aron & S. Corne, Eds.). Harvard University Press.

Matsuno, E., & Israel, T. (2018). Psychological interventions promoting resilience among transgender individuals: Transgender resilience intervention model (TRIM). *The Counseling Psychologist, 46*(5), 632–655. https://doi.org/10.1177/0011000018787261

Mereish, E. H., Peters, J. R., & Yen, S. (2019). Minority stress and relational mechanisms of suicide among sexual minorities: Subgroup differences in the associations between heterosexist victimization, shame, rejection sensitivity, and suicide risk. *Suicide and Life-Threatening Behavior, 49*(2), 547–560. https://doi.org/10.1111/sltb.12458

Meyer, D. (2012). An intersectional analysis of lesbian, gay, bisexual, and transgender (LGBT) people's evaluations of anti-queer violence. *Gender & Society, 26*(6), 849–873. https://doi.org/10.1177/0891243212461299

Mosley, D. V., Neville, H. A., Chavez-Dueñas, N. Y., Adames, H. Y., Lewis, J. A., & French, B. H. (2020). Radical hope in revolting times: Proposing a culturally relevant psychological framework. *Social and Personality Psychology Compass, 14*(1), e12512. https://doi.org/10.1111/spc3.12512

Mosley, D. V., McNeil-Young, V., Bridges, B., Adam, S., Colson, A., Crowley, M., & Lee, L. (2021). Toward radical healing: A qualitative metasynthesis exploring oppression and liberation among Black queer people. *Psychology of Sexual Orientation and Gender Diversity, 8*(3), 292. https://doi.org/10.1037/sgd0000522

Neville, H. A., Ruedas-Gracia, N., Lee, B. A., Ogunfemi, N., Maghsoodi, A. H., Mosley, D. V., LaFromboise, T. D., & Fine, M. (2021). The public psychology for liberation training model: A call to transform the discipline. *American Psychologist, 76*(8), 1248–1265. https://doi.org/10.1037/amp0000887

Noyola, N., Sánchez, M., & Cardemil, E. V. (2020). Minority stress and coping among sexual diverse Latinxs. *Journal of Latinx Psychology, 8*(1), 58–82. https://doi.org/10.1037/lat0000143

Pachankis, J. E., Mahon, C. P., Jackson, S. D., Fetzner, B. K., & Bränström, R. (2020). Sexual orientation concealment and mental health: A conceptual and meta-analytic review. *Psychological Bulletin, 146*(10), 831. https://doi.org/10.1037/bul0000271

Parker-Barnes, L., McKillip, N., & Powell, C. (2022). Systemic advocacy for BIPOC LGBTQIA+ clients and their families. *The Family Journal, 30*(3), 479–486. https://doi.org/10.1177/10664807221090947

Parmenter, J. G., & Galliher, R. V. (2024). Development and initial validation of the LGBTQ+ Community Resilience and Inequity Scale. *Psychology of Sexual Orientation and Gender Diversity, 11*(1), 56–68. https://doi.org/10.1037/sgd0000601

Parmenter, J. G., Galliher, R. V., & Maughan, A. D. (2020). An exploration of LGBTQ+ community members' positive perceptions of LGBTQ+ culture. *The Counseling Psychologist, 48*(7), 1016–1047.

Parmenter, J. G., Gao, S., Khan, N. S., Lê, D., Staton, D. R., & Galupo, M.P. (2024). "My healing journey gives back to my communities": Experiences of intersectional resilience and liberation among queer and trans Black, Indigenous, and People of Color. Psychology of Sexual Orientation and Gender Diversity. Advance online publication. https://doi.org/10.1037/sgd0000750

Portman, T. A., & Garrett, M. T. (2006). Native American healing traditions. *International Journal of Disability, Development and Education, 53*(4), 453–469.

Quandt, K. R., & Jones, A. (2021, March 18). Research roundup: Violent crimes against Black and Latinx people receive less coverage and less justice. *Prison Policy Initiative*. https://www.prisonpolicy.org/blog/2021/03/18/race-and-violence/

Richaud, M. C. (2013). Contributions to the study and promotion of resilience in socially vulnerable children. *American Psychologist, 68*(8), 751–758. https://doi.org/10.1037/a0034327

Romanelli, M., & Hudson, K. D. (2017). Individual and systemic barriers to health care: Perspectives of lesbian, gay, bisexual, and transgender adults. *American Journal of Orthopsychiatry, 87*(6), 714. https://doi.org/10.1037/ort0000306

Russell, S. T., Toomey, R. B., Ryan, C., & Diaz, R. M. (2014). Being out at school: The implications for school victimization and young adult adjustment. *American Journal of Orthopsychiatry, 84*(6), 635–643. https://doi.org/10.1037/ort0000037

Salerno, J. P., Williams, N. D., & Gattamorta, K. A. (2020). LGBTQ populations: psychologically vulnerable communities in the COVID-19 pandemic. *Psychological Trauma, 12*(suppl 1), S239–S242. https://doi.org/10.1037/tra0001254

Singh, A. A., Parker, B., Aqil, A. R., & Thacker, F. (2020). Liberation psychology and LGBTQ+ communities: Naming colonization, uplifting resilience, and reclaiming ancient his-stories, her-stories, and t-stories. In L. Comas-Díaz & E. Torres Rivera (Eds.), *Liberation psychology: Theory, method, practice, and social justice* (pp. 207–224). American Psychological Association. https://doi.org/10.1037/0000198-012

Sostre, J. P., Abreu, R. L., Vincent, D., Lockett, G. M., & Mosley, D. V. (2024). Young Black trans and gender-diverse activists' well-being among anti-Black racism and cissexism during the COVID-19 pandemic. *Psychology of Sexual Orientation and Gender Diversity, 11*(4), 664–678. https://doi.org/10.1037/sgd0000627

Stone, A. L., Nimmons, E. A., Salcido, R., & Schnarrs, P. (2020). "My meemaw is a cool ass person": Family members as role models of resilience for sexual and gender diverse people of color. *Journal of GLBT Family Studies, 16*(2), 241–257. https://doi.org/10.1080/1550428X.2020.1724148

Sweet, J. W. (2009). The subject of the slave trade: recent currents in the histories of the Atlantic, Great Britain, and Western Africa. *Early American Studies*, 1–45. https://www.jstor.org/stable/23546554

Toomey, R. B., Ryan, C., Diaz, R. M., & Russell, S. T. (2018). Coping with sexual orientation–related minority stress. *Journal of homosexuality, 65*(4), 484–500. https://doi.org/10.1080/00918369.2017.1321888

Watkins, M. (2012). *Accompaniment: Psychosocial, environmental, transspecies, earth.* Plenary Panel for Psychologists for Social Responsibility in Washington, DC.

Watts, R. J., Diemer, M. A., & Voight, A. M. (2011). Critical consciousness: Current status and future directions. *New Directions for Child and Adolescent Development, 2011*(134), 43–57. https://doi.org/10.1002/cd.310

Wirtz, A. L., Poteat, T. C., Malik, M., & Glass, N. (2020). Gender-based violence against transgender people in the United States: A call for research and programming. *Trauma, Violence, & Abuse, 21*(2), 227–241. https://doi.org/10.1177/1524838018757749

Wood, A. W., & Conley, A. H. (2014). Loss of religious or spiritual identities among the LGBT population. *Counseling and Values, 59*(1), 95–111.

Zongrone, A. D., Truong, N. L., & Kosciw, J. G. (2020a). *Erasure and resilience: The experiences of LGBTQ students of color, Latinx LGBTQ youth in U.S. schools*. GLSEN.

Chapter 11
Interrupting Cissexism and Binary Conceptualizations of Gender/Sex in Therapy

Jay Bettergarcia, Em Matsuno, Yu-Chi Wang, Emerson Parker Pehl, and M. Paz Galupo

Highlights

In this chapter, we invite readers to think with us about how to interrupt cissexism and binary conceptualizations of gender/sex when conducting therapy. We offer the following in order to provide a framework for understanding the range of experiences that clients may bring to therapy in relation to gender and other intersecting social identities:

- A historical context for understanding the gender binary and how it is related to larger systems of oppression (e.g., cisgenderism, sexism, racism).
- A discussion of gender related normativities (e.g., alignment normativity, cisnormativity, binary normativity, transnormativity and nonbinary normativity) and how they may limit our thinking and shape the experiences of our clients both in and outside of therapy.

J. Bettergarcia (✉)
Department of Psychology and Child Development, California Polytechnic State University, San Luis Obispo, CA, USA
e-mail: jbetterg@calpoly.edu

E. Matsuno
School of Counseling and Counseling Psychology, Arizona State University, Tempe, AZ, USA

Y.-C. Wang
Gay, Lesbian, and Straight Education Network (GLSEN), New York, NY, USA

E. P. Pehl
Gender and Women's Studies Department, University of Illinois Urbana-Champaign, Champaign, IL, USA

M. P. Galupo
Brown School of Social Work, Washington University in St. Louis, St. Louis, MO, USA

N. A. Livingston et al. (eds.), *Addressing Minority Stress and Enhancing Resilience with Diverse LGBTQ+ Clients*, CBT: Science Into Practice, https://doi.org/10.1007/978-3-031-92836-9_11

- A brief review of gender minority stress theory to identify unique proximal (internal) and distal (external) stressors for Two-Spirit, Trans, and Nonbinary (2STNB) folx and how those can be used to explain mental health disparities.
- An overview of three critical frameworks that may help therapists deepen their gender affirmative practices for working with 2STNB clients.
  - Transgender Resilience Intervention Model (TRIM; Matsuno & Israel, 2018)
  - Radical Healing Framework (French et al., 2020)
  - 2STNB Microaffirmation Model (Anzani et al., 2019)
- Two case examples that apply the above models and exemplify interventions that can be used to interrupt cissexism and binary conceptualization of gender when working with clients.

Positionality
We are a group of researchers, clinicians, and sexologists in psychology and social work at various stages of our careers. We represent a range of gender and sexual identities (agender, asexual, bi/pansexual, nonbinary, trans, queer) and racial/ethnic identities (Asian American, American Indian, Biracial, Cherokee Nation of Oklahoma, Filipinx, Japanese, Taiwanese, Mexican American, Multiracial, Native American, white). Despite our different positionalities, we are singular in our professional and personal commitment to supporting the health, wellbeing, and liberation of Two-Spirit, trans and nonbinary people (2STNB). It is from this shared perspective that we invite readers to think with us about what interrupting cissexism and binary conceptualizations of gender/sex might look like in our professional lives in general, and in our therapy relationships in particular. We firmly believe that addressing these issues is critical not only for providing affirming care for 2STNB folx but will help bring awareness to the ways that binary gendered thinking impacts everyone. Finally, we hope that this work can pave the way towards not only trans liberation but liberation for all people from the oppressive forces entangled within cissexism and the gender/sex binary.

Historical Context for the Gender Binary

Gender/sex is a multidimensional construct that encompasses assigned sex, gender identity, gender roles and expectations, social presentation, as well as gender evaluations (Tate et al., 2014; van Anders, 2015). Although gender is increasingly understood to be a nonbinary construct (Hyde et al., 2019), it is important to recognize the ubiquity of the gender binary and its roots in settler colonialism (binaohan, 2014; Feinberg, 1996; Robinson, 2020). For many cultures with a history of European colonization, gender has been conceptualized, and imposed, as two distinct categories of women and men. There has been a strong historical legacy that has codified the gender binary into all aspects of social, legal, and psychomedical practice. In the twentieth century, the concept of the gender binary was further rooted in western culture through scientific theories of human evolution that elevated white supremacy and viewed evolution as stratified by both race and sex (Schuller, 2017). Human evolution was characterized as a hierarchy of different classes of people (i.e., white men, then white women, Asian men, Asian women, Black/Indigenous men, and finally Black/Indigenous women) who were conceptualized as more or less evolved, respectively. Central to this racist construction of evolutionary science was the idea that sex differentiation (i.e., binary distinctions between women and men) is most evident among white people. Therefore, whiteness and the gender binary were portrayed as biologically linked and as the most evolved human states (Schuller, 2017). Because of the marginalization that occurs based on these essentialist assumptions, the gender binary has a deep connection to experiences of trauma for individuals of all genders (Iantaffi, 2020), and it is particularly tied to historical trauma for Black, Indigenous, and People of Color (BIPOC).

Given this historical context, it is impossible to disentangle our understanding of the gender binary from larger systems of oppression including white supremacy, sexism, heterosexism, and cissexism. For this reason, adopting an intersectional understanding of gender diversity (Galupo & Orphanidys, 2022) is key to providing culturally competent gender affirmative care. Intersectionality refers to the interrelatedness between multiple systems of inequality and oppression, such as racism, heterosexism, and cissexism (Crenshaw, 1991; Collins, 1991; The Combahee River Collective, 1977). While intersectionality is primarily about how these systems work together, the practical implications of intersectionality in a clinical setting, can be understood when considering the impacts of these systems across a client's multiple identities. For example, when considering a misgendering incident of a nonbinary Asian American client, a therapist should recognize that the experience may be a manifestation of cissexism or binary gender conceptualizations specific to expected stereotypical Asian American appearance. An intersectional approach is necessary to address the wide range of experiences within 2STNB communities and to consider the ways that those with normative (i.e., cisgender heterosexual) identities may also be impacted by systems of gender.

Definitions of Gender/Sex and Oppressive Systems

In addition to being conceptualized as binary, there is an assumption that the different dimensions of gender/sex (e.g., assigned sex, gender identity, gender roles) should somehow line up neatly with one another. Coined by van Anders (2015), **alignment normativity** provides a context for understanding how some experiences of gender are normalized (e.g., cisgender) and gender and sex diversity (e.g., 2STNB and intersex) are considered non-normative and therefore problematic. For example, **cisnormativity** idealizes cisgender identity precisely because of the alignment of assigned sex and gender identity. In contrast, 2STNB identities are problematized due to the way that assigned sex and gender identity run counter to the larger societal expectation that they should be aligned. Because normative experience is often unlabeled (Galupo et al., 2015; May, 2015), one subtle way that cisnormativity is communicated is when cisgender identity is often unlabeled, yet is assumed (e.g., using "trans women" when talking or writing about trans women, but using "women" to refer to cisgender women). Alignment normativity also underlies **binary normativity** which establishes the expectation that having a gender that falls within the gender binary is the expected ideal. Even within larger 2STNB experience, community assumptions are established that there is only one way to be transgender (**transnormativity**) and only one way to be nonbinary (**nonbinary normativity**) (Lindley & Budge, 2023; Pasley et al., 2018).

Taken together, the reliance on the gender binary system coupled with alignment normativity functions to uphold sexist, cissexist, and heterosexist ideologies (Ansara & Hegarty, 2012; Schilt & Westbrook, 2009). In addition, these normativities impact how people are expected to fit within the community, which may also impact who seeks gender affirming care. Table 11.1 provides additional examples for how these different normativities may impact the way we think about gender/sex generally and how they may also show up in therapy.

Gender Minority Stress

Given the tie to systemic cissexism, it makes sense that one of the dominant psychological frameworks for understanding 2STNB experiences is minority stress theory. Initially proposed to explain mental health inequities experienced by lesbian women (Brooks, 1981) and gay men (Meyer, 1995), the minority stress model was first adapted by Hendricks and Testa (2012) to describe the mental health inequities faced by 2STNB individuals due to their marginalized gender identity and/or gender expression. Researchers have since elaborated key distal (i.e., external) gender minority stressors as gender-based victimization, rejection, and discrimination, and identity non-affirmation and invalidation; proximal (i.e., internal) gender minority stressors include negative expectations for future discriminatory events, internalized transnegativity (internalized negative perceptions and messages about 2STNB people; Rood, et al., 2017), concealment or nondisclosure of gender identity, gender dysphoria, vicarious stress, and mental/emotional burden (Johnson et al., 2020; Lindley & Galupo, 2020; Matsuno et al., 2021; Puckett et al., 2021; Testa et al., 2015; see Matsuno et al., 2023). This model also incorporates the potential for coping and resilience factors, namely community connectedness, belonging, and identity pride, that may attenuate the effects of these minority stressors (Matsuno et al., 2023; Testa et al., 2015).

By and large, 2STNB individuals report higher prevalence of negative mental health outcomes, including but not limited to depression, anxiety, and suicidality when compared to their cis peers (Becerra-Culqui et al., 2018; Johns et al., 2019; Wang et al., 2020). Intersectionality, we see higher rates of depressive symptoms and suicidality among Black and Latinx 2STNB youth compared to Black and Latinx cisgender youth, and higher rates of suicide attempt among BIPOC

Table 11.1 Gender normativities

Concept	Definition	General Example	Therapy-Specific Example
Alignment normativity	The expectation that all dimensions of gender and sex (e.g., sex assigned at birth, gender expression, gender roles, gender identity) and sexual orientation are binary and should align with one another (van Anders, 2015).	The assumption that if someone was assigned female at birth, they are naturally feminine in gender expression, will adopt a feminine gender role, will develop the identity of a girl / woman, and be attracted to men.	Therapist assumes that a trans man desires a "masculine" role in his relationships. Therapist assumes that gender nonconformity is an indication of non-heterosexuality.
Cisnormativity	Cultural norms, messages, and structures that convey that being cisgender is expected, normal, and preferred.	Language that assumes that all men and women have bodies associated with their assigned sex.	Therapist pathologizes trans and nonbinary identities by equating them with gender dysphoria, or assuming they need to be "fixed".
Binary normativity	Cultural norms, messages, and structures that convey that having a binary gender is expected, normal, and preferred.	Facilities including only two bathrooms specifically labeled men and women and language like "ladies and gentlemen" or "sir or madam".	Therapist assumes that a client's nonbinary identity is only a "phase" before adopting a more binary identity.
Transnormativity	Cultural norms and messages that convey that there is one singular normative way to be transgender.	Assuming that all trans individuals desire to medically or socially transition and that transition occurs in a single linear pathway.	Therapist assumes that a trans client desires surgery. Therapist assumes or prescribes a linear path to "coming out" or "transitioning" socially among friends, family, and coworkers.
Nonbinary normativity	Cultural norms and messages that convey that there is one singular normative way to be nonbinary.	Representation of nonbinary people in the media portraying nonbinary people as white, thin, trans masculine and androgynous. Someone doubting the validity of a nonbinary person's identity because they don't fit the normative narrative.	Therapist assumes that a nonbinary client does not want to medically transition and/ or that they only desire a medical transition to achieve an androgynous presentation.

compared to white 2STNB adults (Adams & Vincent, 2019; Vance et al., 2021). In terms of distal stressors, experiences of victimization and discrimination have been linked to depressive symptoms, suicidality, and emotional distress (Eisenberg et al., 2019; Goldblum et al., 2012; Hatchel et al., 2019). Specific to proximal stressors, studies have shown that anti-trans discrimination can lead to internalized transphobia which, in turn, is associated with negative mental health outcomes (Scandurra et al., 2018), and 2STNB individuals with high internalized transphobia were more likely to meet criteria for major depression and generalized anxiety (Chodzen et al., 2019). As for resilience, social connectedness and social support are related to positive self-esteem and reduced anxiety among 2STMB individuals (Austin & Goodman, 2017; Pflum et al., 2015). Qualitative findings show that feelings of identity pride for 2STNB individuals includes the freedom to define gender in their own words rather than having it labeled by others, and this is also understood to be a resilience strategy (Singh et al., 2014).

Clinical Application and Science into Practice

Clinical Frameworks for Addressing Cissexism & Oppression

To date, there are very few evidence-based trans affirming clinical interventions or treatments (see Expósito-Campos et al., 2023 for review) and only a couple of randomized controlled trial studies that test trans affirmative therapy interventions (Budge et al., 2021; Israel et al., 2021). However, there are a few key strength-based psychological frameworks that may be particularly useful for addressing cissexism in therapy with 2STNB clients. These include the transgender resilience intervention model (TRIM; Matsuno & Israel, 2018), the radical healing framework (French et al., 2020), and 2STNB microaffirmations in therapy (Anzani et al., 2019). This section outlines each of the theories and frameworks. In the following section, we draw on these theoretical frameworks to demonstrate affirmative clinical approaches to addressing cissexism and internalized normativity in therapy.

The TRIM (Matsuno & Israel, 2018) is particularly useful for supporting 2STNB clients' development of individual resilience and group resilience. It was developed as an extension of the gender minority stress model (Testa et al., 2015) and theorizes how different types of interventions (i.e., community-based, group-level, and individual interventions) can target either group-level or individual resilience factors (Matsuno & Israel, 2018). Group-level or interpersonal resilience factors include being role models for others, developing a sense of community belonging, having family acceptance, having positive role models, receiving social support, and engaging in 2STNB activism, while individual-level resilience factors include hope, self-acceptance and identity pride, self-definition, self-worth, and transition.

Radical healing is a theoretical framework that can help therapists conceptualize social justice, antiracist, and liberatory approaches to psychotherapy (French et al.,

2020). Radical healing is framed by a dialectic of resisting interlocking systems of hate and oppression, while also moving toward freedom, justice, and liberation (French et al., 2020). The radical healing framework has five main anchors, including critical consciousness, cultural authenticity and self-knowledge, radical hope and envisioning possibilities, strength and resilience, and collectivism (French et al., 2020). *Critical consciousness* is often conceptualized as the ability to critically reflect on and challenge sociopolitical barriers and injustice (Adames et al., 2023; Diemer et al., 2016). For 2STNB clients, this may include learning about gender normativities and their impacts. Developing *cultural authenticity and self-knowledge* includes honoring ancestral and cultural wisdom, knowledge, and self-definition (Adames et al., 2023). This may include learning about 2STNB histories and not needing to be defined by cissexist norms and expectations. *Radical hope* can include imagining futures for 2STNB communities that are free from oppression. *Strength and resistance* acknowledges the strengths that people have to resist oppressive structures and live joy-filled lives, while *collectivism* includes interconnectedness with broader communities as places for validation, social support, and healing (Adames et al., 2023). Although the radical healing framework was originally developed for BIPOC to address racial trauma (French et al., 2020), it has been applied to oppression and liberation among Black queer people (Mosley et al., 2021) and LGBTQ+ young adults experiencing homelessness (Schmitz et al., 2023).

Therapists can also use a framework of microaffirmations when working with 2STNB clients. Microaffirmations can be intentional and unintentional words, gestures, and behaviors that convey validation of a 2STNB person's identity (Anzani et al., 2019). In the therapeutic context, microaffirmations can serve as interventions to build a therapeutic alliance with 2STNB clients by intentionally calling out cisnormativity in their own behavior, in the way gender diversity is pathologized in the field, and in the ways it shows up in clients' lives. Specifically, therapists can affirm 2STNB clients using an affirmation model targeting four main domains: absence of microaggressions, acknowledging cisnormativity, disrupting cisnormativity, and seeing authentic gender (Anzani et al., 2019). Therefore, therapists can support clients by understanding and actively avoiding microaggressions that clients likely encounter in other spaces. Simply avoiding harmful microaggressions, however, does not help 2STNB clients identify their own internalized cissexism. Instead, therapists can help by naming the cisnormative context of clients' experiences and can actively support clients to disrupt cisnormative assumptions about gender norms, such as supporting clients to notice when they're comparing themselves to cisgender ideals. Finally, seeing a client's gender identity as a real and authentic part of who they are is another microaffirmation that can support clients to feel validated and affirmed in therapy (Anzani et al., 2019).

Therapists Challenging Cissexism and Gender/Sex Binaries

Understanding what cissexism is and how it operates across every aspect of our institutions, including healthcare systems and experiences with providers, is an important first step to dismantling cissexism and cisnormativity (McGeorge et al., 2021). Cissexist norms permeate our cultural, social, legal, and educational landscape, and as with all multicultural awareness, mental health professionals should continue doing the work to dismantle these norms for themselves and with their clients. Therapists should be aware of their own attitudes and assumptions about gender and the biases they hold. The unlearning of gendered expectations, stereotypes, and biases is an integral part to challenging cissexism in therapeutic practice with clients (Iantaffi, 2020). Therapists must be willing to reflect on the gendered messages they have received (and likely internalized), their own perceptions of 2STNB people, and challenge their own reliance on cisnormativity and binary gender categories. Moving from theory to practice includes therapists gaining more knowledge about 2STNB lives and experiences, developing skills to challenge cissexism, and engaging in movement toward social justice and liberation.

Challenging Gendered Assumptions

Given that cissexism and binary conceptualizations of gender can permeate nearly every encounter that therapists have with clients, it is important to explore options for challenging cissexist assumptions that may lead to microaggressions with 2STNB clients (Anzani et al., 2019). First, therapists should avoid making assumptions about clients' gender identity based on their clothing, appearance, body shape or size, voice, or other gendered social cues. Therapists can respectfully ask all clients for their name and pronouns, not just those who are perceived as 2STNB or gender diverse. Therapists can also use gender neutral language when speaking with a group of clients. Rather than saying "you guys can find a seat wherever you'd like" or "welcome in ladies and gentlemen", therapists can use more inclusive language including, "feel free to sit wherever you'd like" or "welcome in folks".

It is also important that therapists notice and challenge trans normative and nonbinary normative assumptions. One common assumption is that all transgender people medically transition. However, 2STNB clients are diverse in their desire or need for hormone therapy and gender affirming surgical procedures, which is often dictated by their embodiment goals, or the myriad of ways that a person wants to live into, or embody, their gender identity and/or expression (DuBois et al., 2022; Hastings, et al., 2021). For some 2STNB people, access to medical transition options is life-saving care and can alleviate some aspects of gender dysphoria (Nolan et al., 2023). However, for others there may be less of a desire or need if they have found contentment or satisfaction with their gender embodiment. It is also important to note that some 2STNB people may lack access to gender-affirming medical procedures because of the barriers to accessing care, such as denial of care, financial constraints, or lack of support in their family or communities.

Another common erroneous assumption is that nonbinary people do not medically transition or that nonbinary people want to, or should, look androgynous (Matsuno et al., 2024). It is important for therapists to understand the difference between gender expression and gender identity to avoid making these normative assumptions about 2STNB people's embodiment goals. When clients receive messages outside of therapy about how they should express their gender or whether they should or should not medically transition, therapists can utilize the microaffirmations framework to help clients work through these cisnormative assumptions and expectations (Anzani et al., 2019). This may include authentically seeing and validating a client's identity or gender expression, helping clients notice and acknowledge these messages as cissexist, and supporting clients to challenge and disrupt these messages by focusing on their own gender euphoria and embodiment goals.

Creating Inclusive Clinical Spaces

In addition to challenging assumptions about gender and changing behaviors to be more 2STNB affirming, therapists can also work to make their website, office, bathrooms, and forms more inclusive for 2STNB people. It can be helpful for therapists to do a 2STNB inclusivity audit to explore what clients might see when they browse the clinic's website, complete intake forms, or visit the therapy office. There are several useful resources that can help therapists think about how to create more welcoming and inclusive spaces for 2STNB clients, including the UCSF Gender Affirming Health Program website (Deutsch, 2016).

Supporting Clients: Managing Cissexism and Gender/Sex Binaries

There are several ways that therapists can work with 2STNB clients who are experiencing cisnormativity, binary normativity, transnormativity, or nonbinary normativity. Using the TRIM, radical healing, and microaffirmations frameworks, the following section provides several options for supporting clients encountering cissexism and gender normativity.

First, since cissexist minority stressors can have detrimental impacts on a client's mental health (Pease et al., 2022; Puckett et al., 2021), it can be helpful for therapists to notice when cissexism might be related to a client's mental health struggles and when it might be distinct. Therapists should be careful not assume that all mental health concerns are related to a person's experience of cissexism. Second, it is also important for therapists to find a balance between attending to gender without overly focusing on gender with 2STNB clients (Schmidt et al., 2025). While some clients may share openly about their experiences, others may be exploring whether it is safe to share these experiences with their therapist. It can be helpful to invite clients to share about their experiences of gender to help open the door to these conversations. However, a therapist overly focusing on gender when the client is wanting to talk about other concerns is often felt as a microaggression and should be avoided (Morris et al., 2020).

2STNB clients' experiences of cissexism and gender normative assumptions vary, and although some may be able to identify these as problematic and harmful, others might need help identifying cisnormativity and challenging these assumptions (Anzani et al., 2019). As clients share their experiences of cissexism, therapists can use a framework of microaffirmations (Anzani et al., 2019) to validate their clients' experiences. 2STNB clients may also internalize the cissexist and gender normative messages they receive, in which case therapists can use the radical healing framework to help their clients externalize these negative messages (French et al., 2020). Using the TRIM framework (Matsuno & Israel, 2018) to explore the impact of these cissexist experiences, the client's coping, resilience strategies, and how they might want to move forward can also be helpful for clients. It is important that therapists avoid minimizing the client's experiences of these harms or making excuses for others who invalidate the client as these are common microaggressions that 2STNB people experience (Mizock & Lundquist, 2016).

Therapists can help clients explore the balance between both physical and emotional safety and authenticity. Clients may share their trouble navigating gendered spaces at school, in the workplace, at social events, on forms, and when using public restrooms. They might have worries, concerns, and fears about ambiguous interactions in which they are uncertain about their physical safety or whether they experienced cisnormative expectations, or microaggressions. Clients may feel empowered to advocate for themselves or they may choose to avoid these situations when possible, depending on safety and their need for authenticity. It can be helpful to know how a client has coped with biases and cisnormativity in the past, and what individual and group resilience strategies they've developed (Matsuno & Israel, 2018), and how they are coping with any current and ongoing cissexism. Therapists should also be carefully attending to intersectionality as they explore the client's experiences of safety (physical and emotional) and authenticity given the client's multiple social identities and the interlocking oppression they may be navigating. There are a variety of responses clients can have when facing cissexism and gender normative expectations, and therapists can support clients to explore their options for navigating these complex situations. Clients might need help considering these possible routes forward, their level of discomfort, and their emotional and physical safety in a variety of contexts.

Working with Internalized Cisnormativity and Binary Normativity

Similar to internalized transphobia, clients may also internalize cisnormative messages that being cisgender is the ideal and default state. Relatedly, clients may internalize binary normativity, or the assumption that the gender binary is natural, normal, and more desirable. These messages are pervasive throughout society; however, therapists can support clients by identifying the sources of these messages, including family, school, media, and pop culture. This may also include an exploration of early messages about gender and the reification of those messages across time. As clients begin to identify the messages they have received and the source of those messages, they can then begin to externalize and reject these messages. Supporting clients to reject these negative and damaging messages can be liberating, but it can also be challenging to acknowledge the internalization of these messages and to counter them. It may be easier for 2STNB clients to reject these messages as they connect with more affirming and validating people and spaces. Therapists can also explore and process any shame that 2STNB people may experience either about their identity specifically, or about the internalization of cisnormativity and binary normativity.

Working with Internalized Transnormativity and Nonbinary Normativity

Clients may also experience internalized transnormativity or nonbinary normativity, or the societal messages that there is one singular normative way to be transgender and a singular normative way to be nonbinary. As with cisnormativity and binary normativity, therapists can support clients to explore these narratives about trans and nonbinary people, where they come from, and support clients in countering these messages. Clients can develop a critical consciousness about the history and medicalization of transgender people across the past several decades, which promulgated and institutionalized the need for trans people to fit a specific binary narrative to access care (see Marrow, 2023). Knowing this history and the role it plays in transnormative narratives can be helpful as clients try to externalize these beliefs and reject these messages.

Sometimes clients feel that they are not trans enough if they do not want to pursue aspects of a medical transition, do not present their gender in specific ways, did not know they were trans from a young age, or otherwise do not fit within a "normative" trans narrative. Clients may also struggle with the pressure of trying to be "trans enough" that they try to prove it to others, which may or may not be in alignment with their embodiment goals. Some clients might find it helpful to explore the variety of gendered expressions, identities, and transition options that trans people may take, which can help expand their views of 2STNB people. This can include an exploration of diverse gendered experiences and expressions like seeing a diversity of 2STNB representation on social media, in books, or in various 2STNB communities. Reading about gender diversity across cultures and history can help challenge the notion that there is one "correct" way to be trans. Helping clients to realize and internalize that there is no one "right way" to be trans or nonbinary can help clients to break free from some of the transnormativity. Helping clients find more authentic gendered ways of being may also help to alleviate some of the internalized stigma and shame they may be experiencing about how they identify, feel embodied in their gender, or present their gender externally to others.

For people who identify as nonbinary, these normativity messages function in similar but unique ways to the transnormative messages. Nonbinary normativity may include beliefs that nonbinary people are always androgynous, that they do not want or need medical transition, and the erroneous belief that all nonbinary people who seek medical transition do so to be more androgynous. Nonbinary people who internalize these messages may struggle to feel that they can be nonbinary while also presenting masculinity or femininity that is in alignment with their gender assigned at birth. Similarly, nonbinary people who do want to transition and whose embodiment goals include a gender presentation that is perceived as less androgynous may struggle to feel that they can still maintain their nonbinary identity, especially if they are being perceived by others as a binary trans man or trans woman. However, it is also important to remember that 2STNB people can hold multiple gender identity labels, such as someone who is a nonbinary transmasculine person or a nonbinary transfeminine person. For some clients, the lines between being a nonbinary or binary trans person are more blurred and it can be helpful for therapists to work with clients to be as flexible or fluid as their embodiment goals may warrant. Gender identities, presentations, and embodiment goals may change over time and clients can be supported through the process of rediscovery rather than trying to fit within trans or nonbinary normativities. As therapists help clients explore the nuances of their clients' gendered identities, gendered presentation, and embodiment goals, these internalized nonbinary normative messages can be explored and challenged.

Connecting to Cultural and Historic Conceptualizations of Gender Diversity

There are several cultural considerations in supporting 2STNB clients as they navigate systems of oppression and gender-based normativities (Schmidt et al., 2025). It is important for therapists to consider the intersectional experiences and cultural background of their clients and how these identities may be influencing the client's presenting concerns. However, it's also critical that therapists acknowledge their own cultural background and consider how their biases may be impacting their work with clients. It's often helpful to work on cultural competence and humility in consultation with other therapists or with a supervisor. Taking time to intentionally consider all aspects of a client's identity and cultural background, with cultural humility, can help therapists avoid making inaccurate assumptions about their clients which may result in microaggressions or cultural misunderstandings in therapy. The following table (Table 11.2) provides some cultural considerations when working with 2STNB clients and recommendations for therapists.

Table 11.2 Cultural considerations when working with 2STNB clients

Cultural Consideration	Recommendations for Therapists
2STNB people have different experiences based on their gender and gender expression	Learn about the unique experiences of trans masculine, trans feminine, and nonbinary people. Understand how gender expression and gender conformity influence 2STNB experiences (e.g., invisibility vs. hypervisibility). Attend to how the gender binary and normativity impact the client's life.
2STNB people have different experiences based on other systems of oppression they face (e.g., racism, classism, ableism)	Ask clients about their intersectional experiences of oppression. Consider how privilege and oppression impact the client's experience. Reflect on your own areas of privilege and how that may influence your view of the client's presenting concerns.
Communities and resources may affirm some identities, but not others	Consider whether a client would feel included, affirmed, etc. in all of their identities before offering resources or referrals (e.g., is the event accessible? Does the support group include other BIPOC 2STNB people?) Understand the nuance in support systems. Some support systems may both be supportive and unsupportive (e.g., family members who invalidate one's gender, but provide a strong racial/ethnic community). Help clients maximize the benefits and minimize the harms from support systems.
Culture influences understandings of gender and gender norms	Reflect on your own understanding of gender and the cultural messages you received about gender. Understand that gender identities and gender roles are socially constructed and that different cultures have different cultural meanings of various gender identities. Recognize that the gender binary and rigid gender roles largely stem from Christian European contexts and have been forcibly spread through colonization.
Cultural values may influence decisions about transition and coming out	Help the client understand their own values and support their decisions regarding transition and coming out. Avoid projecting your own values onto the client's decisions.
2STNB clients are experts in their own experiences, but not responsible for educating their therapists	Ask questions that aim to benefit the client vs. the therapist. For example, asking questions that will help the client gain greater insight into their own emotions rather than questions that are motivated by the therapist's own curiosity or lack of knowledge.

Strengths-Based Approaches to Combating Cissexism

In addition to supporting clients to manage the negative effects of cissexism, therapists can take a strengths-based approach in their clinical work with 2STNB clients. While it is important to understand and acknowledge the role of minority stress, what has unfortunately developed is a "damage-centered" narrative that may create a one-dimensional view of the pain and struggle of living as a 2STNB person (Levitt et al., 2023; Tuck, 2009). For both 2STNB people and therapists, these narratives can perpetuate misconceptions that focus primarily on violence and suffering. However, 2STNB people also find affirmation, healing, pride, gender euphoria, and joy in their 2STNB identities and within communities (Holloway, 2023; Shuster & Westbrook, 2022; Tebbe et al., 2022).

Supporting clients with strengths-based approaches that attend to their joy, pride, and gender euphoria can help to alleviate or offset the negative impacts of living as a 2STNB person in a cissexist world (Holloway, 2023; Tebbe et al., 2022). Therapists can engage clients in an exploration of the positive aspects of the client's gender identity and gender expression. For example, therapists can ask clients about their experiences of gender euphoria, or the positive feelings that come from their gender identity (Beischel et al., 2022), rather than focusing primarily on the client's gender dysphoria. 2STNB people describe gender euphoria as a sense of "rightness", joy, elation, or positive feelings associated with being gendered correctly, feeling "at home" in one's gender, or content with aspects of a 2STNB identity or gender expression (Austin et al., 2022; Beischel et al., 2022). Gender euphoric experiences can be internal, external, or social (Beischel et al., 2022). Therapists should find a balance between exploring and processing a client's gender dysphoria, or what feels most wrong, upsetting, and challenging, with conversations about how and when they feel gender euphoria. It can also be helpful to help clients identify when and with whom they feel joy, contentment, and ease around their gender and create a gender euphoria plan to increase these experiences and feelings.

Case Studies

The following two case studies illustrate the ways that cissexism and systems of normativity may show up in the lives of 2STNB clients. Each case does not represent a real client, but rather were inspired by a combination of clients that the authors have worked with in therapy. We aim to demonstrate how cultural biases and mistakes are inevitable, but also how they can be addressed. We also aim to give examples of how the theoretical frameworks and clinical interventions discussed previously can be applied in therapy.

Case Study #1: Arielle

Arielle (they/them) is a 20-year-old Black, trans feminine, nonbinary first-generation college student who is attending community college in an urban area. Arielle is referred to their current clinician Chris, by their college counselor. Chris (he/him) is a 35-year-old white, trans man who works in a group practice which is advertised as being LGBTQ+ friendly.

Arielle comes to therapy to discuss feelings of anxiety and stress about their gender and wanting to make decisions about future medical interventions. Arielle explains that they aren't sure if they are "a trans woman" or "nonbinary" and they feel like they "need to know" to decide whether to begin taking hormones. Arielle reports that they hate being perceived as a man or being read as trans. Arielle reports spending a lot of time getting ready and evaluating whether they "pass" as a cis woman before leaving their house for class each day. They disclose that one reason they are invested in "passing" as a cis woman is because they were harassed and followed by a group of men when taking the bus one of the first times they went in public dressed in feminine attire and makeup. Arielle described being terrified and feeling ashamed afterwards. They stopped wearing feminine clothes after this incident for 6 months and have not disclosed what happened to anyone.

Arielle reported that although being perceived as a woman felt much better than being perceived as a man, they were still unsure if being a woman is the right fit. They also felt like if they really were a trans woman, they would have known this about themselves as a child and they didn't start exploring their gender until they were 18. They reported researching nonbinary identities online and joining a few social media groups for nonbinary people. However, when other members posted pictures or described themselves, Arielle didn't feel that they related to them as they were mostly white trans masculine individuals. Arielle also shared that they loved makeup and wearing feminine clothing, so they worried that they were too feminine to be nonbinary. Arielle said, "I think I'm not trans enough to be a trans woman, but I'm not nonbinary enough to be nonbinary. I don't know why I can't settle on one or the other."

Clinician's Assumptions and Biases

Through intentional self-reflection and case consultation with other clinicians in the group practice, Chris was able to recognize some of his assumptions and biases in Arielle's case. First, Chris noticed that he assumed Arielle was a trans woman based on their feminine appearance and name as opposed to being nonbinary. Chris accidently used "she/her" pronouns a few times in Arielle's first clinical note, which Chris was able to correct before finalizing. As therapy progressed, Chris also became aware that he assumed that Arielle was either a trans woman or nonbinary and did not consider that Arielle could be both or that their gender may be fluid or evolve over time. Many nonbinary people identify to some extent with binary genders. For example, the identity of demi-girl or demi-women means partially or sometimes being a woman (Matsuno et al., 2021). Chris was not able to realize he had this bias until this was pointed out by another clinician during a case consultation. Chris also reflected on his own experiences as a white trans man and considered how he may be projecting his own experiences onto Arielle. He realized that he hoped Arielle would start hormones, because in his own experience, taking hormones was life changing. Chris recognized this bias was driven by the intention to help Arielle experience the relief that he experienced but recognized that he needed to support what was the best decision for Arielle and make sure that Arielle didn't feel pressured into a certain direction.

During group case consultation, a Black clinician asked Chris how race played a role in the client's decision-making process. This prompted Chris to realize that he had not explored how Arielle's race, cultural background, or other social identities were influencing their presenting concerns. Chris was so focused on Arielle's experience of gender that he overlooked their other identities. Chris reflected on how his whiteness, class background, education, and other privileged identities contributed to his lack of focus on these other dimensions. He became aware of how his privilege as a white trans man influenced his transition decisions and how this may differ from Arielle's experience. As a white person, Chris had the privilege to base his decision primarily on seeking authenticity and did not have to consider his physical safety. When Chris began taking testosterone in his mid-twenties, he had an established friend group of queer and trans people who supported and validated his identities. He had family support and the financial resources to access care. As a trans man seeking hormone therapy, he did not experience the barriers that many nonbinary people experience such as medical providers questioning his decision (Puckett et al., 2018).

Clinical Approach and Interventions

Gender Affirmative Approach and Identifying Embodiment Goals

In line with the principles of a gender affirmative approach (Matsuno, 2019; Singh & dickey, 2017), Chris validated and affirmed Arielle's experiences of gender and actively worked on his own gendered assumptions and biases to prevent them from influencing his work with Arielle. For example, Chris was able to correct himself when he thought or wrote the wrong pronouns. Chris also explicitly told Arielle that he supported whatever decisions were right for them and that he did not have a desired outcome in terms of Arielle's gender or decisions about transitioning. Chris monitored his own body language to show that he was open and non-judgmental about the client's desires and decisions. Chris also explored with Arielle why it was important for them to come to a decision about their identity and why this was necessary before deciding about hormone therapy. Chris and Arielle uncovered some transnormative and nonbinary normative messages that Arielle had internalized about what it meant to be a trans woman or a nonbinary person. Arielle felt that if they were a trans woman then they would need to "fully transition" and that if they were nonbinary then they shouldn't medically transition whatsoever. These expectations were adding significant stress and limited options for Arielle.

Chris helped Arielle expand their perspective on this decision from being that of one of two options (identifying as a trans woman and undergoing every medical intervention or identifying a nonbinary and not going through any medical interventions) to many options. Chris shared some examples of trans people who didn't fit these normativity narratives, which Arielle expressed felt relieving and validating. Rather than focusing on choosing an identity to then dictate a transition path, Chris suggested reflecting on Arielle's experiences of gender euphoria and dysphoria to guide their decision-making path. Chris provided Arielle with the framework of gender embodiment (DuBois et al., 2022; Hastings, et al., 2021) and asked Arielle to reflect on how they would like to embody their gender, noting that it was okay to want to femininize or masculinize some aspects of themselves and not others.

Attending to Intersectionality

After reflecting on his own experiences, Chris intentionally tried to explore other social and cultural factors that were influencing Arielle. Chris explicitly asked Arielle about how their experience of race and their cultural background were influencing them and their decision stating, "This may not be relevant, but I wanted to check in and see if any other parts of your identity – such as being Black – impacted your decision-making process at all. I apologize for not attending to this earlier. I think my privilege as a white trans man made me less aware of how these aspects may be influencing you." Arielle noted that they appreciated Chris bringing this into the conversation and disclosed that as a Black person, they are always thinking about their safety. Arielle stated, "I think it's much harder as a Black person to 'be in the middle' gender wise. I already get people looking at me all the time as a Black person, it makes me hesitant to do anything that would draw more attention to myself." Chris validated Arielle's reality as a Black trans person and created space for Arielle to feel the sadness and anger associated with needing to always be cognizant of how others are perceiving them.

Chris acknowledged the unjust nature of Arielle having to balance their own authenticity with protecting their safety and collaboratively discussed ways that Arielle could attend to both needs. Chris and Arielle reviewed Arielle's embodiment goals and Chris asked Arielle to rate how safe each goal would be to enact. They expanded further by identifying the levels of safety they felt in various situations. For example, Arielle shared they didn't feel safe using public transportation while dressing in a feminine manner and having facial hair, whereas this was an embodiment goal that they felt safe exploring in their apartment with their roommates. Arielle agreed to try out the safest embodiment goals first. Additionally, Chris engaged in collaborative safety planning to identify strategies Arielle could use if there ever was a situation in which they felt unsafe such as being accompanied by a friend when using public transportation.

Case Study #2: Andi

Andi (they/them) is a queer, gender questioning, 27-year-old member of the Confederated Salish and Kootenai Tribes of the Flathead Reservation. Andi moved from a small town in Montana to an out-of-state urban city for their organizational psychology graduate program 6 months ago. Andi self-refers for individual bereavement counseling at the local 2SLGBTQIA+ health center after having a negative experience at their university bereavement group. They have been assigned to work with one of the staff clinicians, Lindsey, who is a 40-year-old cisgender, bisexual second-generation Chinese American woman.

Andi comes to therapy in the wake of their Kootenai mother's death a few weeks prior and reports feeling grief, guilt, remorse, anxiety, and an exacerbated isolation since then. They explained that prior to their mother's sudden death, they were already having a difficult time transitioning to graduate school and the new city since it was their first time being away from their family and community in Montana. With their mother's death, Andi reports feeling guilt and remorse for not being at home when their mother had died and that they experience intense sadness when reflecting on how they had "abandoned" their mother and family during that time.

They report that their feelings of loss of their mother also extend to feelings of grief related to the Kootenai knowledge that their mother held within their family. Andi explained to Lindsey that while they had identified as queer since their adolescence, they had recently begun exploring their gender identity. At the time, Andi had not felt ready to "come out" about their gender to their family because they were unsure of how to describe and label their gender, but that they had intended to speak to their mom at the end of the semester to learn about how their gender identity would be understood in Kootenai culture and language. With the death of their mother, Andi is mourning the cultural loss of ascertaining guidance from their mother about their gendered role in their community. Andi believed their mother to be an understanding Kootenai woman but reported feeling hesitant and uncertain about reaching out to their extended Kootenai family members about their gender identity exploration, as they feared their extended family would not be accepting of their gender.

Prior to starting therapy with Lindsey, Andi had a negative experience at their university's bereavement group. Andi reported an incident where after vulnerably explaining how their mother's loss also felt like a loss of cultural context and support about their gender identity exploration, one of the attendees questioned the validity of Andi's current gender exploration by commenting "I would have never guessed you were trans." The group counselor then attempted to interject on this microaggression by describing Andi as a Native American Two-Spirit person who had "both" male and female spirits inside them. Andi responded that they had ambivalent feelings about using a pan-Native term, like Two-Spirit, to describe themself before understanding and describing their gender in Kootenai language. Andi reported feeling very alienated and hurt by the interaction, which is why they decided to attend individual therapy at a 2SLGBTQIA+ center.

Clinician's Assumptions and Biases

Lindsey recognized that she did not have much experience working with indigenous clients and had only worked with Native American clients in group counseling settings. She noticed her own discomfort related to having a lack of knowledge and familiarity with indigenous cultures. Therefore, she sought out extra case consultation from a trusted colleague Gary, who had identified working with indigenous clients as one of his areas of expertise and had previously offered to consult with others about this topic. During her first consultation, Lindsey realized that she held the desired outcome that Andi would come out to their extended family members and that she hoped connection to family would help Andi through their grieving process. When questioned about where this desire came from, Lindsey reflected on how her own cultural values of connection to family and her own previous experience with coming out as bisexual influenced what she expected would happen if Andi were to come out to their extended family. Lindsey also realized that she had an assumption that all indigenous people were accepting of 2SLGBTQIA+ people due to learning about the history of colonization and understanding that 2SLGBTQIA+ bias was rooted in Western European Christian ideology that was spread through colonization. Gary praised Lindsey for having this knowledge and explained that through colonization much of the knowledge of indigenous history was lost even within the same tribe and that indigenous cultural norms, roles, values, and practices were erased through colonialism.

Lindsey suggested that Andi could find out more about how gender was conceptualized by the Kootenai people through doing their own research online or at the library. Gary explained that this information may be difficult to find as much of indigenous history is passed down orally and not through written text. This gave Lindsey a better understanding of and more empathy for the cultural loss that Andi was experiencing due to the loss of their mother.

Clinical Approaches and Interventions

In the first session with Andi, Lindsey acknowledged and validated the harm done in Andi's university bereavement group. Lindsey reflected Andi's thoughts and feelings by stating, "it sounds like you felt really misunderstood," and "you felt like an outsider in that group." Lindsey was careful not to diminish or make excuses for the behaviors of the other group members or group therapist. Lindsey focused on the impact on the client rather than the intent of the enactors of the microaggressions. By doing this in the first session, Lindsey was able to build a strong rapport with Andi, who was understandably, more cautious about being vulnerable due to their past negative therapy experience.

Throughout the course of therapy, Andi was able to process their grief at multiple levels. Lindsey validated and reflected back the multiple losses Andi was experiencing including the loss of their mother, moving away from their home and community in Montana, the loss of the opportunity for Andi to share their gender with their mother, and the loss of the cultural knowledge of gender within the Kootenai tribe. Given that Lindsey had worked towards educating herself more about indigenous communities and the impact of colonization, she was comfortable bringing up the role of colonization in her sessions with Andi. Lindsey gently asked Andi, "I'm wondering if you have ever had the chance to process the many losses that occurred from colonization?" Approaching this topic and allowing Andi space to express their grief, anger, and resentment led to a powerful clinical moment. Andi uncovered a deeper collective grief about how things "could have been" if colonization didn't happen. As a non-native person, Lindsey was able to hold space and be a witness to Andi's experiences and emotions.

Throughout therapy, Andi had the chance to explore their gender further. They shared that they never connected to the terms trans or nonbinary and felt out of place when attending 2SLGBTQIA+ community events or support groups. Andi expressed how the role of being a man or being a woman never fit, but they also didn't relate to trans or nonbinary people they saw on social media, who were predominately white. Lindsey recognized and validated that it was difficult for Andi to find spaces where they could be fully seen and understood in terms of both their indigenous cultural heritage and their gender. Lindsey acknowledged her own lack of knowledge about native 2SLGBTQIA+ communities, and humbly inquired about whether Andi was able to find others who they may be able to relate to more in terms of gender and cultural background. Andi reported that they planned on attending an upcoming two-spirit powwow. After attending the event, Andi and Lindsey were able to process the impact. Andi reported that this was a powerful experience as they had never been surrounded by so many native 2SLGBTQIA+ people before. Although the attendees came from several different tribes, Andi said they felt a sense of belonging, community, and shared sense of knowing. Andi also connected with one of the organizations that sponsored the event and said they were considering getting more involved.

Future Directions

This chapter provides a roadmap for understanding the role of cissexism and binary conceptualizations of gender in the lives of 2STNB clients and utilizing this knowledge to inform clinical practice. Through a lens of intersectionality and 2STNB liberation, we explored the historical context and cultural underpinnings of cissexism, therapeutic frameworks that can be used across multiple therapeutic orientations and modalities, examples of how to translate the science of psychotherapy with 2STNB people into therapeutic practice, and two case studies to help bring these concepts to life.

There are several interventions utilized throughout the chapter that can be helpful for therapists working to dismantle cissexist ideology, binary conceptualizations of gender, and gender-based normativities in clinical practice with 2STNB clients. First, therapists must interrogate their own conceptualization of gender, including their own reliance on cisnormativity and other gender-based normativities. Examination of personal biases and normative beliefs about gender are ongoing processes for therapists as we all work to unlearn cissexist norms and reduce microaggressions with 2STNB clients.

Therapists also play a role in helping clients manage the negative impacts of cissexism. With the TRIM framework, therapists can support the development of a client's individual and group resilience factors and identify specific therapeutic interventions to help address and bolster the client's resilience (Matsuno & Israel, 2018). The radical healing framework provides a model for addressing oppressive systems, like cissexism, in therapy with 2STNB clients with interventions aimed at raising critical consciousness, exploring cultural authenticity and self-knowledge, and collectivism within 2STNB communities (French et al., 2020). Using a framework of microaffirmations in therapy, therapists can work to avoid microaggressions, acknowledge cisnormativity, disrupt cisnormativity, and see a client's authentic gender (Anzani et al., 2019). Each of these strength-based models provides therapists with options for interventions that not only dismantle cissexist ideology to reduce minority stressors for 2STNB clients, but also increase resilience, connection with communities, and ideally, provide opportunities for gender euphoria and joy.

References

Adames, H. Y., Chavez-Dueñas, N. Y., Lewis, J. A., Neville, H. A., French, B. H., Chen, G. A., & Mosley, D. V. (2023). Radical healing in psychotherapy: Addressing the wounds of racism-related stress and trauma. *Psychotherapy, 60*(1), 39–50. https://doi.org/10.1037/pst0000435

Adams, N. J., & Vincent, B. (2019). Suicidal thoughts and behaviors among transgender adults in relation to education, ethnicity, and income: A systematic review. *Transgender Health, 4*(1), 226–246. https://doi.org/10.1089/trgh.2019.0009

Ansara, Y. G., & Hegarty, P. (2012). Cisgenderism in psychology: Pathologizing and misgendering children from 1999 to 2008. *Psychology & Sexuality, 3*(2), 137–160. https://doi.org/10.1080/19419899.2011.576696

Anzani, A., Morris, E. R., & Galupo, M. P. (2019). From absence of microaggressions to seeing authentic gender: Transgender clients' experiences with microaffirmations in therapy. *Journal of LGBT Issues in Counseling, 13*(4), 258–275. https://doi.org/10.1080/15538605.2019.1662359

Austin, A., & Goodman, R. (2017). The impact of social connectedness and internalized transphobic stigma on self-esteem among transgender and gender non-conforming adults. *Journal of Homosexuality, 64*(6), 825–841. https://doi.org/10.1080/00918369.2016.1236587

Austin, A., Papciak, R., & Lovins, L. (2022). Gender euphoria: A grounded theory exploration of experiencing gender affirmation. *Psychology & Sexuality*, 1–21. https://doi.org/10.1080/19419899.2022.2049632

binaohan, b. (2014). *Decolonizing trans/gender 101*. Biyuti Publishing.

Becerra-Culqui, T. A., Liu, Y., Nash, R., Cromwell, L., Flanders, W. D., Getahun, D., Giammattei, S. V., Hunkeler, E. M., Lash, T. L., Millman, A., Quinn, V. P., Robinson, B., Roblin, D., Sandberg, D. E., Silverberg, M. J., Tangpricha, V., & Goodman, M. (2018). Mental health of transgender and gender nonconforming youth compared with their peers. *Pediatrics, 141*(5). https://doi.org/10.1542/peds.2017-3845

Beischel, W. J., Gauvin, S. E. M., & van Anders, S. M. (2022). "A little shiny gender breakthrough": Community understandings of gender euphoria. *International Journal of Transgender Health, 23*(3), 274–294. https://doi.org/10.1080/26895269.2021.1915223

Brooks, V. R. (1981). *Minority stress and lesbian women*. Lexington Books.

Budge, S. L., Sinnard, M. T., & Hoyt, W. T. (2021). Longitudinal effects of psychotherapy with transgender and nonbinary clients: A randomized controlled pilot trial. *Psychotherapy, 58*(1), 1–11. https://doi.org/10.1037/pst0000310

Chodzen, G., Hidalgo, M. A., Chen, D., & Garofalo, R. (2019). Minority stress factors associated with depression and anxiety among transgender and gender-nonconforming youth. *Journal of Adolescent Health, 64*(4), 467–471. https://doi.org/10.1016/j.jadohealth.2018.07.006

Collins, P. H. (1991). *Black feminist thought: Knowledge, consciousness, and the politics of empowerment*. https://www.routledge.com/Black-Feminist-Thought-Knowledge-Consciousness-and-the-Politics-of-Empowerment/Collins/p/book/9780415964722

Combahee River Collective. (1977). *The Combahee river collective statement*. https://americanstudies.yale.edu/sites/default/files/files/Keyword%20Coalition_Readings.pdf

Crenshaw, K. W. (1991). Mapping the margins: Intersectionality, identity politics, and violence against women of color. *Stanford Law Review, 43*(6), 1241–1299. https://doi.org/10.2307/1229039

Deutsch, M. (2016, June 17). *Creating a safe and welcoming clinic environment*. UCSF Gender Affirming Health Program. https://transcare.ucsf.edu/guidelines/clinic-environment

Diemer, M. A., Rapa, L. J., Voight, A. M., & McWhirter, E. H. (2016). Critical consciousness: A developmental approach to addressing marginalization and oppression. *Child Development Perspectives, 10*(4), 216–221. https://doi.org/10.1111/cdep.12193

DuBois, L. Z., Puckett, J. A., & Langer, S. J. (2022). Development of the gender embodiment scale: Trans masculine spectrum. *Transgender Health*. https://doi.org/10.1089/trgh.2020.0088

Eisenberg, M. E., Gower, A. L., McMorris, B. J., Rider, G. N., & Coleman, E. (2019). Emotional distress, bullying victimization, and protective factors among transgender and gender diverse adolescents in city, suburban, town, and rural locations. *Journal of Rural Health, 35*(2), 270–281. https://doi.org/10.1111/jrh.12311

Expósito-Campos, P., Pérez-Fernández, J. I., & Salaberria, K. (2023). Empirically supported affirmative psychological interventions for transgender and non-binary youth and adults: A systematic review. *Clinical Psychology Review, 100*, 1–20. https://doi.org/10.1016/j.cpr.2022.102229

Feinberg, L. (1996). *Transgender warriors: Making history from Joan of Arc to Dennis Rodman*. Beacon Press.

French, B. H., Lewis, J. A., Mosley, D. V., Adames, H. Y., Chavez-Dueñas, N. Y., Chen, G. A., & Neville, H. A. (2020). Toward a psychological framework of radical healing in communities of color. *The Counseling Psychologist, 48*(1), 14–46. https://doi.org/10.1177/0011000019843506

Galupo, M. P., & Orphanidys, J. C. (2022). Transgender Black, Indigenous, and People of Color: Intersections of oppression. *International Journal of Transgender Health, 23*(1–2), 1–4. https://doi.org/10.1080/26895269.2022.2020035

Galupo, M. P., Mitchell, R. C., & Davis, K. S. (2015). Sexual minority self-identification: Multiple identities and complexity. *Psychology of Sexual Orientation and Gender Diversity, 2*(4), 355–364. https://doi.org/10.1037/sgd0000131

Goldblum, P., Testa, R. J., Pflum, S., Hendricks, M. L., Bradford, J., & Bongar, B. (2012). The relationship between gender-based victimization and suicide attempts in transgender people. *Professional Psychology: Research and Practice, 43*(5), 468–475. https://doi.org/10.1037/a0029605

Hastings, J., Bobb, C., Wolfe, M., Amaro Jimenez, Z., & Amand, C. S. (2021). Medical care for nonbinary youth: Individualized gender care beyond a binary framework. *Pediatric Annals, 50*(9), e384–e390. https://doi.org/10.3928/19382359-20210818-03

Hatchel, T., Valido, A., De Pedro, K. T., Huang, Y., & Espelage, D. L. (2019). Minority stress among transgender adolescents: The role of peer victimization, school belonging, and ethnicity. *Journal of Child and Family Studies, 28*(9), 2467–2476. https://doi.org/10.1007/s10826-018-1168-3

Hendricks, M. L., & Testa, R. J. (2012). A conceptual framework for clinical work with transgender and gender nonconforming clients: An adaptation of the minority stress model. *Professional Psychology: Research and Practice, 43*(5), 460–467. https://doi.org/10.1037/a0029597

Holloway, B. T. (2023). Highlighting trans joy: A call to practitioners, researchers, and educators. *Health Promotion Practice, 24*(4), 612–614. https://doi.org/10.1177/15248399231152468

Hyde, J. S., Bigler, R. S., Joel, D., Tate, C. C., & van Anders, S. M. (2019). The future of sex and gender in psychololgy: Five challenges to the gender binary. *American Psychologist, 74*(2), 171–192. https://doi.org/10.1037/amp0000307

Iantaffi, A. (2020). *Gender trauma: Healing cultural, social, and historical gendered trauma.* Jessica Kingley Publishers.

Israel, T., Matsuno, E., Choi, A. Y., Goodman, J. A., Lin, Y.-J., Kary, K. G., & Merrill, C. R. S. (2021). Reducing internalized transnegativity: Randomized controlled trial of an online intervention. *Psychology of Sexual Orientation and Gender Diversity, 8*(4), 429–439. https://doi.org/10.1037/sgd0000447

Johns, M. M., Lowry, R., Andrzejewski, J., Barrios, L. C., Demissie, Z., McManus, T., Rasberry, C. N., Robin, L., & Underwood, J. M. (2019). Transgender identity and experiences of violence victimization, substance use, suicide risk, and sexual risk behaviors among high school students—19 states and large urban school districts, 2017. *MMWR. Morbidity and Mortality Weekly Report, 68*(3), 67–71. https://doi.org/10.15585/mmwr.mm6803a3

Johnson, K. C., LeBlanc, A. J., Deardorff, J., & Bockting, W. O. (2020). Invalidation experiences among non-binary adolescents. *Journal of Sex Research, 57*(2), 222–233. https://doi.org/10.1080/00224499.2019.1608422

Levitt, H. M., Kehoe, K. A., & Hand, A. B. (2023). Beyond minority stress: Toward a multidimensional psychology of trans/nonbinary gender. *Current Opinion in Psychology, 49*, 101515. https://doi.org/10.1016/j.copsyc.2022.101515

Lindley, L., & Budge, S. L. (2023). Challenging and understanding gendered narratives: The development and validation of the transnormativity measure (TM). *International Journal of Transgender Health*. https://doi.org/10.1080/26895269.2023.2218365

Lindley, L., & Galupo, M. P. (2020). Gender dysphoria and minority stress: Support for inclusion of gender dysphoria as a proximal stressor. *Psychology of Sexual Orientation and Gender Diversity, 7*(3), 265–275. https://doi.org/10.1037/sgd0000439

Marrow, E. (2023). "I hope that as our selection becomes more accurate, the number … will be very few": The creation of assessment criteria for gender-affirming care, 1960s–1980s. *Psychology of Sexual Orientation and Gender Diversity*. Advance online publication. https://doi.org/10.1037/sgd0000633

Matsuno, E. (2019). Nonbinary-affirming psychological interventions. *Cognitive and Behavioral Practice, 26*(4), 617–628. https://doi.org/10.1016/j.cbpra.2018.09.003

Matsuno, E., & Israel, T. (2018). Psychological interventions promoting resilience among transgender individuals: Transgender resilience intervention model (TRIM). *The Counseling Psychologist, 46*(5), 632–655. https://doi.org/10.1177/0011000018787261

Matsuno, E., Webb, A., Hashtpari, H., Budge, S. L., Krishnan, M., & Balsam, K. F. (2021). Nonbinary fact sheet. Society for the Psychological Study of Lesbian, Gay, Bisexual, and Transgender Issues. https://www.apadivisions.orgision-44/resources/nonbinary-fact-sheet.pdf

Matsuno, E., Puckett, J. A., & Barr, S. M. (2023). Stigma and mental health inequities: The gender minority stress and resilience framework. In T. G. Goetz & A. S. Keuroghlian (Eds.), *Gender-affirming psychiatric care for transgender and gender diverse people*. American Psychiatric Association.

Matsuno, E., Bricker, N. L., Collazo, E. N., Mohr Jr., R., & Balsam, K. F. (2024). "The default is just going to be getting misgendered": Minority stress experiences among nonbinary adults. *Psychology of Sexual Orientation and Gender Diversity, 11*(2), 202–214. https://doi.org/10.1037/sgd0000607

May, V. M.(2015).*Pursuing intersectionality: Unsettling dominant imaginaries.Routledge.*

McGeorge, C. R., Coburn, K. O., & Walsdorf, A. A. (2021). Deconstructing cissexism: The journey of becoming an affirmative family therapist for transgender and nonbinary clients. *Journal of Marital and Family Therapy, 47*(3), 785–802. https://doi.org/10.1111/jmft.12481

Meyer, I. H. (1995). Minority stress and mental health in gay men. *Journal of Health and Social Behavior, 36*(1), 38–56. https://doi.org/10.2307/2137286

Mizock, L., & Lundquist, C. (2016). Missteps in psychotherapy with transgender clients: Promoting gender sensitivity in counseling and psychological practice. *Psychology of Sexual Orientation and Gender Diversity, 3*(2), 148–155. https://doi.org/10.1037/sgd0000177

Morris, E. R., Lindley, L., & Galupo, M. P. (2020). "Better issues to focus on": Transgender microaggressions as ethical violations in therapy. *The Counseling Psychologist, 48*(6), 883–915. https://doi.org/10.1177/0011000020924391

Mosley, D. V., McNeil-Young, V., Bridges, B., Adam, S., Colson, A., Crowley, M., & Lee, L. (2021). Toward radical healing: A qualitative metasynthesis exploring oppression and liberation among Black queer people. *Psychology of Sexual Orientation and Gender Diversity, 8*(3), 292–313. https://doi.org/10.1037/sgd0000522

Nolan, B. J., Zwickl, S., Locke, P., Zajac, J. D., & Cheung, A. S. (2023). Early access to testosterone therapy in transgender and gender-diverse adults seeking masculinization: A randomized clinical trial. *JAMA Network Open, 6*(9), e2331919. https://doi.org/10.1001/jamanetworkopen.2023.31919

Pasley, A., Hamilton, T., & Veale, J. (2018). Transnormativities: Reterritorializing perceptions and practice. In P. Doan & L. Johnston (Eds.), *Rethinking transgender identities: Reflections from around the globe* (pp. 124–147). Routledge.

Pease, M., Williams, N. D., Iwamoto, D. K., & Salerno, J. P. (2022). Minority stressors and their associations with severe psychological distress among gender-diverse people. *American Journal of Orthopsychiatry, 92*(5), 578–589. https://doi.org/10.1037/ort0000635

Pflum, S. R., Testa, R. J., Balsam, K. F., Goldblum, P. B., & Bongar, B. (2015). Social support, trans community connectedness, and mental health symptoms among transgender and gender nonconforming adults. *Psychology of Sexual Orientation and Gender Diversity, 2*(3), 281–286. https://doi.org/10.1037/sgd0000122

Puckett, J. A., Cleary, P., Rossman, K., Newcomb, M. E., & Mustanski, B. (2018). Barriers to Gender-Affirming Care for Transgender and Gender Nonconforming Individuals. *Sexuality Research & Social Policy: Journal of NSRC: SR & SP, 15*(1), 48–59. https://doi.org/10.1007/s13178-017-0295-8

Puckett, J. A., Aboussouan, A. B., Ralston, A. L., Mustanski, B., & Newcomb, M. E. (2021). Systems of cissexism and the daily production of stress for transgender and gender diverse people. *International Journal of Transgender Health, 24*(1), 113–126. https://doi.org/10.1080/26895269.2021.1937437

Robinson, M. (2020). Two-spirit identity in a time of gender fluidity. *Journal of Homosexuality, 67*, 1675–1690. https://doi.org/10.1080/00918369.2019.1613853

Rood, B. A., Reisner, S. L., Puckett, J. A., Surace, F. I., Berman, A. K., & Pantalone, D. W. (2017). Internalized transphobia: Exploring perceptions of social messages in transgender and gender-nonconforming adults. *International Journal of Transgenderism, 18*(4), 411–426. https://doi.org/10.1080/15532739.2017.1329048

Scandurra, C., Bochicchio, V., Amodeo, A. L., Esposito, C., Valerio, P., Maldonato, N. M., Bacchini, D., & Vitelli, R. (2018). Internalized transphobia, resilience, and mental health: Applying the psychological mediation framework to Italian transgender individuals. *International Journal of Environmental Research and Public Health, 15*(3). https://doi.org/10.3390/ijerph15030508

Schilt, K., & Westbrook, L. (2009). Doing gender, doing heteronormativity: "Gender normals," transgender people, and the social maintenance of heterosexuality. *Gender & Society, 23*, 440–464. https://doi.org/10.1177/0891243209340034

Schmidt, C. K., Bettergarcia, J. N., Matsuno, E., & Galupo, M. P. (2025). Cultural humility with transgender and gender diverse clients. *Practice Innovations.* 10(3), 203–220. https://doi.org/10.1037/pri0000263

Schmitz, R. M., Amjadi, S., Tabler, J., & Ishoy, J. (2023). Radical healing in Precarity: LGBTQ+ Young people's approaches to life challenges and aspirations through pet caregiving in the context of homelessness. *Youth, 3*(1), Article 1. https://doi.org/10.3390/youth3010004

Schuller, K. (2017). *The biopolitics of feeling: Race, sex, and science in the nineteenth century*. Duke University Press.

Shuster, S. M., & Westbrook, L. (2022). Reducing the joy deficit in sociology: A study of transgender joy. *Social Problems*, spac034. https://doi.org/10.1093/socpro/spac034

Singh, A. A., & dickey, l. m. (2017). Affirmative counseling with transgender and gender nonconforming clients. In K. A. DeBord, A. R. Fischer, K. J. Bieschke, & R. M. Perez (Eds.), *Handbook of sexual orientation and gender diversity in counseling and psychotherapy* (pp. 157–182). American Psychological Association. https://doi.org/10.1037/15959-007

Singh, A. A., Meng, S. E., & Hansen, A. W. (2014). "I am my own gender": Resilience strategies of trans youth. *Journal of Counseling and Development, 92*(2), 208–218. https://doi.org/10.1002/j.1556-6676.2014.00150.x

Tate, C. C., Youssef, C. P., & Bettergarcia, J. N. (2014). Integrating the study of transgender spectrum and cisgender experiences of self-categorization from a personality perspective. *Review of General Psychology, 18*(4), 302–312. https://doi.org/10.1037/gpr0000019

Tebbe, E. A., Bell, H. L., Cassidy, K., Lindner, S., Wilson, E., & Budge, S. (2022). "It's loving yourself for you": Happiness in trans and nonbinary adults. *Psychology of Sexual Orientation and Gender Diversity*. https://doi.org/10.1037/sgd0000613.supp

Testa, R. J., Habarth, J., Peta, J., Balsam, K., & Bockting, W. (2015). Development of the gender minority stress and resilience measure. *Psychology of Sexual Orientation and Gender Diversity, 2*(1), 65–77. https://doi.org/10.1037/sgd0000081

Tuck, E. (2009). Suspending damage: A letter to communities. *Harvard Educational Review, 79*(3), 409–427. https://doi.org/10.17763/haer.79.3.n0016675661t3n15

van Anders, S. M. (2015). Beyond sexual orientation: Integrating gender/sex and diverse sexualities via sexual configurations theory. *Archives of Sexual Behavior, 44*(5), 1177–1213. https://doi.org/10.1007/s10508-015-0490-8XXXX

Vance, S. R., Boyer, C. B., Glidden, D. V., & Sevelius, J. (2021). Mental health and psychosocial risk and protective factors among Black and latinx transgender youth compared with peers. *JAMA Network Open, 4*(3), 1–13. https://doi.org/10.1001/jamanetworkopen.2021.3256

Wang, Y., Yu, H., Yang, Y., Drescher, J., Li, R., Yin, W., Yu, R., Wang, S., Deng, W., Jia, Q., Zucker, K. J., & Chen, R. (2020). Mental health status of cisgender and gender-diverse secondary school students in China. *JAMA Network Open, 3*(10), e2022796. https://doi.org/10.1001/jamanetworkopen.2020.22796

Chapter 12
Countering Anti-Bisexual Prejudice and Monosexism in Therapy with Bisexual Clients

Jade Wilkinson, Tom Carter, and Brendan J. Dunlop

Highlights

- We provide an overview of the social context in which bisexual people live, considering bisexual erasure and stereotypes, emphasising that bisexual mental health is a social problem.
- We consider the experiences of bisexual individuals through the lens of Queer Theory, Minority Stress Theory and social discourse. We explore affirmative therapy and consider the current evidence base, and suggested adaptations to Cognitive Behavioural Therapy for bisexual individuals are presented.
- A clinical vignette is presented towards the end of this chapter, to allow readers the opportunity to see how theoretical considerations may be applied in practice.

Positionality

Dr. Jade Wilkinson is a white woman and Clinical Psychologist working in the United Kingdom in the National Health Service within adult neurorehabilitation and paediatric neurodisability teams. She recently completed her thesis in affirmative interventions for LGBTQ+ young people. She has developed and delivered an affirmative self-esteem intervention for young bisexual people who self-injure as part of this. She views gender and sexuality through a post-structuralist lens.

Dr. Thomas Carter is a bisexual Clinical Psychologist working in the United Kingdom. He recently completed a doctoral thesis investigating how discourses of gender and sexuality are used by bisexual men to construct their mental wellbeing and distress. He constructs his own gender and sexuality as liberated from

J. Wilkinson · B. J. Dunlop (✉)
University of Manchester, Manchester, UK
e-mail: brendan.dunlop@manchester.ac.uk

T. Carter
University of Leeds, Leeds, UK

N. A. Livingston et al. (eds.), *Addressing Minority Stress and Enhancing Resilience with Diverse LGBTQ+ Clients*, CBT: Science Into Practice,
https://doi.org/10.1007/978-3-031-92836-9_12

mainstream binary views of sexuality and gender, emphasising the importance of Queer Theory. He works in the National Health Service offering therapy to adults with severe and enduring mental health difficulties.

Dr. Brendan J Dunlop is a white gay cisgender man, Consultant Clinical Psychologist, author, lecturer, and researcher. Brendan is based in the United Kingdom, and his research mainly centres on bisexual mental health, in particular the relationship between bisexuality and self-injury behaviour. Brendan approaches research, teaching and lecturing on LGBTQ+ mental health from a political perspective; that is, LGBTQ+ mental health is inherently tied to cultural, political, and societal discourse, policy and law. He is the author of The Queer Mental Health Workbook (Dunlop, 2022), which is the first resource of its kind specifically designed to support LGBTQ+ people with their own mental health and wellbeing.

Introduction

This chapter will explore anti-bisexual prejudice and monosexism (see Table 12.1) and consider this in the context of the therapeutic environment. Key theoretical considerations for working with bisexual people will be presented, including the importance of understanding socially created narratives in the context of informing the ways in which bisexual people make sense of their internal worlds. Ways of enhancing therapeutic practice and an illustrative clinical vignette are also presented. This chapter specifically focuses on bisexual clients; while much of the content is likely relevant to clients who use other labels to describe multi-gender attractions (e.g., pansexual, queer, fluid), there may be differences as well (see Galupo, 2020).

Bisexuality has been defined in various ways over time. It is important to acknowledge that identifying as bisexual can mean many things to different people. A good definition for encompassing various personal definitions is ‘sexual and/or romantic attraction to more than one sex or gender’. However, there is variability in the sexes and genders various bisexual people are attracted to.

Within the context of a society in which monosexism is prevalent, bisexuality can be understood as identifying with and behaving in ways that differ from societal norms and expectations of both heterosexuality and monosexism. Additionally, some bisexual people might identify with a gender that does not conform to the gender binary, or their sex assigned at birth. Consequently, this places one in a position of greater vulnerability to social erasure and oppression.

Table 12.1 Glossary of terms

Monosexuality	Romantic or sexual attraction to members of one sex or gender only (typically heterosexual, gay or lesbian).
Monosexism	Social assumption or belief that monosexuality is superior.
Bi-erasure	Social assumption or belief that only monosexuality exists, excluding bisexual experiences and identities.

Over the last decade, the increased visibility of bisexual people in academic research has unveiled their disproportionate risk of poor physical and mental health outcomes (e.g., Cross et al., 2023; Dunlop et al., 2020; Feinstein & Dyar, 2017). This includes higher risk of anxiety and mood disorders, suicidality, self-injury, long-term health conditions and substance use. However, research focussing on bisexual people's specific experiences and treatment needs is significantly under-represented, particularly research on adapting therapy and the therapy process. This backdrop makes the writing of a practical chapter on working with bisexual people in therapy a difficult task, relying a great deal on speculation from the research we do have of bisexual people's experiences, particularly of social oppression. A great deal of implications can be taken from the literature on Queer Theory (Butler, 1990), which proposes that both sexuality and gender norms are socially constructed thus vary across historical and cultural contexts. Queer Theory can help therapists and bisexual people in therapy to understand the social contexts in which they exist, including understanding concepts such as bi-erasure. However, it can become more difficult to apply to therapy, particularly when people in therapy (or therapists alike) have not come to understand gender and sexuality as socially constructed. Additionally, whilst Queer Theory is congruent with definitions of bisexuality which understand sex/gender identity as existing outside of binary definitions, it struggles to conceptualise bisexual people who define their sexuality according to an exclusive gender binary (Feldman, 2009).

The Minority Stress Theory (MST), first applied to sexual minority groups by Virginia Brooks in 1981 and later applied to gender minorities (Testa et al., 2015), helps to explain a potential pathway to this increased risk of poorer health outcomes (Meyer, 1995; Meyer, 2003). It suggests that unique stressors give rise to hypervigilance and the internalisation of prejudice or negative societal attitudes which contributes to this disparity in health outcomes. For people who are attracted to more than one gender, these unique stressors, such as bi-negativity, may come from heterosexual people as well as from within the queer community (Pachankis et al., 2020a; Feinstein et al., 2020). Work by Israel and Mohr in 2004 highlighted attitudes towards bisexual people which are rooted in monosexism, the belief that people can only be gay or heterosexual, and stereotypes about bisexual people. For instance, the belief that bisexual people are "just confused" about their sexuality, are only bisexual to maintain their heterosexual privilege and are promiscuous and unfaithful. These attitudes and beliefs can lead to microaggressions and verbal or non-verbal messages that reinforce these stereotypes, such as people questioning the validity of a bisexual person's identity or their loyalty (Bostwick & Hequembourg, 2014). For instance, asking whether bisexual individuals are "in transition" to being gay, describing them as "halfway out of the closet", or not wanting to date them for fear of them cheating. Unsurprisingly, these experiences of biphobia are associated with increased psychological distress, and bisexual individuals may develop a heightened sense of anxiety in anticipation of further biphobic experiences (Doan Van et al., 2019; Meyer, 2003).

This double discrimination and stigma can make it difficult for bisexual people to feel a sense of connectedness and community to either the LGBTQ+ or heterosexual communities, therefore leading to social isolation (McLean, 2008). If bisexual people become socially isolated, they are less visible in society which perpetuates bi-erasure and continues the societal narrative that sexuality exists as a binary. The internalisation of heterosexism and double discrimination can mean that bisexual people choose to conceal their identity, perhaps to mitigate the unique stressors they face, or to align themselves with one side of the sexuality binary (i.e., gay or heterosexual) to be accepted into those spaces or communities. Bisexual people may do this intentionally by code switching–that is, changing gestures, body language, clothing and other forms of non-verbal communication, to imitate the dominant culture in social settings where they feel uncomfortable communicating their bisexual identity (Winn, 2021). Unfortunately, in a society that naturally favours a binary, identity concealment may also come in the form of being ascribed a sexual orientation based on the gender of one's current partner and choosing not to correct it. Although there may be some perceived benefits to identity concealment (i.e., mitigation of prejudice and access to community support), doing so prevents people from living in line with their authentic selves, is associated with negative mental health outcomes, and is detrimental to overall health (Pachankis et al., 2020b). Given the unique stressors bisexual people face, it follows that they are reported to conceal their identity more than their gay/lesbian peers which, again, means they may be less visible, thus contributing to bi-erasure within society.

In general, psychotherapy practitioners tend to have greater social privilege than the people with whom they work. Of course, it would be unreasonable to expect psychotherapists to fully understand the lived experience of all marginalised groups, especially intersectional and idiosyncratic experiences. However, greater awareness of the causes of oppression of marginalised groups can help us as therapists from perpetuating social problems. This is paramount as psychotherapy has been criticised for perpetuating social inequality through its own discourse of problems being located, and resolved, within individuals (Greenleaf & Bryant, 2012). Additionally, such awareness might even help us to build insight with people in therapy into the causes of their distress, or even begin to build more resilient internal experiences in our bisexual clients against the social contexts in which they exist. Many people in therapy present believing that they are the problem, struggling to locate the cause of their distress as external to them; Although, it is worth recognising that cognitive and/or behavioural processes can inadvertently perpetuate the client's core problem(s). Beginning to disrupt this might involve locating the 'problem' within its social context, building new beliefs or stories based on positive self-worth, rather than oppressive experience, or encouraging engagement with less oppressive, safer aspects of the world. When considering how to work with bisexual people in therapy there is a need to recognise that the social context of being a bisexual person within a monosexist, heteronormative, cissexist world creates significant predisposing and perpetuating factors in their mental lives.

In any person-centred Cognitive Behavioural Therapy, it is helpful for psychotherapists to establish the systems around a person that may be contributing to their difficulties, and this can be done without making assumptions about a person's experiences. Bronfenbrenner's (2005) Ecological Systems Model (Fig. 12.1;

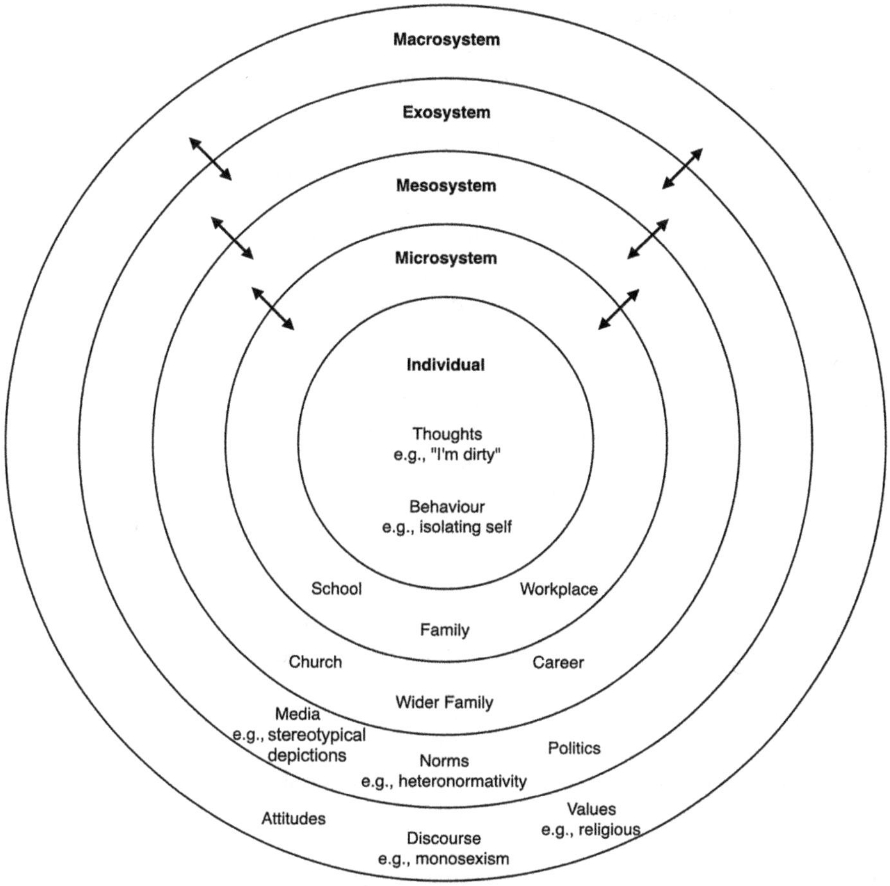

Fig. 12.1 Ecological Systems Model. Adapted from Bronfenbrenner (2005) and informed by Dunlop (2022). Each system influences and is influenced by the others. Each circle of influence can impact upon a bisexual person's mental health in a variety of different ways, and some bisexual-specific examples are included above

informed by Dunlop, 2022) outlines the ways in which various levels of society influence a person in therapy. Whilst this is not strictly a cognitive-behavioural model, it has implications for the ways in which cognition and behaviour can be influenced by the external world. The largest structure represented in the model is the macrosystem. The macrosystem represents societal attitudes and values. Now, it is well known and understood that LGBTQ+ populations exist within a context of societal attitudes of monosexism, homophobia, transphobia, and misogyny. Whilst it is true that early life experiences can form core beliefs and rules for living that can perpetuate mental health difficulties, it can be damaging to ignore the wider messages and experiences that also trigger and perpetuate these difficulties. An acknowledgement and validation of these experiences that is weaved into the seams of therapy can be a really powerful, and crucial, therapeutic tool.

Thinkers who take a more systemic view, considering intersectionality, social privileges, and their effects on the psyche, often relate internal cognition to social context, including external discourse, in which a person lives. Post-structural thinkers, such as Foucault (1972), have defined discourse as the various social systems which create meaning itself, influenced by the attitudes and values of those in power (dominant discourses). A variety of dominant and alternative discourses exist socially, though dominant discourses are relied upon more regularly by people when constructing meaning. Taking this holistic viewpoint, it becomes clear that anti-bisexual prejudice and monosexism can be understood and represented within dominant discourses in which the lives of bisexual people are understood by themselves and others.

Bisexual people, particularly bisexual men or trans/nonbinary bisexual people, have been largely invisible and/or invalidated in exosystems, such as societal discourse and the media (Glaad Media Institute, 2023). This has been traced back to the emergence of early definitions of sexuality, in which sexuality was seen as a binary in which people are categorised as gay/lesbian or heterosexual (Hayfield, 2020). Such definitions manifest little understanding or representation of people who might otherwise be defined as outside of this binary. This binary understanding of sexuality has been elaborated and replicated by biological, psychological, and social explanations of sexuality in which the concept of a 'bisexual' has been largely invisible. It is tempting here to assume that this is because bisexual people simply have not existed, at least openly, once again placing the blame on them. However, evidence suggests this is not the case; bisexuality has existed throughout history, despite being largely underrepresented (Shaw, 2022). Where there are bisexual representations, these are often misrepresentations of the bisexual experience, built on harmful stereotypes (Johnson, 2016). For example, of bisexuals as immoral, or mysticised. The 1914 movie *'A Florida Enchantment'* is the first known film representation of bisexuality. Constructing a bisexual experience as an *'enchantment'* implies that it occurs in the context of an external, magical influence. Thus, implying a lack of validity.

In more mainstream representations of bisexuality, bisexual people are often understood through prejudiced discourse, such as being regarded as promiscuous, dishonest, or denying of their bisexuality (i.e., that they are really gay or lesbian). For example, when a character on Sex and the City finds out her partner is bisexual, she says "I'm not even sure bisexuality exists, I think it's just a layover on the way to Gay Town" (Parker & Thomas, 2000).

Common misperceptions of bisexuality have also been reported in the literature. For example, Hayfield et al. (2014) interviewed 20 bisexual women about their marginalisation. The bisexual women interviewed reported common cultural misunderstandings of bisexuality, including:

1. Bisexuality is an attention-seeking strategy for women to attract men;
2. Bisexuality is a temporary developmental phase and bisexual people are unable to commit to an identity;

3. Bisexual people are confused, cowardly, and unable to commit to LGBTQ+ communities;
4. Bisexual people are sex-obsessed, promiscuous, and unable to commit to monogamous relationships;
5. Bisexual people are greedy.

Living amongst prejudiced discourse about one's identity will inevitably affect people. If a bisexual person believes or identifies with these discourses, they might struggle to develop new perspectives of themselves outside of them. To manage this, they may suppress their bisexuality, or seek out pride-affirming discourse, such as from the queer community. Seeking acceptance from the queer community is not risk-free and might inadvertently create fractures within a variety of bisexual people's support systems, particularly as bisexuality is not the only part of one's identity. For example, if they previously had positive relationships with mesosystems, such as anti-LGBTQ+ family, religious communities, and professional networks. This is particularly difficult for men, whose male friends often perpetuate homophobia through discourse, leaving bisexual men with the choice between suppressing their sexuality, losing friends, or contending with the dissonance between these prejudicial attitudes and their sense of self. Instead, many bisexual people, particularly men, choose to conceal their bisexual identity and exclusively date women. Doing so can create internal dissonance between parts of themselves, lead to feeling isolated, and inadvertently expose them to biphobic discourse, which can take a toll on their mental health.

This indicates that this problem is a social one which a bisexual client may choose to avoid, as they may be used to appearing monosexual and face erasure or oppression when not. Therefore, it is important for the therapist to normalise and affirm bisexuality within the therapeutic relationship and remain open to potential bisexuality throughout therapy. This might sound unusual; however, it is not uncommon for bisexual people to be assumed to be either exclusively heterosexual or exclusively gay/lesbian in therapy, particularly if they have only referred to sexual and/or romantic attraction to one gender, without referencing another.

Bisexuality and Gender

Gender is of course one of the many intersectional identities by which bisexual people might vary. It is the one which will be discussed in more depth here for two reasons. First, gender is a concept which like bisexuality is affected by a dominating binary-based discourse of gender. Secondly, it is an area of expertise for the authors contributing to this chapter. However, it is important to state that gender is no more or less important or impactful than other elements of diversity across the bisexual population, of which there are many—too extensive indeed to fully cover in a single chapter.

We recognise that whilst dominant and inherent to some people's experiences of their bisexuality, a binary view of gender is deeply flawed and invalidating for many people's lived experience of gender. However, we shall first consider disparities between broadly bisexual men and women first. Whilst bisexual men and women typically define themselves using the same (broad) definitions of bisexuality, the way in which bisexual men and bisexual women are seen by society is vastly different. Bisexual behaviour in women is typically fetishized (particularly by heterosexual men), albeit through discourse which objectifies women's bodies and sexuality as being for male pleasure and for the male gaze. Conversely, bisexual behaviour in men is typically feared and perceived as to be avoided. A prominent example of this was during the HIV/AIDS epidemic in which bisexual men were constructed in the media as carriers of the disease from men to women. This construction creates prejudice today, with many members of the public thinking bisexual people are more likely to transmit HIV than heterosexual people, despite this being untrue (Dodge et al., 2016). McCormack and Anderson (2014a, 2014b) describe the concept of 'homohysteria', in which men express fear that being thought of as gay would pose a risk to their masculinity. Consequently, they defensively protect them being seen as masculine by avoiding anything which might be perceived as gay, including bisexuality. This creates a social context in which it is incredibly difficult to be both bisexual and be seen as male/masculine, particularly in the eyes of heterosexual men. His matters as men's voices continue to dominate discourse (e.g., in politics, business, the media, etc.). Perhaps making sense of these competing social narratives and how they limit clients' engagement with different parts of themselves (e.g., both their bisexuality and masculinity) would make a suitable goal in a cognitive behavioural therapy for bisexual men. Of course, albeit a less-dominant view, a non-binary view of gender allows for more fluidity between two (or several) genders. Such alternative frameworks for understanding gender, for example those found in Queer Theory and the writings of Judith Butler (Butler, 1990), can help both clinicians and people in therapy to redefine their identity. This could be done in accordance with their lived experience, and within the context of more or less influential discourses of gender. Alternative conceptualisations, drawing on Queer Theory, can support all gender and sexuality diversity by offering non-normative conceptualisations of expression. Whilst this work is typically outside of the reading of a psychotherapist, it is undoubtedly important for psychotherapists working with people in therapy who identify according to societally non-dominant genders and sexualities, including those who describe their bisexuality using these terms.

Affirmative Practice in Therapy

Affirmative practice is a way to enhance an existing model of treatment by acknowledging and validating the impact of systemic factors (such as monosexism, biphobia and bi-erasure), promoting self-acceptance and positive identity, and enhancing coping and strengths. Of the affirmative interventions literature in the past two decades, only three papers have explored whether the efficacy differs by sexual orientation (Craig et al., 2012; Craig et al., 2014; Craig & Furman, 2018). These three papers explored two interventions: ASSET (Affirmative Supportive Safe and Empowering Talk) and Strengths First. ASSET is a school-based group intervention, offering an affirmative context for young LGBTQ+ people to discuss a range of issues whilst promoting their strengths and coping. Strengths First is a strengths-based care coordination model for LGBTQ+ young people, offering a one-to-one care coordination intervention to promote strengths, self-efficacy, and overall well being. Whilst not strictly psychotherapy, these interventions yielded similar benefits for bisexual individuals compared to other LGBTQ+ participants in the studies, suggesting that we can draw from the affirmative therapy literature, albeit tentatively, to consider how to culturally apply or adapt CBT for bisexual individuals. This is particularly important when considering that some studies of interventions which were not adapted for LGBTQ+ people found that bisexual people may have worse treatment outcomes than both heterosexual and lesbian/gay people (Crawford et al., 2016; Rimes et al., 2018).

Misunderstanding or misrepresentation of the sexuality of a person in therapy is likely to impact the therapeutic relationship. There are several things that psychotherapists can do to adapt therapy to make it affirmative for bisexual individuals, and thus increase the quality of the therapeutic relationship. First and foremost, it is important to establish the extent to which a person's sexual orientation is linked to their reason for seeking support. Experiences cannot be assumed based on their sexual orientation, or any other single aspect of their identity. For some people, internalised biphobia may be driving low self-esteem and thus contributing to mental health problems; this may take some careful assessment and tentative guided discovery to identify and understand. For others, bisexuality could be a resilience factor which is unrelated to the difficulties they are facing. For example, somebody's sexuality may be a characteristic that is embraced by themselves and those around them, and may form a core part of their positive sense of self. As with any psychotherapeutic alliance, time should be taken to get to know and understand an individual's experiences through a holistic, person-centred lens. Therapists who assume monosexuality are likely to inadvertently limit the likelihood of their client feeling comfortable challenging this, given it is such a prevalent discourse. It is undoubtable that the therapeutic relationship is of paramount importance to the effectiveness of therapy, with feelings of being understood characteristic of effective therapy.

Suggestions have been published for how CBT can be adapted for sexual minority youth (Craig et al., 2013; Nakamura et al., 2022; Proujansky & Pachankis; 2014), some of which may be novel to affirmative practice, and some of which should be applied principles regardless of the client but are particularly important with this client group. Consolidated and applied to bisexual people in Table 12.2, they act as a helpful guide or starting point for ensuring therapy is affirmative:

Clinical Vignette

The following vignette is a fictitious case example that consists of an amalgamation of the similar experiences of numerous previous clients.

Jamie (he/him) is a 32-year-old White cisgender man, living in Hull in the East Riding of Yorkshire. Jamie grew up in Hull in the North of England, and had recently moved back, after he spent the previous 14 years living in Camden, North London. Jamie is bisexual and had been in relationships with men and women, and had been living with his boyfriend of 2 years, Antonio.

Jamie has a mother, Christine, and stepfather, Tony. Jamie's birth father (Ian) left the family unit when he was 10 years old and has not maintained contact with him. When Jamie was younger, he was described by friends and family as an 'effeminate young lad', and he had interests in school related to tennis, musical theatre and tap dance. Jamie is an only child, and after completing high school in Hull, he went to study contemporary dance in central London. Jamie did not tell anyone about his bisexuality whilst in Hull, though many people asked him if he was gay whilst growing up. Jamie recalled feeling embarrassed and anxious whenever the prospect of dating, or romantic relationships, came up in conversation.

When Jamie first arrived in London aged 18, he had a traumatic experience following a night out drinking with friends. He was spiked in a night club (had drugs unknowingly put into his drink) and woke up in a stranger's house, and it was evident he had been sexually assaulted. The perpetrator of this assault was a 52-year-old man, who told Jamie when he woke up that Jamie 'really enjoyed it' and was 'all over him' in the club. Jamie did not report this to the police.

Jamie dated women publicly at university, though had sex with men in private. Jamie felt unable to share his bisexuality with friends, even though he had several close friends male friends who were bisexual themselves. Jamie wanted to join his friends when they attended LGBTQ+ socials, but felt he was "not bisexual enough", because of his publicly-facing relationships with women. After finishing university, Jamie's most invested relationship was with a woman called Amina; they were together for 6 years. They had started discussions around starting a family, and getting married, though Jamie had become 'withdrawn' after these conversations.

Ultimately, this ended with Jamie breaking up with Amina, telling her that he felt he had to 'work on himself' before he could fully commit to her. Jamie is now in a relationship with a man called Antonio, though Antonio thinks Jamie is gay, and Jamie has never corrected him, and has never disclosed dating women previously. Jamie thinks it is too late in their relationship now to tell him and worries that Antonio will leave him if he does share his sexuality with him.

Jamie experiences hypervigilance, anxiety, flashbacks, and low mood. He does not think very highly of himself and has recently started scratching his inner thigh. Jamie says that this helps remind him where he is when he becomes hypervigilant, or when he experiences a flashback, though sometimes he notices that when he is very anxious or angry, he begins to scratch his legs too. It is important to assess each of these concerns and their relation to past trauma and/or minority stress experiences, as well as the nature and severity to determine if, for instance, scratching or similar coping strategies are self-injurious (as illustrated below).

Table 12.2 Bi-affirmative adaptations

Adaptation	Bi-specific example
Validate the impact of minority stress on mental health	Acknowledge and address the impact of biphobia, heterosexism and monosexism on their lived experiences, including feelings of guilt and shame, fears of negative evaluation, self-silencing and identity concealment.
Identify and validate personal and unique strengths	This could include asking clients to list positive feelings about identifying as bisexual, discussing their favourite bisexual cultural icons, or identifying positive traits about other bisexual people they know. Moving from acceptance of identity to embracing identity. Examples can be taken from the previous point, e.g., using how they have overcome or withstood experiences of discrimination to draw out personal strengths.
Help to identify and build supportive relationships and support networks	This should include identifying the client's chosen and biological family, informal supports, formal peer supports, community groups, and events or rituals that help celebrate their identity. Also, particularly where social support is lacking, supporting individuals to build supportive connections and relationships, such as community groups or bisexual-specific groups or organisations.
Ensure that homework assignments are congruent with the client's culture and current circumstances	Between-session therapeutic tasks should align with the individual's personal experience. For instance, if a client has not "come out" to their family or friends, they may not be comfortable accessing bisexual-specific supports or groups to foster social connectedness, and the function of this exercise should be considered and applied to a more appropriate task, e.g., spending time with a friend/ally.
Empower assertive communication	Assertiveness training can be a core part of CBT. Empowering clients to advocate for themselves and express their feelings and needs comfortably without significant anxiety can have significant benefits, particularly with difficulties such as low self-esteem, identity concealment, internalised biphobia, or people-pleasing tendencies. This may be applied to conversations in which monosexuality is assumed and a client wants to challenge this or correct somebody regarding their sexuality but feels unable to.
Facilitate emotion awareness, regulation, and acceptance	Internalised societal messages may lead clients to feel like their natural feelings are "wrong" and therefore not to be trusted. For example, questioning their sexuality because of the dominant societal narrative around monosexuality. Therefore, clinicians may support clients to identify, accept and regulate their emotions with healthy expressions of emotion. Mindfulness and mood-labelling exercises may be helpful, as well as creative expressions of emotions such as expressive writing.
Decrease avoidance	Clinicians may support clients to decrease avoidance of accessing supportive spaces or sharing parts of themselves with others. For example, clients may wish to access LGBTQ+ spaces but may avoid this due to not feeling "queer enough". This should be done carefully and driven by the client, ensuring that clients are making these decisions. Encouragement and motivational interviewing may be helpful to support the client to understand whether they want to engage in certain activities, however the safety of the client should also be considered.

(continued)

Table 12.2 (continued)

Adaptation	Bi-specific example
Restructure minority stress cognitions	Bisexual individuals may hold cognitions about themselves based on internalised biphobia or monosexism, therefore identification of this through guided discovery can be helpful to empower clients to gain critical distance from some of these thoughts. Their identified personal strengths may be used to generate some cognitive flexibility.
Distinguish between problems that are environmental and those that stem from unhelpful thinking patterns	For bisexual people for whom biphobic discrimination or family rejection may be impacting their well being, it would be invalidating and dismissive to suggest that they challenge or restructure thoughts about their external circumstances. Alternatives to thought challenging here may be more helpful, such as techniques in compassion Focussed therapy (CFT) or acceptance and commitment therapy (ACT). For environmental or systemic problems and consequential thoughts, it would be more appropriate to question the helpfulness of the thought/belief rather than the validity. Then, support the client to make changes that decrease stress and increase personal supports and strengths.
Consider positive social action as a contributor to social change	Whilst the onus should not be on minoritized groups to drive social change, individuals could be supported to consider how to engage in activism or advocacy to use their skills to promote and encourage social change. For example, supporting bisexual organisations and campaigns, or advocating for more inclusivity.

Countering Anti-Bisexual Prejudice and Monosexism in the Clinical Vignette of Jamie

Considerations for formulation development and treatment planning for Jamie should adopt an affirmative, systemic, and strengths-based perspective. Consideration and integration of context ('systemic' ideas) alongside CBT-specific models, is important. What follows is a Systemic-informed CBT formulation, based on the circles of influence (Bronfenbrenner, 2005; Dunlop, 2022; Dunlop & Lea, 2023) and Padesky and Mooney's (1990) 'hot cross bun' model (that is, an understanding of a person's difficulties which considers the systems around the individual, and their related thoughts, feelings, behaviours and physiology), to demonstrate how principles discussed in this chapter can be applied to a client. A diagrammatic formulation is presented for Jamie's experiences in Fig. 12.2, with a narrative explanation of this formulation following.

Prominent narratives in Jamie's life connect to masculinity, and what it means to be a man, and monosexuality. From a young age he had been labelled 'effeminate' by those around him, and there is an assumption of homosexuality within his current relationship with Antonio. There is also perhaps a narrative connected to heritage and place of birth, whereby in British culture being 'Northern' has connotations of being strong, gritty, working class and poorer than 'Southern' counterparts. It may therefore be tricky for Jamie to reconcile numerous aspects of his ascribed identity which seem to be at odds with his feelings, especially his bisexuality and

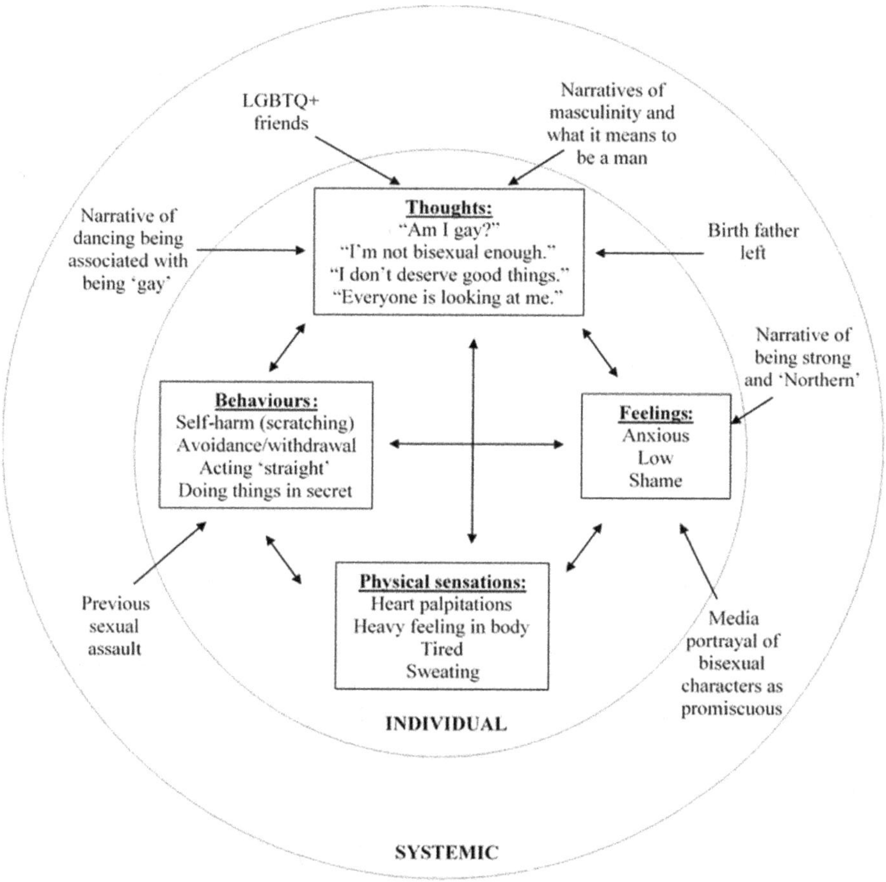

Fig. 12.2 Jamie's developing psychological formulation. Adapted from Bronfenbrenner (2005) and informed by Dunlop (2022) and Padesky and Mooney (1990)

the very binary-focussed world he finds himself in. Coupled with his experience of sexual assault at university, at a time when young people are still developing and figuring out their identity, it is unsurprising that this may have exacerbated Jamie's feelings of internalised biphobia and self-blame ("I must have wanted to have sex with him, because maybe I am just gay"; "I hate myself for not just being gay or straight like everyone else"). Resulting feelings of shame were reinforced by the double life Jamie was leading; dating women in public and having sex with men in private, further solidifying the position that the synthesis of sexual and/or romantic relationships with men and women was not possible. Perhaps the fixation of keeping these parts of his identity separate led to intense feelings of anxiety, and certain hypervigilant behaviours (such as watching people carefully to make sure they did not 'discover' his secret life). Withdrawing from relationships, friendships and previously enjoyed activities was one way to manage these intense anxiety sensations. Whilst this decreased the hypervigilant behaviour, Jamie was not engaging in any pleasurable or enjoyable activities, and hence became low in mood. When he did leave the house, his hypervigilance seemed to be a lot worse; to the point where he thought other people were staring at him, almost as if they could 'sense' Jamie was bisexual, which perpetuated his worry about the fact that he had not told Antonio about his sexuality, and solidified the fact that telling him was not the right thing to do. Jamie had not found space to vocalise his true feelings or identity, nor embrace this with safe people, internalising the fact that he is not deserving of this, and his feelings of low mood, anxiety and shame remain in his life. Jamie was, however, very athletic and a very talented dancer. Whilst Jamie had moved back to Hull, he was often contacted by friends and ex-colleagues in London to come and perform with them. He did not always take up this invitation, despite the fact that Antonio thought this would give them a good excuse to have a weekend away together.

A Bisexual-Affirmative CBT Intervention

Whilst socialising Jamie to the CBT model, attention was brought to Jamie's cognitions that were likely influenced by minority stress, such as "I am not bisexual enough". Naming the development of these as perhaps originating through distal stressors, such as media portrayal of bisexuality, or probing questions about sexuality from friends, provided Jamie with an alternative perspective to attribute blame for this elsewhere. Jamie may have had few positive representations of bisexuality in his life, so sourcing this in external media may be a good starting point (and perhaps a between session task for Jamie) to witness positive bisexual representation.

Some of Jamie's behaviours have been driven by shame, such as withdrawal, avoidance, and keeping information/behaviours to himself. A mood diary is a helpful starting point to understand the temporal relationship between shame, physical sensation, and behaviour, with the aim of helping Jamie understand, name, and encourage self-reflection when feelings occur. Highlighting the reinforcing nature of shame-based behaviours is likely to help Jamie develop motivation to break this. Once Jamie was more able to recognise his shame feelings, he was able to try to do something different. An affirmative CBT intervention for bisexual people must crucially understand the individual's context, and within this, what is and is not behaviourally possible. At this stage of Jamie's therapeutic journey, encouraging him to break his shame cycle by telling people about his bisexuality may not be clinically useful, nor clinically safe, if his immediate home/hometown environments are not conducive to sharing this. Whilst this may be a useful goal to work towards, if Jamie would like to do this, a more realistic CBT technique may be a self-affirmation exercise. After Jamie began to recognise some of his thoughts as being influenced by earlier minority stress, and after engaging with some alternative experiences of positive bisexual representation, Jamie was supported to develop a list of self-affirmation statements that he read to himself when he noticed feeling ashamed. These included "I am bisexual enough" or "There is no right or wrong way to be bisexual" or "Other people having a problem with bisexuality does not mean I have to have a problem with it".

Jamie described experiencing some trauma symptoms, which we may reasonably attribute to the sexual assault he experienced. There is enough evidence to suggest an assessment, and perhaps intervention, for Posttraumatic Stress Disorder (PTSD) would be useful. Flashbacks can be common following a traumatic experience, and techniques aligned to CBT for trauma should be utilised, such as grounding exercises. In working together, it became clear that Jamie scratched himself to stop the flashbacks, though this can obviously have unwanted secondary effects of bleeding, infection, eventual scarring, etc. Helping Jamie to develop alternative grounding techniques, such as the smelling of a fragrance on the sleeve of his jumper, that reassures him he is in the present moment, is an important first step. Hypervigilance and paranoia can also be common experiences following a traumatic event, though if we adopt a minority stress lens, cumulative distal and proximal stressors can reasonably lead a bisexual person to develop hypervigilant thoughts and behaviours. CBT may conceptualise these as 'maladaptive behaviours', though an affirmative position would be to reframe these as necessary safety behaviours. This provides Jamie with a more congruent explanation for their existence and increases the likelihood of continued 'buy-in' to the therapeutic endeavour to source healthier (yet equally as effective) safety-seeking behaviours. Such alternate behaviours could be mindfulness/grounding techniques, connection with others (perhaps contacting a "safe person" or reading something from a loved one) and conscious re-focusing on the present moment.

Jamie is a strong dancer, so it makes sense within our intervention to capitalise on this strength. Jamie was encouraged to utilise movement or dance to process his anxiety or feelings of shame; which could be a type of exposure-based exercise, allowing him to experience threatening emotions in a safer way, that he can do with safe people or in places that he currently avoids, thereby providing opportunities for corrective learning and a decrease in avoidance behaviours.

Other behaviourally based intervention techniques may include ways to decrease Jamie's shame and situate blame where it should be placed. For example, Jamie never reported the sexual assault he experienced whilst at university. Filing a police complaint following sexual assault can be very difficult, and this can be made even more difficult for men following discourses relating to masculinity, power, and responsibility. This is likely only a suggestion that a therapist might make to Jamie after the therapeutic relationship had been established, there was a collaborative understanding (formulation) of Jamie's experiences, and some evidence of change strategies proving successful (to provide further motivation). If Jamie wished to report this, our role as therapists should be to support in this process, perhaps even allowing him to do so on the phone to the police whilst in our session. Unfortunately, nothing might come of the report, though the exercise of reporting itself may be what was needed for Jamie to distance himself from feelings of blame associated with the assault. Other behavioural interventions of this ilk include letter writing, which again serves as an emotion-processing (as well as a valid means of reattributing blame) exercise. Caution should be exercised if using these techniques; clients with internalised and unacknowledged biphobia may use such exercises as opportunities to reinforce negative self-views or inadvertently self-blame, and as such, therapists should be reasonably certain that these exercises will likely disrupt or break reinforcing cycles, rather than inadvertently maintain them.

Jamie's invitations to go to London with friends and ex-colleagues provides an excellent 'in-vivo' opportunity to connect with people, whilst doing something he really enjoys. Such 'behavioural activation' may help lift Jamie's mood, which increases the chance of him wishing to do this again. If Jamie has multiple opportunities to go and see his friends in London, the therapist may suggest that Jamie uses this opportunity to talk to a friend whilst he is there about his sexuality. This allows 'safe sharing' away from his hometown and perhaps away from Antonio, and Jamie would hopefully be met with validation that sharing this was not as scary as he thought it was, hence increasing the chance that he feels able to share this (in his own time, and at his own pace) with others, including Antonio.

Conclusion

This chapter has presented various key theoretical considerations for countering anti-bisexual prejudice and monosexism in therapy. This has included a key focus on the development and maintenance of dominant discourses within society, and how this trickles through into the therapy space. Some intersectional considerations have been provided (namely the intersection between bisexuality and gender), and a clinical vignette has highlighted how practitioners may formulate and subsequently intervene therapeutically with bisexual clients. Future research is needed to continue to explore the efficacy and implementation of bisexual-specific therapies, and bisexual-specific adaptations to current models, to ensure models remain responsive and sensitive, as well as theoretically coherent.

References

Bostwick, W., & Hequembourg, A. (2014). 'Just a little hint': Bisexual-specific microaggressions and their connection to epistemic injustices. *Culture, Health & Sexuality, 16*(5), 488–503.

Bronfenbrenner, U. (2005). Ecological systems theory (1992). In *Making human beings human: Bioecological perspectives on human development* (pp. 106–173). Sage Publications Ltd..

Brooks, V. R. (1981). *Minority stress and lesbian women*. Lexington Books.

Butler, J. (1990). *Gender trouble: Feminism and the subversion of identity*. Routledge.

Craig, S. L., & Furman, E. (2018). Do marginalized youth experience strengths in strengths-based interventions? Unpacking program acceptability through two interventions for sexual and gender minority youth. *Journal of Social Service Research, 44*(2), 168–179. https://doi.org/10.1080/01488376.2018.1436631

Craig, S. L., McInroy, L., Austin, A., Smith, M., & Engle, B. (2012). Promoting self-efficacy and self-esteem for multiethnic sexual minority youth: An evidence-informed intervention. *Journal of Social Service Research, 38*(5), 688–698. https://doi.org/10.1080/01488376.2012.718194

Craig, S. L., Austin, A., & Alessi, E. (2013). Gay affirmative cognitive behavioral therapy for sexual minority youth: A clinical adaptation. *Clinical Social Work Journal, 41*, 258–266. https://doi.org/10.1007/s10615-012-0427-9

Craig, S. L., Austin, A., & McInroy, L. B. (2014). School-based groups to support multiethnic sexual minority youth resiliency: Preliminary effectiveness. *Child and Adolescent Social Work Journal, 31*, 87–106. https://doi.org/10.1007/s10560-013-0311-7

Crawford, M. J., Thana, L., Farquharson, L., Palmer, L., Hancock, E., Bassett, P., Clarke, J., & Parry, G. D. (2016). Patient experience of negative effects of psychological treatment: Results of a national survey. *The British Journal of Psychiatry, 208*(3), 260–265. https://doi.org/10.1192/bjp.bp.114.162628

Cross, H., Bremner, S., Meads, C., Pollard, A., & Llewellyn, C. (2023). Bisexual people experience worse health outcomes in England: Evidence from a Cross-sectional survey in primary care. *The Journal of Sex Research, 1-9*. https://doi.org/10.1080/00224499.2023.2220680

Doan Van, E. E., Mereish, E. H., Woulfe, J. M., & Katz-Wise, S. L. (2019). Perceived discrimination, coping mechanisms, and effects on health in bisexual and other non-monosexual adults. *Archives of Sexual Behavior, 48*(1), 159–174.

Dodge, B., Herbenick, D., Friedman, M. R., Schick, V., Fu, T. J., Bostwick, W., Bartelt, E., Muñoz-Laboy, M., Pletta, D., Reece, M., & Sandfort, T. G. (2016). Attitudes toward bisexual men and women among a nationally representative probability sample of adults in the United States. *PLoS One, 11*(10), e0164430. https://doi.org/10.1371/journal.pone.0164430

Dunlop, B. J., Hartley, S., Oladokun, O. & Taylor, P. (2020). Bisexuality and Non-Suicidal Self-Injury (NSSI): a narrative synthesis of associated variables and a meta-analysis of risk. *Journal of Affective Disorders, 276*, 1159 –1172. https://doi.org/10.1016/j.jad.2020.07.103

Dunlop, B. J. (2022). *The queer mental health workbook: A creative self-help guide using CBT, CFT and DBT*. Jessica Kingsley Publishers.

Dunlop, B. J., & Lea, J. (2023). It's not just in my head: An intersectional, social and systems-based framework in gender and sexuality diversity. *Psychology and Psychotherapy, 96*(1), 1–15. https://doi.org/10.1111/papt.12438

Feinstein, B. A., & Dyar, C. (2017). Bisexuality, minority stress, and health. *Current Sexual Health Reports, 9*, 42–49. https://doi.org/10.1007/s11930-017-0096-3

Feinstein, B. A., Xavier Hall, C. D., Dyar, C., & Davila, J. (2020). Motivations for sexual identity concealment and their associations with mental health among bisexual, pansexual, queer, and fluid (bi+) individuals. *Journal of Bisexuality, 20*(3), 324–341. https://doi.org/10.1080/15299716.2020.1743402

Feldman, S. (2009). Reclaiming sexual difference: What queer theory can't tell us about sexuality. *Journal of Bisexuality, 9*(3–4), 259–278. https://doi.org/10.1080/15299710903316562

Foucault, M. (1972). *The archaeology of knowledge and the discourse on language* (A. M. S. Smith, Trans.). Tavistock Publications Limited.

Galupo, M. P. (2020). Mental health for individuals with pansexual and queer identities. In E. D. Rothblum (Ed.), *The Oxford handbook of sexual and gender minority mental health* (pp. 331–342). Oxford University Press.

Glaad Media Institute. (2023). *Where we are on TV report 2022–2023*.

Greenleaf, A. T., & Bryant, R. M. (2012). Perpetuating oppression: Does the current counseling discourse neutralize social action? *Journal for Social Action in Counseling & Psychology, 4*(1), 18–29.

Hayfield, N. (2020). *Bisexual and pansexual identities: Exploring and challenging invisibility and invalidation* (1st ed.). https://doi.org/10.4324/9780429464362

Hayfield, N., Clarke, V., & Halliwell, E. (2014). Bisexual women's understandings of social marginalisation: 'The heterosexuals don't understand us but nojohnr do the lesbians'. *Feminism & Psychology, 24*(3), 352–372. https://doi.org/10.1177/0959353514539651

Israel, T., & Mohr, J. J. (2004). Attitudes toward bisexual women and men: Current research, future directions. *Journal of Bisexuality, 4*(1–2), 117–134.

Johnson, H. J. (2016). Bisexuality, mental health, and media representation. *Journal of Bisexuality, 16*(3), 378–396. https://doi.org/10.1080/15299716.2016.1168335

McCormack, M., & Anderson, E. (2014a). Homohysteria: Definitions, context and intersectionality. *Sex Roles, 71*, 152–158. https://doi.org/10.1007/s11199-014-0401-9

McCormack, M., & Anderson, E. (2014b). The influence of declining homophobia on men's gender in the United States: An argument for the study of Homohysteria. *Sex Roles, 71*(3), 109–120. https://doi.org/10.1007/s11199-014-0358-8

McLean, K. (2008). Inside, outside, nowhere: Bisexual men and women in the gay and lesbian community. *Journal of Bisexuality, 8*(1–2), 63–80. https://doi.org/10.1080/15299710802143174

Meyer, I. H. (1995). Minority stress and mental health in gay men. *Journal of Health and Social Behavior, 36*(1), 38–56. https://doi.org/10.2307/2137286

Meyer, I. H. (2003). Prejudice, social stress, and mental health in lesbian, gay, and bisexual populations: Conceptual issues and research evidence. *Psychological Bulletin, 129*(5), 674–697. https://doi.org/10.1037/0033-2909.129.5.674

Nakamura, N., Dispenza, F., Abreu, R. L., Ollen, E. W., Pantalone, D. W., Canillas, G., Gormley, B., & Vencill, J. A. (2022). The APA guidelines for psychological practice with sexual minority persons: An executive summary of the 2021 revision. *American Psychologist, 77*(8), 953–962. https://doi.org/10.1037/amp0000939

Pachankis, J. E., Clark, K. A., Burton, C. L., Hughto, J. M. W., Bränström, R., & Keene, D. E. (2020a). Sex, status, competition, and exclusion: Intraminority stress from within the gay community and gay and bisexual men's mental health. *Journal of Personality and Social Psychology, 119*(3), 713. https://doi.org/10.1037/pspp0000282

Pachankis, J. E., Mahon, C. P., Jackson, S. D., Fetzner, B. K., & Bränström, R. (2020b). Sexual orientation concealment and mental health: A conceptual and meta-analytic review. *Psychological Bulletin, 146*(10), 831–871. https://doi.org/10.1037/bul0000271

Padesky, C. A., & Mooney, K. A. (1990). Clinical tip: Presenting the cognitive model to clients. *International Cognitive Therapy Newsletter, 6*, 13–14. Available from https://www.padesky.com/clinical-corner/publications

Parker, S. J. (Producer) & Thomas, P. (Director). (2000). *Sex and the city*. [Television Broadcast].

Proujansky, R. A., & Pachankis, J. E. (2014). Toward formulating evidence-based principles of LGB-affirmative psychotherapy. *Pragmatic Case Studies in Psychotherapy: PCSP, 10*(2), 117. https://doi.org/10.14713/pcsp.v10i2.1854

Rimes, K. A., Broadbent, M., Holden, R., Rahman, Q., Hambrook, D., Hatch, S. L., & Wingrove, J. (2018). Comparison of treatment outcomes between lesbian, gay, bisexual and heterosexual individuals receiving a primary care psychological intervention. *Behavioural and Cognitive Psychotherapy, 46*(3), 332–349. https://doi.org/10.1017/S1352465817000583

Shaw, J. (2022). *Bi: The hidden culture, history and science of bisexuality*. Canongate Books.

Testa, R. J., Habarth, J., Peta, J., Balsam, K., & Bockting, W. (2015). Development of the gender minority stress and resilience measure. *Psychology of Sexual Orientation and Gender Diversity, 2*(1), 65–77. https://doi.org/10.1037/sgd0000081

Winn, B. (2021). *Pass/codes: Code switching for survival* (Doctoral dissertation). University of North Carolina at Greensboro).

Chapter 13
Supporting Asexual- and Aromantic-Spectrum Individuals in Therapy: Challenging Community-Specific Hardships and Compulsory Sexuality and Romanticism

Caroline Bauer

Highlights

Asexuality and aromanticism are two distinct identities and communities with considerable overlap. This chapter will work to recognize their independence from one another and how individuals can be both. Each are on spectrums that can layer with many other aspects of queer identity. This chapter will outline:

- Definitions and descriptions of what asexuality and aromanticism are, and examples of lived experiences.
- Intersectional lenses that affect each community, specifically gender, race, and other LGBTQIA (lesbian, gay, bisexual, trans, queer, intersex, asexual/aromantic/agender) identities.
- Challenges people on the asexual spectrum (ace) and aromantic spectrum (aro) face, particularly around minority stress or not conforming to societal and relationship expectations, and the stress of masking their identities or pushing themselves to conform.
- How to be supportive of someone who identifies as ace or aro as a therapist.

Positionality

I am a self-identified ace therapist working in Affirmative and Relational Therapy, a Licensed Clinical Social Worker (LCSW), an ace community organizer, founder of Aces NYC, a member of the Ace Community Survey Team, and an ace researcher. My identity has drawn many ace and aro clients to my therapeutic practice, which has also allowed me to run therapeutic ace identity exploration groups. As a white,

C. Bauer (✉)
Bauer Therapy; The Ace Community Survey Team; Aces NYC, Brooklyn, NY, USA

N. A. Livingston et al. (eds.), *Addressing Minority Stress and Enhancing Resilience with Diverse LGBTQ+ Clients*, CBT: Science Into Practice,
https://doi.org/10.1007/978-3-031-92836-9_13

mostly cis, mostly able bodied woman with experience in polyamory, this chapter includes content informed by my own experience as well as the experiences others have shared with me. While there is a limited but growing presence of published research and reports on asexuality, research and publications on aromanticism is much more limited. Some of the institutional knowledge in this chapter comes from being engrained in these communities for over a decade but is not yet in publications. This chapter aims to provide an introduction to affirming therapy with ace and aro clients. However, it only addresses a small slice of the diversity within each community, and there is hope for entire therapeutic books on each aromanticism and asexuality separately in the future.

Introduction

The spectrums for each asexuality and aromanticism follow a similar base structure, with tremendous diversity that has bloomed out of them (see Table 13.1). Whereas asexuality is most often described as a "lack of sexual attraction," there are those who have experienced sexual attraction, but have no interest in having sex, who still use the term asexual. Aromanticism follows a similar frame with "not experiencing romantic attraction." From there, the most standard related terms are gray and demi. Gray relates to the colloquial gray area, something nearby to asexuality or aromanticism. That could include infrequent experiences of attraction, very low intensity, a preference to not engage in that way, along with a variety of other experiences.

A demi modifier indicates additional intersections and specificity. It requires an emotional connection before sexuality or romanticism can emerge. Instead of, 'I know I want to connect to this person before the potential of a sexual or romantic experience,' it is more similar to, 'now that I am connected to this person I *might* want to get to know them in a different (romantic or sexual) way.'

The ace and aro communities are currently known to comprise about 1% of the general population, with considerable overlap between the two communities. It is likely that this is an underestimate of the size of each community. The percentage of those who identify as either or both ace/aro may grow over time with additional

Table 13.1 Asexuality and aromanticism terminology

Modifier	Sexual Orientation	Romantic Orientation
A-	Asexual: Lack of sexual attraction	Aromantic: Lack of romantic attraction
Gray-	Gray-asexual: In the gray area around asexuality, e.g. infrequent, low levels of attraction, or a desire not to engage sexually	Gray-aromantic: In the gray area around aromanticism, e.g. infrequent or low levels of attraction, or a desire not to engage romantically
Demi-	Demi-sexual: Requires an emotional bond to experience sexual attraction	Demi-romantic: Requires an emotional bond to experience romantic attraction
Allo-	Allosexual: Describes people who are not on the asexual spectrum	Alloromantic: Describes people who are not on the aromantic spectrum

visibility and knowledge of the communities, as well as increased inclusion in research (e.g., including ace/aro identity options in surveys). The Aromantic-spectrum Union for Recognition, Education, and Advocacy found a larger percentage of aro people report also identifying as ace (~70%), while the Ace Community Survey finds about 40% of ace people identify as aro, with an additional 20% unsure if they are on the aromantic spectrum (Hermann et al. 2022; Aromantic-spectrum Union for Recognition, Education, and Advocacy [AUREA], 2019).

Currently, the majority of each community identifies as aromantic *and* asexual (aroace), and there is also considerable overlap with other sexual and romantic minority identities. For the ace community, 31% identify as queer, 13% as bisexual or pansexual, 8% as gay or lesbian, and 7% as straight (percentages are not exclusive; Hermann et al., 2022). The Aro Census finds similar non-exclusive proportions with aro community members identifying as queer (23%), followed by bisexual (13%), unsure or questioning (12%), gay (5%), lesbian (4%), and straight (3%; AUREA, 2019). Relatedly, the 2015 U.S. Trans Survey also found a high overlap; 10% of people who identified as nonbinary also identified as asexual (James et al., 2016).

Each community has a larger online presence than in person, as the internet has helped people find one another. There are more and more local groups being created, most of which are accepting of both ace and aro people. Some LGBTQIA+ organizations are explicitly inclusive of ace and aro people, and more are opening up to ace/aro inclusion. However, it is still common for people to live far away from an ace or aro group in the U.S. This can cause clients to feel lonely and lack a sense of community. If there are no local groups, LGBTQIA+ organizations with a younger demographic, university LGBTQIA+ centers, and trans-run organizations are often the most welcoming.

Minority Stress

A common experience for ace and aro people is thinking they were broken or that something was wrong with them prior to learning about asexuality and aromanticism. It is not uncommon for healthcare and mental healthcare providers to treat ace or aro people as though the lack of sexual or romantic attraction is a symptom of another disorder, to indicate that there is something wrong with them, or to suggest ways to fix them (Hermann et al. 2022; Benoit & Santos, 2023, Schneckenburger et al., 2024). Both ace and aro individuals report having trouble accessing or being accepted by mental and physical healthcare providers (Hermann et al. 2022; AUREA, 2021). While curiosity and openness are encouraged, most ace and aro people have experienced excessive or inappropriate personal questions due to their identity, and will likely be hyper attuned to questions assessing for issues with their identities (Hermann et al. 2022).

A stereotype is that ace and aro people cannot love others. In a study on bias towards asexual people, "asexuals were relatively denied uniquely human and human nature emotions" and seen as "more machine-like than heterosexuals, homosexuals, or bisexuals" (MacInnis & Hodson, 2012, pp. 13–14). Further, aromantic individuals have experienced assumptions that they cannot feel love and are missing out on it (Fowler et al., 2024). Aces and aros may misattribute their distinct internal experiences as an inability to love, when their feelings and what they feel comfortable offering are different from what they see others display. There can be assumptions they can't receive love, either because of their lack of attraction, or because there are so few people who would be willing to love them that they do not have access - coined by David Jay as a lack of relational agency (2024). Sexual desire with a lack of romantic attraction can also be hypersexualized and assumed that sexuality without romance is inherently less connecting or loving. This fear of not providing enough love is beautifully illustrated in Rebecca Wenson's poem, An Aromantic Love Letter (2022):

> … You fear that everyone else's love
> is a torrential rainfall
> or a raging river
> and yours is just a trickling stream
> and that they will all leave you
> because you cannot quench their thirst …

Research comparing aces to heterosexual cisgender individuals has shown higher depressive and anxiety levels in asexual people (Borgogna et al. 2019; Xu et al., 2023; Wichaidit et al., 2023; Yule et al., 2013). While research comparing asexual individuals to lesbian, gay, and bisexual individuals has a mix of indistinguishable differences (Yule et al., 2013; Rothblum et al., 2020; Xu et al., 2023) and increased negative symptoms for asexual individuals (Zheng & Su, 2022, McInroy et al., 2020; Lyons et al., 2022; Pitcher et al., 2023). Concealment motivation, the motivation to conceal one's minority identity, shows up for aces and aros in the hopes of being more accepted. Research has shown asexual individuals with higher concealment motivation than gay and lesbian people (Zheng & Su, 2022). Societal expectations or a lack of knowledge that healthy alternatives exist can also encourage ace and aro people to conceal or mask their identities.

For ace and aro clients exploring their identity, a maladaptive coping mechanism is testing one's potential attraction, or repeatedly questioning one's potential attraction; assessing their asexuality or aromanticism as a threat and constantly being on alert for potential attraction shows up as a form of hypervigilance. Suggesting that they have not met the right person yet can intensify this testing. Repeatedly considering if they are really ace or aro (e.g., asking oneself "could I be attracted to this person, or that person?") seems to have similar invalidating consequences. That they are invalidating their own experience does not seem to soften the invalidation. When working with ace and aro clients, I strongly encourage not suggesting that they might become romantic or sexual in the future as a preferable outcome and to pay attention to any hypervigilant behavior around assessing their identity.

Sexual Violence

Sexual violence unfortunately affects many people in the ace and aro community. The 2020 data from the Ace Community Survey found that 54% of survey respondents had experienced some form of sexual contact they did not want, 26% had experienced sexual coercion, and 19% had experienced rape (Hermann et al., 2022). In addition, those with nonbinary genders have been reported to have higher rates of sexual trauma within the ace community (Fink, 2022). In addition, approximately 12% of ace individuals, who have had consensual sex, reported feeling pressured as a reason for having sex. This pressure from partners is further supported in Kristina Gupta's (2015) work, reporting from one of her interviews, "I should have said no [to sex]. I could have said no, but I didn't. I thought that this is what everybody did in their free time, and so I was trying to be like everybody else." Here, Gupta illustrates the concept of compulsory sexuality, "the assumption that all people are sexual" (2015, p.132). This desire to change one's own or someone else's asexuality or aromanticism extends to pressure from outside sources. The UK's National LGBTQ Survey from 2018 found asexual respondents to be the most likely to have undergone conversion therapy (10%), aka sexual orientation change efforts (SOCE), out of all sexual minority respondents, in an attempt to make them experience attraction (Government Equalities Office, 2018). Hopefully with more acceptance these rates can decline, especially since ace individuals who are out to more of their partners and ex-partners have been found to experience less coercion, physical threats, or force of sexual violence (Mollet & Black, 2023). SOCE interventions can increase depression and suicidality, and have no proof of changing one's sexual orientation (American Psychological Association, 2021).

Gender

The intersection most disproportionate to the general population is the intersection with gender. There is a tremendous overlap with the trans and specifically nonbinary communities and asexuality and aromanticism. While a non-generalizable survey, the Ace Community Survey reported that in 2020, 25% of their respondents only identified with a nonbinary gender; when including those that chose both man or woman plus a nonbinary gender, the number jumps to 42% (Hermann et al., 2022). In contrast, 48% of survey respondents identify as only female and 10% identify as only male (Hermann et al., 2022). In response to a separate question, 15% of respondents reported identifying as trans and 9.5% were unsure (Hermann et al., 2022). The dearth of self-identified men in the community stands out. Tori Bianchi (2018) posits that "socialization and expectations placed on individuals throughout childhood is a factor in asexual identification, and that expectations of masculinity [inhibit] masculine individuals from identifying as asexual" (p. 51).

Race

Whiteness has overshadowed the racial diversity of the ace and aro communities, historically and currently. The Asexual Visibility and Education Network (AVEN) (2024) came online in 2001 and for many years the predominant, if not exclusive, representation of the community was white. As Ianna Hawkins Owen describes, "[A]sexuality is initially racialized as white through associations with innocence, purity, and abstinence, it is recognized by the popular discourse as non deviant, but as deserving of grief, care, support, and rehabilitation. Were asexuality not racialized as white, the public attitude toward it might be markedly different" (2014, p. 126). While the visibility of aces and aros of color is growing, white aces and aros are still overrepresented. This can act as a self-fulfilling prophecy where aces and aros of color feel less comfortable joining or participating in the communities, and those who do receive less visibility than their white counterparts.

Some communities have markedly different attitudes toward asexuality and aromanticism including the Pawnee, who have an acknowledgement of a lack of romance and sexuality in their heritage and mythologies. Deanne Linn Grant describes two protagonists in this mythology: "[the] characters are understood as queer because they show no interest in boys or girls … [and] they are seemingly uninterested in finding a partner" (2019, p. 160). While the lack of interest is notable in the myth it is not negatively portrayed and the characters are encouraged to meet one another, because they are similar.

Unfortunately, Black asexual people face additional stressors. Sherronda J. Brown (2022, p. 53) illustrates: "Black asexuals, in our impossible existence, are up against multiple overlapping narratives: the blanket hypersexuality imposed on Black bodies, the simultaneous adultification and sexualization of Black youth, the infantilization of asexuality and Blackness in tandem, and the pressure to conform to white cisheteropatriarchal[1] chrononormative[2] ideals while never being able to meet the standards of whiteness, which is continually defined against Blackness." The ace and aro community, as well as clinicians who work with them, must work to make sure we do not continue to "in both friendly and hostile manners, [urge Black asexuals] to yield the desire for multidimensional senses of belonging in the name of neutral space (a familiar tactic used in other identity-based movements)" (Owens, 2018, p. 76).

In recent years, people of color have contributed invaluable work to the ace and aro communities. Contributions from authors such as Angela Chen, Sherronda J. Brown, Claire Kann, Nilah Magruder, and Cam Awkward-Rich, and scholars such as Ianna Hawkins Owen, Michael Paramo, Kristina Gupta, Eunjung Kim, Aasha Foster, Jasmine Stork, Brittany Miles, Justin Smith, and others have been tremendous. Some ace and aro communities have created spaces exclusively for

[1] Cisheteropatriarchal refers to the idea that cisgender heterosexual men have authority over those who are not cisgender, heterosexual, or male.

[2] Chrononormative is the expectation that everyone is on the same timeline.

people of color, which allows more people of color who do, or might, identify as ace or aro to participate. This work and recognition must continue.

Relationship Considerations

A frequent concern in ace and aro communities is losing important relationships, or the depth of those relationships, when friends or close loved ones begin committed relationships. Research has shown that single people, and even more so single people who do not desire a relationship, prioritize and value their friends more than those who are married or living with a partner (DePaulo, 2023). While it is a strength of single people to value and prioritize friendships, the inverse of this means that those who are married or living with a partner are not prioritizing their single friends the same in return. This fear and loss intensifies as individuals grow older and especially as they grow out of structured community settings such as school or university. This is not a uniquely ace or aro issue, but is compounded by the increased frequency of being single in both communities, and the expectation that they may not find a partner. It heightens the feeling of being alone and potential loneliness, as it lowers their relational agency.

Ace and aro people engage in relationships, in a variety of forms, including with a partner who may not be asexual (known as allosexual) or who may not be aromantic (known as alloromantic). Most of the couples I see in my practice that include an ace or aro person, only include one ace or aro person. Often, they have been in a long-term partnership before one of them realized that they or their partner might be ace or aro. The motivation to pursue therapy often revolves around different levels of sexual or romantic desire. This can also show up as feeling disconnected from their partner, because they can each tell that the other is having a fundamentally different experience when they engage in sexual or romantic experiences. The ace or aro partner may be described as not being present, or not as invested as their partner. It can make the allosexual or alloromantic partner uncomfortable to engage with their ace or aro partner in a sexual or romantic way, or make them feel undesired. Recognizing that what makes one partner feel close to the other does not reciprocally make the other partner feel close back can be disconcerting or even off putting. On the other hand, ace or aro partners can fear that they are not "good" at sex or romantic gestures and fear that they are not satisfying to their partners. Compromising by engaging in more sexual or romantic experiences than any participant wants is not recommended. Compromising by exploring and expanding a couple's repertoire of sexual activities, romantic gestures, communication of care, consideration, and love, beyond what is promoted in the media, can help provide more options that both partners feel comfortable with. Activities that have inherently different levels of sexual stimulation can be helpful. For example, sexual acts where one partner gives and the other receives, or using toys, hands, or other explicit set ups where the focus is more heavily on one partner.

Building Community and Strengths

The ace and aro communities are small but readily available online, and in-person groups are growing. As so many issues, fears, and concerns revolve around loneliness, community can be a resource to help with those issues. I make sure to mention local groups to all prospective ace or aro clients, because connection is so vitally important. I have seen multiple friend groups blossom out of ace and aro community groups, transforming the lives of those individuals. Therapeutic identity groups can be more accessible than community groups to some aces and aros. They can create spaces that allow for greater depth in identity exploration. These groups explore many of the challenges mentioned above, but also fostered pride, understanding, and strengths of their identities. Much of the group sessions focused on relationships of all kinds, and what the participants' lives could look like as they moved through life stages. People of all identities, including ace and aro people, can intentionally or unintentionally diminish what ace and aro people bring to a relationship. However, many aspects of a relationship are not necessarily sexual nor romantic. The Relationship Anarchy Smorgasbord can help lay out aspects of a relationship as if it were a menu to help people identify what aspects someone wants or does not want to engage with (Phoenyx, n.d.).

Case Studies

The cases presented in this chapter will focus on some, but not most, of the issues present in the ace and aro communities expressed online, in person, during social groups, at workshops, conferences, in individual, couple, and group therapy. They intentionally and explicitly include intersections with other identities to provide a variety of experiences. Consideration for additional intersections and common issues can be explored in the additional resources table at the end. Each case study is an amalgamation of multiple clients and/or community members. All names are made up.

Case Study 1

Daren (he/him), a 24-year-old cis aroace Black man, referred himself for counseling for feelings of loneliness and mourning the loss of a close friendship. He learned about asexuality and aromanticism in high school through the LGBTQ club. During high school, he would frequently test himself to see if he might be attracted in some way to other people. He would constantly question if how he felt towards people could be attraction. While in the LGBTQ group he would question if he was possibly gay or queer but unwilling to acknowledge it. From his descriptions it seemed like a form of hypervigilance. This checking came up again, although not as strongly, in the work we did in the present. While many well-meaning loved ones and strangers would reinforce this idea by saying things like "you just haven't met the right person yet!" these experiences of questioning him and his orientation seemed to create more stress and strife than a helpful curiosity. Encouraging self-reflection was particularly helpful to learn more about Daren and create rapport. Boot-Haury et al. (2024) recommend their adaptation of Lefevor et al.'s (2022) sexual identity confusion and conflict model for ace and aro clients: asking what labels clients use for their sexuality, how consistently they use them, and how satisfied they are with them. I also found collaboratively exploring how he knew himself opened up the conversation, for example with questions such as, "What moments, thoughts, or experiences let you know that you are asexual and/or aromantic?" and "Are there experiences others have shared that resonate with you?"

In college, he met other ace and aro people, but most of his friends were a variety of other kinds of queer (not ace and aro). While he was not drawn to the drama of his friends' dating sagas, he learned that he appreciated the closeness and emotional intimacy of being confided in and having someone to confide in. A relationship with one friend, Alex, grew especially close. They bonded over their similar family lives and childhoods. Both were only children, who helped take care of their young cousins. Daren's mother was explicit in her love and appreciation for Daren, and hoped he would provide many grandkids he would not have to raise on his own. For Daren, this was not necessarily an issue, but it was very difficult for him to express to his mother how hard it was to hear her hope for him to find a partner.

With Alex, Daren felt for the first time that he had the space and support to share how much he wanted to be a parent, and how much he valued the time with his cousins. Most of his other friends did not want kids, and were kind, but did not grasp how impossible it seemed to Daren to find someone to raise kids with. Daren felt seen by Alex in a way he'd never felt before. He still didn't want to date Alex, but the shared understanding of one another was incredibly valuable to Daren. During college their relationship was organic and they saw each other often. Daren was also friends with Alex's partners and Alex having a partner didn't impact their relationship very much. It was after college, when Alex got a serious partner and they moved in with one another, that Daren felt like he lost the aspect of being able to really share a deep understanding of one another.

It became clear quite quickly that Daren felt abandoned and was heartbroken and grieving the most significant relationship he had ever had. Alex was always the first person Daren thought to contact, the one Daren most cared about and for, and the one he by far preferred to be vulnerable with. It just wasn't sexual nor romantic. It resembled the platonic care and affection long-term partners might have after limerence has long faded. At first, I was not sure how much Daren was aware of this or not, but it felt that it would be more powerful if Daren was able to verbalize that on his own. His own realization seemed especially important, because he was concerned that he was deficient in his ability to love people.

After Alex started living with a partner, Daren felt like his relationship with Alex was much more valuable to him than it was to Alex. He felt like he had been easy to replace, while he had no other examples or hopes to find that kind of connection with someone else. He was convinced that he would not be able to make someone else feel loved in the way they needed to be loved. He felt like there was something wrong with him in a way that was familiar, but now much stronger. Where before he was worried, now he was convinced there was a key piece missing within him. He started testing himself again to see if he could be attracted to someone. All the while, he felt confident that if he couldn't be attracted to Alex sexually or romantically then there was no hope for him to be attracted to anyone. That devastated him. He felt like it was proof that he was fated to end up alone and lonely.

Our work's most reliable throughline was this continual struggle and desire to be connected, to try to be connected, and the grief from the loss of that connection. Cultivating a "holding environment" fostered a reparative relationship as Daren risked being seen at his most vulnerable and risked sharing his own understanding of himself with me (Neimeyer, 2012). I took care to not recreate the dynamic of trying to comfort him by telling him that he'll find someone. Validating that he does have less options than his allosexual and alloromantic peers and that it is unfair was helpful. Our work focused on being able to be known, seen, and appreciated for who he was, instead of a hope for a different future. It is still unusual for ace and aro people to find therapists who do not view or indicate that being ace or aro are symptoms of another issue. Steadfast acceptance that there is nothing wrong with an ace or aro person's sexual or romantic orientation is still rare enough that experiencing it from a therapist can be transformational. My hope is that it becomes a given.

To help expand Daren's exposure to other ace and aro people I provided resources of local groups for asexual and aromantic people, larger regional events, books, and media. It took months before Daren explored any of the resources I provided. Angela Chen's book "Ace: What Asexuality Reveals About Desire, Society, and the Meaning of Sex" (2020a) spoke to him. The variety of perspectives helped Daren see different parts of himself represented. When Sherronda J. Brown's "Refusing Compulsory Sexuality: A Black Asexual Lens on Our Sex-Obsessed Culture" came out in 2022, it gave him an outlet for many frustrations, and hardships he had struggled with. It was particularly meaningful for him that it is written from a Black asexual lens. We discussed what experiences shared in these books resonated with him the most, which were hardest, and what life experiences he might want to work towards.

At first he was somewhat unconvinced he would connect with people at an ace or aro group, since he had occasionally met ace/aro people in college. He went a couple times to social events. He felt somewhat comforted that a group existed, but he found it hard to connect with people since different people attended each event. He was open to joining a therapeutic group for people exploring ace identity. The group's goals were to make space for people to share their experience navigating their identity and to hear from others in the group. He appreciated that he was in a space with other people where he did not have to teach where he was coming from. The experience of friends pairing off and no longer being available was prevalent and validating of how he had been feeling. It was helpful to be heard and understood around learning that you are not prioritized in the same way as a partner.

Through the therapeutic group Daren started to make connections and budding friendships with other people. Not most, but a few also wanted children and had a hard time imagining a way to raise them, besides being a single parent. Someone had heard about David Jay, an asexual activist raising a child with a couple David was friends with (Chen, 2020b). Those interested in having kids debated how possible or not this seemed for each of them. Others hoped they could raise a child in community or with other single parents. Daren appreciated having people to talk to who also shared the same fears.

Daren's participation in the group allowed us to do additional work individually. Alex used to be an integral part of Daren's support system, and now was still present but not available to be foundational. With this framework we were able to explore who else and what other groups would be able to add to structural support for Daren, and what aspects of relationships were particularly important to him. Using David Jay's (2024) three step approach to building relationships: (1) explore ways to spend time with someone, (2) express how you feel about that time, and (3) commit to spending more time together, we outlined how he could build new relationships and strengthen ones he already had.

He became more willing to participate in other group social activities. This was particularly important because connection to community has been shown to improve aces' wellbeing (Schneckenburger et al., 2024). This allowed him to be a part of something larger, and not feel so dependent only on individual relationships. A local writers group for ace and aro people allowed him to express creativity and create new friendships. The writing group also encouraged sharing of the members' thoughts and work, which helped recreate some of the intimacy he had appreciated with his LGBTQ group in college and Alex.

We explored how he had love to offer and that he deserved to receive it himself. Reflecting what he valued in himself helped us create a template for what kinds of relationships he might want. For example, he wanted quality time on a regular basis, including consistent time one on one, not just in groups, depth of emotional intimacy, collaborative and committed planning for the future together, and the possibility to co-parent. As he started to build up other sources of reliable support and connection he was more able to engage with Alex in a way that did not distress him, which relieved some tension and strengthened their relationship.

Case Study 2

This second case study focuses on a couple where one partner is aro and she thinks her partner is ace. Allegra and Marcy have been together for 8 years, married for 4. They live together in a queer-friendly city. At the time they sought couple's therapy they were having sex every few months or so and attributed their waning sex life as a reason to seek counseling.

Allegra (she/her) is 38 and identifies as a cis, bisexual, and aromantic South Asian, or Desi, woman. She grew up in a neglectful household and was often passed around to different family members. She found the physical aspects of her relationships beneficial, but the expectations of romanticism to be difficult.

Allegra's immediate family grew to be supportive of her relationship and now adores Marcy, but entering a queer relationship was rough at first. As Allegra finds sex to be a strong part of her connection to others, she feels unfulfilled leading a largely sexless life. She is attuned to and considerate of Marcy's needs, but is unsure how to advocate for her own. She is very concerned about recreating any scenarios that are similar to Marcy's previous sexual assault. Her own history of neglect exacerbates her anxiety around advocating for her own needs. She feels like she is the only one thinking about the fact that they aren't having sex.

Marcy (they/them) identifies as a gender non-conforming, queer, indigenous person, but has been deemed asexual by their partner Allegra. Marcy thinks they agree but is unsure. They have a few extended family members who are also queer and together they have helped create a strong support network for each other, along with Marcy's mom and siblings.

Marcy has been aware of their lower sex drive for some time, but had not considered themselves asexual until Allegra suggested the idea. They had assumed it was always going to be a requirement to have sex to be able to have a partner. This resulted in relationships where Marcy would "perform" desire and have sex, even if they preferred not to have a sexual experience. Approximately 10 years ago, Marcy experienced sexual assault from a previous partner. Their partner had been sexually frustrated from a drop off in their sexual encounters and blamed their own assaulting actions on Marcy's sexual withdrawal. Marcy felt so caught up in the relationship that when it came crashing down, they questioned themselves, their worth, and their ability to assess relationships. The familial support and close friendships Marcy had were integral in working through the experience. There are a number of sexual acts Marcy no longer participates in. They are untrusting of large or intense romantic gestures due to the reminder of this previous partner and the assault itself.

For Allegra, the expansiveness of queer sex was very exciting, as opposed to a previous series of penile-vaginal sex with ejaculation as the main goal. Marcy was interested in the more affectionate aspects of sex that Allegra had felt were often rushed with her previous sexual partners. It made Allegra feel less objectified and more seen as a whole person with her pleasure as a focal point, as opposed to an afterthought. She found that Marcy was non-judgmental, never upset about not orgasming, and capable of sharing wants and needs.

Marcy was relieved to have a sexual partner interested and willing to explore things very slowly. It felt much easier for Marcy to focus on Allegra's pleasure and desire than to be the focus. They felt comfort and security in being able to focus on more affectionate parts of sex, which felt romantic and sweet to them. The physical and emotional closeness created a deep intimacy for them, while the sexual aspects were not Marcy's focus – so long as they were not triggering. Their time together outside of sex felt like Marcy had regained a best friend.

As they each became more familiar with one another and secure in their relationship, their sex life became monotonous and less frequent. Allegra began initiating more in-depth conversations about what sex means to each of them, and what they each get out of it. Marcy started to feel interrogated and shut down. Allegra was confused by how her previously willing sexual partner now seems uninterested. If Marcy is on the asexual spectrum, why would Marcy have been willing before? I worked to slow them down and make space for Marcy to explore their potential asexuality: "Let's choose both. If you're asexual, what lets you know that you are? If you're not asexual, what lets you know that you're not?" Explicitly creating room for Marcy to disagree that they might be asexual helped Marcy put their guard down.

We began exploring what was working in their sex life, what was not, and what used to work. This included asking each to describe a fulfilling sexual experience with the other, what parts were the easiest, what parts make them feel fulfilled, which aspects are a bonus but not required, and what they each miss, both in their sexual life and in their relationship as a whole.

Marcy pieced together that their sexual experiences created a sense of romance from Allegra. The idea that Marcy had been interested in sex, as a way to feel romance, was new information for both of them. As a romantic person, Marcy knew about Allegra's identity as being aromantic, but had generally thought of sex as a romantic experience when there was palpable care, consideration, and love in the experience. While Allegra had been the initiator to explore Marcy's potential asexuality, Allegra now considered that Marcy might not experience sexual attraction to her, including while they were having sex. Allegra was unsure how she felt. She had already been feeling sexually undesirable for a few months and she felt overwhelming emotions and spiraled at times between sessions. She would jump from a new understanding of Marcy's identity to interpretations such as, "Marcy never desired me", and felt retroactively undesirable in the beginning of their relationship. Marcy in turn would shut down and avoid sharing more about their identity with Allegra outside of therapy sessions.

To slow down some of Allegra's assumptions and interpretations, I shifted to exploring her experience by asking questions such as: "Allegra, would you be willing to expand more on your experiences? Both so that we can get to know more about you, and also to see if there is potential overlap with Marcy that has become hidden?" "What makes you feel desired?" "Are there additional benefits that feeling desired gives you?" We also explored how she felt she had met Marcy's romantic needs. I intentionally stayed with what was already working since that seemed to get lost. "Marcy, what makes you feel desired by or special to Allegra?"

Through Allegra's exploration of her own sexuality, she was able to name aspects of sex that were desirable. Marcy initiating was the most surefire way for Allegra to feel desired. Learning that many of Marcy's initiations were more romantic for Marcy, even though they felt sexual for Allegra, was uncomfortable at first. Both eased into the idea of affection. We worked together to make a list of all possible romantic actions, such as buying flowers, holding hands, emotional intimacy, hugging Allegra from behind, massaging her shoulders, etc., and then assessed if each was comfortable for both of them. Allegra was able to start integrating more nuance and accept gray areas, as opposed to the black and white thinking she started with.

We dug deeper into what was going on for Marcy. I asked questions such as: What circumstances made Marcy more open to a sexual experience? Had either of them noticed anything that might diminish or increase the likelihood for a sexual experience? Were there times when they had sex more frequently? Less frequently? Marcy started to recognize that some of the romantic aspects of their sexual experiences with Allegra had been less present, which made Marcy less interested in participating. The experiences had become less emotional and more detached. The less sex they were having, the more Allegra became sexually frustrated, but disinclined to ask for her own needs based on her family history. She felt like a nag and a burden, which made her even more detached and provided less of the aspects that encourage Marcy to engage sexually. Naming this cyclical dynamic helped take the blame off of either one of them and made them each more open to move towards the other in ways that would reverse or slow down the cycle.

We traced the pattern of monotonous sexual slumps which they have worked through previously in their relationship. This time felt different. Together, they were able to identify that while their sexual frequency had declined from their initial limerence-filled start, they had a significant drop off between 6 and 8 months ago. We explored what aspects around that time had made either of them feel more distant from the other.

As they put this into practice Allegra started to feel more emotionally connected to Marcy and she became more open to some of the romantic aspects they previously had in their relationship. To help find new overlaps, we explored the Relationship Anarchy Smorgasbord developed by Lyrica Lawrence and Heather Orr, and edited by Maxx Hill and Phoenyx (Phoenyx, n.d.). This allowed them to consider some ways of relating.

Marcy shared that they were insecure that Allegra was sexually unsatisfied because she had less and less frequently orgasmed when they had sex. Allegra was flabbergasted at how Marcy could think that Allegra did not enjoy their sexual encounters. While at first bashful, she emphasized how she assumed that she woke the neighbors with how emphatically she verbally expressed her pleasure. I wanted to make sure I did not shame Allegra for her expressions of pleasure, but I also wanted to explore how she was consistently dismissive of Marcy's concern. I validated that Allegra was the expert on whether or not she was satisfied, but even so, would she consider with me that there was some kernel of truth to Marcy's fears, even if it was not related to Allegra. She was skeptical but willing to humor me.

Marcy seemed to avoid being vulnerable. We paused to acknowledge that Marcy was scared, and Allegra reassured them. With trepidation, Marcy started to outline how their previous partners most frequently disengaged from them when sex started to seem less satisfying. Sometimes a relationship would fizzle because Marcy lost interest. However, when Marcy wanted to continue a relationship but could not fulfill their partner's sexual needs, that was when Marcy lost relationships they were hoping to keep.

During our work together, Marcy and Allegra both learned a variety of ways they had been taught to mask the aspects of themselves that reflected their ace and aro identities. This unmasking revealed ways they were less compatible. They recognized how they supported one another and can create a loving and healthy relationship. Rebuilding their emotional connection helped each of them reach back towards the other. This did not take away their different levels of desire for sexual and romantic attention, but brought them closer together. They each grew to be more aware of what encourages disconnection and what encourages connection between the two of them. Their couple's therapy gradually transitioned from regular sessions focusing on the conflict between the two of them, to a less frequent co-therapy opportunity to support one of the partners and bear witness to struggles they each had.

Discussion

These case studies illustrate how ace and aro people's identities and connections with others are unknown and invalidated by mainstream society, which encourages masking of those identities and creates an unequal burden to carry. We must work to allow ace and aro people to choose how they identify and to show how asexuality and aromanticism are valuable aspects of who they are. There are challenges with each of them, and those challenges can create stressful and distressing situations. That does not mean that being asexual and/or being aromantic is inherently stressful or distressing. Focusing on the client's resilience and pride for their identity, or understanding of themselves, can help tease out what aspects they want to hold onto and what aspects do not serve them (Chang et al., 2018). These potentially stressful situations can cause fear or doubt in a client. As *A Clinician's Guide to Gender-Affirming Care* encourages trans clients, "normalize[ing] doubt or fear can convey that being able to have candid discussions can be helpful and validating, [and the clinician is] willing to explore challenging emotions" (Chang et al., 2018, p. 90). As clinicians, we need to create a space that can hold the complexities that seem overwhelming for our clients.

Working with ace and/or aro clients can look like providing space to explore asexuality and/or aromanticism, or it can be allowing them to know they are ace and/or aro and move onto other areas of their lives. This distinction will be client directed. Clients can clearly indicate if they felt comfortable in their identity and want to move to other topics. I still have ace and aro clients seek me out so that they can talk about the aspects of their lives that they do have an issue with and would like to change, but they need someone who understands and believes that asexuality or aromanticism is not part of the problem. Leaning on the stance to affirm trans clients, we can create this space by saying "I come from an affirming stance that is informed by the evidence and belief that [ace/aro] people should be supported in their identities and goals... I am not here to evaluate... I believe you are who you say you are, and no one else can decide that for you" (Chang et al., 2018, p. 143). Here in this affirming stance ace and aro people can relax and allow themselves to more fully open up in order to dive into challenges they have not been able to process on their own and use therapy to its full advantage.

Asexuality and aromnaticism are unfortunately still commonly treated as symptoms of other issues, or a phase. Treating asexuality and aromanticism as healthy identities is the basis for all affirming therapeutic work. If there is an underlying hint of a preference for another sexual or romantic orientation, it will generally not only be noticeable but familiar and will reinforce default societal expectations. Questions and phrases I go back to over and over center around exploring the client's world together where I am a co-pilot, but they are in charge:

- Let's choose both and explore each; what things let you know that you might be asexual or aromantic? Which things indicate to you that you might not be?
- If asexuality or aromanticism was widely known and accepted, would you still have these anxieties/fears/concerns?
- Are there any experiences that have shaped your connection to your identity?
- Do you know what kinds of relationships work for you or which ones do not work for you? Are there relationships, friendships, partnerships, family members, or characters in a show or book that illustrate a connection that is particularly valuable to you?
- Do you know what your ideal future would look like? Does it seem attainable? Which parts are within reach and which parts seem out of reach?
- What would you want to hear to know that you are accepted?

Regarding sex specifically, if someone understands themselves to be on the asexual spectrum and is not interested in having sex at a particular time, that is not a distorted experience and this lack of interest in sex is not something to try to fix. If there are disordered behaviors or feelings, such as anxiety around sex, performance, feeling rejected, or anything they feel like they have lost and would like to regain, those areas are appropriate to work on. This is easier to address with an individual client, as the individual client's experience and comfort is the focus. When working with a couple or partnership, where one person is on the asexuality spectrum and another is not, it is not a compromise to have the asexual spectrum person have sex more often than they want to. This can be hard with a couple where the allosexual partner feels like their sexual needs are not being met, feels lonely, undesirable, or less loved than they had before. Those unmet needs engender empathy and understanding, but does not change the fact that there should not be pressure or insinuation that the asexual spectrum partner should have sex more often. If the asexual partner is more likely to be open to sex under circumstances and less open to it in others, establishing those expectations and working on increased comfort may make sex more attainable, but it may not.

When ace or aro clients are interested in talking about relationships of all kinds, it is important to acknowledge that societal, familial, and peer expectations are often not aligned with what would work for them. This may be obvious with a partnership, but accepting that the ace or aro person's preferences and comfort are equally important is not yet obvious to many people and therapists. In addition, aces and aros often prioritize friendships or platonic relationships more than allosexual or alloromantic people and this imbalance can be very painful. Especially outside of schools, or other structural environments that encourage frequent spontaneous interaction, there is often a feeling of loss when friends enter romantic and/or sexual relationships and become much less available for these important friendships. While the communities are growing, the small size of each community can be isolating and they may feel encouraged or pressured to conform or acquiesce to those expectations to be able to build or keep connections with others. Sharing ways to access online or in person communities with other ace and/or aro people is an important psychoeducational component of therapy. Clients will move at their own pace, but because so many areas of life may teach or reinforce that they are not behaving as expected, not fitting in, or are often viewed as childish or immature, it is crucial for ace and aro clients to have access to others ace and aro first person perspectives. Some resources currently available are included below (see Table 13.2).

Table 13.2 Additional Resources

Type/Topic of Resource	Specific Resource
Referrals for Ace & Aro Friendly Professionals	AceRecommended.org AroRecommended.org
Groups for Aces & Aros	Acesandaros.community
Micro-label descriptions	The Ace and Aro Advocacy Project (TAAAP) (n.d.) at taaap.org The Aromantic-Spectrum Union for Recognition, Education, and Advocacy (AUREA) at aromanticism.org The Asexual Education and Visibility Network (AVEN) at asexuality.org
In depth look at asexuality	"The Invisible Orientation" (2015) by Julie Sondra Decker
Asexual lived experiences	"Ace: What Asexual Reveals about Desire, Society, and the Meaning of Sex" (2020a) by Angela Chen
Societal expectations, intersectionality, hardships, and interpersonal concerns for aces	"Refusing Compulsory Sexuality: A Black Asexual Lens on Our Sex-Obsessed Culture" (2022) by Sherronda J Brown "Relationality" (2024) by David Jay
Platonic relationship exploration	"The Other Significant Other" (2024) by Rhaina Cohen
Legal concerns for aces	"Compulsory Sexuality" (2014) by Elizabeth Emens
Demographic descriptive statistics	The Ace Community Survey Team's annual reports at acecommunitysurvey.org The Aro Census by AUREA at aromanticism.org/aro-census
Media	AZE, interdisciplinary journal of asexual, aromantic, and agender creators at azejournal.com Sounds Fake But Okay: Podcast focused on a sexual and aromantic content at soundsfakepod.com
Historical	"Against Sex: Identities of Sexual Restraint in Early America" (2021) by Kara French

References

American Psychological Association. (2021). *APA resolution on sex- ual orientation change efforts*. https://www.apa.org/about/policy/resolution-sexual-orientation-change-efforts.pdf

Aromantic-spectrum Union for Recognition, Education, and Advocacy [AUREA]. (2019). *AUREA—About AUREA*. AUREA. https://www.aromanticism.org/en/about-aurea

Asexual Education and Visibivility Network. (2024). *Home*. https://asexuality.org

AUREA Aro Census Team 2020. (2021). *The Aro census 2020 report*. AUREA. https://aromanticism.org/aro-census

Benoit, Y. & Santos, R. (2023). *Ace in the UK report*. Stonewall. https://www.stonewall.org.uk/resources/ace-report

Bianchi, T. (2018). *Gender discrepancy in asexual identity: The effect of hegemonic gender norms on asexual identification*. WWU Honors College Senior Projects.

Boot-Haury, J., Brennan, J. M., & Joseph, K. M. (2024). Asexual-affirming care: Recommendations for practice. *Journal of Health Service Psychology, 50*, 137–147. https://doi.org/10.1007/s42843-024-00115-1

Borgogna, N. C., McDermott, R. C., Aita, S. L., & Kridel, M. M. (2019). Anxiety and depression across gender and sexual minorities: Implications for transgender, gender nonconforming, pansexual, demisexual, asexual, queer, and questioning individuals. *Psychology of Sexual Orientation and Gender Diversity*. https://doi.org/10.1037/sgd0000306

Brown, S. J. (2022). *Refusing compulsory sexuality: A black asexual lens on our sex-obsessed culture*.

Chang, S. C., Singh, A. A., & Dickey, L. M. (2018). *A clinician's guide to gender-affirming care: Working with transgender and gender nonconforming clients*. New Harbinger Publications.

Chen, A. (2020a). *Ace: What asexuality reveals about desire, society, and the meaning of sex*. Beacon Press.

Chen, A. (2020b) 'The Rise of the Three Parent FamilyAngela', *The Atlantic*, 22 September. Available at: https://www.theatlantic.com/family/archive/2020/09/how-build-three-parent-family-david-jay/616421/ (Accessed: 23 September 2024).

Decker, J. S. (2015). *The invisible orientation: An introduction to asexuality*. Skyhorse Publishing.

DePaulo, B. (2023). Single and flourishing: Transcending the deficit narratives of single life. *Journal of Family Theory & Review, 15*(3), 389–411. https://doi.org/10.1111/jftr.12525

Emens, E. F. (2014). Compulsory sexuality. *66 Stanford Law Review, 303*.

Fink, B. N. (2022, October 14). *Sexual trauma, suicide, and post-traumatic stress disorder among the asexual adult population: An analysis of the 2020 ace community census — AZE*. AZE. https://azejournal.com/article/2022/10/13/sexual-trauma-suicide-and-post-traumatic-stress-disorder-among-the-asexual-adult-population-an-analysis-of-the-2020-ace-community-census

Fowler, J. A., Mendis, M., Crook, A., Chavez-Baldini, U., Baca, T., & Dean, J. A. (2024). Exploring aromanticism through an online qualitative investigation with the aromantic community: "freeing, alienating, and utterly fantastic". *International Journal of Sexual Health, 36*(1), 126–143. https://doi.org/10.1080/19317611.2024.2311158

Government Equalities Office. (2018). *National LGBT survey: Research report*. https://assets.publishing.service.gov.uk/government/uploads/system/uploads/attachment_data/file/721704/LGBT-survey-research-report.pdf

Grant, D. L. (2019). *Indigenous women at the heart: An imagining of indigenous Decolonial sexualities*. PhD Thesis. University of Colorado. https://scholar.colorado.edu/downloads/pk02cb68r. Retreived May 15, 2023.

Gupta, K. (2015). Compulsory sexuality: Evaluating an emerging concept. *Signs: Journal of Women in Culture and Society, 41*(1), 131–154.

Hermann, L., Baba, A., Montagner, D., Parker, R., Smiga, J. A., Tomaskovic-Moore, S., Walfrand, A., Miller, T. L., Weis, R., Bauer, C., Campos, A., Jackson, E., Johnston, M., Khan, S., Lutz, G., Nguyen, H., Niederhoff, T., van der Biezen, T., Ventresca, C. & Volvoredra. (2022). *2020 ace community survey summary report*. The Ace Community Survey Team. https://acecommunitysurvey.org/2022/10/27/2020-ace-community-survey-summary-report/

James, S. E., Herman, J. L., Rankin, S., Keisling, M., Mottet, L., & Anafi, M. (2016). *The report of the 2015 U.S. transgender survey*. National Center for Transgender Equality.

Jay, D. (2024). *Relationally*. North Atlantic Books.

Lefevor, G. T., Goldblum, P., Dowling, K. T., Goodman, J. A., Hoe-flein, B., & Skidmore, S. J. (2022). First do no harm: Principles of care for clients with sexual identity confusion and/or conflict. *Psychotherapy, 59*(4), 487–497. https://doi.org/10.1037/pst0000426

Lyons, A., Hill, A. O., McNair, R., Carman, M., Morris, S., & Bourne, A. (2022). Demographic and psychosocial factors associated with recent suicidal ideation and suicide attempts among lesbian, gay, bisexual, pansexual, queer, and asexual (LGBQ) people in Australia: Correlates of suicidality among LGBQ Australians. *Journal of Affective Disorders, 296*, 522–531. https://doi.org/10.1016/j.jad.2021.09.105

MacInnis, C. C., & Hodson, G. (2012). Intergroup bias toward "Group X": Evidence of prejudice, dehumanization, avoidance, and discrimination against asexuals. *Group Processes & Intergroup Relations, 15*(6), 725–743. https://doi.org/10.1177/1368430212442419

McInroy, L. B., Beaujolais, B., Leung, V. W. Y., Craig, S. L., Eaton, A. D., & Austin, A. (2020). Comparing asexual and non-asexual sexual minority adolescents and young adults: Stressors, suicidality and mental and behavioural health risk outcomes. *Psychology & Sexuality, 13*(2), 387–403. https://doi.org/10.1080/19419899.2020.1806103

Mollet, A. L., & Black, W. (2023). Coercive rape tactics perpetrated against asexual college students: A quantitative analysis considering students' multiple identities. *Journal of College Student Development, 64*(1), 96–101. https://doi.org/10.1353/csd.2023.0004

Neimeyer, R. A. (2012). Presence, process, and procedure: A relational frame for technical proficiency in grief therapy. In R. A. Neimeyer (Ed.), *Techniques of grief therapy: Creative practices for counseling the bereaved*. Routledge/Taylor & Francis Group.

Owen, I. (2014). On the racialization of asexuality. In K. Cerankowski & M. Milks (Eds.), *Asexualities feminist and queer perspectives*. Routledge.

Owen, I. (2018). Still, nothing: Mammy and black asexual possibility. *Feminist Review, 120*(1), 70–84.

Phoenyx. (n.d.). *Conscious authentic relating*. Phoenyx Enterprising - Relating. https://www.phoenyxenterprising.com/relating.html

Pitcher, K. J., Smith, R. L., & Watson, R. J. (2023). Outness and social–emotional adjustment among asexual and demisexual adolescents. *Journal of LGBT Youth, 21*(3), 507–525. https://doi.org/10.1080/19361653.2023.2200385

Rothblum, E. D., Krueger, E. A., Kittle, K. R., & Meyer, I. H. (2020). Asexual and non-asexual respondents from a U.S. population-based study of sexual minorities. *Archives of Sexual Behavior, 49*(2), 757–767. https://doi.org/10.1007/s10508-019-01485-0

Schneckenburger, S. A., Tam, M. W. Y., & Ross, L. E. (2024). Asexual competent practices in healthcare: A narrative review. *Journal of Gay & Lesbian Mental Health, 28*(3), 314–334. https://doi.org/10.1080/19359705.2023.2214528

The Ace and Aro Advocacy Project. (n.d.). *Identity terminology—The Ace and Aro advocacy project*. Retrieved May 15, 2023, from https://taaap.org/learn/identity-terminology/

Wenson, R. (2022, April 8). *An aromantic love letter — AZE*. AZE. https://azejournal.com/article/2020/8/19/an-aromantic-love-letter

Wichaidit, W., Mattawanon, N., Somboonmark, W., Prodtongsom, N., Chongsuvivatwong, V., & Assanangkornchai, S. (2023). Behavioral health and experience of violence among cisgender heterosexual and lesbian, gay, bisexual, transgender, queer and questioning, and asexual (LGBTQA+) adolescents in Thailand. *PLoS One, 18*(6), e0287130. https://doi.org/10.1371/journal.pone.0287130

Xu, Y., Ma, Y., & Rahman, Q. (2023). Comparing asexual with heterosexual, bisexual, and gay/lesbian individuals in common mental health problems: A multivariate meta-analysis. *Clinical Psychology Review, 105*, 102334. https://doi.org/10.1016/j.cpr.2023.102334

Yule, M. A., Brotto, L. A., & Gorzalka, B. B. (2013). Mental health and interpersonal functioning in self-identified asexual men and women. *Psychology & Sexuality, 4*(2), 136–151. https://doi.org/10.1080/19419899.2013.774162

Zheng, L., & Su, Y. (2022). Sexual minority identity and mental health among individuals on the asexuality Spectrum in China: A longitudinal study. *Archives of Sexual Behavior, 51*, 3627–3636. https://doi.org/10.1007/s10508-022-02395-4

Chapter 14
Addressing Relationship Stigma and Supporting LGBTQ+ Individuals in Consensually Non-Monogamous Relationships

Alexander K. Tatum, Sharon M. Flicker, and Jessi M. Schroeder

Highlights

- This chapter provides an introduction to therapy with LGBTQ+ clients who practice consensual non-monogamy (CNM).
- Readers will understand motivations for engaging in CNM, stigma and discrimination faced by individuals in CNM relationships, and the importance of examining internal biases toward CNM.
- We describe anti-oppressive and positive psychology-based interventions for working with LGBTQ+ clients in CNM relationships, and we offer specific clinical recommendations and two case examples.
- Last, we identify strategies to improve clinical training on the topic of CNM.

Positionality

We are a group of researchers, educators, and clinicians in counseling and clinical psychology at various stages in our career (assistant professor, associate professor, and doctoral student). We represent a range of gender and sexual identities (cisgender man, cisgender women, queer, gay, bisexual, straight). We also represent a range of relationship orientations (polyamorous, relationship anarchy, monogamous). We identify as mostly White (including one biracial White/Hispanic author). Two of the authors work in psychology departments. All authors either currently or previously

A. K. Tatum (✉)
Department of Psychology, Illinois State University, Normal, IL, USA
e-mail: aktatum@ilstu.edu

S. M. Flicker
Department of Psychology, California State University, Sacramento, Sacramento, CA, USA

J. M. Schroeder
Department of Counseling Psychology, Social Psychology, & Counseling, Ball State University, Muncie, IN, USA

N. A. Livingston et al. (eds.), *Addressing Minority Stress and Enhancing Resilience with Diverse LGBTQ+ Clients*, CBT: Science Into Practice,
https://doi.org/10.1007/978-3-031-92836-9_14

engaged in clinical practice providing individual and relationship therapy to LGBTQ+ clients. The authors collectively adopt interpersonal, humanistic, cognitive behavioral, systems, and acceptance and commitment modalities to sensitively and compassionately work with clients from diverse backgrounds. All authors share a passion for promoting the health and wellbeing of LGBTQ+ people and people engaged in consensually non-monogamous relationships.

Introduction

Consensual non-monogamy (CNM) is an umbrella term that includes any relationship agreement between partners other than sexual and emotional monogamy (Barker & Langdridge, 2010). The most common forms of CNM include open relationships, in which partners negotiate sexual non-monogamy while maintaining emotional monogamy (Levine et al., 2018); swinging, in which couples pursue sex with other partners in a social or recreational setting (Kimberly & Hans, 2017); and polyamory, which incorporates multiple romantic, intimate, and/or sexual relationships (Sheff, 2014). Although CNM is practiced by people of all sexual orientations and genders, higher rates of engagement in CNM have been noted among lesbian, gay, bisexual, transgender, and queer (LGBTQ+) individuals (Levine et al., 2018). We note that the research summarized in this chapter is a reflection of the current state of the literature, which continues to rapidly evolve.

Mononormativity reflects the common belief that sexually and emotionally exclusive intimate relationships are normal, natural, healthy, and successful whereas relationships that deviate from this norm are unhealthy and symptomatic of poor relationship quality or poor mental health of the partners involved (Barker & Langdridge, 2010). Mononormativity shows up in therapy rooms with the common assumption that monogamy is the goal for all individuals (Cassidy & Wong, 2018) and that any deviations from monogamy may be the root of unrelated problems within the client's life (Schechinger et al., 2018). Providing biased treatment to people in CNM relationships can lead to harmful consequences, such as early termination (Schechinger et al., 2018) and worsening client symptoms (Graham, 2014). In an effort to reduce negative outcomes and support therapists' efforts to work more effectively with their clients, in this chapter, we provide an introduction to therapy with LGBTQ+ clients who practice CNM. We begin by discussing some motivations for engaging in CNM and the stigma and discrimination faced by individuals in CNM relationships both in and out of therapy. We then discuss the importance of examining internal biases toward CNM before transitioning into anti-oppressive and positive psychology-based interventions for working with LGBTQ+ clients in CNM relationships. We conclude by providing specific clinical recommendations for therapists (including two case examples), and we identify strategies to improve clinical training on the topic of CNM. Throughout this chapter we focus on addressing minority stressors and relational challenges that often show up in clinical work with LGBTQ+ individuals in CNM relationships.

Motivations for Engaging in CNM

In order to connect and relate with people in CNM relationships, it is important to first understand some common motivations that initially lead people to seek out a CNM relationship. Research on this topic is typically conducted through the lens of self-determination theory (Ryan & Deci, 2000). Self-determination theory is a motivational theory that posits people are motivated to engage in behaviors that meet three core psychological needs: autonomy (the desire to feel agency and personal choice when making decisions), relatedness (the desire to connect meaningfully with others and experience a sense of belonging), and competence (the desire to feel effective and proficient in navigating one's environment). These motivations encapsulate many of the reasons that individuals cite for their interest in CNM, which we discuss below.

Autonomy

Two qualitative studies examined the motivations of individuals engaged in CNM (Wood et al., 2021) and polyamory specifically (Tatum et al., 2024), and both of these studies included samples that were predominantly (over 50%) LGBTQ+ participants. Results include several themes consistent with self-determination theory's autonomy motivation, including the autonomy to make independent decisions about sexuality and relationships, beliefs and value systems associated with authenticity and relatedness, and the desire to explore sexual identities and behaviors that they are unable to explore within their monogamous relationships.

Consistent with self-determination theory, mental health and well-being are promoted when people feel like they have control over their lives, and that includes the freedom to consider what types of relationships best serve their needs. Many CNM practitioners seek to challenge society's norms around gender, sexuality, and relationship structures. For instance, CNM inherently challenges the concept of the "relationship escalator," which Gahran (2017, p. 19) defines as "the default bundle of societal expectations for intimate relationships" in which "[t]he goal at the top of the Escalator is to achieve a permanently monogamous relationship. … Common related (but no longer heavily required) Escalator milestones include shared ownership of a home, combined finances and having kids together." CNM practitioners often work through significant self-reflection to undo the mononormative and heteronormative assumptions imbued through socialization and address the shame that they may experience around not conforming to society's relationship expectations (Bergstrand & Sinski, 2010).

Relatedness

Wood et al. (2021) also found relational themes in their data on motivations for engaging in CNM, including the desire to develop intimacy with multiple partners and/or create families of choice, the desire to meet sexuality-related goals (such as experiencing sexual novelty or managing discrepant sexual desires in partnered relationships), relational growth and expansion, and pragmatism associated with relationship idiosyncrasies (e.g., engaging in open relationships to fulfill sexual desire in long-distance relationships).

Similar to individuals involved in monogamous relationships, those engaged in CNM report their relationship style affords benefits such as love, trust, and sex (Conley et al., 2013). However, expectations of monogamous relationships have morphed over time from fulfilling one's partner's physiological needs, such as housing and food, to fulfilling psychological needs and facilitating self-growth (Finkel et al., 2014). These greater, and possibly unreasonable, expectations can set the stage for disappointment and lower relationship satisfaction. In contrast, individuals engaged in CNM have the potential to disperse their needs (e.g., emotional, sexual, recreational) among multiple partners, resulting in a greater likelihood of having those needs fulfilled (Finkel et al., 2014). Some research suggests that individuals in polyamorous relationships experience more nurturance from their primary partners and more eroticism with their secondary partners (Balzarini et al., 2017).

CNM can also provide opportunities to explore or fully express one's sexuality, including the opportunity to explore romantic, intimate, and/or sexual connections with partners of diverse genders (Moors et al., 2017). Having multiple partners can help manage sexual discrepancies between partners and can also be a way to engage with individuals who share non-sexual mutual interests. Additionally, CNM practitioners report that a benefit of engaging in CNM is the opportunity to form a community of connected intimate partners (Moors et al., 2017).

Self-Growth and Competence

Competence is less frequently mentioned as a motivation for engaging in CNM, yet some individuals mention motivations that do fit within this theme. For instance, for some, the variety of non-sexual activities they engage in with their partners is an important benefit of CNM (Moors et al., 2017). These activities include sharing hobbies with one partner that they may not share with another, as well the ability to have new experiences, socialize, and engage in a wide variety of activities, all opportunities for the development of new competencies.

Consistent with self-expansion theory (Aron & Aron, 1986), individuals report that the potential for personal growth and development is an important benefit of CNM (Wood et al., 2021). Self-expansion theory posits that individuals have an inherent desire to expand their knowledge, skills, and abilities and that a primary strategy for doing so is through forming intimate relationships and including the other (i.e., the partner) in the self. It follows that having multiple partners may facilitate greater self-expansion. The process of engaging in CNM may establish facilitative conditions for self-growth. Given the lack of traditional relationship scripts, successful CNM relationships require honest communication to establish consensual relationship agreements. CNM relationships also tend to foster trust between partners, equality of power within relationships, and the maintenance of independent identities, conditions which Peabody (1982) suggests are ripe for both personal and interpersonal growth. Indeed, engaging in CNM can facilitate the development of competence in intrapersonal skills such as emotion regulation (e.g., skills to manage jealousy) and interpersonal skills such as effective communication (e.g., to express emotions and negotiate time and other resources as well as relational boundaries).

Stigma and Prejudice Experienced by LGBTQ+ People Involved in CNM Relationships

LGBTQ+ clients who practice CNM may experience multiple forms of stigma and may face repercussions in various areas of their lives for not fitting within the heteronormative and mononormative standards of our society (Stults et al., 2022). LGBTQ+ clients in CNM relationships commonly experience rejection from their family of origin upon coming out as LGBTQ+ and/or CNM (Emens, 2004), and this rejection may extend to their chosen families (an alternate network of kinship not necessarily dictated by biology or sexual connections; Sheff, 2011). Beyond this, CNM families may be exposed to systemic barriers that harm their family. The presumed superiority of monogamous relationships is reflected in the legal protections conferred to monogamous couples as well as a societal structure that confers benefits to monogamous couples (e.g., the ability to marry, share insurance plans, visit one another in the hospital; inheritance law) while failing to extend such benefits to those who do not fit within these norms. Nearly one-quarter of CNM practitioners in one study reported experiencing discrimination based on their relationship style in the last 10 years (Cox et al., 2013), and a large online study found that nearly two-thirds of people engaged in CNM have experienced at least one instance of discrimination based on their relationship type, such as isolation from friends and family, being fired from their job, or losing custody of their children (Witherspoon & Theodore, 2021). Reduced access to the social and financial benefits available to monogamous individuals can have a direct negative impact on the well-being of those who fall outside those norms (Weitzman, 2006).

LGBTQ+ people engaged in CNM may experience dual forms of sexuality-based prejudice—stigma based on their sexual orientation and engagement in CNM. Recent research with a large sample of LGBTQ+ individuals involved in CNM found high rates of both enacted and anticipated stigma, and those with intersecting identities that carry less privilege (e.g., disabled, poor) are at particular risk for both forms of stigma (Stults et al., 2022). CNM gay and lesbian couples have been found to be viewed less favorably than monogamous gay and lesbian couples by heterosexual participants (Moors et al., 2013). Relatedly, recent qualitative research found that in a predominantly LGBTQ+ sample participants felt pressured to conform to mononormativity (Willis, 2019).

In relation to LGBTQ+ individuals, the minority stress model provides a framework with which to understand the impact of multiple forms of minority-specific stressors (such as those noted above) on physical and mental health (Brooks, 1981; Meyer, 2003). Some evidence suggests that this model applies to individuals who practice CNM as well (Moors et al., 2021). For instance, people in CNM relationships may experience shame and fear discussing their intimate relationships with family and friends because of stigma associated with their relationship type. To avoid anticipated stigma, CNM practitioners may selectively disclose their relationship status to others, a strategy which may shield individuals from discrimination and other negative experiences, but also holds disadvantages, such as the strain of living inauthentically and having to hide important parts of oneself (Meyer, 2003). Furthermore, individuals who practice CNM have been found to internalize societal stigma about their relationship style (i.e., internalized CNM negativity). These relationship-based stressors are linked with harmful outcomes, including lower relationship quality, depression, and anxiety (Moors et al., 2021). Therapists who lack awareness of the stigma and prejudice faced by individuals who practice CNM could erroneously attribute the source of their clients' psychological distress to individual- or relationship-level factors, rather than responses to discriminatory environments, which can hinder effective treatment. By automatically attributing psychological distress to a client's CNM relationship, the therapist is actually creating a biased environment that LGBTQ+ clients in CNM relationships are hoping to seek refuge from. Thus, the need for LGBTQ+ individuals engaged in CNM to have access to well-trained, unbiased therapists is a pressing one.

Despite rampant stigma and prejudice experienced by LGBTQ+ people in CNM relationships, one recent qualitative study by Füllgrabe and Smith (2023) examined the resilience of 11 (mostly) LGBTQ+ participants in CNM relationships. Results from this project revealed that participants engaged in a non-linear process of recognizing an interest in CNM, accepting this interest, and communicating this interest to other people. By doing so, participants mindfully unlearned habitual monogamous practices that intersect with societal heterosexist narratives (Füllgrabe & Smith, 2023). Consequently, participants spoke about seeking out polyamorous and queer social supports that reinforced their resilience against internalized narratives about the way relationships "should" look. These findings are congruent with a large-scale quantitative analysis of over 1100 polyamorous adults, most of whom identified as bisexual or pansexual (Witherspoon & Theodore, 2021). Specifically, the authors found that participants who reported low levels of mindfulness exhibited a much stronger relationship between minority stress and psychological distress than more mindful participants. Taken together, these findings provide empirical support for therapists to intentionally, compassionately, and nonjudgmentally promote the development and integration of clients' intersecting LGBTQ+ and CNM identities.

Adopting an Anti-Oppressive Stance

Therapy with LGBTQ+ individuals engaged in CNM must come from an anti-oppressive stance to be effective. By definition, an anti-oppressive stance consists of any behaviors that work to disrupt and dismantle systems of oppression, from acknowledging potential impacts of oppression on the client in the therapy room to engaging in systems-level advocacy work. This section will discuss positive psychology interventions and best practices that therapists can utilize with their LGBTQ+ clients in CNM relationships. Then, we will provide two case examples that illustrate these concepts in practice.

Integrating Positive Psychology Interventions with CNM Relationships

Consistent with the APA Guidelines for Psychological Practice with Sexual Minority Persons (2021a) and Guidelines for Psychological Practice with Transgender and Gender Nonconforming People (2015), interventions with LGBTQ+ clients in CNM relationships should adopt an affirming stance with the intention of promoting well-being and reducing minority stress. APA's Guidelines further specify that practitioners should adopt a respectful approach toward diverse relationships among the LGBTQ+ community. Positive psychology is a fitting orientation that can be flexibly applied in therapy with LGBTQ+ people, and is consistent with the above-mentioned guidelines. Positive psychology is rooted in three pillars: cultivating positive emotions, fostering positive individual traits, and promoting supportive environments (Lytle et al., 2014). Although these approaches show up across many orientations and evidence-based practices, we choose to anchor our interventions in positive psychology due to its explicit emphasis on depathologizing the experiences of LGBTQ+ people and intentional cultivation and reinforcement of client strengths.

Cultivating positive emotions such as hope and joy plays a crucial role in buffering against the negative effects of minority stressors (Lytle et al., 2014), thereby promoting resilience against ongoing stressors. Therapists may consider focusing on the positive aspects associated with an LGBTQ+ or CNM identity, such as the possibilities for personal growth and access to a community of people who can empathize with similar experiences of stigma and rejection (Lytle et al., 2014). Additionally, facilitating the conditions under which compersion (positive feelings about a partner's romantic, intimate, and/or sexual involvement with another partner; Flicker et al., 2021) can flourish, such as feeling secure in one's relationship and that one's needs are being met, and developing positive relations with one's metamour (the partner of one's intimate partner with whom one is not involved; Flicker & Sancier-Barbosa, 2024), can enhance relationship quality and has the potential to reduce or improve the management of jealousy. Relatedly, partners can be encouraged to engage in activities that bring each other joy (Moors et al., 2017). Examples include pursuing shared interests, spending quality time together, or surprising each other with meaningful gifts or experiences.

Fostering positive individual traits may further enhance well-being and resilience, which in turn can offset minority stressors. Conducting strengths-based assessments can help LGBTQ+ people identify their own character strengths that facilitate problem solving (Lytle et al., 2014). Peterson and Seligman (2004) identify 24 character strengths that therapists may draw on to facilitate clients' development of positive individual traits. Lytle et al. (2014) highlight several strengths (e.g., creativity, integrity, love, citizenship, gratitude) that are particularly applicable to LGBTQ+ people. These same strengths have been identified in studies of the motivations (Tatum et al., 2024; Wood et al., 2021) and benefits (Bergstrand & Sinski, 2010; Conley et al., 2013) of CNM engagement. For example, people in CNM relationships may consider engaging in regular gratitude practice strategies such as expressing appreciation for their partners' presence and support. Relatedly, therapists may consider providing psychoeducation on self-compassion when working with clients who struggle to identify positive individual traits. Self-compassion is a central construct of positive psychology and involves treating oneself with kindness, recognizing one's experiences of stress and suffering as part of the common human experience, and mindfully remaining present of one's thoughts, emotions, and physiological experiences without judgment (Neff, 2011).

Promoting supportive environments for LGBTQ+ people in CNM relationships inherently minimizes exposure to and/or buffers against heteronormative and mononormative messages (e.g., "People in CNM relationships cannot commit to relationships") that create internalized CNM negativity (e.g., "My relationships are flawed simply because they are CNM"). It can be helpful for people in CNM relationships to build community with other people in CNM relationships as a source of support and understanding. Fortunately, many CNM communities exist online (e.g., Reddit and Facebook) and are readily accessible. Other sources of support can include therapy groups or local communities geared toward CNM. We encourage providers to join listservs that can provide direct links to community resources, and we recognize the most appropriate listservs may be local (such as a state psychological association or local social media groups for therapists). Promoting supportive environments for LGBTQ+ people in CNM relationships also requires that all interventions are rooted in anti-oppression strategies.

Knowledge and Skills to Work Effectively with LGBTQ+ Clients Engaged in CNM

Mental health practitioners are in a unique position to either exacerbate or combat the minority stress experienced by their clients with minoritized and/or stigmatized identities, such as LGBTQ+ clients and clients who practice CNM (Schechinger et al., 2018). Unfortunately, clinical training rarely includes CNM in the curriculum (Ramos et al., 2022) and national clinical guidelines did not address this population until 2021 (APA, 2021b). Research has documented inappropriate practices experienced by clients in therapy, including assumption of a monogamous identity/relationship type, lack of basic knowledge about CNM, and, in extreme cases, framing CNM as sick or immoral and applying pressure to renounce their CNM relationships (Schechinger et al., 2018).

It is the ethical responsibility of mental health practitioners to demonstrate sensitivity and respect for the diversity of their clientele (Cassidy & Wong, 2018). At a minimum, this involves educating oneself about the lived experiences and perspectives of their clients as well as examining one's own biases concerning individuals whose identities and experiences may differ from the majority. Therapists can expand their own knowledge regarding CNM, such as exploring both non-fiction (e.g., academic research, documentaries) and fiction (e.g., young adult, romance) books, movies, podcasts, and blogs to better understand the experiences of those engaged in CNM and to learn relevant terms and laws. Another important strategy is to become aware of personal beliefs about CNM and begin to challenge misconceptions about CNM that might otherwise impede communication, therapeutic alliance, and therapy. To this end, in Table 14.1, we share some common misconceptions about CNM, how these may show up in the therapeutic context in the form of therapist microaggressions, and we provide relevant research findings that challenge the validity of these assumptions. Additionally, we provide questions in the table below that can be used to guide your self-reflective practice. These questions are designed to help generate insight into automatic biases you may hold about CNM relationships. Before proceeding to the case examples, we recommend you pause to write down your responses to the following questions:

- What beliefs or misconceptions in Table 14.1 do you hold about CNM relationships? How did those beliefs develop? In your work with clients, do you think it would be helpful to challenge those beliefs? Why or why not?
- What would your first reaction be if your child (or another loved one) disclosed they were in multiple CNM relationships? How might this reaction show up in your clinical work (e.g., how would you react if a long-term client came out as CNM)?
- How can you create an honest and supportive environment that allows clients, and their partner(s), to explore CNM?

Table 14.1 Misconceptions that can underpin clinician microaggressions and relevant empirical findings

Misconception about CNM	Example of a clinician's microaggression	Evidence
A certain type of person engages in CNM	"You're polyamorous? That's surprising. You don't seem like the type."	People who practice CNM do not differ from those who do not across age, race/ethnicity, religion, education level, political affiliation, income, or geographic region (Fairbrother et al., 2019). However, LGBTQ+ individuals are twice as likely as non-LGBTQ+ people to have engaged in CNM.
Couples turn to CNM to save their relationships	"Instead of opening up your marriage, I encourage you to pursue couples counseling to address what you feel is lacking in your relationship."	The decision to pursue CNM relationships is often an individual one that predates relationship formation. Additionally, those who open up their monogamous relationships do so for a variety of reasons. One study of monogamous couples planning to open up their relationships found that *more* satisfied couples were more likely to open up their relationships by the end of the study period than were less satisfied couples (Murphy et al., 2021).
CNM relationships have lower relationship quality than monogamous relationships	"Perhaps you would be more satisfied if you focused on your primary relationship and ended your other intimate connections."	Those in CNM relationships have similar relationship quality to individuals in monogamous relationships, including relationship satisfaction, commitment, trust, intimacy, passion, and sexual satisfaction, and those in CNM have reported higher rates of relationship quality on some metrics (e.g., less jealousy and lower attachment avoidance; Conley et al., 2017; Conley et al., 2018; Morrison et al., 2013; Rubel & Bogaert, 2015).
People engaged in CNM spread STIs	"You should probably get tested for STIs. This lifestyle puts you at high risk."	Individuals in monogamous and CNM relationships report similar rates of STIs (18–20% over their lifetimes; Lehmiller, 2015).
CNM practitioners are not fit to be parents	"I wonder if your child's depression is related to your open marriage?"	CNM practitioners and their children report numerous benefits to having multiple adults serving as parents and parental figures, including sharing a larger pool of resources across multiple parents, such as finance and time/attention (Sheff, 2014; Pallotta-Chiarolli et al., 2013).

Clinical and Training Recommendations

We will conclude this chapter by highlighting important clinical recommendations to create affirming environments that help clients feel comfortable openly discussing CNM. In the spirit of adopting an anti-oppressive stance, we also believe it is important to highlight recommendations for proactively improving graduate training on CNM topics. We note that APA's Division 44's Committee on Consensual Non-Monogamy contains a comprehensive list of additional resources for therapists, educators, and researchers (https://www.div44cnm.org/resources).

Clinical Recommendations

The process of providing CNM-affirming therapy begins with structural elements that signal a provider's knowledge and awareness of diverse relationships. For example, intake forms can serve as a litmus test of therapists' attunement to CNM relationships. In their content analysis of clinical intake paperwork, Cook et al. (2020) reported clinicians used the term "marital status" far more often than "relationship status." These findings contrast with Moors and Schechinger's (2014) CNM-inclusive recommendation of using the term "relationship status," which signals therapists' awareness of relationship configurations outside of legally recognized structures. In general, it is best practice to use open-ended questions to allow clients to self-identify where possible. However, therapists may also consider allowing clients to select multiple choices (e.g., partnered and open-relationship) to minimize arbitrary restrictions on identity labels. At the same time, any configuration of relationship checkbox categories will never be an exhaustive list. Thus, gathering this information both through intake forms and verbal discussions in therapy, while avoiding making assumptions of monogamy, is preferred.

Another way to ensure one's practice is inclusive of LGBTQ+ people in CNM relationships is by accommodating the unique needs of polyamorous clients. For instance, one- hour sessions may not be sufficient for treatment of larger systems (Weitzman, 2006). In both individual and relationship therapy, the clinician should attend to each relevant relationship within client systems and accommodate scheduling concerns of all members of the system who will be attending the session. When scheduling sessions with multiple partners, clinicians should also consider the number of seats and possible seating configurations so as not to unintentionally create or reinforce power differentials between partners. Observing where partners choose to sit in relation to each other can be an important piece of data that organically highlights relationships dynamics in the therapy room, such as power and connection among partners. Adjusting seating arrangements can be a powerful intervention to potentially modify dysfunctional relationship processes by physically centering partners who may not feel empowered to take up space in their relationship and de-centering partners who take up too much space.

When providing psychotherapy, therapists should be alert for and compassionately attend to clients' internalized negativity toward CNM relationships. This includes exploring client sources of internalized shame about engaging in—or curiosity toward—CNM relationships, challenging negative beliefs or stereotypes about CNM relationships, and/or examining underlying speech patterns that inherently assign greater value to monogamous relationships over CNM relationships. "Should" statements can be potential indicators of shame, belief systems, or stereotypes. Therapists can help clients identify where they learned this messaging and assess clients' interest in challenging the corresponding belief.

Drawing on Meyer's (2003) minority stress model, therapists have several opportunities to address these stressors. Notably, the presence of social support can prevent or lessen the negative impacts of minority stress on mental health. Therapists are encouraged to work with clients to identify connections to in-person or virtual CNM-centered community groups that are LGBTQ+ focused or inclusive. Simply being around other people involved in CNM may offset feelings of isolation for clients who are entirely surrounded by people oriented toward monogamy. Similarly, clients are encouraged to minimize time in environments that foster general or minority stressors. Therapists may consider working with clients to mindfully attend to their internal experiences across their daily environments (e.g., work, school, home) for symptoms associated with a threat to safety (e.g., hypervigilance, chest tightness, racing thoughts). Therapists can help identify strategies to minimize these symptoms, such as spending time in alternative, more affirming environments and finding social supports (e.g., allies) in environments that cannot be immediately changed (such as a workplace). Conducting a body scan of what it feels like to exist in these alternate environments provides the therapist and client with information about safety relative to existing environments.

Finally, it is imperative for therapists working with CNM clients to practice within the scope of their respective ethical codes. While none of the governing practice bodies' ethical codes explicitly address CNM (Duke, 2022), all of them address cultural humility and multiple relationships. There are many possible ethical dilemmas that can arise when working with CNM clients, such as working with clients from the same polycule (a network of polyamorous people linked through their connecting intimate relationships) who come in separately, especially if their presenting problems overlap (thereby impairing objectivity). Additionally, therapists need to reflect on whether or not they are able to sufficiently challenge their own internalized biases against CNM in order to ethically work with members of this population. Clinicians working with CNM clients should consult with their profession's ethical code, along with peers and supervisors who have expertise with this population when navigating ethical dilemmas.

Below are some reflection questions meant to spur thinking about anti-oppression, CNM-affirming approaches. As you think about working with CNM clients, write down your responses to the following questions:

- What are some specific, measurable, achievable, realistic, and timely goals you can develop to further your own education of CNM?
- How do you want to hold yourself accountable for improving your cultural competence on topics related to CNM?
- How would you approach a colleague who reveals a biased view of CNM (such as "people in open relationships have commitment issues")?

Case Example: Jennifer

Jennifer (she/her/hers), a 28-year-old, White, bisexual, cisgender woman, has been struggling with low mood, overeating, and insomnia. She has neglected her household duties, and she is finding it difficult to connect with her loved ones. Upon closer inspection, it becomes clear that Jennifer has been experiencing a lot of life stress. She and her two partners, Kiri and Soren, are trying to find ways to pay their medical bills. Kiri, a 32-year-old, Japanese, cisgender woman, has recently been diagnosed with endometriosis and needs surgery but does not have health insurance to cover the exorbitant cost. Despite being in a relationship for many years, the triad is unable to get married due to legal restrictions, and Jennifer's insurance will only cover a spouse. Therefore, despite having decent health insurance, Jennifer is unable to add Kiri and Soren to her plan. Ultimately, she is feeling forced to either marry Kiri to provide health benefits or maintain her values and equal relationship with both of her partners. This decision has not only exacerbated her symptoms of depression, but it has also made it more difficult for her to connect with her partners because she worries about what the future holds for them. Due to these stressors, Jennifer decides to see a therapist named Kris. Kris is a 31-year-old, White, cisgender woman who, while not polyamorous herself, has completed many trainings on how to provide affirming care to polyamorous individuals.

The following example illustrates how a therapist may talk to Jennifer about the stress she is experiencing:

Jennifer: I just feel so lost, you know? It's like I'm struggling with this decision, and I'm so frustrated at myself for not just doing something about it.

Kris: I can see how hard it's been for you to grapple with this decision, and I'm hearing some self-blame in how you've responded thus far.

Jennifer: I mean, yeah, I should be able to figure out a solution.

Kris: It can be pretty easy to blame ourselves when we don't know what to do, but it sounds to me like you have such a difficult decision to make. Ultimately, you deserve to feel secure in your life and your love, but prejudiced insurance regulations have pressured you to make a decision you should not have to make.

Jennifer: Exactly. And it's like, I can't even share this stress with some of my other family or friends because they judge me for my relationships. It really sucks. I mean, my parents don't mind that I'm dating another woman, which is highly frowned upon by some of my other relatives. But they always tell me they "don't get" why I have more than one partner. I'm not even comfortable to come out to some of my friends because I don't want them to react the same.

Kris: Unfortunately, there is so much stigma surrounding polyamory, and that stress is only compounded when you also have to worry about how people will respond to being attracted to someone of the same gender. And it's really common for this stress to manifest in the ways it has for you. All-in-all, it's completely understandable why you would be so upset.

Jennifer: Yeah, most people don't get it. It's really nice to sort of get everything off of my chest. I just wish there was something I could do.

Kris: It seems to me like you're feeling the weight of the world on your shoulders and, despite all of these societal barriers that are making this decision so difficult, you're expecting yourself to produce some magical solution. That sounds like a lot of undue pressure you're placing on yourself, when we just spoke about everything that is hindering your decision.

Jennifer: Yeah, I guess you're right. I just want to help out my partner without having to get married because I worry that would create an unnecessary hierarchy, and I really don't view my relationships that way.

Kris: I can tell you really value all of your relationships and worry about how the dynamic might change if you are pressured into a decision. Have you spoken to your partners yet about your dilemma?

Jennifer: No, I'm too worried what they'll say. What if Kiri decides to leave me if I don't marry her? Or what if Soren leaves me if I do?

Kris: You really want to make sure everybody is happy and loved, and you worry whatever decision you make will disrupt that to the point of someone leaving.

Jennifer: Exactly.

Kris: I can see how real this fear must feel in this moment. I do wonder, however, how realistic it is that talking about your concerns will lead to a break up with one of your partners?

Jennifer: Honestly, now that I think about it, the likelihood of that happening is really low. I mean, we all really focus on being honest and open to discomfort in our relationships.

Kris: It sounds like, by not communicating with them, you're hiding from that honesty and openness you try to cultivate.

Jennifer: Yeah, you're right. Do you think I could have them come in for a session to talk through this?

Kris: Yeah, let's discuss what that might look like. I want to make sure we address what you're comfortable or not comfortable with discussing with them and how we can include them in a way that works with your communication style with each of them. For example, if you would prefer to have both partners come in for the same session or if you usually discuss difficult topics with them separately. I also have some local resources that you could share with Kiri that may cover some of the cost of the surgery or assist her in finding low-cost insurance. *(Here, Kris is fostering a supportive environment.)*

Jennifer: That sounds wonderful! I'm already feeling that weight get a little less heavy.

Case Example: Mateo

Mateo (he/him/his), a 37-year-old, Latino, gay, cisgender man, has been in a relationship with his partner, Lucien, for 7 years. Although he loves his partner and considers his metamour (his partner's partner), Levi, a friend, he has found himself becoming jealous of his partner's relationship and decides to see a CNM-affirming therapist to address these unwanted feelings. James is a 43-year-old therapist who received his master's degree in marriage and family therapy. Because his academic experiences focused solely on monogamous couples, James recently received his certification through the American Association of Sexuality Educators, Counselors, and Therapists to be a sex therapist, which has expanded his competency in working with diverse sexual and romantic identities.

The following dialogue illustrates how a therapist may attend to Mateo's feelings of jealousy utilizing a positive psychology framework:

Mateo: I just feel really upset that they're spending so much time together. It's like, I love Lucien, and Levi is such a good friend, but I find myself struggling to be excited for their love.

James: It sounds like you have such a strong relationship with both of them, and I'm hearing that you feel left out when they spend time without you. Is that correct?

Mateo: Yeah, I guess I am. I don't want to lose either of my relationships, but I can't shake this feeling like I'm losing both of them.

James: When thinking about your relationship with Lucien, how have you been spending time together and connecting?

Mateo: You know, I don't think we really have been lately. We've just gotten complacent, I guess.

James: Think back to a time when you felt connected with him. What are some things that brought you joy in your relationship? *(Here, James is cultivating/eliciting positive emotions.)*

Mateo: We both love playing board games, so we used to schedule game nights with each other.

James: That sounds like a wonderful time.

Mateo: Yeah! I miss doing stuff like that. We would have time to just be ourselves where we could share about our jobs or the dates we've been on.

James: What was it like to hear about Lucien's dates at that time?

Mateo: I was always so happy to hear how much fun he was having on his dates then. I felt a lot of compersion [positive feelings about one's partner's intimate relations with others], not jealousy.

James: It sounds like it was easier to feel compersion when you felt more connected with Lucien.

Mateo: Yeah. It's like the connection I felt at the time was connected to a sense of relationship security.

James: What would it look like if you shared your current feelings of disconnection with him?

Mateo: I think he'd be motivated to spend more time together, and we'd be able to put more effort into making our relationship better. But a part of me worries he will think I'm being too clingy or unsupportive.

James: Would you mind telling me more about these worries?

Mateo: I guess I'm just worried that he won't also feel disconnected from me, which would make everything a "me problem" and not an "us problem." Does that make sense?

James: You're worried he's happy with the way the relationship is and will think you're clingy for wanting more.

Mateo: Yes! And I don't want to cause any problems between him and me or him and Levi.

James: I can see where you're coming from, and I'm hearing that you would rather put yourself in discomfort than potentially cause waves in your relationship.

Mateo: I guess, yeah.

James: So, you mentioned your worries about what could happen if you speak to Lucien. How do you see staying silent affecting your relationships?

Mateo: I hope things would just settle down, but I think I'll just continue to be upset. I already notice feeling more upset toward him.

James: Okay, so you stay upset. Then what happens between you and Lucien? Or even you and Levi?

Mateo: Well, we'd probably fight more and maybe even spend less time together.

James: And that's the opposite of what you want.

Mateo: Yeah. I guess it'll really be better if I tell him.

James: It sounds like it to me. How about we spend some time practicing what you might want to say and how you want to express yourself to alleviate some of your anxiety about facing this unknown? Of course, we cannot prepare for every situation, but there are some strategies we can discuss to communicate effectively and empathically.

Mateo: That sounds good. I already feel like I can breathe a bit better.

Training Recommendations

Unfortunately, therapists do not currently receive adequate (if any) training related to CNM (Grunt-Mejer & Łyś, 2022). CNM-related training and knowledge is vital to provide licensed mental health professionals with the tools needed to provide affirming care and such training should occur as part of standard training curricula for students in these fields. To start, we suggest that educators incorporate CNM into pre-existing required coursework on multiculturalism, as well as family and relationship counseling and sexuality courses. Updating course titles to include phrases like "relationship counseling" or "relationship diversity" is a low-effort, high-impact action that decenters monogamous relationships before students arrive at the classroom. Additionally, educators should work through their own mononormative assumptions and biases and provide the structure for students to challenge their pre-existing biases, beginning early in their training. Instructors who are less familiar with CNM may consider inviting (and compensating) guest lecturers with expertise on the topic to expose students to a greater instructional diversity. Beyond graduate coursework, there are various training opportunities open to mental health professionals and students, such as those provided by The Affirmative Couch (n.d.) and Sexual Health Alliance (n.d.). Finally, the American Association of Sexuality Educators, Counselors, and Therapists (AASECT, n.d.) maintains a list of continuing education providers. Mental health professionals who wish to specialize in sexual or relationship therapy may wish to pursue certification via AASECT, which provides a pre-established set of requirements that demonstrates an understanding of diverse sexual and relationship health topics, including CNM.

References

American Association of Sexuality Educators, Counselors, and Therapists. (n.d.). *Certification overview*. https://www.aasect.org/aasect-certification

American Psychological Association. (2015). Guidelines for psychological practice with transgender and gender nonconforming people. *American Psychologist, 70*(9), 832–864.

American Psychological Association. (2021a). *American Psychological Association guidelines for psychological practice with sexual minority persons*. www.apa.org/about/policy/psychological-practice-sexual-minority-persons.pdf

American Psychological Association. (2021b). *Equity, diversity, and inclusion framework*. https://www.apa.org/about/apa/equity-diversity-inclusion/equity-division-inclusion-framework.pdf

Aron, A., & Aron, E. (1986). *Love and the expansion of self: Understanding attraction and satisfaction*. Hemisphere.

Balzarini, R. N., Campbell, L., Kohut, T., Holmes, B. M., Lehmiller, J. J., Harman, J. J., & Atkins, N. (2017). Perceptions of primary and secondary relationships in polyamory. *PLoS One, 12*(5), e0177841. https://doi.org/10.1371/journal.pone.0177841

Barker, M., & Langdridge, D. (2010). Whatever happened to non-monogamies? Critical reflections on recent research and theory. *Sexualities, 13*(6), 748–772. https://doi.org/10.1177/1363460710384645

Bergstrand, C. R., & Sinski, J. B. (2010). *Swinging in America: Love, sex, and marriage in the 21st century*. Praeger.

Brooks, V. R. (1981). *Minority stress and lesbian women*. Lexington Books.

Cassidy, T., & Wong, G. (2018). Consensually nonmonogamous clients and the impact of Mononormativity in therapy. *Canadian Journal of Counselling and Psychotherapy, 52*(2) Retrieved from https://cjc-rcc.ucalgary.ca/article/view/61124

Conley, T. D., Moors, A. C., Matsick, J. L., & Ziegler, A. (2013). The few the merrier?: Assessing stigma surrounding consensually non-monogamous romantic relationships. *Analyses of Social Issues and Public Policy, 13*(1), 1–30. https://doi.org/10.1111/j.1530-2415.2012.01286.x

Conley, T. D., Matsick, J. L., Moors, A. C., & Ziegler, A. (2017). Investigation of consensually nonmonogamous relationships: Theories, methods, and new directions. *Perspectives on Psychological Science, 12*(2), 205–232. https://doi.org/10.1177/1745691616667925

Conley, T. D., Piemonte, J. L., Gusakova, S., & Rubin, J. D. (2018). Sexual satisfaction among individuals in monogamous and consensually non-monogamous relationships. *Journal of Social and Personal Relationships, 35*(4), 509–531. https://doi.org/10.1177/0265407517743078

Cook, J. M., Skaistis, S. M., Borden, S., & Nair, D. (2020). Inquiring about client cultural identities: A content analysis of intake paperwork. *Journal of Mental Health Counseling, 42*(3), 220–233. https://doi.org/10.17744/mehc.42.3.03

Cox, D. W., Fleckenstein, J., & Bergstrand, C. R. (2013). *What do polys want? An overview of the 2012 loving more survey*. Loving More Magazine. Retrieved from http://www.lovemore.com/polyamory-articles/2012-lovingmore-polyamory-survey/

Duke, E. A. (2022). Ethical clinical practice with consensual non-monogamous clients. In M. D. Vaughan & T. R. Burnes (Eds.), *The Handbook of Consensual Non-Monogamy: Affirming Mental Health Practice* (pp. 266–282). Rowman & Littlefield.

Emens, E. F. (2004). Monogamy's law: Compulsory monogamy and polyamorous existence. *New York University Review of Law & Social Change, 29*(2), 277–376.

Fairbrother, N., Hart, T. A., & Fairbrother, M. (2019). Open relationship prevalence, characteristics, and correlates in a nationally representative sample of Canadian adults. *The Journal of Sex Research, 56*(6), 695–704. https://doi.org/10.1080/00224499.2019.1580667

Finkel, E. J., Hui, C. M., Carswell, K. L., & Larson, G. M. (2014). The suffocation of marriage: Climbing Mount Maslow without enough oxygen. *Psychological Inquiry, 25*, 1–41.

Flicker, S. M., Vaughan, M. D., & Meyers, L. S. (2021). Feeling good about your partners' relationships: Compersion in consensually non-monogamous relationships. *Archives of Sexual Behavior, 50*(4), 1569–1585. https://doi.org/10.1007/s10508-021-01985-y

Flicker, S. M., & Sancier-Barbosa, F. (2024). Your happiness is my happiness: Predicting positive feelings for a partner's consensual extra-dyadic intimate relations. *Archives of Sexual Behavior, 53*(3), 941–958. https://doi.org/10.1007/s10508-023-02766-5

Füllgrabe, D., & Smith, D. S. (2023). "Monogamy? In this economy?": Stigma and resilience in consensual non-monogamous relationships. *Sexuality & Culture, 27*, 1–22.

Gahran, A. (2017). *Stepping off the relationship escalator: Uncommon love and life*. Off the Escalator Enterprises, LLC.

Graham, N. (2014). Polyamory: A call for increased mental health professional awareness. *Archives of Sexual Behavior, 43*(6), 1031–1034. https://doi.org/10.1007/s10508-014-0321-3

Grunt-Mejer, K., & Łyś, A. (2022). They must be sick: Consensual nonmonogamy through the eyes of psychotherapists. *Sexual and Relationship Therapy, 37*(1), 58–81. https://doi.org/10.1080/14681994.2019.1670787

Kimberly, C., & Hans, J. D. (2017). From fantasy to reality: A grounded theory of experiences in the swinging lifestyle. *Archives of Sexual Behavior, 46*(3), 789–799.

Lehmiller, J. J. (2015). A comparison of sexual health history and practices among monogamous and consensually nonmonogamous sexual partners. *The Journal of Sexual Medicine, 12*(10), 2022–2028. https://doi.org/10.1111/jsm.12987

Levine, E. C., Herbenick, D., Martinez, O., Fu, T.-C., & Dodge, B. (2018). Open relationships, nonconsensual nonmonogamy, and monogamy among US adults: Findings from the 2012 National Survey of Sexual Health and Behavior. *Archives of Sexual Behavior, 47*(5), 1439–1450.

Lytle, M. C., Vaughan, M. D., Rodriguez, E. M., & Shmerler, D. L. (2014). Working with LGBT individuals: Incorporating positive psychology into training and practice. *Psychology of Sexual Orientation and Gender Diversity, 1*(4), 335–347.

Meyer, I. H. (2003). Prejudice, social stress, and mental health in lesbian, gay, and bisexual populations: Conceptual issues and research evidence. *Psychological Bulletin, 129*(5), 674–697. https://doi.org/10.1037/0033-2909.129.5.674

Moors, A. C., & Schechinger, H. (2014). Understanding sexuality: Implications of Rubin for relationship research and clinical practice. *Sexual and Relationship Therapy, 29*(4), 476–482. https://doi.org/10.1080/14681994.2014.941347

Moors, A. C., Matsick, J. L., Ziegler, A., Rubin, J. D., & Conley, T. D. (2013). Stigma toward individuals engaged in consensual nonmonogamy: Robust and worthy of additional research. *Analyses of Social Issues and Public Policy, 13*, 52–69. https://doi.org/10.1111/asap.12020

Moors, A. C., Matsick, J. L., & Schechinger, H. A. (2017). Unique and shared relationship benefits of consensually non-monogamous and monogamous relationships: A review and insights for moving forward. *European Psychologist, 22*(1), 55–71. https://doi.org/10.1027/1016-9040/a000278

Moors, A. C., Schechinger, H. A., Balzarini, R., & Flicker, S. (2021). Internalized consensual non-monogamy negativity and relationship quality among people engaged in consensual non-monogamy. *Archives of Sexual Behavior, 50*(4), 1389–1400. https://doi.org/10.1007/s10508-020-01885-7

Morrison, T. G., Beaulieu, D., Brockman, M., & Beaglaoich, C. O. (2013). A comparison of polyamorous and monoamorous persons: Are there differences in indices of relationship well-being and sociosexuality? *Psychology & Sexuality, 4*(1), 75–91. https://doi.org/10.1080/19419899.2011.631571

Murphy, A. P., Joel, S., & Muise, A. (2021). A prospective investigation of the decision to open up a romantic relationship. *Social Psychological and Personality Science, 12*(2), 194–201. https://doi.org/10.1177/1948550619897157

Neff, K. D. (2011). Self-compassion, self-esteem, and well-being. *Social and Personality Psychology Compass, 5*(1), 1–12.

Pallotta-Chiarolli, M., Haydon, P., & Hunter, A. (2013). "These are our children": Polyamorous parenting. In A. E. Goldberg & K. R. Allen (Eds.), *LGBT-parent families: Innovations in research and implications for practice* (pp. 117–131). Springer. https://doi.org/10.1007/978-1-4614-4556-2_8

Peabody, S. A. (1982). Alternative life styles to monogamous marriage: Variants of normal behavior in psychotherapy clients. *Family Relations, 31*, 425–434.

Peterson, C., & Seligman, M. E. (2004). *Character strengths and virtues: A handbook and classification* (Vol. 1). Oxford university press.

Ramos, A., Moors, A. C., Dours, N. O., & Jonathan, N. (2022). Surface and complex representation of diverse intimate relationships: Insights from a content analysis of marriage and family therapy resources. *Sexuality & Culture*. https://doi.org/10.1007/s12119-022-09956-8

Rubel, A. N., & Bogaert, A. F. (2015). Consensual nonmonogamy: Psychological well-being and relationship quality correlates. *The Journal of Sex Research, 52*(9), 961–982. https://doi.org/10.1080/00224499.2014.942722

Ryan, R. M., & Deci, E. L. (2000). Self-determination theory and the facilitation of intrinsic motivation, social development, and well-being. *American Psychologist, 55*(1), 68–78. https://doi.org/10.1037/0003-066X.55.1.68

Schechinger, H. A., Sakaluk, J. K., & Moors, A. C. (2018). Harmful and helpful therapy practices with consensually non-monogamous clients: Toward an inclusive framework. *Journal of Consulting and Clinical Psychology, 86*(11), 879–891. https://doi.org/10.1037/ccp0000349

Sexual Health Alliance. (n.d.). *Certified consensual non-monogamy certificate program*. https://sexualhealthalliance.com/consensual-non-monogamy-certification

Sheff, E. (2011). Polyamorous families, same-sex marriage, and the slippery slope. *Journal of Contemporary Ethnography, 40*(5), 487–520. https://doi.org/10.1177/0891241611413578

Sheff, E. (2014). *The polyamorists next door: Inside multiple-partner relationships and families*. Rowman and Littlefield.

Stults, C. B., Abreu, R. L., Tjia, L., Kaczetow, W., Brandt, S. A., Malavé, D. M., & Chumpitaz, M. (2022). Enacted and anticipated stigma related to consensual nonmonogamy among LGBTQ+ adults. *Psychology of Sexual Orientation and Gender Diversity*. Advance online publication. https://psycnet.apa.org/doi/10.1037/sgd0000546.

Tatum, A. K., Flicker, S. M., Peralta, I., & Kubicki, R. J. (2024). Initial motivations for polyamory engagement. *Archives of Sexual Behavior, 53*(2), 629–644. https://doi.org/10.1007/s10508-023-02750-z

The Affirmative Couch. (n.d.). *CNM, kink, & LGBTQIA+ continuing education courses*. https://affirmativecouch.com/courses/

Weitzman, G. (2006). Therapy with clients who are bisexual and polyamorous. *Journal of Bisexuality, 6*(1–2), 137–164. https://doi.org/10.1300/J159v06n01_08

Willis, A. S. (2019). "One among many"? Relational panopticism and negotiating non-monogamies. *Sexualities, 22*(4), 507–531. https://doi.org/10.1177/1363460718756569

Witherspoon, R. G., & Theodore, P. S. (2021). Exploring minority stress and resilience in a polyamorous sample. *Archives of Sexual Behavior, 50*, 1367–1388. https://doi.org/10.1007/s10508-021-01995-w

Wood, J., De Santis, C., Desmarais, S., & Milhausen, R. (2021). Motivations for engaging in consensually non-monogamous relationships. *Archives of Sexual Behavior, 50*(4), 1253–1272. https://doi.org/10.1007/s10508-020-01873

Chapter 15
Addressing Interpersonal and Systemic Bias Among LGBTQ+ Veterans

Tiffany M. Lange, Sarah M. Wilson, and Nicholas A. Livingston

Highlights

- LGBTQ+ veterans face unique challenges relative to non-LGBTQ+ veterans and LGBTQ+ people who do not have military backgrounds.
- Person-centered care for LGBTQ+ veterans requires dual consideration of military culture and training and pre-, peri-, and post-military (e.g., deployment) experiences; as well as minority stressors that pertain to LGBTQ+ people that are covered in this chapter.
- We review concepts and skills necessary for effectively addressing interpersonal and systemic bias among LGBTQ+ veterans such as relevant military history and culture, impacts of minority- and military-related stressors on health, and nuances at the intersection of LGBTQ+ and veteran identities relevant to providing person-centered care.

T. M. Lange (✉)
Defense Health Agency, Medical Affairs, Falls Church, VA, USA
e-mail: tiffany.m.lange.civ@health.mil

S. M. Wilson
Mental and Behavioral Health Service, Durham VA Health Care System, Durham, NC, USA

Department of Psychiatry & Behavioral Sciences, Duke University School of Medicine, Durham, NC, USA

N. A. Livingston
National Center for PTSD, Behavioral Science Division, VA Boston Healthcare System, Boston, MA, USA

Department of Psychiatry, Boston University Chobanian & Avedisian School of Medicine, Boston, MA, USA

N. A. Livingston et al. (eds.), *Addressing Minority Stress and Enhancing Resilience with Diverse LGBTQ+ Clients*, CBT: Science Into Practice,
https://doi.org/10.1007/978-3-031-92836-9_15

Positionality
The author team has drawn upon lived experiences relating to their own respective identities related to gender (cisgender, demigender women), sexual orientation (bisexual/pansexual, queer, heterosexual/straight), and race/ethnicity (White and racially minoritized with experiences of White/light-skinned privilege). We have privileged aspects of identity and aspects of identity that contribute to passing privilege in society (queer sexual orientation in a mixed gender romantic relationship). We are each mid-career researchers and clinicians in psychology with experience in mental health care for LGBTQ+ U.S. military veterans, and collectively have experience within and outside of the Veterans Health Administration. We individually occupy unique identities, but we are unified in our commitment to supporting the health and wellbeing of LGBTQ+ veterans.

Introduction

Military veterans who identify as lesbian, gay, bisexual, transgender, and queer/questioning (LGBTQ+) face unique challenges at the intersection of these identities that differ in important ways from people with either identity alone. Veterans have been shown to experience high rates of psychiatric disorders, including posttraumatic stress disorder (PTSD), substance use disorder, anxiety and depression, and suicide (Trivedi et al., 2015). People who identify as LGBTQ+, compared to non-LGBTQ+ people, likewise evidence higher rates of adverse mental health outcomes, including anxiety, depression, PTSD, and substance use disorders (Meyer, 2003; Hatzenbuehler, 2009; Hendricks & Testa, 2012). Although additional research is needed, LGBTQ+ veterans appear to evidence added disparities compared to non-LGBTQ+ veterans, including higher rates of military sexual trauma, PTSD, hazardous substance use, substance attributable death, and suicide (Blosnich et al., 2014; Livingston et al., 2023; Livingston et al., 2022; Shipherd et al., 2021; Tucker, 2019). Minority stress theory provides an orienting framework for understanding health disparities among LGBTQ+ veterans and attributes adverse health outcomes and maladaptive coping mechanisms (e.g., substance use) to stigma and social stress that is not experienced by the larger cisgender, heterosexual population (Brooks, 1981; Livingston et al., 2019; Meyer, 2003; Hendricks & Testa, 2012; Shipherd et al., 2019). In this chapter, we outline considerations pertaining to military culture and veteran experience in general, LGBTQ+ health and minority stress, and providing person-centered care for LGBTQ+ veterans.

U.S. Military Structure and Culture

Military veterans are an incredibly diverse group, yet there are foundational military concepts that are key to understanding the cultural context for many LGBTQ+ veterans. Although this chapter concerns military veterans, who are no longer active-duty service members but civilians following active military service, it is important to understand military structure and culture when caring for veterans. There are six main branches of the U.S. military: Army, Navy, Marine Corps, Air Force, Coast Guard, and Space Force. In addition, the U.S. has the National Guard (State-Based Military Force; Army or Air National Guard) and Armed Forces Reserves (Army, Naval, Marine Corps, Air Force, and Coast Guard Reserves). Each military branch has its own unique culture and norms.

Across all branches, military culture emphasizes camaraderie, which is the shared understanding of mutual self-sacrifice in order to function cohesively as a whole. Military camaraderie is a unique bond among service members that is built on shared experiences, mutual respect, community, and for some can provide an unparalleled sense of belonging. Camaraderie is important during peace times and is essential, and even lifesaving, in times of conflict and war (McCormick et al., 2019). These qualities of military culture are appealing to many people, including LGBTQ+ people who join the armed forces for similar reasons as their non-LGBTQ+ counterparts (e.g., patriotism; Meade, 2021), but who may be additionally drawn to the assumed closeness and connection with fellow service members in the military. Camaraderie may be especially potent for LGBTQ+ people who have experienced rejection from close friends or relatives, who crave a sense of shared connection and purpose, or who joined the military to distance themselves from unhealthy people and relationships, or to combat gender dysphoria (e.g., Parco & Levy, 2014). In a qualitative study of transgender and gender diverse veterans, one participant joined the military in the hopes that "my dysphoria [would] go away since the military is so focused on everyone being the same and equal." (Parco & Levy, 2014; p. 12).

On the other hand, aspects of military culture and norms are at odds with the diversity present within the military and among veterans. Notably, the military system is based on a binary view of sex (male/female), which informs many standards and requirements (e.g., medical fitness for duty, uniform and grooming standards; Department of Defense, 2022). The hyper-masculine culture of the military may be appealing for some people; for example, some military veterans have reported that the culture of the military assisted in "burying" feelings of gender incongruence or dysphoria (e.g., McDuffie & Brown, 2010). However, repressing such important aspects of one's identity can contribute to immediate and lasting adverse psychiatric outcomes (Pachankis et al., 2020). In a qualitative study of transgender and gender diverse service members, participants cited examples of double standards, noting that despite aims that men and women are treated equally, each has different appearance and performance standards that align with sex assigned at birth and not gender (and generally are more lenient for people assigned female at birth), and that military culture is male-dominated and favors masculine gender expression (Parco & Levy, 2014). Transgender service members also felt that there was greater pressure to exceed performance standards to overcompensate, expressing sentiments such as "As long as you do your job and you do it well, a lot of people are willing to look the other way," and "I knew that so many people were watching me and that everybody was pretty much waiting for me to slip up." (Parco & Levy, 2014, p. 13).

The hierarchy of the military maintains power differentials that are often not experienced in other settings, conferring greater authority among higher (e.g., commissioned officers such as generals, colonels, lieutenants) versus lower ranking service members (e.g., enlisted: private, airman, seaman). Military service members may also have vastly different career and cultural experiences depending on category of rank: enlisted (i.e., can advance to status of non-commissioned or warrant officer), a non-commissioned officer (i.e., earned the officer title through promotion in the military), or a commissioned officer (i.e., earned the officer title before entering the role, usually due to having a bachelor's degree). Rank establishes and maintains the chain of command, order, and deference to authority, and can be a source of stress and isolation for LGBTQ+ service members. For example, the hierarchical nature of the military may also have an impact on LGBTQ+ service members' degree of outness, with officers being less likely to disclose identity than their LGBTQ+ enlisted counterparts (McNamara et al., 2021).

Although each U.S. military branch has its own unique characteristics, U.S. military culture in general supports values related to communal orientation (i.e., others over self), hierarchical and organized structure (i.e., chain of command), and order/discipline (i.e., responsibility and accountability; Soeters et al., 2006). Additionally, veterans are more likely than non-veterans to believe in traditional gender roles, which has been theorized to lead to the promotion and reward of stereotypically masculine traits, such as strength, stoicism, and dominance (Boyce & Herd, 2003; Hinojosa, 2010). It is important to note that these are features of military culture that can confer support and protection, particularly communion and unit cohesion, but that support and protection is not without risk of harm among LGBTQ+ veterans who may be targeted and discriminated against on the basis of their identity (Livingston et al., 2019).

History of LGBTQ+ Discrimination and Exclusion in the U.S. Military

Dating back to the Revolutionary War, U.S. military history includes many LGBTQ+ individuals who served with pride and advocated for progress and honoring the LGBTQ+ people who have served in the military (e.g., Nell "Johnnie" Phelps, Fannie Mae Clackum, Leonard Phillip Matlovich, Patricia King, Bree Fram, Tammy Smith, Dr. Rachel Levine). Unfortunately, these honorable narratives are often unknown or overshadowed by the military's history of anti-LGBTQ+ policies (e.g., Don't Ask, Don't Tell [DADT], Transgender Military Ban), which often led to systemic discrimination through formal discipline, career consequences, dishonorable discharges, harassment, violence, retaliation, and fear (Gates, 2010; National Defense Research Institute, 2010; McNamara et al., 2021). Exact numbers are not known, but it is estimated that more than 100,000 individuals were subjected to other-than-honorable discharges due to sexual orientation or gender identity with 13,000 of those during DADT (1993–2011; The Williams Institute, 2010). This type of discharge is given when a service member has been found to have committed a serious departure from conduct, protocol, or performance expectations. A less-than-honorable discharge impacts Veterans Affairs benefits, employment prospects, as well as perceptions of their military service. Even though LGBTQ+ veterans discharged under these previous policies are now eligible to apply for an upgrade to their military discharge to "honorable", it is believed that less than 8% have pursued this option (McDermott, 2016).

It is crucial for mental health providers to understand the era in which the veteran served, as specific time-bound policies had bearing on what systems-level experiences of discrimination may have occurred (Table 15.1).

LGBTQ+ open service in the U.S. military has not led to significant problems related to unit cohesion, recruitment, retention, or morale (Belkin et al., 2013; Dietert & Dentice, 2023). However, many LGBTQ+ service members continue to report that the military environment—at both the institutional and interpersonal level—is still not inclusive for sexual and gender minorities (McNamara et al., 2021; Livingston et al., 2019). For example, even with transgender open service in

Table 15.1 Shifts in military policy toward LGBTQ+ service by era

Pre-1993:	*Complete LGBTQ+ Exclusion.* Common belief that "homosexuality" was "incompatible with military service" (United States General Accounting Office, 1992). Invasive investigations and other-than-honorable discharges of about 1500 LGBTQ+ military service members occurred each year between 1980 and 1990.
1993–2011:	*DADT.* Same-sex sexual behavior was banned in the military, but investigations into sexual orientation were also not allowed without "evidence" (Borch, 2010). Continued widespread investigations and other-than-honorable discharges of those accused of having LGBTQ+ identities.
2011:	*Repeal of DADT (No Change to Transgender Exclusion).* Continued widespread social stigma towards LGBTQ+ identities in the military. Inconsistent rules around inclusion of transgender and nonbinary individuals upon entry (McNamara et al., 2021).
2016–2018:	*Transgender Open Service.* Transgender service members could no longer be separated, solely on the basis of gender identity. Military policy established guidelines for Transgender Open Service, with the requirement that they meet the same military standards as others (Department of Defense, 2016).
2017:	*President Trump Social Media Announcement.* President Trump announced on social media that transgender service members would not be able to serve in the military "in any capacity" (Manuel, 2020).
2018–2020:	*Transgender Service Restrictions and Ban.* A series of multiple memoranda from the White House severely limited the ability for transgender service members to remain in the military. These memoranda ranged from at first an all-out ban on military service members with diagnoses of gender dysphoria to later allowing transgender service members to remain in military service only if they use the "uniforms, pronouns, and sleeping and bathroom facilities for their biological sex" (Manuel, 2020).
2021–2024:	*Inclusion of All Gender Identities in Military Service.* An executive order by the Biden Administration (Exec. Order No. 14004, 2021) reversed previous policy and allowed individuals to serve openly as transgender or nonbinary. Previously discharged transgender service members were allowed to re-enlist. Provision of military healthcare support for gender affirming care and surgical procedures (Defense Health Agency, 2023; Suits, 2021).

the U.S. military, difficulties remain with gender affirmation due to ongoing stigma about gender diversity and challenges with accessing gender affirming interventions (e.g., Johnson et al., 2023; Klein et al., 2024; Schvey et al., 2020).

LGBTQ+ Veteran Overview

The intersectionality of LGBTQ+ identity and veteran identity poses several unique considerations and there are specific impacts of navigating a cultural environment historically known to be discriminatory towards sexual and gender diversity. Mental health care for LGBTQ+ veterans involves familiarizing oneself with the "basics" of military culture and the role of systemic bias in health disparities and identity development. Culturally responsive therapy with LGBTQ+ veterans encompasses a thorough understanding of veteran and LGBTQ+ affirmative care, the historical and systemic contributors to health, ability to culturally adapt evidence-based approaches, as well as a commitment to advocate for systemic improvements. In the context of affirmative care, mental health providers are tasked with adopting a stance of cultural humility while identifying key opportunities to integrate therapeutic strategies aimed at reducing the negative impact of minority stressors (e.g., micro- and macro-aggressions) on psychological and emotional functioning. The following ten recommendations (Table 15.2) are provided to inform and guide care considerations for LGBTQ+ veterans:

While attending to the significance of veteran and LGBTQ+ identities and intersectional stressors that impact their health, and aligning care in accordance with the recommendations above, it is also important to acknowledge individual differences. U.S. culture tends to express formalities to those who served in the military ("Thank you for your service") but not every individual will feel connected to a veteran identity and their service, and some may have received conflicting messages about their service (e.g., receipt of hostility upon return from deployment, most notably among Vietnam veterans). People who identify as LGBTQ+ also differ in the salience and prominence of their LGBTQ+ identity, with some regarding it as central and others regarding it as less central or irrelevant to their mental health concerns and healthcare needs. Mental health providers must be aware that there are a wide range of perceptions and emotions about the military among LGBTQ+ veterans and it is not the role of the mental health provider to interject their opinions. As such, it is important to ask open-ended questions of LGBTQ+ veterans to prevent making assumptions based on well-intentioned albeit stereotyped notions of what it means to be LGBTQ+ or a veteran.

Table 15.2 Ten recommendations to guide care considerations for LGBTQ+ veterans

1. Embrace an affirmative care stance	Adopt and demonstrate a commitment to affirmative care through recognition of the intersectionality of LGBTQ+ and veteran identity as well as delivering best practice interventions to address the impact of minority stressors (e.g., micro- and macro-aggressions).
2. Demonstrate cultural humility	Culturally responsive therapy involves recognition of one's knowledge gaps, ongoing professional training to address those gaps, affirmative skill development, and routine engagement in self-reflection.
3. Ask about sexual orientation, gender identity, and veteran status	As a standard of practice, mental health providers should ask about sexual orientation, gender identity, and veteran status in addition to creating a welcoming environment that promotes identity self-disclosure.
4. Acknowledge intersectional sources of discrimination	Develop a thorough understanding of military culture and LGBTQ+ identity to enhance ability to acknowledge and intervene on sources of discrimination that can impact well-being. Effective therapeutic engagement and treatment involves conceptual considerations of intersectional stressors (military- and minority- related) in order to facilitate identity development and protect against unwarranted diagnostic labeling (i.e., overpathologizing emotional reactions to discrimination-based experiences).
5. Support the coming out process and identity development	Explore the development of LGBTQ+ identity as well as factors that hindered or promoted the coming out process (e.g., serving under anti-LGBTQ+ military policy).
6. Identify and address inequities and sources of resilience	Culturally responsive therapy with LGBTQ+ veterans should strive to balance attending to health inequities, while at the same time emphasizing sources of resilience. This balance can promote proactive healthcare engagement.
7. Identify and address risk for self-harm	Identifying specific sources of risk for self-harm that are more common among LGBTQ+ veterans is essential. Mental health providers should seek out and maintain training and competency in evidence-based practices for reducing suicide risk (e.g., safety planning intervention).
8. Recognize the heightened risk for interpersonal bias, discrimination, and trauma	Providing trauma-informed care to LGBTQ+ veterans involves proactively and purposefully addressing the chronic stress experienced from microaggressions, discrimination, overt harm, and stigma.
9. Use evidence-based approaches, best practice guidelines, and cultural adaptations	Prioritize familiarity with field best practice standards, cultural adaptations to evidence-based practices (EBPs), emerging intervention and program development, as well as reputable health literacy materials to share with LGBTQ+ veterans for shared decision-making during development of the treatment plan.
10. Address systemic biases and barriers to care	Compile resources known to be inclusive of the LGBTQ+ community, be knowledgeable of systemic healthcare services and referrals that can aid in accessing care (e.g., LGBTQ Veteran Care Coordinator [VCC] at the Veterans Health Administration [VHA]), and advocate for systemic progress (e.g., creation of safe zones, updating organizational policies and procedures).

Minority Stress and Case Conceptualization

LGBTQ+ veterans face military-specific stressors, such as deployment or combat experiences that increase risk for psychiatric disorders and interpersonal problems (Hoge et al., 2006). LGBTQ+ veterans experience additional stressors in relation to their sexual orientation and/or gender identity, both within and outside of their military and deployment experiences. These veterans can also feel as though they are doubly estranged, feeling a lack of belonging among service members and veterans because they are LGBTQ+, and a lack of belonging in the LGBTQ+ community given their veteran status (Livingston et al., 2019). Below are illustrations of some of the minority stress processes that relate to many LGBTQ+ people, but that are also specific to or more pronounced among LGBTQ+ veterans, that are important to consider in case conceptualization.

Trauma Exposure and Reactions

Trauma, as classically defined, can be an event or circumstance that involves exposure to death, threatened death, actual or threatened physical harm, or sexual assault experienced directly or indirectly (e.g., witnessed or learned about the event happening to a close friend of relative [American Psychiatric Association, 2013]). LGBTQ+ veterans are exposed to the same types of trauma as other veterans, particularly in combat situations, but are also exposed to higher rates of trauma in relation to their LGBTQ+ identity. In interviews with trauma-exposed LGBTQ+ veterans, Livingston et al. (2019) reported bias-related accounts ranging from veterans having M16 rifles pointed at them by fellow service members, causing them to fear more their unit than enemy combatants; and witnessing and learning about gay friends getting beaten to death for being gay or for suspicion of dating LGBTQ+ people. There were also cases of discrimination from providers. One gay veteran reported that he was questioned excessively about his sexual and romantic interests, then subjected to an unnecessary digital rectal exam during a routine office visit. These veterans also reported extreme distress resulting from being investigated by the military for homosexuality under DADT and having to defend themselves against the United States of America, and in relation to being denied admission to residential treatment because of their transgender identity. Although some of these events are consistent with Criterion A trauma, some are not but nevertheless produced similar reactions among LGBTQ+ veterans, and some regarded their experiences of discrimination as higher impact than their Criterion A trauma(s). As shared by one veteran, "Being in the closet is itself a traumatic event, but it doesn't fit the definition of trauma, which is problematic, because how do you treat something that … I mean, and there's no [diagnostic] code for 'traumatized by the closet.'" (p. 699).

Although it is beyond the scope of this chapter to advocate for an expanded definition of Criterion A trauma (see Marx et al., 2024), we do encourage careful assessment of the full range of traumatic and potentially traumatic events that disproportionately befall LGBTQ+ veterans, as well as careful assessment of their subjective impacts. It may not be the case that someone presenting with Criterion A trauma and non-traumatic minority stressors will regard the former primary or central to their presenting distress. These experiences, as well as the reactions to these experiences, are often intertwined (e.g., experiencing a violent hate crime in the military but also dealing with chronic discrimination and microaggressions in their daily lives). Exposure to extreme or repeated exposures to any potentially traumatic event can condition people to anticipate threat and rejection; experience intrusive thoughts and rumination; feel shame and doubt; and increase identity concealment efforts aimed at preventing further harm and emotional pain. These reactions resemble the intrusive thoughts, avoidance, negative alterations in cognition and mood, and hyperarousal criterion of PTSD (i.e., Criteria B, C, D, and E; Livingston et al., 2020). The point of this illustration is not to equivocate PTSD and minority stress reactions, only to shine light on similarities that are worth clinicians' attention in working with LGBTQ+ veterans. One important contrast, however, is that PTSD reactions are residual effects of past trauma that persist in the absence of current threat (e.g., PTSD symptoms in relation to combat experienced years prior). For LGBTQ+ veterans, threat may persist and their symptoms may be an amalgamation of reactions to past trauma and adaptations to persistent and chronic threats in their environment (Livingston et al., 2020).

In conceptualizing LGBTQ+ veteran distress, it is important for providers to be aware of the potential of traumatic invalidation, or the repeat occurrence of having one's experiences discredited or dismissed, in framing their responses to minority stressors (Cardona et al., 2022). This can be an easy misstep to make among even the most well-intentioned providers who do not share lived experience with LGBTQ+ veterans, or who are more accustomed to providing trauma-focused therapy in relation to classically defined Criterion A trauma. Notably, minority stressors have been demonstrated to trigger the same physiological stress response (fight-flight-freeze) as other Criterion A stressors (Forrester et al., 2019), and a PTSD diagnosis is not a requirement for providing trauma-focused therapy or adapting these interventions for use among LGBTQ+ veterans who are experiencing minority stress.

Moral Injury

No one is immune to moral injury, yet unique features of military culture and military exposures (e.g., combat) make it a particularly salient concern among LGBTQ+ veterans. The military upholds high moral and conduct standards, shared expectations, and emphasizes duty to others. These include explicit codes pertaining to loyalty, duty, respect for others, selfless service, honor, integrity, and personal courage; as such, the morality of the individual could become interwoven with the morality of the organization (Molendijk et al., 2018). Moral injury "involves an act of transgression that creates dissonance and conflict because it violates assumptions and beliefs about right and wrong and personal goodness" due to actions or inactions by self or others (Litz et al. 2009, p. 689). For LGBTQ+ veterans, moral injury may arise from military-related stressors (e.g., engaging in combat, training accidents, military sexual trauma) or situations that involve self-preservation or engagement in institutional harm/betrayal towards fellow LGBTQ+ service members (Livingston et al., 2019). In interviews, LGBTQ+ veterans have recounted highly morally injurious events caused by acts of commission (e.g., participating in the investigation and eventual discharge of other LGBTQ+ service members while remaining concealed themselves) or omission (e.g., failing to intervene to prevent hate crimes lest they also become targets of violence) that have enduring and deleterious psychological effects on LGBTQ+ veterans (Livingston et al., 2019).

There is increased recognition that being subjected to conversion therapy practices can result in or perpetuate a sense of moral injury or inferiority, and religious trauma due to the existential distress that can arise from the perspective that LGBTQ+ identity is a moral "failing" within certain spiritual viewpoints (Jones et al., 2022). The intersection of LGBTQ+ identity and spiritual identity is a salient matter for many LGBTQ+ veterans, many of whom have deeply held religious and spiritual beliefs (Kopacz et al., 2019). On the one hand, studies suggest that religion and spirituality can contribute to resilience and enhanced emotional well-being (e.g., Akerman et al., 2020; Lichter & Min, 2013) and buffer against adverse psychiatric outcomes such as PTSD among veterans (Sharma et al., 2017). However, religion and spirituality can be a source of significant distress for the LGBTQ+ community (e.g., Kocet & Curry, 2011), especially for those with prior experiences of religious abuse or orientation change efforts (e.g., sexual orientation or gender identity change efforts, or "conversion therapy"; Super & Jacobson, 2011), which have been shown to increase risk for depression, suicide, and other negative outcomes (e.g., Fish & Russell, 2020; Higbee et al., 2022). Even without exposure to such abuses, reconciling religious beliefs with LGBTQ+ identity and authentic expression can be very challenging, potentially contributing to guilt, shame, and moral injury (Bogel-Burroughs, 2024).

Minority Stress

Some LGBTQ+ veterans report high levels of internalized stigma (Livingston et al., 2019), which is the internalization of "stigma, stereotypes, and negative views into one's self concept as a product of social bias" (Puckett & Levitt, 2015, p. 329). For LGBTQ+ veterans, these messages come from the same national and state-level laws and policies that discriminate against LGBTQ+ people generally, as well as military-specific policies such as DADT and the residual effects of these repealed policies on military culture (i.e., ongoing prejudice). Messages that convey second-class standing force LGBTQ+ veterans to reconcile these messages with their own basic needs for autonomy, respect, and authenticity. In Livingston et al. (2019), one LGBTQ+ veteran coped with this by living a "double life," which involved using alcohol and drugs to cope with stressors but also to express himself in ways that were difficult without substances, resulting in a split self. "I was going to school and working and being straight, and pretending I wasn't involved in drugs, and I had a second life where it was all about drugs. I had my straight clean life that I was living simultaneously with a straight drug life, and then a gay drug life, and then just a gay life, so it was like multiple personality syndrome [*sic*]." (p. 699).

Concealment of identity among LGBTQ+ veterans can be a means of self-preservation in an environment in which disclosure of identity could have led to negative consequences (e.g., harassment, abuse, or discharge; Livingston et al., 2019). For LGBTQ+ veterans, reasons may be due to sociopolitical and geographical factors, military policies, direct or vicarious victimization experiences in the military, or lack of trust and uncertainty about safety (Cramer et al., 2022; Lattanner et al., 2021; Livingston et al., 2019; Model, 2013; Moradi, 2009; Trivette, 2010). A poignant example from Livingston et al. (2019) highlights an LGBTQ+ Vietnam veteran's experience: "pretty much the whole year in Vietnam I was more afraid of being killed by somebody in my unit [than my enemy]" (p. 697). LGBTQ+ veterans in this study recounted experiences of extreme violence, and strategies to conceal their identity to prevent assault, and efforts aimed at preventing military investigations and discharge from the military, such as participating in the investigation of other LGBTQ+ service members while remaining concealed themselves, choosing not to intervene when they witnessed anti-LGBTQ+ hate crimes, or getting married to someone of a different sex for dual concealment. One veteran shared his experience (gay man) with a friend (lesbian woman), "We were both gay but we didn't want to get fired and we wanted to make a career out of it, so we got married [to each other]." (Livingston et al., 2019; p. 699).

Although the repeal of DADT ostensibly should have helped ease some minority stress for LGBTQ+ service members, this has not been documented in the literature and many continue to report "strategic disclosure" (Van Gilder, 2017), and some continue to suffer the psychological consequences of DADT years later (Livingston et al., 2019). Prior to transgender open service in the U.S., an example from a transgender service member highlights the difficult balance of identity concealment and disclosure in the military: "I decided that if anyone ever asked me I would not lie about it… I'd rather just be upfront with them and honest about it… it is a little nerve racking because you don't want to tell the wrong person because they could kick you out of the military for it which is scary. This is supposed to be my career" (Okros & Scott, 2015, p. 9). Even with recent progress towards open service, LGBTQ+ veterans may continue to be hesitant in sharing their identity with others even when it matters in healthcare. Providers are encouraged to consider the impact of the military environment in how an individual manages their identity in various situations.

Affirmative LGBTQ+ Veteran Treatment

LGBTQ+ veterans often mistrust healthcare settings and have negative expectations about the healthcare they will receive (e.g., Johnson & Federman, 2013). As such, providers are encouraged to consider the treatment context and setting where care is being delivered, its reputation regarding LGBTQ+ affirmation and inclusion, and how that may impact treatment expectations. For instance, service delivery within government healthcare settings (e.g., VA) may arouse feelings of institutional betrayal or understandable suspicion or mistrust on the client's part that stems from prior military service or healthcare experiences. Interventions targeting cultural change in practice settings involve a proactive approach to addressing systemic bias, such as modifying processes that maintain inequities (e.g., policy), as well as careful attention toward establishing and maintaining trust and providing what for many may be a corrective healthcare experience.

In terms of care delivery, research shows that "evidence-based treatments for distinct cultural groups yield better outcomes, including engagement, retention, and satisfaction in therapy" (Soto et al., 2019). There is increased attention on the need for integrating LGBTQ+ and/or veteran identity into evidence-based practices (EBPs), which has led to new intervention development (e.g., Lange et al., 2020; Pachankis et al., 2019; Rider et al., 2019), theory-driven adaptations and treatment modifications (e.g., Chang, 2022; Lange, 2020; Livingston et al., 2020) as well as practice recommendations (e.g., American Psychological Association, 2009; Chang & Singh, 2018).

Given the confluence of minority and military-related stressors, effective engagement of LGBTQ+ veterans often entails addressing interpersonal and systemic biases throughout the course of treatment. For LGBTQ+ veterans, this calls for due diligence and careful consideration of the unique macro-level factors that have and continue to impact LGBTQ+ service members (i.e., historical military bans and the legacy of these policies that continue to impact LGBTQ+ veterans; Livingston et al., 2019), more immediate stressors that may relate to LGBTQ+ or veteran identity or both, and unique trauma and morally injurious experiences. It is also important to consider thwarted trust and belonging among LGBTQ+ veterans, the potential for a basic mistrust of government systems with their privileged information (e.g., LGBTQ+ identity), and the relatively masculine nature of military service which may discourage help seeking and vulnerable disclosure in ways that are also unique to veterans. Providers are tasked with adopting a stance of cultural humility while identifying key opportunities to make the "invisible" visible through effectively intervening during instances of bias.

There are an encouraging number of recent and ongoing projects to develop new or adapt existing treatments for LGBTQ+ veterans, such as expressive writing interventions for minority stress (Harper et al., 2024) and Trans-Affirmative Narrative Exposure Therapy (TA-NET; Lange, 2020). We focus on the latter for the remainder of the chapter to illustrate key considerations in providing affirming and trauma- and minority stress-focused care. TA-NET is a trans-affirming adaptation to

Narrative Exposure Therapy (NET), which is an evidence-based treatment trauma-focused treatment (Schauer et al., 2011). TA-NET builds on NET in that it is designed to address minority- and trauma-related stress among transgender and gender-diverse individuals, with applicability to LGBTQ+ veterans broadly. It is a time-limited treatment (12–16 sessions) that emphasizes healing through storytelling. In TA-NET, clients construct a written timeline of their lives, by chapter, which provides a chronological structure for identifying key moments in their life that can become the target of therapeutic processing in session. Key moments can include (but are not limited to) positive moments, attempts and outcomes of gender identity exploration, traumatic experiences, institutional betrayal, instances that have contributed to or exacerbated internalized stigma and shame. Construction and exploration of clients' written narrative also provides a means of articulating and highlighting protective factors or events (e.g., achievements, supportive relationships, resiliency factors), and helping them make meaningful connection between their life experiences, outcomes, and how they would like their life story to progress following completion of the treatment.

TA-NET consists of three treatment phases: (1) creation of the autobiographical timeline, (2) written chapter narratives that are read and processed in session to identify themes, and (3) conclusion of the autobiography and therapeutic process. The therapeutic tasks vary across the three phases yet consistently emphasize the individual's exploration of identity within an environment that recognizes and affirms gender diversity (see Table 15.3).

Table 15.3 TA-NET treatment phases and therapeutic tasks

	Phase One: Constructing the Timeline	Phase Two: Chapter Narratives	Phase Three: Treatment Completion
	Sessions 1–2	*Sessions 3–10*	*Sessions 11–12*
Purpose and structure	The timeline provides a structured approach to identifying key moments throughout life (positive moments, traumatic experiences, gender identity exploration). The timeline determines the number of sessions, or "chapters", that will structure the next phase.	The chapter narratives encourage identity exploration within the context of one's entire life. The session structure begins with the client reading the previously assigned chapter narrative and the majority of the session is spent in therapeutic processing of emerging content and themes. The session concludes with the assignment of the next chapter.	At this point, the narratives should have brought the client to the present day providing a natural transition to discussion about goals for the future and how to maintain therapeutic gains following the completion of treatment. The final session structure includes the client sharing the title of their autobiography and reflection on the treatment process.

(continued)

Table 15.3 (continued)

	Phase One: Constructing the Timeline	Phase Two: Chapter Narratives	Phase Three: Treatment Completion
	Sessions 1–2	*Sessions 3–10*	*Sessions 11–12*
Therapeutic tasks	The main therapeutic tasks are to create a safe place for identifying key moments in the timeline, validate when memories may not be recalled, normalize and challenge avoidance, encourage a steady pace to identifying key moments, and gently redirect back to the purpose of the timeline.	Within an affirmative care stance, mental health providers should be prepared for psychoeducation, validation and normalization, identity integration techniques (such as fostering identity exploration in safe environments), challenging avoidance and internalized stigma, promoting resiliency (such as identifying strengths), and identification of themes (such as recurring coping patterns or interpersonal relationships).	As treatment completion nears, the mental health provider begins to mention the upcoming conclusion with the aim to maintain treatment gains autonomously. Other therapeutic tasks include coordinating referrals for follow-up or additional services, assisting with community resources, and empowering autonomy.
Homework assignments	Homework is not required during the construction of the timeline. If the timeline is not completed during the first session of TA-NET then the client has the option to complete it during session two or for homework. After the completion of the timeline, the client is assigned the first chapter narrative to write in between sessions.	Each session of this phase includes assignment of writing the next chapter narratives. Additionally, it is common for clients to "self-select" additional homework assignments, such as exploring gender identity with new clothing or attending a social event. While not required, these are encouraged.	Clients may find it beneficial to complete treatment by choosing a title for their autobiography and writing a "letter from the author", which allows for an opportunity to summarize insights gained.

Clinical Application

The following case vignette provides an example of addressing interpersonal and systemic bias through TA-NET and the application of the above ten recommendations for culturally responsive therapy with an LGBTQ+ veteran. The case vignette utilizes a pseudonym and is a compilation of information that is not based on a specific person.

Background

Brianna is a 29-year-old Biracial (African American and White) Navy veteran who identifies as a transgender lesbian woman (pronouns she/her). She was raised in a single parent household with her biological mother and had minimal contact with her biological father; Brianna spoke about how these early childhood experiences contributed to a deep emotional longing for a "normal" family and that she "missed out" on having a "real dad." Childhood was described as a lonely time due to her mother's employment schedule, yet Brianna spoke about the freedom to explore her own interests and self-expression (e.g., wearing clothing typically regarded as feminine). Although she recognized dissatisfaction with her gender at age 6, she indicated gender dysphoric feelings were not prominent in her early years because of the ability to express her femininity and her mother's support for individuality. At the age of 11, the ability to explore her gender identity was impacted by an instance of childhood sexual abuse perpetrated by her mother's boyfriend, which Brianna did not disclose due to a belief that it was her fault ("if I wasn't different, this wouldn't have happened to me") and contributed to distrust in others ("I can't let anyone know who I am or get close to me because they'll hurt me"). Throughout adolescence, Brianna experienced romantic attraction towards cisgender women yet denied significant relationships and expressed a tendency to "run" when "things got serious." After high school, Brianna enlisted in the Navy to "escape" and received an honorable discharge after four years of military service. She did not publicly identify as a transgender woman during military service and adhered to the military's standards for men (e.g., fitness and grooming requirements). Brianna spoke about fears of being "discovered" when the Transgender Military Ban on military service occurred in 2019 and coped with these concerns through overt displays of masculinity and excessive alcohol consumption despite negative consequences (e.g., exacerbated interpersonal problems). Since military discharge, Brianna has come out in all domains of life (e.g., social, employment) and pursued gender affirming care (i.e., hormone therapy, feminizing voice therapy).

Brianna self-referred to a VA outpatient psychotherapy clinic and was scheduled with a mid-career White psychologist who identifies as a cisgender woman (pronouns she/her). Brianna expressed a desire to address the impact her childhood traumatic experiences had on her emotions and relationships. She had a history of substance use treatment, with recent completion of a 90-day residential program, active involvement in 12-Step programming (Alcoholics Anonymous, AA), and was abstinent from all substances. At intake, Briana denied suicide ideation, plan, intent, had no history of suicidal behaviors or attempts, and had no immediate access to lethal means. During the intake appointment, Brianna received diagnoses of PTSD, alcohol use disorder (in early remission), and had a historical diagnosis of borderline personality disorder (see below for explanation).

Treatment

The treatment plan was established after review of several "gold-standard" EBPs (e.g., Cognitive Processing Therapy, Prolonged Exposure), with Brianna electing to engage in Trans-Affirmative Narrative Exposure Therapy (TA-NET; Lange, 2020). The treatment plan also included integration of 12-Step AA programming, with particular attention to timing of Step 4 ("Made a searching and fearless moral inventory of ourselves"; AA, 2001, p. 59) to prioritize ongoing progress with recovery.

Phase One: Constructing the Timeline

The first phase of TA-NET, construction of the timeline, helped to set the pace and determine the number of sessions needed to complete the narratives and treatment. With guidance from the provider, Brianna identified key moments throughout her life that were positive, negative, and impactful for gender identity development; these events were captured on a written chronological timeline that framed the course and duration of psychotherapy, with an anticipated 12 sessions for completion of the treatment approach. This phase of treatment also included review of coping strategies for potential moments of emotional overwhelm (e.g., contact AA sponsor, Veterans Crisis Line, breathing techniques) and identifying ways to maintain treatment engagement. With the completion of the timeline during the therapy sessions, Brianna was assigned homework of writing her first chapter narrative focused on early childhood years.

Phase Two: Chapter Narratives

The session structure in this phase involved Brianna reading her previously assigned narrative written homework, emotional processing of the content, and identifying themes that emerged to promote identity development. During the early chapter narratives, it was observed that Brianna tended to read aloud at a rapid pace or not complete the written homework. Rather than view these behaviors as resistance or disengagement, the provider prioritized strengthening rapport and trust through affirming verbal and non-verbal communication (e.g., active listening, leaning forward, acknowledging strengths), validation of gender identity (i.e., use of appropriate pronouns), and providing psychoeducation about minority stressors and trauma reactions. Over the course of care, Brianna displayed enhanced willingness to be emotionally vulnerable and reveal details of her experiences that contributed to distress. For example, she shared that her perpetrator of sexual abuse would communicate homophobic/transphobic views and connected the assault to identity ("no one will believe someone like you"). These disclosures provided therapeutic opportunities to challenge internalized stigma while appropriately shifting blame away from Brianna.

Brianna's revelations about the impact of these early experiences shaped her approach to future narrative chapters, which noticeably included more compassionate language and identification of minority stressors. A prominent example of this occurred when Brianna described the impact of the ban on transgender military service and enduring guilt about "hiding in the closet" while others were publicly impacted by the change in policy. She spoke about racial tensions within her naval unit and fleet, which increased concerns about being ostracized from others. Through writing, she was able to challenge her feelings of shame and guilt by acknowledging the safety functions of her identity concealment in the military. Although she denied being targeted for her gender or racial identity, treatment focused on the impact of witnessing discrimination against others, guilt about not intervening, and her developed sense of mistrust in others as a result of these experiences.

Processing of chapter narratives highlighted past experiences of discrimination that contributed to maladaptive coping (i.e., alcohol consumption) or aggressive outbursts previously believed to be consistent with borderline personality disorder (per history). During therapy, it became clear that following Brianna coming out to others and pursuing gender-affirmative care (i.e., hormone therapy, vocal coaching), she experienced an increase in social rejection (e.g., previous relationships from military service have ceased communication) and developed a tendency to become verbally aggressive with others, especially when misgendered. Through processing these experiences, and examining historical antecedents to her dysregulated moods and behaviors, it was determined that her dysregulation was not consistent with a pattern of core dysregulation or a diagnosis of borderline personality disorder. Rather, her dysregulation was acquired and an understandable reflection of the trauma and chronic discrimination she had experienced throughout life, which when triggered led to dysregulated moods and behaviors. Briana experienced this conceptualization as deeply validating and therapy was then able to shift toward helping Brianna improve emotion regulation skills in response to triggers.

The provider encouraged Brianna to consider how her experiences with minority- and trauma-related stressors impacted the way she tends to interact with others and build relationships. She was able to readily identify how emotional distancing from relationships was connected to intersectional sources of discrimination and trauma; yet she voiced pessimism in others accepting and embracing her identity. Interventions targeting these expressions of internalized stigma included identifying and challenging negative self-talk and encouraging engagement with others in the LGBTQ+ community. These conversations led to Brianna reconsidering her AA sponsor who had limited knowledge and familiarity with the LGBTQ+ community, had no military experience, and was reported to be overly focused on Step 3 ("Made a decision to turn our will and our lives over to the care of God as we understood Him"). At Brianna's request, the provider shared several resources about 12-Step programming that served the LGBTQ+ and/or military community.

Phase Three: Treatment Completion

With the chapter narratives completed, therapeutic attention shifted to termination with the final phase of TA-NET, which involved completing a "letter from the author" and selecting a title for the autobiography. The final homework assignments provided Brianna with an opportunity to reflect upon the therapeutic process as well as the insights and progress gained during treatment. Brianna's letter from the author reflected enhanced identity development ("I wanted to define who I am, there are all these good things about me and I feel proud of that") and a reduction in intensity of symptoms stemming from minority- and trauma-related stress ("I own my story now… I realize as I've been writing this that I'm not obligated to have my trauma take up so much of my story now"). The autobiography was titled, *Brianna's Story: Unapologetically and Bravely Herself.*

By the conclusion of TA-NET and the therapeutic relationship, Brianna reported a reduction in trauma-related symptom intensity, enhanced confidence in her ability to build a support system, and maintenance of recovery with continued abstinence from substances. Notably, she had recently increased frequency of contact with her biological mother who, while supportive, Brianna had distanced from in previous years. Brianna continued to experience internalized stigma yet voiced enhanced confidence in her ability to identify and challenge those thoughts in the future ("I am worthy of love"). The aftercare plan involved continued involvement with a newly obtained AA sponsor (who also identified within the LGBTQ+ community) and remaining active with her AA homegroup (that had several members of both the LGBTQ+ and military community).

The favorable treatment progression with Brianna was largely due to the individual strengths she brought to therapy, such as a high degree of motivation and insight that led to deeper processing of experiences. The provider recognized the heightened risk of trauma exposure and prioritized addressing risk factors (i.e., history of alcohol use) that could impact trauma-focused therapy and purposefully integrating protective factors (i.e., 12-Step programming, review of coping skills). Further, the provider's understanding of military culture and history facilitated the therapeutic alliance and allowed for deeper understanding of Brianna's heightened identity concealment during the ban on transgender service. Within the framework of a culturally adapted treatment, the provider supported and affirmed identity development while attending to the impacts of minority- and trauma-related stressors without overpathologizing Brianna's emotional reactions.

Conclusion

There are important considerations when working with LGBTQ+ veterans that overlap with LGBTQ+ non-veterans and non-LGBTQ+ veterans but that are also distinct. Military culture can have a profound effect on LGBTQ+ people, positive (e.g., shared purposes, camaraderie) and negative (e.g., prejudice, within unit aggression, gender performance pressure and hypermasculinity). LGBTQ+ veterans are susceptible to experiencing more frequent and severe trauma and minority stressors, compared to people with either identity alone. Despite these challenges and perhaps because of them, it is important to understand that LGBTQ+ service members and veterans have often developed a sense for and prioritize camaraderie and loyalty, show strong moral fortitude, and are uniquely trained to act prudently and selflessly in high-stress situations. These adaptations can be the source of resilience but can also become sources of treatment interference to the extent that clients struggle to share concerns that might distinguish them from other veterans (e.g., breaking away from the "military unit"), or to the extent that the masculinity norms inherent with military service discourage sharing openly. The considerations and recommendations provided in this chapter are aimed to shine light on some of these underlying considerations in the hopes that providers can become more keenly aware of not only what may be driving distress among LGBTQ+ veterans, but also some of the LGBTQ+ affirming ways of redressing the harms of trauma and minority stress among them.

Disclaimer Statement The views expressed in this chapter are those of the authors and do not necessarily reflect the official policy or position of the Defense Health Agency, Department of Defense, Department of Veterans Affairs, nor the U.S. Government.

References

Akerman, M., Mendes, R., Lima, S., Guerra, H. L., Silva, R. A. D., Sacardo, D. P., & Fernandez, J. C. A. (2020). Religion as a protective factor for health. *Einstein (Sao Paulo, Brazil), 18*, eED5562. https://doi.org/10.31744/einstein_journal/2020ed5562

Alcoholics Anonymous (AA). (2001). *Alcoholics Anonymous: The story of how thousands of men and women have recovered from alcoholism* (4th ed.). Alcoholics Anonymous World Services, Inc., New York.

American Psychiatric Association. (2013). *Diagnostic and statistical manual of mental disorders* (5th ed.). APA. https://doi.org/10.1176/appi.books.9780890425596

American Psychological Association, Task Force on Appropriate Therapeutic Responses to Sexual Orientation. (2009). *Report of the American Psychological Association task force on appropriate therapeutic responses to sexual orientation.* Retrieved from http://www.apa.org/pi/lgbc/publications/therapeutic-resp.html

Belkin, A., Ender, M. G., Frank, N., Furia, S. R., Lucas, G., Packard, G., et al. (2013). Readiness and DADT repeal: Has the new policy of open service undermined the military? *Armed Forces & Society, 39*(4), 587–601. https://doi.org/10.1177/0095327X12466248

Blosnich, J. R., Mays, V. M., & Cochran, S. D. (2014). Suicidality among veterans: Implications of sexual minority status. *American Journal of Public Health, 104*(S4), S535–S537.

Bogel-Burroughs, N. (2024, October 2). *Millions of LGBTQ Americans have religious trauma. Psychiatrists want to help.* NBC News. https://www.nbcnews.com/nbc-out/out-health-and-wellness/millions-lgbtq-americans-religious-trauma-psychiatrists-want-help-rcna135728

Borch, F. L. (2010). The history of "Don't Ask, Don't Tell" in the Army: How we got to it and why it is what it is. *Military Law Review, 203*, 189–206.

Boyce, L. A., & Herd, A. M. (2003). The relationship between gender role stereotypes and requisite military leadership characteristics. *Sex Roles, 49*, 365–378.

Brooks, V. R. (1981). *Minority stress and lesbian women*. Lexington Books.

Cardona, N. D., Madigan, R. J., & Sauer-Zavala, S. (2022). How minority stress becomes traumatic invalidation: An emotion-focused conceptualization of minority stress in sexual and gender minority people. *Clinical Psychology: Science and Practice, 29*(2), 185–195. https://doi.org/10.1037/cps0000054

Chang, S. C. (2022). EMDR therapy as affirmative care for transgender and nonbinary clients. In M. Nickerson (Ed.), *Cultural competence and healing culturally based trauma with EMDR therapy: Innovative strategies and protocols* (2nd ed.). Springer.

Chang, S. C., & Singh, A. A. (2018). *A clinician's guide to gender-affirming care: Working with transgender and gender nonconforming clients*. New Harbinger Publications.

Cramer, R. J., Kaniuka, A., Lange, T. M., Brooks, B. D., Feinstein, B. A., & Hilgeman, M. M. (2022). A pilot evaluation of sexual and gender minority identity measures in a treatment-seeking military veteran sample. *American Journal of Orthopsychiatry., 92*. https://doi.org/10.1037/ort0000627

Defense Health Agency (DHA). (2023, May 12). *Guidance for gender-affirming health care of transgender and gender-diverse active and reserve component service members* (DHA Procedural Instruction 6025.21). Retrieved from: https://www.health.mil/Reference-Center/DHA-Publications/2023/05/12/DHA-PI-6015-21

Department of Defense (DoD). (2016, June). *Military service of transgender service members*. (DoD Directive-type Memorandum 16-005). Retrieved from: https://dod.defense.gov/portals/1/features/2016/0616_policy/dtm-16-005.pdf

Department of Defense (DoD). (2022, December 20). *In-service transition for transgender service members* (DOD Instruction 1300.28, Change 1). Retrieved from: https://www.esd.whs.mil/Portals/54/Documents/DD/issuances/dodi/130028p.pdf

Dietert, M., & Dentice, D. (2023). Transgender military experiences: From Obama to Trump. *Journal of Homosexuality, 70*(6), 993–1010.

Exec. Order No. 14004, 86 FR 7471. (2021). *Enabling all qualified Americans to serve their country in uniform*. https://www.federalregister.gov/documents/2021/01/28/2021-02034/enabling-all-qualified-americans-to-serve-their-country-in-uniform

Fish, J. N., & Russell, S. T. (2020). Sexual orientation and gender identity change efforts are unethical and harmful. *American Journal of Public Health, 110*(8), 1113–1114. https://doi.org/10.2105/AJPH.2020.305765

Forrester, S. N., Gallo, J. J., Whitfield, K. E., & Thorpe, R. J., Jr. (2019). A framework of minority stress: From physiological manifestations to cognitive outcomes. *The Gerontologist, 59*(6), 1017–1023.

Gates, G. J. (2010). *Discharges under the Don't ask, Don't tell policy: Women and racial/ethnic minorities*. UCLA: The Williams Institute. Retrieved from https://escholarship.org/uc/item/45h8x98t

Harper, K., Kelton, K., Livingston, N.A., Iverson, K., & Marx, B. (2024). *Community-based feedback on an expressive writing intervention for LGBQ+ veterans*. Paper presented at the 58th Annual Association for Behavioral and Cognitive Therapies Convention. Philadelphia, PA.

Hatzenbuehler, M. L. (2009). How does sexual minority stigma "get under the skin"? A psychological mediation framework. *Psychological Bulletin, 135*(5), 707–730.

Hendricks, M. L., & Testa, R. J. (2012). A conceptual framework for clinical work with transgender and gender nonconforming clients: An adaptation of the Minority Stress Model. *Professional Psychology: Research and Practice, 43*(5), 460–467.

Higbee, M., Wright, E. R., & Roemerman, R. M. (2022). Conversion therapy in the Southern United States: Prevalence and experiences of the survivors. *Journal of Homosexuality, 69*(4), 612–631.

Hinojosa, R. (2010). Doing hegemony: Military, men, and constructing a hegemonic masculinity. *The Journal of Men's Studies, 18*(2), 179–194.

Hoge, C. W., Auchterlonie, J. L., & Milliken, C. S. (2006). Mental health problems, use of mental health services, and attrition from military service after returning from deployment to Iraq or Afghanistan. *JAMA, 295*(9), 1023–1032.

Johnson, L., & Federman, E. J. (2013). Pathways and barriers to care for LGBT veterans in the US Department of Veterans Affairs (VA). *Journal of LGBT Issues in Counseling, 7*(3), 218–235.

Johnson, N., Pearlman, A. T., Klein, D. A., Riggs, D., & Schvey, N. A. (2023). Stigma and barriers in health care among a sample of transgender and gender-diverse active duty service members. *Medical Care, 61*(3), 145–149.

Jones, T. W., Power, J., & Jones, T. M. (2022). Religious trauma and moral injury from LGBTQA+ conversion practices. *Social Science & Medicine (1982), 305*, 115040. https://doi.org/10.1016/j.socscimed.2022.115040

Klein, D. A., Gonzalez, X. B., Highland, K. B., Thornton, J. A., Sunderland, K. W., Funk, W., et al. (2024). Variation in time-to-gender-affirming hormone therapy in US active duty service members. *Medical Care, 62*(7), 481–488.

Kocet, M. M., & Curry, J. (2011). Finding the spirit within: Spirituality issues in the LGBT community. *Journal of LGBT Issues in Counseling, 5*(3–4), 160–162.

Kopacz, M. S., Nieuwsma, J. A., Wortmann, J. H., Hanson, J. L., Meador, K. G., & Thiel, M. M. (2019). The role of chaplaincy in LGBT veteran healthcare. *Spirituality in Clinical Practice, 6*(3), 213–217.

Lange, T. M. (2020). Trans-affirmative narrative exposure therapy (TA-NET): A therapeutic approach for targeting minority stress, internalized stigma, and trauma reactions among gender diverse adults. *Practice Innovations, Special Issue on Evidence Based Relationship Variables, 5*(3), 230–245. https://doi.org/10.1037/pri0000126

Lange, T. M., Hilgeman, M. M., Portz, K. J., Intoccia, V. A., & Cramer, R. J. (2020). Pride in All Who Served: Development, feasibility, and initial efficacy of a health education group for LGBT veterans. *Journal of Trauma & Dissociation, Special Issue on Trauma, Advocacy, and Social Movements, 21*(4), 484–504. https://doi.org/10.1080/15299732.2020.1770147

Lattanner, M. R., Ford, J., Bo, N., Tu, W., Pachankis, J. E., Dodge, B., & Hatzenbuehler, M. L. (2021). A contextual approach to the psychological study of identity concealment: Examining direct, interactive, and indirect effects of structural stigma on concealment motivation across proximal and distal geographic levels. *Psychological Science, 32*(10), 1684–1696.

Lichter, D. A., & Min, D. (2013). Studies show spiritual care linked to better health outcomes. *Health Progress, 94*(2), 62–66.

Litz, B. T., Stein, N., Delaney, E., Lebowitz, L., Nash, W. P., Silva, C., & Maguen, S. (2009). Moral injury and moral repair in war veterans: A preliminary model and intervention strategy. *Clinical Psychology Review, 29*(8), 695–706. https://doi.org/10.1016/j.cpr.2009.07.003

Livingston, N. A., Berke, D. S., Ruben, M. A., Matza, A. R., & Shipherd, J. C. (2019). Experiences of trauma, discrimination, microaggressions, and minority stress among trauma-exposed LGBT veterans: Unexpected findings and unresolved service gaps. *Psychological Trauma: Theory, Research, Practice, and Policy, 11*(7), 695–703. https://doi.org/10.1037/tra0000464

Livingston, N. A., Berke, D., Scholl, J., Ruben, M., & Shipherd, J. C. (2020). Addressing diversity in PTSD treatment: Clinical considerations and guidance for the treatment of PTSD in LGBTQ populations. *Current Treatment Options in Psychiatry, 7*(2), 53–69. https://doi.org/10.1007/s40501-020-00204-0

Livingston, N. A., Lynch, K. E., Hinds, Z., Gatsby, E., DuVall, S. L., & Shipherd, J. C. (2022). Identifying posttraumatic stress disorder and disparity among transgender veterans using nationwide veterans health administration electronic health record data. *LGBT Health, 9*(2), 94–102.

Livingston, N. A., Gatsby, E., Shipherd, J. C., & Lynch, K. E. (2023). Causes of alcohol-attributable death and associated years of potential life lost among LGB and non-LGB veteran men and women in Veterans Health Administration. *Addictive Behaviors, 139*, 107587.

Manuel, V. (2020). Trump's transgender military ban: Policy, law, and litigation. *Tulane Journal of Law and Sexuality: Review of Sexual Orientation and Gender Identity in the Law, 29*, 75–92.

Marx, B. P., Hall-Clark, B., Friedman, M. J., Holtzheimer, P., & Schnurr, P. P. (2024). The PTSD Criterion A debate: A brief history, current status, and recommendations for moving forward. *Journal of Traumatic Stress, 37*(1), 5–15. https://doi.org/10.1002/jts.23007

McCormick, W. H., Currier, J. M., Isaak, S. L., Sims, B. M., Slagel, B. A., Carroll, T. D., Hamner, K., & Albright, D. L. (2019). Military culture and post-military transitioning among veterans: A qualitative analysis. *Journal of Veteran Studies, 4*(2).

McDermott, J. (2016). *Few vets expelled under 'don't ask' seek remedy.* The Associated Press: AP NewsBreak. Retrieved from: https://apnews.com/article/801324c48838400f9aa49c8c5efa3e44

McDuffie, E., & Brown, G. R. (2010). 70 US veterans with gender identity disturbances: A descriptive study. *International Journal of Transgenderism, 12*(1), 21–30.

McNamara, K. A., Lucas, C. L., Goldbach, J. T., Castro, C. A., & Holloway, I. W. (2021). "Even if the policy changes, the culture remains the same": A mixed methods analysis of LGBT service members' outness patterns. *Armed Forces & Society, 47*(3), 505–529.

Meade, V. (2021). Patriotism as a construct for understanding military service among LGBTQ+ veterans: A call for research grounded in institutional oppression. *Journal of Veterans Studies, 7*(3).

Meyer, I. H. (2003). Prejudice, social stress, and mental health in lesbian, gay, and bisexual populations: Conceptual issues and research evidence. *Psychological Bulletin, 129*(5), 674–697.

Model, B. M. S. (Director). (2013). *The Camouflage Closet: LGBT Veteran Educational Resource.* [Short Film]. Retrieved from: https://www.camouflagecloset.com/

Molendijk, T., Kramer, E. H., & Verweij, D. (2018). Moral aspects of "moral injury": Analyzing conceptualizations on the role of morality in military trauma. *Journal of Military Ethics, 17*(1), 36–53.

Moradi, B. (2009). Sexual orientation disclosure, concealment, harassment, and military cohesion: Perceptions of LGBT military veterans. *Military Psychology, 21*(4), 513–533. https://doi.org/10.1080/08995600903206453

National Defense Research Institute. (2010). *Sexual orientation and U.S. military personnel policy: An update of RAND's 1993 study*. RAND Corporation. http://www.jstor.org/stable/10.7249/mg1056osd

Okros, A., & Scott, D. (2015). Gender identity in the Canadian forces: A review of possible impacts on operational effectiveness. *Armed Forces & Society, 41*(2), 243–256. https://doi.org/10.1177/0095327X14535371

Pachankis, J. E., McConocha, E. M., Reynolds, J. S., Winston, R., Adeyinka, O., Harkness, A., et al. (2019). Project ESTEEM protocol: A randomized controlled trial of an LGBTQ-affirmative treatment for young adult sexual minority men's mental and sexual health. *BMC Public Health, 19*(1), 1–12.

Pachankis, J. E., Mahon, C. P., Jackson, S. D., Fetzner, B. K., & Bränström, R. (2020). Sexual orientation concealment and mental health: A conceptual and meta-analytic review. *Psychological Bulletin, 146*(10), 831–871.

Parco, J. E., & Levy, D. A. (2014). *Evolution of government policy towards homosexuality in the US military*. Routledge.

Puckett, J. A., & Levitt, H. M. (2015). Internalized stigma within sexual and gender minorities: Change strategies and clinical implications. *Journal of LGBT Issues in Counseling, 9*(4), 329–349.

Rider, G. N., Vencill, J. A., Berg, D. R., Becker-Warner, R., Candelario-Pérez, L., & Spencer, K. G. (2019). The gender affirmative lifespan approach (GALA): A framework for competent clinical care with nonbinary clients. *International Journal of Transgenderism, 20*(2–3), 275–288.

Schauer, M., Neuner, F., & Elbert, T. (2011). *Narrative exposure therapy: A short term treatment for traumatic stress disorders* (2nd ed.). Hogrefe Publishing.

Schvey, N. A., Klein, D. A., Pearlman, A. T., Kraff, R. I., & Riggs, D. S. (2020). Stigma, health, and psychosocial functioning among transgender active duty service members in the US military. *Stigma and Health, 5*(2), 188–198.

Sharma, V., Marin, D. B., Koenig, H. K., Feder, A., Iacoviello, B. M., Southwick, S. M., & Pietrzak, R. H. (2017). Religion, spirituality, and mental health of U.S. military veterans: Results from the National Health and Resilience in Veterans Study. *Journal of Affective Disorders, 217*, 197–204. https://doi.org/10.1016/j.jad.2017.03.071

Shipherd, J. C., Berke, D., & Livingston, N. A. (2019). Trauma recovery in the transgender and gender diverse community: Extensions of the Minority Stress Model for treatment planning. *Cognitive and Behavioral Practice, 26*(4), 629–646. https://doi.org/10.1016/j.cbpra.2019.06.001

Shipherd, J. C., Lynch, K., Gatsby, E., Hinds, Z., DuVall, S. L., & Livingston, N. A. (2021). Estimating prevalence of PTSD among veterans with minoritized sexual orientations using electronic health record data. *Journal of Consulting and Clinical Psychology, 89*(10), 856–868.

Soeters, J. L., Winslow, D. J., & Weibull, A. (2006). Military culture. In G. Caforio (Ed.), *Handbook of the sociology of military* (pp. 237–254). Springer. https://doi.org/10.1007/0-387-34576-0_14

Soto, A., Smith, T. B., Griner, D., Rodríguez, M. D., & Bernal, G. (2019). Cultural adaptations and multicultural competence. In J. C. Norcross & B. E. Wampold (Eds.), *Psychotherapy relationships that work: Evidence-based therapist responsiveness* (pp. 86–132). Oxford University Press. https://doi.org/10.1093/med-psych/9780190843960.003.0004

Suits, D. (2021). *Change to policy allows transgender soldiers to serve openly*. United States Army News Service. Retrieved from: https://www.army.mil/article/247785/change_to_policy_allows_transgender_soldiers_to_serve_openly

Super, J. T., & Jacobson, L. (2011). Religious abuse: Implications for counseling lesbian, gay, bisexual, and transgender individuals. *Journal of LGBT Issues in Counseling, 5*(3–4), 180–196.

The Williams Institute. (2010). *Discharges under the Don't Ask/Don't Tell policy*. Retrieved from: https://williamsinstitute.law.ucla.edu/wp-content/uploads/Discharges-DADT-Women-Race-Sep-2010.pdf

Trivedi, R. B., Post, E. P., Sun, H., Pomerantz, A., Saxon, A. J., Piette, J. D., et al. (2015). Prevalence, comorbidity, and prognosis of mental health among US veterans. *American Journal of Public Health, 105*(12), 2564–2569.

Trivette, S. A. (2010). Secret handshakes and decoder rings: The queer space of Don't Ask/Don't Tell. *Sexuality Research & Social Policy: A Journal of the NSRC, 7*(3), 214–228. https://doi.org/10.1007/s13178-010-0020-3

Tucker, R. P. (2019). Suicide in transgender veterans: Prevalence, prevention, and implications of current policy. *Perspectives on Psychological Science, 14*(3), 452–468.

United States General Accounting Office. (1992). *Defense force management DOD's policy on homosexuality*. Washington, D.C.

Van Gilder, B. J. (2017). Coping with sexual identity stigma in the U.S. military: An examination of identity management practices prior to and after the repeal of "Don't Ask, Don't Tell". *Identity, 17*(3), 156–175. https://doi.org/10.1080/15283488.2017.1340162

Index

N. A. Livingston et al. (eds.), *Addressing Minority Stress and Enhancing Resilience with Diverse LGBTQ+ Clients*, CBT: Science Into Practice,
https://doi.org/10.1007/978-3-031-92836-9

GPSR Compliance
The European Union's (EU) General Product Safety Regulation (GPSR) is a set of rules that requires consumer products to be safe and our obligations to ensure this.

If you have any concerns about our products, you can contact us on

ProductSafety@springernature.com

In case Publisher is established outside the EU, the EU authorized representative is:

Springer Nature Customer Service Center GmbH
Europaplatz 3
69115 Heidelberg, Germany

www.ingramcontent.com/pod-product-compliance
Lightning Source LLC
Chambersburg PA
CBHW060339311025
34791CB00003B/39
* 9 7 8 3 0 3 1 9 2 8 3 5 2 *